Dirty Shirt

The 'Dirty Shirt' series:

Dirty Shirt
A Green Bough
The World in a Sandbag
Household Gods

***

John Ware used to work in the construction industry until they made him stop. He now lectures in history in his home town of Cork.

Join John's mailing list for news, updates and **a free book**.

www.pagedor.co.uk/johnware

Dirty Shirt

John Ware

PAGE D'OR
MMXX

Page d'Or is an imprint of Prosperity Education Limited
Registered offices: 58 Sherlock Close, Cambridge CB3 0HP,
United Kingdom

© John Ware 2020

First published 2020
Revised edition: 2025

All rights reserved. No part of this book may be reprinted or reproduced or utilised in any form or by any electronic, mechanical, or other means, now known or hereafter invented, including photocopying and recording, or in any information storage or retrieval system, without permission in writing from the publisher.

The right of John Ware to be identified as the author has been asserted in accordance with sections 77 and 78 of the Copyright, Designs and Patents Act 1988.

A catalogue record for this book is available from the British Library

ISBN: 978-1-9138250-4-1

Typeset in Times New Roman and Garamond by ORP Cambridge
Cover designed by Siantura
Cover photo by 2nd Lieutenant Cyril Drummond RFA in 1914
(reproduced with permission from the Imperial War Museum's 'Brigadier CAF Drummond Collection')
Frontispiece: Royal Munster Fusiler cap badge. Image courtesy of the National Army Museum, London.

For further information visit: www.pagedor.co.uk

Ad infinitum et ultra.

The Regiment, of which this Battalion formed a part, has now ceased to exist, but its records in the Great War [...] sustain its ancient reputation, and its deeds will not be forgotten.

—Lieut. General H.G. Miles, Colonel. Royal Munster Fusiliers,
10th November 1922

EXPLANATORY NOTE

A battalion is a sub-unit of a regiment. A regiment is a body of regular troops sharing a common corporate identity. A battalion (meaning roughly 'battle formation') might number anywhere between five hundred and a thousand personnel, and there might be one, or two, or three battalions to a regiment. It all depends on the time and the place.

In the United Kingdom of Great Britain and Ireland, in the last decade of its existence as such, there was a minimum of two battalions to each regiment, but it wasn't quite that simple. For a start, a British regiment was not a tactical unit, but a family united by shared insignia and tradition rather than by organisational structure.

Each battalion lived its own life, largely independent of its sisters, regarding its own lieutenant colonel as its supreme regimental authority. Even when a higher formation was demanded, battalions were not grouped together according to regiment, as in other armies, but were joined together in brigades of unassociated battalions in marriages of geographical convenience. For instance: in 1914, the 1st Battalion of the Royal Munster Fusiliers was scattered across Burma. The 2nd Battalion was half the world away in Aldershot, where it was brigaded alongside battalions from English and Scottish regiments.

Each of these two units could and did claim to be the Munster Fusiliers, without mentioning that it was really only a battalion thereof. Each was the embodiment of the regiment.

There were three other bodies in Ireland claiming to be the 3rd, 4th and 5th Battalions of the regiment respectively. These featured on the Army List but were not factored into the army's fighting strength. They upheld the regiment's traditions, but they did not usually go out into the world and emulate on the battlefield the actions of the two 'regular' battalions. When the war came and the army vastly expanded, no new regiments were raised, but existing regiments were enlarged, so that a 6th, 7th, 8th and 9th Battalion of the Munsters were formed for foreign service.

In a four-battalion British brigade an untrained eye might spot few differences between one unit and the next, but it was in the differences that regimental identity was cherished.

A regiment jealously treasured its eccentricities as a mark of privileged individuality in an otherwise uniform world. Examples are legion, so much as to almost make nonsense of the very pretence at uniformity. The officers and warrant officers of the Royal Welch Fusiliers (not only insisting on spelling Welsh with a C) delighted in affixing their eighteenth-century hair ribbons to the collars of their twentieth-century tunics. But even if you factor their regimental goat into the reckoning, the oddities of the Royal Welch are not so remarkable.

The 4th Gurkha Rifles, a regiment of Nepalese mercenaries raised in the nineteenth century, proudly wore as their badge the three feathers that the Black Prince of Wales had taken from the blind King of Bohemia on the field of Crècy in 1346. Better yet, the Gurkhas also played the bagpipes and took careful precautions at dinner against the spread of Jacobitism (this was done by assiduously removing the water glasses from the mess table before the drinking of the Loyal Toast so that, when the wine glasses were raised, there might be no sly turning of 'The King' into 'The King over the water'). Thus, even in the twentieth century, no officer of this largely Hindu regiment might surreptitiously toast the restoration of the Catholic Stuart monarchy.

The Gurkhas tended to dress rather soberly though, favouring – even at their dressiest – an elegant dark green that traced its origin to the forests of England's American colonies. Even with their bagpipes the Gurkhas could never match the barbaric flamboyance of soldiers from the Scottish highlands, with their pleated kilts of hunting tartan and their white spats and their tall bonnets made of ostrich feathers.

If for pure outlandishness none of His Majesty's regiments of the United Kingdom could match the Highlanders, none could be called sombre either. As late as 1914, there were regiments of Irish cavalry dressed, with romantic theatricality, as Polish and Hungarian horsemen, in costumes that had been first designed in the eighteenth century, when the fashion was all for something evoking the wild men of the great steppe. Headgear of sable or bearskin that added twelve or more inches to a man's stature was commonplace.

Ireland's four fusilier regiments wore towering caps of black sealskin or raccoon skin above their uniforms of scarlet and blue. This distinguished them from the other Irish line regiments in their spiked helmets with gleaming gilt fittings. None of this, by the way, was an Irish, or even a British peculiarity: every army in Europe had similar costumes. These were peacetime dress uniforms though.

Since the South African War (usually remembered as the Boer War and technically the Second Boer War) the British service uniform was a utilitarian khaki, and most of the world's armies were likewise adopting military clothing in greys and browns and dull greens.

The older Irish regiments celebrated a seventeenth-century heritage, when they had held the kingdom for Good King

Billy against the Catholic James. The younger regiments were largely Catholic themselves, but, whether Catholic or Protestant, Methodist or Presbyterian or, in the regiments of Indian army, Hindu, Muslim, Sikh or Buddhist, the real religion – the true unifying faith in the armies of the king and king-emperor – was ancestor worship.

A man coming to the end of his enlistment might be only twenty-five, but still he boasted of the deeds he had done a hundred years before. The fact that he himself had not been alive then was the merest technicality. His regiment had been there, and it had done mightily. As with the Prince of Wales's feathers from Crècy, so with the Egyptian sphinxes and Napoleonic eagles: the trophies from those days were blazoned on badges, the names of the battlefields embroidered on flags, and the memories of the dead heroes toasted in overflowing cups.

Our fathers' names are remembered. Let our deeds be great that our names too be so celebrated.

There were tales that grew in the telling. The portraits, red-coated and bewigged, listened from where they hung in the mess, and they didn't mind.

A government might be cruelly heedless of a regiment's pride, might abolish or amalgamate or disband at a whim. They might trample on tradition, but they could not erase history. Men died. Their successors lived, and soldiered on.

In 1914, the Royal Munster Fusiliers had been in existence for all of thirty-three years, yet they proudly held to two and a half centuries of history. Had it all been true, their earliest claimed ancestors, a band of English and Portuguese mercenaries guarding a trading post on the Bay of Bengal, might have looked down the centuries and wondered how their distant descendants could possibly have ended up, of all places, in Tralee.

I

CELTIC TWILIGHT

Some say the devil is dead,

The devil is dead, the devil is dead,

Some say the devil is dead and buried in Killarney.

More say he rose again, more say he rose again,

More say he rose again,

And joined the British Army.

—Traditional

1

Let us go forth, the tellers of tales, and seize whatever prey the heart longs for, and have no fear.

—W.B. Yeats, *The Celtic Twilight*

It was raining in Tralee.

Wyndham was thinking that perhaps he should have gone to Killarney after all. They'd all advised him to go to Killarney. Killarney was mentioned in the guidebooks. It was represented on the poster he'd seen in Queenstown and again in Cork. It had promised vistas of green and blue, and more green again, but Wyndham had never cared for that sort of sentiment. He didn't want to be the foreign visitor come for the quaint scenery: the tourist that the ticket inspector and the hotel desk clerk thought they saw. That said, it was at the shore of one of Killarney's lakes that the Fianna had met Niamh Golden-haired, who had ridden across the western sea from the Land of the Young. Perhaps though it was from here at Tralee, the Strand of the Lee, that she had returned across the waves, carrying Oisin with her.

Perhaps indeed, thought Wyndham, but Killarney could probably promise a better class of hotel.

The place he had chosen here was perfectly acceptable in its way, but then so was walking aimlessly through this wet provincial town after dinner, with everything shut and little enough to see.

He'd walk a little farther – to that turn in the road anyway. He'd surely be able to see beyond the town from there, to the grey sea and the mountains.

He walked, but it wasn't worth it. Across the slate roofs there may have been sea and mountain, but there was a low mist obscuring the mountains, and the only evidence of the invisible sea was a stiff wet breeze that tasted vaguely of salt.

When I was a child I had only to climb the hill behind the house to see long, blue, ragged hills flowing along the southern horizon. What beauty was lost to me, what depth of emotion is still perhaps lacking in me, because nobody told me, not even the merchant captains who knew everything, that Cruachan of the Enchantments lay behind those long, blue, ragged hills!

Mr Yeats had said that. Wyndham had read those words on the train, when the weather had made the view from the window unrewarding. He'd read them on his own journey across the western sea, in his cabin and in the 2nd Class lounge. And of course he'd almost had them by heart before then, so many times had he read Mr Yeats, and Lady Gregory, and their marvellous stories of an Ireland that was so distant from tourism advertisements and songs about Kathleen Mavourneen.

He'd tried to explain it to friends, this new enthusiasm of his, but their perspective of Ireland was twisted by what they knew of the lowering poor of cities like Boston, and by the cloying songs and the comical rogues of the stage. They could not comprehend him, and had laughed. It had been hopeless, of course, to make his family see it. The Irish? With their riotous ways and Romish faith? The very idea.

In the end he'd just gone – just upped and left them with their mouths agape at his wilfulness. Of course it wasn't as if he hadn't tried to explain things. He spoke of broadening his horizons, of stretching his wings a little. This modest inheritance was just the thing for giving a young man some finish. He'd implied (and he'd had no firm notion to the contrary) that once back he'd apply himself to the job that Uncle Henry had been so good to furnish him with, and he'd no doubt marry whomever they found for him after that, too. He'd tried to convince them that it wasn't about Ireland. He'd mentioned Oxford and Canterbury, and had made himself appear as strait-laced and priggish as he knew how when his friends ragged him about Paris and showgirls.

He didn't tell them. He wasn't after showgirls: he was looking for legends and heroes. He was looking for their shadows in the stories the people still told of ghosts and fairies.

Even here in Ireland now, he doubted that people would see things his way. That poster of Killarney was one indication of that. The attitude of the hotel clerk in Cork was another. On learning that the guest was an American gentleman, the clerk had perceptibly become just a little comical, a little roguish in his demeanour. Again in Cork, that very morning, when the train's destination was announced, some idler on the platform was inspired to break into that song about the Rose of Tralee.

Wyndham wasn't here for the Rose of Tralee, nor did he care for the wearin' of the green. Danny Boy was nothing to him. His instinct told him that these tawdry fictions were a consequence of the Irish being taken out of their true habitat and made to live in cities. They had forgotten the gods and fighting men and had made mock of the folk tales.

And that must have been why he had chosen Tralee and not Killarney. He was closer to the truth here. He knew that Cruachan of the Enchantments lay in Connacht, somewhere to the north, but there in front of him were other blue ragged hills, disdained by tourists, and there he would find the true Irish, working their stony fields and telling their true stories.

They might look at him with suspicion, but that was surely better than some picturesque local with a stage wink and the offer of a jaunt round the beautiful lakes.

The small part within Daniel Wyndham's soul that used strong language said Hell with That.

Tomorrow his real journey would begin. No trains and no hotels. Thatch instead of slate roofs, and an ancient magic still to be sensed in the misty air.

There was no magic on this street, where the twentieth century was already staking its claim. No magic. What there was, though, was a certain air of unreality – of wrongness. It was a few days past midsummer, but he could feel the damp chill through his overcoat. It was almost nine o'clock in the evening, but there was little sign of the daylight fading.

The resolve that fixed his mind on tomorrow pushed him further now. Why postpone his quest any more? This wasn't the countryside he'd been seeking, but here he was in Ireland, already in an unknown land. He had passed perhaps a half-dozen small public houses on his walk – places where the men gathered and talked. He could just walk in to any of them, and sit, and listen.

At the very least he would get out of the rain.

2

On Field Service Helmet and Forage Cap: In gilt or gilding metal, a grenade. On the ball, in silver, the Tiger and scroll inscribed 'Royal Munster'.

—*Dress Regulations for the Army*, 1911

'The Bengal tiger,' said Moriarty, licking beer from his moustache, 'is not an animal commonly associated with the counties of Kerry, Limerick, or even Cork.'

He set his glass down on the bar with the emphasis of a judge sounding his gavel, and fixed the publican with a look. The glass was refilled.

Wyndham was barely in the door and already he had fallen in with bad company.

The place had looked so inviting from the outside, and for the most part this modest bar had lived up to its promise. There was the soft yellow light from the paraffin lamps, and the warmth and fragrance of the turf fire. The men in soft hats, with strong hands gripping their glasses, with rough clothes smelling of livestock and the fields, were almost as he'd envisioned them.

The two redcoats at the bar were out of place.

Daniel Wyndham had come to Ireland in search of old stories. Well this story had tigers in it.

Growing up in New England, Wyndham had been nurtured on prejudices older than a disgust of the teeming Catholic slum-dwellers of the cities. Older yet was the inherited fear of King George's men – the redcoats of Lexington and Concord – who'd burned and murdered up and down the country, from Massachusetts to Virginia. But then, if you only listened to any Irishman for more than a moment, you'd know that what the British soldiery had done in the American colonies was a mere nothing compared to the rapine and slaughter and starvation inflicted upon God's Holy Ireland by these same uniformed savages.

And now here he was: drinking with two of them, because they were the only men in the place who'd talk to him.

In truth it was just the one of them – this man Moriarty – who was doing the talking. The other man, Lynch, was content to mind his drinking, and only added the odd animal sound to the conversation; not that it was a conversation. Moriarty was giving a performance, and Wyndham and Lynch were merely props.

It had begun the moment Wyndham opened the door. Everyone looked up, of course, but only the barman and the two soldiers failed to look down again.

Wyndham had ordered a glass of whiskey because he had been brought up to believe that decent people did not drink beer in saloons. Of course he had also been brought up to believe that decent people did not drink ardent spirits either, but he was a man now, independent of his teetotal Episcopalian home. He had proved that on his very first evening aboard the *Laconia*, when he'd tasted alcohol for the first time. Whiskey was something that men drank. Respectable men in well-tailored coats ordered it from stewards before dinner. They seemed to prefer it with soda, but fizz was a little too fast for the young Mr Wyndham, who took it with water.

All the better, for this did not look like the sort of establishment acquainted with the sophistication of soda water.

The barman was civil, but if the locals were not evidently hostile, there was a stoniness in the air. It didn't take Wyndham long to know that he was not the cause of it. The realisation reassured him but little, because in this small room the only place to stand was in the wide berth that the locals had given the two soldiers, and thus Wyndham was now clearly with the foreigners' party.

The taller soldier had waited no more than a few seconds after Wyndham's change had been given to him before he opened the game. He was a lean young man, and was probably no more than a couple of years older than Wyndham, though his moustache and his worldly-wise confidence added half a generation to him in Wyndham's eyes.

He'd begun by asking, in an easy way, if he was right in supposing that the gentleman was a visitor to these shores. A travelled gentleman? A transatlantic gentleman, even?

He'd thought as much.

He didn't say so, but his look was of one who knew a fellow cosmopolitan when he met one.

The accent was marked, but the soldier spoke slowly and deliberately, including the whole room in his audience.

And had the gentleman in his travels ever visited Alexandria by chance? No? The soldier had.

In elaborating, he half turned to face the room in general, both his elbows against the bar, his cap pushed far back on his head.

Alexandria. There was the place. Especially if you were just a young fella who'd never seen anything more exotic than Aldershot. Oh, but he could tell stories! he said.

But did they know? Did they know that there was better than Alexandria? Well there was. For hadn't he been shipped out all the way from Egypt to Calcutta, and seen it with his own two eyes? And hadn't he met fellas in Alexandria, and hadn't they told this poor young gawm that the place wasn't a patch on Calcutta? And weren't they right?

And here he turned to Wyndham and added, 'And sure you know yourself, sir.'

Although it had clearly been established that the visitor did not know, Wyndham kept his peace. In this soldier's theatre he hoped he was being set up as the straight man, and not the butt.

'Calcutta! Jesus!'

The soldier made it known that that was the place to see. It was, he averred, not just grand, but the grandest place altogether. He took a long pull on his cigarette and stared into the rising smoke for a moment, remembering no doubt the smoke that rose in the different air of India.

But did the gentleman know that there was some to be met in India who had no love for the place at all any more? Not for the splendours of Calcutta even? It wasn't good enough for them, they'd said. There was, they'd sworn, a place that'd beat Calcutta hollow: a place that was more livelier and more beautiful, and even where the girls were prettier.

He paused a few beats to let the notion of such a place be encompassed by the narrow and parochial minds of his audience.

'And I asked them, didn't I? I asked them where that might be. And do you know what they said to me?'

Wyndham wore a tight and civil smile. He was the only one.

'"Tralee!" they said!'

Wyndham made the motion of a brief silent laugh.

'And do you know something, sir?' – and now the soldier's voice was too loud entirely. He was back facing Wyndham, but his eyes were on the men near the fire.

'They were all bloody liars!'

The publican wiped the bar vigorously, and declined to look the soldier in the eye as he told him that they didn't want that class of language in here.

'Sure I was only codding,' said the soldier. 'Only codding,' he said to the room at large. 'Only codding,' he murmured to Wyndham as he tilted his pint down his open throat. The other soldier did likewise, and that was when Wyndham realised that the unspeaking man had not moved, nor turned his gaze away from the locals all the while his companion was speaking.

The silence that followed the soldier's performance demanded something to fill it, and the locals were being of no help. Wyndham took a sip of his whiskey and resolved not to do such a thing again without due care. At least his voice was now roughened enough to speak to this widely travelled warrior beside him at the bar.

'You're a long way from home,' said Wyndham, referring to the man's exile in this miserable backwater, without, of course, implying to anyone for the least moment that it was at all miserable or in any way a backwater.

The soldier looked philosophical. 'Ah, sure,' he said. 'It could be worse. A few hours on the train. You know yourself, sir.'

A few hours? Wyndham made a rapid calculation, and the answer turned him up far short of England's shore.

'You're Irish, then?' he said, unable to keep the surprise from his voice.

'And why wouldn't I be?' said the soldier, heading towards indignation.

'Ah. Yes. I do beg your pardon. The red coat, you see. The English uniform. I thought... well.'

The soldier straightened himself, and took a step closer to Wyndham, but this was no threat. He spoke with stern patience.

'Do you see that now, sir?' he said, pointing to the bright buttons. 'Can you read that at all?' He pushed his cap forward and tilted his head until the peak was nearly touching Wyndham's nose. The tone of voice suggested that it might have been an honest question, but before Wyndham could admit that he didn't know what he was looking for, nor could he see it in this light, the soldier read it for him.

'Royal Munster,' he said. 'Do you see that, sir?'

And with that he straightened up again, and the light caught the cap badge, and Wyndham did see it: a globe, or a sunburst or something, and a heraldic beast of some description, and a scroll that read Royal Munster.

Munster was Ireland's southernmost province, and the soldier wasn't going to hit him after all.

'Of course! Yes!' said Wyndham. 'Yes!'

'So not English at all, sir, do you see?'

'Of course. Yes. I do beg your pardon, Mister –.'

'Private –.'

'Private –.'

'Moriarty.'

'Moriarty.'

'And that's Private Lynch.'

'How do you do? My name is Wyndham. May I buy you gentlemen – you men – a drink?'

'Delighted, Mr Wyndham.'

Private Francis Moriarty was only too happy to talk, and talk all night. The sullen locals weren't rising to his bait, and Lynch, if he spoke at all, didn't seem to Wyndham as though he spoke English. Like Moriarty, he had a moustache like a yard brush, but it never once twitched from a smile beneath, and his pale eyes stared the whole time at Wyndham with no emotion whatever. He leant on the bar as if with his last strength, and only ever took the cigarette out of his mouth to pour beer in.

Moriarty would have been having a dull old evening if it had just been him and Lynch. Wyndham was a godsend.

The American gentleman was new to the country and needed to be filled in on all manner of things of which Moriarty had both wide knowledge and strong opinions. Best of all, like all true Americans, this Mr Wyndham had deep pockets and, if he seemed to be only a bit of a moderate drinker himself, he had proper regard to the needs of two of His Majesty's thirsty men.

The red coat (more of a tunic, really) was the chief obstacle to Wyndham's understanding. Everyone – even the decent people who kept the Irish at arm's length – knew that Ireland was a troubled land. Wyndham's fascination with the place had already informed him that besides being the bright warriors of Finn's war-band, the Fenians were also a black-handed secret society, sworn to wrest Ireland from the British crown by dynamitings and rick-burnings, and murders with knives in public places. This was in answer to, and answered by, more burnings and murders, as well as hangings and transportations. Even if an outsider disregarded all the more lurid elements of this tale, he could see from any newspaper that Ireland's difficult relationship with England, although mostly now conducted by men in collars and ties in Westminster, was a very real issue, with the alarmists even rumbling about open rebellion.

What puzzled Wyndham therefore, was how two Irishmen – nay, a whole regiment of Irishmen – could wear the king's uniform in their own country, and even drink fearlessly in public houses, outnumbered by the hostile peasantry? It was a difficult question to pose without giving offence, but Moriarty had no reluctance in tackling the answer. At the very tentative broaching of the Irish Question, he was in like a shot.

'A conflict of interest, Mr Wyndham? I follow you exactly. You're talking about Fenians, aren't you?'

Wyndham noticed the barman wince. Moriarty must have noticed too, for he soothingly assured the man that there'd be no talk of politics, only that he was just explaining things to the foreign gentleman, a visitor to these shores. He turned back to the visitor.

'I will put your mind at rest, sir. We are not Fenians.' Then, raising his voice to the wider audience, 'And we're not Orangemen either! But that said,' – more conversational again – 'there's a few that are.'

The army, as it turned out, was a complex and splendid thing, and the way Moriarty presented it, each regiment was a nation unto itself, with customs and loyalties all of its own. There were a considerable number – or, as Moriarty had it, a rake – of Irish regiments in the British army, and while all loyal to the king, God bless him, they maintained other and more peculiar loyalties too. Moriarty knew it all, and he did not spare Wyndham.

To begin with, there was, apparently, the Royal Irish Regiment – the 18th Foot as was – and even if they'd been called Paddy's Blackguards, you could take it that the 'Royal' bit meant what it said. Not outright Orangemen, mind. Not as could be proven anyhow. But they thought themselves a cut above the rest on account of having been around as long as the army practically. So that was them, and no more need be said about them.

And then there was the Skins. That's the Enniskillen Fusiliers, only they called it 'Inniskilling' because, as the audience might readily have guessed, they couldn't bloody spell, which was fitting, because they couldn't bloody speak at all either, except for that bloody awful way Ulstermen might talk.

Orangemen. Black Orangemen. Every man jack of them. Sashes and lodges and the whole damned lot.

There were the Royal Irish Rifles too. Orange. As orange as the day was long.

After that came a 'shower' referred to as the Faughs, known in polite company as the Royal Irish Fusiliers. Not especially orange – not so's you'd notice, mind, but terrible men for giving themselves airs. There followed a long digression that began with the capture (or 'theft', as he called it) of one of Napoleon's eagles and then somehow ended up in an aggrieved anecdote about a fight in Portsmouth, in which certain Irishmen had not seen fit to deliver their fellow countryman from the hands of the Marines. Anyway, fierce men for putting on airs were the Faughs, bad luck to them.

Then the Connaught Rangers. No 'Royal' there. And why? Moriarty's answer was unreserved. Hooligans the lot of them. Hooligans! Why the army had let them in at all one might never know. Indeed, anyone looking for Fenians might find them there, but if the Fenians had any sense they'd have damn all to do with that mob. 'The Devil's Own' the Rangers were called, and that they were in a perpetual state of mutiny and filthy indiscipline was not down to Fenianism but to blackguardism.

May God and the War Office keep them far hence.

The great regimental history also included, in the interest of completeness and fairness, bodies from Leinster and Dublin, which were rather beneath a Munster man's consideration, and several regiments of cavalry that were hardly worth a mention, with their frilly uniforms and their horses and all. No need to dwell on these. Let's get to the main event.

'The Royal Munster Fusiliers!' announced Moriarty, as if the whole regiment had just arrived and was standing at the door. Lynch raised his glass, proclaimed what could only have been a toast or a motto in God-knew-what language, and sank the best part of a pint without seeming to move his throat.

Wyndham politely joined in the toast, ignoring the scowls from some of the men around the fire. It then seemed only fair to honour the occasion by ordering another round.

The Munster Fusiliers were, as it turned out, the finest regiment in the army. They were both loyal to the core and Irish through and through, and had held the empire together for centuries. Sure wouldn't they all be speaking Boer in South Africa now if it hadn't been for the Munsters? Saved the day there, when all the English regiments, and the Scots, and half the bloody Irish regiments as well, if truth be told, were ready to run like rabbits. Sure everyone knew that.

Wyndham listened to all this and sipped his whiskey, and paid for even more drink for the soldiers. He had no idea what the large coins pushed across the bar in change were worth, but as he recklessly ordered even a second drink for himself, he thought it a cheap price for the steady dispelling of his shyness and an evening in the company of men.

He peered more closely at Moriarty's badge, which was replicated on either side of his collar and all down his buttons. The learned Moriarty, happy to continue all night in his dissertation, explained that the flaming orb was not, as the American gentleman had first supposed, a globe, but a bursting grenade. The silver beast embossed thereon was clearly, on examination, a tiger.

Wyndham asked why.

Moriarty glanced at the clock, drank his pint, and cleared his throat.

Tigers were not native to the province of Munster. Wyndham had guessed as much.

Tigers came from India.

3

'I have nothing to say to the 1ˢᵗ Fusiliers: they will do as they always do.'

—Colonel John Nicholson, Delhi 1857

Tigers came from India. So did the Munster Fusiliers.

'Hundred an' first Foot, so we were, once upon a time, but before that – before that – we were the Bengal European Fusiliers, and proud of it, boy.'

Wyndham wondered if the 'boy' were rhetorical, or whether Moriarty was sliding down the scale through familiarity towards contempt.

'We were the first white men in India. Long before there ever was a Royal Irish Regiment, or even an army for that matter, there we were, out in India, fighting the bloody wogs. We were at Plassey with Clive. You know Plassey? Big battle there, boy. Big huge battle. And we won it. Naturally we won it. Chillianwalla too. And Goojerat and all. Length and breadth of India, the Dirty Shirts were there.'

He was watching for the inquiry to be formed on Wyndham's lips and forestalled it.

'The Dirty Shirts? That's us. And why? Let me tell you why.'

He looked again at the clock and declared they'd better call for another round. 'And you'll need one.'

Wyndham would have been content to stay with the glass he had, but Moriarty insisted that his fibres would require fortification if he were to follow the Bengal Europeans down the blazing road from Dagshai to Delhi. He did not insist that Wyndham pay for the drinks, but didn't make any demur when the American put his hand in his pocket either.

'Right,' said Moriarty, after he had wiped his moustache on the back of his hand. 'Eighteen hundred and fifty-seven. The Great Mutiny. You've heard of that. That was when all the Indian regiments rose up and killed all their officers, and all the white men, and all the women and children too, the dirty bastards. And any of the white people that they didn't kill escaped into forts, or barricaded themselves into residences, or just dug themselves into trenches in their own cantoonments like they did at Cawnpore – and weren't they nearly all killed? – until there wasn't a loyal soldier left hardly that wasn't dead or besieged. But there was us, d'you see. So they called us and they sent us to fight.

'Now if you were ever in India, or even if you weren't, you'd know that it's hot. In winter it's like a grand summer's day. In summer it would kill a man dead. Dead! You can't fight in summer. You can't even march in summer. You can't even get out of your cot and stroll around a bit any more than you can stroll into a brick oven and have a lie down and expect to be all right after. The army always heads to the hills in the summer. But not this summer. There was fighting to be done. "March to Delhi," was the order, "and damn the heat." So we did.'

He took a deep swallow of his beer. 'The heat, lads. Jesus.'

The sky was like hot steel and it was filled with wheeling vultures. The commander squinted at the blurred image in his telescope. The dust and the heat haze and the intense glare from the summer sun rendered a telescope almost useless, more especially since the distance was not so great after all, but the commander had appearances to keep up. The men at his back were mostly regular troops, many of whom had seen hard service in the Punjab and even as far away as the

Afghan frontier. To them, a general without a horse and a sword and a brass telescope was no general at all, and the commander had to convince them that his credentials were genuine. In truth, he had never commanded troops in battle before, but he was a high-born gentleman and there was no question that men should not obey his orders.

And such men to obey! The troops behind him were assembled from half of the regiments of India, from the Presidency of Bengal, which had soldiered through a hundred years and a hundred hard campaigns under the flag of the English East India Company. And now the English had broken faith, and shown how they despised their Indian soldiers, and the soldiers had risen up against them and then the whole country had risen in anger also. It was as if the old days were returned, with all the men of India fighting together in common cause, and rallying to the standard of the Mughal emperor, shorn of his power and dignity by the English, but soon to come into the glories of his great ancestors. Joining him were the disinherited heir to the Peshwa of Bithur, the disregarded queen of Jhansi, and a host of Maratha princelings remembering the days of their grandfathers, now with armies behind them again.

Ah yes, by God, thought the commander proudly, the army at his back would fill the meanest man with pride. But what of the army before him?

The ranks of the infidel were formed up for attack, and menacing they looked, but menacing like a host of bandits. This was not an army that the Maharani Victoria would have had parade before her. Where was their shine and their polish and their splendour? Where were the gaudy uniforms of blue and scarlet? All gone in the killing heat.

The red woollen coat was hardly to be seen, and would, it was certain, have killed the white men faster than the cholera, had

*it been worn. In its place were cotton and canvas in a dozen
shades of drab. The Urdu word was khaki. Dust-coloured.
Dung-coloured. A pitiful substitute for infantry red and
cavalry blue and rifle green.*

*Who were these barbaric men to his front? They looked
all alike in their colourless motley, with their skins burned
the colour of red brick and their beards bleached like dead
grass, but the commander knew that they were not all the
same. Those ruffianly men at the left of the line – were they
a scratch collection of civil servants and settlers, hastily
outfitted as soldiers? Or maybe an elite regiment toughened
from fighting the Russians in the Crimea?*

*To the commander, all of them were Franks, but he knew
that, like the Indians, the Franks were many nations, and the
queen of the English ruled over races that were not English.
Those grim ranks in grey jackets: they might be nobody, but
they might just as well be fearsome Scottish men from the
mountains. Without their skirts and plumed war bonnets
it was impossible to tell. No. No, it wasn't. The Highland
men were over there. There to the right, dressed in brown,
with one man in feathers and goatskin and all, making the
bagpipes howl. They'd need watching.*

*But there were worse than the Scots. When the British line
swept down on them, the Indians would need to hold hardest
against those bloody mercenaries from the cold wastes of
Ireland. The commander found them at last. Their shot-torn
battle flags proclaimed them. They wore no coats. Each man
had come to the battlefield in his shirtsleeves, like a man
accustomed to look on fighting as his daily work, and those
same shirts, dyed to an inconspicuous blue-grey, were all
begrimed with dust and sweat and powder. The men beneath
those colours would come with their glittering bayonets
down on the Indian ranks like a storm on a field of wheat.*

Courage alone could not stop them. Every gun, every rifle, every blade must be brought to bear against those terrible Irishmen of the Bengal Fusiliers. They would not falter. They would not flee. To be stopped, they must be killed, every one. The first guns rumbled somewhere behind the haze and the first rounds blossomed in white smoke over the Indian ranks. The Frankish line came forward. God had already granted the victory. It was written. The Indian commander shut his telescope, turned in his saddle, and gave the order.
'Kill the men in the dirty shirts,' he said.

'"Kill the men in the dirty shirts," begod,' said Moriarty, gazing deep into his glass and shaking his head at the memory of something that was dead and done with thirty years before he'd even been born. 'I'm telling you, lads: they were men then. What time is it? We'll have another.'

And they did.

How many was that? wondered Wyndham. Certainly enough to forget that he'd ever felt the cold.

The room had thinned out. The older men had all made their goodnights by now, and only a group of four young men remained by the fire, watchful and truculent under the gaze of the two fusiliers.

Lynch said something to the barman, but was given a firm answer concerning the licence. Wyndham guessed that it was closing time and was glad. He had passed his test. He had stood and drunk with hard men in a barroom and had held his own. He would be leaving on his feet.

Lynch didn't seem to cotton on to the notion of leaving at all. There was a threatening, wheedling tone to his exchange with the publican, even though Wyndham couldn't understand a word. Out of curiosity, and to diffuse the rancour in the air, he politely inquired if, like Lynch, Moriarty also spoke Gaelic.

Everybody looked at Wyndham. He was putting his question in a different way before Moriarty answered him, scoffing.

'Him? Speak Irish? Devil a word!' He grinned at Lynch and punched him on the shoulder. 'A word of Hindustani, wha'? But not so's the blacks could understand, hah?'

Lynch took it more seriously. He fixed on Wyndham, and then jerked his thumb towards the local men, now gathering up to leave.

'Them,' he said. 'Them fellas,' and Wyndham could understand the words, but not immediately the meaning. Moriarty was there before him. He called to the men, who had halted on their way out.

'The gentleman here was wondering if any of you might speak Irish?' he said, a grin on his face.

They made no reply, but looked at Moriarty, and at Wyndham. Lynch helped them along. Maybe he was enunciating properly for the benefit of all, or perhaps Wyndham, aided by whiskey, had finally penetrated the accent, but Lynch's words rang out clear.

'On account of yis all being fucking culchies, do y'know.'

'Out! Get out now!' shouted the barman. 'I've had enough of you! I'll have the police out on ye!'

'Ah, would you ever mind yourself?' said Moriarty lazily, his eyes not leaving the men by the door.

'You'll forgive my comrade his uncivil language, I'm sure,' he said to them. 'Only he'd be unused to the genteel company now.'

'That's enough!' said the barman. 'Go on out! And go quietly, for Jesus's sake!'

Reluctantly, the four civilians moved edgewise out the door, jaws set and fists clenched. Wyndham stayed with the soldiers, who, despite the barman's unceasing protests, made no move until the door closed. Then they drained the last of their glasses and straightened themselves. Moriarty set his cap exactly.

'You stupid Dublin gobshite,' he said.

Lynch merely laughed.

Wyndham, light-headed, followed them out.

The fresh air of the street made Wyndham dizzy. For a moment he couldn't even see that the four men were waiting for them.

Lynch started it.

Wyndham watched the wild Irish as they brawled in the street, his heart pounding and his head swimming. He saw Moriarty's fist, wrapped in his belt, swing and strike. He saw a man down on his knees, his hands to his face, felled by Lynch's head-butt. He thought in his dizziness of the heroes who fought with Finn and the Hound of Cullann, and of the laments of Cathleen, the daughter of Houlihan, bowed beneath an English yoke. The words of Mr Yeats came to him unbidden, and he spoke them aloud in a faraway voice.

On the flaming stones, without refuge, the limbs of the
Fenians are tost.

Lynch looked at him with joyful and bloody face, and laughed, and kicked his man while he was down.

4

Who hath woe? Who hath sorrow? Who hath contentions? Who hath babbling? Who hath wounds without cause? Who hath redness of eyes?
They that tarry long at the wine; they that go to seek mixed wine

—Proverbs XXIII, 29–30.

Tralee,
Kerry County,
Ireland.

June 28th 1914

Dear Sarah,

You'd laugh if you could see me now. For myself, I almost feel like weeping.
O Sarah! I wish—

He wished he was dead.

Wyndham lay curled on a wooden shelf. There was a blanket, so the shelf was probably supposed to serve as a bed. The blanket did not quite keep out the chill, nor did it hide him from the world, but he had it drawn close about him just the same.

Besides the shelf there was a bucket, and these made up the room's entire furnishings.

The bucket had become the focus of his consuming shame, which was too huge to be contemplated in its entirety. He had been sick into that bucket. He believed he would be so again. He was stuck in what looked like a cell with a bucket of sick. And on a Sunday.

June Something, 1914

Sunday

Dear Sarah,

By the time you read this I will be dead. Tell Mother whatever you think fit, but—

Would he and the noisome bucket be together all day? And all the next day? And all through his long incarceration? No. Surely not. Worse than that. Someone would come. Someone in heavy boots would come and open that door and glance in disgust at that bucket before turning the same look on Wyndham, and Wyndham would be judged: not by his Maker before the Throne, but by a terrible figure in heavy boots and a uniform.

What sort of a uniform? The man in his imagination wore the coat of the town constable from back home when Wyndham was a little boy, but, as he thought about it, the nightmare vision reclothed itself in the dark green coat and peculiar spiked helmet of the Irish police. An Irish policeman in heavy boots, filling up that stark room, and looking down at Wyndham with disgust – with utter disgust. And he deserved it.

How long had he been lying here? What time was it? All the light there was came from the small grey square of daylight showing through the barred window near the ceiling. He imagined that it might be possible to reach the bars by jumping and then to hoist himself up to get a view of the outside, but his head still swam sickeningly and such gymnastics were beyond him.

He was afraid even to sit up straight because that only made him dizzy, and that meant the bucket again.

Outside a bugle sounded. He didn't know what it meant, but it was no stretch of the imagination on this blighted Sabbath to hear the angel sounding his trumpet. Judgement was coming.

He must have slept again then, because he woke up. The thudding headache was still with him. There was the sound of many nailed boots going to and fro, but they were their own business and not his.

He thought again of his sister, and in his mind started yet another letter to her, but his earlier delirium was fading away and he could no longer lose himself in his bitter little fantasy.

Dear Sarah,

I am in jail.

Yours Ever,

    Daniel.

He left it at that. He was fully awake now, and the pain and the queasiness were all he had. He discovered that he could almost take his mind off it all by concentrating absolutely on the chattering of his teeth.

He had no idea where his overcoat had got to.

Lord, but he was thirsty.

What would they be saying of him back in Lowell when they learned of his fate? Would they speak of him at all? There would be gossip around the town for a year and more, but it would be hushed out of respect for the Wyndhams. The family, after the initial shock, would become tight-lipped, and stay tight-lipped for evermore. Maybe in years to come one of Sarah's children would find a fading photograph in the back of some bureau, and be told with a sudden sob that, 'That is your poor Uncle Daniel,' and the bureau would be hastily locked, while in a distant land the clean young face from the photograph grew ever more grey and dissipated in who knew what wretched circumstances.

They had been right. He'd dismissed them in his heart as fussing women, smothering him with their petty concerns, but they'd been right. He had damned himself with his foolish dreams.

At some incalculable hour he drifted again into unconsciousness. Then later he was awake again and sick again.

It was dark when they came for him.

5

III, 30. In the offence of simple drunkenness there are practically various grades, for the purpose of the amount of punishment; and evidence should be given as to the circumstances of the drunkenness, and as to whether the drunken man was riotous or not, so that punishment may be apportioned accordingly.

—*Manual of Military Law*, 1907

Francis Moriarty was feeling rotten altogether. It wasn't just the bad head on him, which was bad enough, but one of those big dirty Kerrymen must have hit him a dig in the side of his neck as well. He hadn't noticed it at the time, but it hurt to swallow now. Not that he wanted to swallow. The smell of brass polish was in his nose, and the taste of it in his mouth. He wouldn't want his breakfast at all. The bread and tea would only taste of Brasso and Blanco. But it wasn't just the bad head that was making him bad. He was nervous and jittery and more nervous still with trying to hide it.

They'd got into trouble last night, and it couldn't be long before they got found out.

The business about the fight wouldn't matter. A hundred-odd men in barracks, all looking the same to a stranger. It had been dark. Better men had got away with worse.

But Lynch had only had to go and act the maggot with that American. Bloody Lynch would get them both landed in the glasshouse. Bloody Lynch and that bloody overcoat.

Look at him sitting there on his cot cleaning his belt and giving little peeks around the room like the thief he is.

'Howya, Moriarty! How's the head, Francie boy?'

That was Harrington, the dirty hoor. Either not so hungover, or still drunk enough to be cheerful at this hour. Moriarty made the effort, and put cheer enough into his own voice.

'You know yourself, boy.'

'Grand night?'

'Great night altogether. A bit of neck-oil in the bar, a bit of skirt in the alley, and a bit of ear in the street.'

Harrington laughed. 'Sets a man up for the week.'

'It does, mate, it does.'

Just your typical Sunday morning: cleaning kit like mad and telling big lies. That said, mind, a few pints of the purge went without saying, and they had managed to get a bit of ear from those lads outside the pub, even if it hadn't been very satisfying nor memorable. Give that bowsie Lynch his due, but he couldn't go home of a night without blood on his knuckles. He just wouldn't sleep easy. There'd be hardly a peep out of him all evening, but he could say three filthy things about your sister in the time it took him to unhook his collar and bring his fists up. He was grand and dependable that way.

But oh, boys! Hadn't he gone too far last night?

That bloody American. The pair of them would swing for that Yank yet.

And the worst of it was that Moriarty had only a few months to go before his discharge. Seven years with the colours next October and then a new suit and a handshake and walk out into the world a free man. Maybe get a job with the brother. Maybe not. Wouldn't matter. He'd be a free man. Mister Moriarty.

And then he came back to earth with a sickening bang. Mister

Moriarty. That's what the American had called him at first. Oh Jesus. Would he remember the name? In his state? Would it matter? Moriarty had been on an identity parade once before, years ago, when some poor shamed housemaid had walked along the ranks to pick out the man who'd taken her good name. That had been a bit of entertainment at least. Getting a girl into trouble was something that more than a few fellas would have been proud of. Robbing a respectable civilian, though? That was a low and common crime, and Moriarty would bet that even some of the worst hard cases would act all sanctimonious over that, and spout on about the honour of the regiment.

And then the orderly room, and then the cells. Oh God! The cells! That had seemed funny last night. That had seemed clever. How the blazes could he have gone along with Lynch like that? How could he have thought that was a good idea, or that they might somehow get away with it?

He must have had drink taken.

Did they transfer you from military to civil prison when your enlistment was up?

This would never have happened if he'd stayed with the battalion out in Burma. No American tourists in Shwebo, and no overcoats for that matter.

He'd thought himself the cutest man alive to get his transfer back to Ireland. He'd laughed at those other fellows with their seven years turning into eight before they got home, because the army always somehow managed to get those ten or twelve extra months out of you if your time expired while you were out east. The troopships sailed at their fixed season, and the army wasn't going to let you go early so you could catch this year's boat, so they kept you on until the next trooping season came around.

But Moriarty had somehow pulled the great stroke of getting posted to the depot to serve out his last months at home and so be free and clear of the army right on time. He'd guessed that Tralee wouldn't match up to Rangoon, but a year ago he'd thought he was at the end of his tether, and would have done anything to get away from the heat and the big huge creepy-crawlies and that bastard Sergeant O'Sullivan. Now, free of all that, he hadn't expected that the boredom would take such a heavy toll. The Devil truly made work for idle hands, or at least made idle soldiers hang around with animals like Lynch. Sometimes you'd almost prefer the company of the scorpion-spiders in Burma.

He breathed on his collar badge and buffed it one last time. It'd do. Bloody Sunday. Bloody church parade. Bloody marching through the streets to Mass in your best kit, with a bad head and everyone gawking at you, and more than a few dirty looks. Bloody day of rest, my arse. And somehow, somehow they had to get that Yank out of the guardroom. He couldn't leave it to Lynch. Lynch was mad. You couldn't trust him

Last night they could have left the Yank out cold in the road, but what does Lynch do? He only goes and tries to help the poor eejit.

'Give him a bed for the night,' he'd said. 'He's after buying us drink.' And he'd tenderly patted the unconscious man's cheek before hauling him up onto his shoulders.

Sergeant Conway was away at a funeral beyond Limerick, and that left Shiels in charge, and if Shiels was true to form, he'd be mouldy drunk, and maybe not even fit enough to write 'All in Order' in the report book, never mind inspect the cells. That, if Lynch was capable of reason at all, must have been the bottom of Lynch's plan.

How in the name of God had it ever seemed like a good idea?

Their only hope was that Shiels would be too sick to shift himself today, and might be out taking the cure as soon as he was able. But Christ, it was a risky business. How they didn't get caught last night was a bloody miracle. How could they pull it off in broad daylight, even on a Sunday?

His heart and stomach were fluttering like mad. He'd have to get Lynch on his own, without letting on that it was a conspiracy.

Surely be to God the man would see the fix they were in. If he had any conscience at all he'd see the necessity of sorting things out. Hadn't he shown conscience last night when he'd wanted to help the American?

Mind you, he'd only just been after walloping the man over the head and robbing his overcoat.

6

Only such officers as are likey to set an example of soldierly bearing, and to ensure the efficient training of young soldiers, will be selected...

—*King's Regulations*, 1912 (Regular Establishment of Special Reserve Units and of Depôts)

Major Hugh Fitzmullen-Brophy was fiftyish and had lost most of his hair, but for all that he was still hale and hearty.

Keeping fit. That was the ticket.

Other men might show their age, and run to fat, and wheeze on the stairs, and claim to be growing old gracefully, but what sort of example were they setting the younger generation? So here he was, on this splendid summer morning, striding briskly to Ballymullen Barracks along a road where another man might ride.

Nothing wrong with riding, of course, but there was nothing either like a two-mile stretch of the legs for setting a chap up of a morning. Clearing the cobwebs. Getting the juices flowing. That sort of thing. Especially after the weekend he'd just had.

A perfectly dismal weekend, cooped in the house with the rain not letting up, and the few topics of conversation soon exhausted, and the sitting-room fireplace smoking dreadfully with the wind out of the west like that. It wasn't that their guests were dreary – not really dreary – but Susan had been fussing and Molly fretting, and Fitzmullen-Brophy himself had been acutely conscious of having to be on his best behaviour. Then there'd been that business with the dogs. Turned out the Bryant boy didn't care for dogs at all. Stupid business really, but Fitzmullen-Brophy thought that far too great a to-do had been made over one torn trouser cuff and, although he didn't like to say it, he could hardly be expected to warm to any young man who reacted in that fashion to a couple of dogs who'd been only a trifle over-eager.

No. Say what you might, but Sidney Bryant was not ideal son-in-law material.

Shame, that, because young Molly seemed to have her heart set on him, and Molly's happiness was the main thing, of course.

Fitzmullen-Brophy doted on his daughter, his only child. Dearest girl any father could want. But it was only natural that a man should want a son. Follow him into the regiment. That sort of thing. Now it looked as if he were to be disappointed in the matter of a son-in-law too.

Still though – there was always a grandson to look forward to. Think of it! Rambling around these fields with a cheerful youngster on a morning like this. Fitzmullen-Brophy couldn't for the life of him think of anything better.

He'd met General Sir Robert Baden-Powell once. South Africa. There was a man with proper notions about child-rearing. Took all that was best about boyhood, about manliness, about the army, and distilled it all into a single simple philosophy. By God, that was something that made it worth waiting for grandsons.

They'd take the dogs and be out after rabbits before breakfast, and have the jolliest times. They'd come back with wet feet and sunburnt faces and the women would make a fuss, but it wouldn't matter a jot, because they'd all be so very *healthy*, do you see? A well-brought-up lad – one who's not mollycoddled – can withstand anything provided he gets enough fresh air, and as for the old man? Why a chap should still be puffing along admirably into his sixties if he kept himself fit.

Hugh Fitzmullen-Brophy was not a man who feared to show his knees in public. What a first-class grandfather he'd make.

Ridiculous thought, though, being a grandfather, when he was still a man in his prime. Damned pity he'd never had the chance to exercise himself fully in the fatherhood stakes. He'd done his best with Molly, but there was only so much that one could do with a girl.

At this particular moment, his knees, for the most part decently clad since the Mohmand expedition in '08, were snugly cased in whipcord breeches above a pair of deeply polished Stohwasser gaiters. His khaki service dress was clearly designed for riding, but besides Fitzmullen-Brophy's delight in vigorous walking, he'd never been thoroughly at ease with horses. He saw himself as an infantryman through and through, and disdained even the spurs that befitted his rank.

South Africa. That had been the proof of it. Only two sorts of officer in South Africa: those who insisted that the army needed more horses, and those who went and got the job done regardless.

He hunted, of course, but only out of duty. Then there was the dashed expense of the brutes. Say what you liked about living in Ireland: you were never short of a neighbour willing to sell you a horse, but it could be a deuced tricky business getting a fair bargain even from a trusted friend. The Fitzmullen-Brophys possessed but a single animal at the moment, and Susan needed it for the trap, and her husband was only too happy to let her have the beast. Nothing wrong with an officer of field rank walking. Sets a good example.

If there was only one thing wrong with County Kerry it was the nature of the landscape, and the enclosed fields with all their hedges and ditches. Capital country for raising children or livestock, of course, but not very practical when it came to teaching fieldcraft to young officers. Here was the training season come round again, and not a patch of ground even remotely resembling the rolling veldt.

Listowel was not Bloemfontein. MacGillycuddy's Reeks were not the North-West Frontier. The Regulars at least had the breadth of the Curragh for their playground. No such luxury for the Reserve.

Still. Couldn't be helped. This was the army, and one did what one had to with whatever was available, and Fitzmullen-Brophy was itching to get back to doing just that, to feeling useful again. That was the one drawback to being an officer on the Special Reserve: too much time with too little to do. The Major Fitzmullen-Brophys of this world were made for action. In that respect, South Africa had been the most tremendous experience of his life, hands down, bar none. Adventure, broad horizons, comradeship, purpose, and promotion. If it hadn't been unpatriotic, Fitzmullen-Brophy would have wished the war could have gone on forever.

And for a while there were hints that the merry life might indeed continue indefinitely, for hadn't the battalion been posted directly to India from Cape Town, with trouble brewing up on the Afghan border any time one looked in that direction? But promotion came slow in peacetime, and the great Mohmand expedition had not been fruitful for the Munsters' glory. Too much marching, a few shots fired from the rocks, and an epidemic in camp to bring the whole unsatisfactory business to an early close.

'The Brigadier General feels he cannot express his admiration for the pluck and patience of the Battalion under the late distressing circumstances...'

That was all very well, but it was a poor consolation prize for a campaign that had never fulfilled its promise.

Fitzmullen-Brophy was invalided home in '09. Shabkadr. Touch of the cholera. Didn't get over it as quick as a younger man might have. Bad luck.

Still, Ireland had been good.

Chance to get reacquainted with the place. Plenty of work to be done with 3rd Battalion. There were clouds on the horizon. All this talk of Home Rule was heating tempers. But the men were steady, loyal to the backbone. Nothing to fear there.

Still though, there were troubled times ahead.

Pluck and patience.

A chap had to keep fit.

He was a picture of military energy and enthusiasm by the time he turned in the barrack gate, and the sentry matched his spirit with the most creditable salute. After such a splendid entrance, the general emptiness that met the eye once inside the gate might have deflated a lesser man but, far from being deterred, Fitzmullen-Brophy gladdened at the sheer potential he saw in this blank canvas that was the depot of the regiment and the home of the 3rd (Special Reserve) Battalion of the Royal Munster Fusiliers.

Hardly anyone about today, but that was the very reason he was here. The reservists would be arriving for their annual training the week after next, and he knew that Lieutenant Colonel Brasier-Creagh, commanding the battalion, probably wouldn't arrive until then. He also knew that Major Worship, the officer commanding the depot, was taking advantage of this lull with a long weekend in Dublin. Nothing wrong with the man, of course, but Major Verelst Turner Worship DSO was *technically* junior to Fitzmullen-Brophy and didn't quite appreciate the guidance and advice of his more experienced elder as much as he might.

Naturally, Fitzmullen-Brophy would obey his superiors in all matters once the battalion was formed up, but if he could have a free hand today and possibly even tomorrow, perhaps he could put his stamp on things in a way that didn't look like meddling and that Worship and the Colonel might recognise as beneficial.

Also, in showing up early like this, Fitzmullen-Brophy could thrill to the feeling of being the senior officer in the barracks, if only for a day or so.

At that precise moment, the only living creature to be seen failed to recognise the authority of this senior officer.

It was the dog Bobs, idling in a patch of sunshine.

Fitzmullen-Brophy stopped and leant forward, slapping his knees.

'Bobs! Here boy! There's a good fella!'

The well-groomed mongrel looked his way and got to its feet but, instead of coming forward in greeting, it merely stared a moment and padded off in another direction. It cast a small cloud on Fitzmullen-Brophy's otherwise fine morning. He had done his damnedest over the past two years to cast the stray as a battalion mascot. It was he who had christened it after Field-Marshal Lord Roberts, whose father had had the regiment eighty years ago and who was sometimes pleased to call himself 'the oldest Munster'. Lord Roberts was still doing his duty like a good 'un. The dog his namesake was, frankly, something of a dashed disappointment. The next figure to appear promised better. It was Crosbie, the adjutant, very brisk and correct, approaching at speed, and with no time for pleasantries.

'Ah, Major,' he said. 'Glad to see you. Very glad.'

He didn't look glad. He looked rather grim, rather urgent. He stood confidentially close to Fitzmullen-Brophy, to impress him with the importance of the matter, and spoke rapidly.

'Slight problem. Rather sticky situation as a matter of fact. Had a spot of trouble yesterday. Haven't notified the CO. Fewer people know the better. Doing our best to sort it out ourselves. Major Belcher is here, of course, but I thought you'd be better suited to help.'

He did not preen to the adjutant's words, nor did he puff himself up, but Fitzmullen-Brophy felt the mantle of command settle again upon his shoulders, and it was light.

'Very wise, Crosbie. Perfectly correct. You can leave it with me. Now tell me what exactly is the matter.'

Good heavens. What a ghastly pickle.

Captain Crosbie had efficiently summarised the facts of the case as they hurried towards the officers' unmarried quarters.

079 Private Lynch had been apprehended on Sunday afternoon in leaving barracks without permission. That was the start of it. Private Lynch was found in unauthorised possession of a civilian overcoat, most likely with the intention of pawning or selling it. Although Private Lynch had claimed ownership of said garment, a tag on the coat was seen to bear the name D.P. Wyndham. Private Lynch was in close confinement pending Monday's company orders. The coat was confiscated by Corporal Shiels, Sergeant Conway being on three day's leave for family business.

Although acting-provost, it transpired that Corporal Shiels did not conduct an inspection of the cells that morning. No arrests having been made the previous night, it was assumed the cells were unoccupied. Corporal Shiels claimed an indisposition, but this should not excuse a clear negligence of duty. Matters were not addressed until Sergeant Conway returned, at which point a man – a civilian – was found occupying the rearmost cell in the guardroom. This civilian, since identified as Mr D.P. Wyndham of the United States, was in a distressed state, having been confined against his will without food or water for more than twenty hours. Furthermore, the Medical Officer, on examining the gentleman, diagnosed a concussion, and Mr Wyndham was duly put to bed. At this time, it was far from clear what circumstances had brought about this unhappy situation, and Captain Crosbie thought it best that discretion should prevail.

This morning, only half an hour before Fitzmullen-Brophy's arrival, an officer of the Royal Irish Constabulary appeared at the barracks, making enquiries after an American visitor named Wyndham, who had disappeared from his hotel on Saturday evening and was last thought to have been seen in the company of two soldiers in a public house off Lower Castle Street.

For the good of the regiment, Crosbie had lied through his teeth to the good constable.

Now perhaps Major Fitzmullen-Brophy might be decent enough to have a quiet word with Mr Wyndham, who was much recovered by now, and persuade him to take it all in good part, and thus keep the RIC, the Home Office, and the United States Embassy from utterly humbling the pride and destroying the reputation of the Royal Munster Fusiliers.

Fitzmullen-Brophy's gaze grew steely. He thought of the action at Slabbert's Nek. The colours of the regiment hadn't been waving in his face that day either, but they didn't need to be. He saw his duty clear.

'This is a serious business, Crosbie,' he said. 'Damned serious.'

'Quite,' said Crosbie. 'Hellish scandal.'

'Hellish. And that is why it must stay between the two of us, the MO, and Conway. Under no circumstances must the CO or the Colonel ever find out. There mustn't even be a formal reprimand for whomever was on sentry duty that night.'

'What do you suggest?'

Fitzmullen-Brophy had no plan whatsoever, but he knew better than to hesitate in a crisis.

'We must hang on to this Wyndham. It won't do at all to let him out of our sight until he sees things our way. How ill is he? Not very? Jolly good. No need for hospital, but the doctor can tell him he's at death's door and can't be moved.

'Send word to that policeman. Tell him you didn't know, but that Wyndham is a personal guest of mine. Then send round to whichever hotel and have Wyndham's things sent along to barracks. A roomful of abandoned baggage will only have people noticing his absence, and the sooner people stop talking about him in the town the better. Also the poor fellow might as well be made comfortable with a change of linen.'

Crosbie could only admire the Major's decisiveness. He was agog to know how the injured civilian himself might be disposed of.

'As I say, leave it with me. In here, is he? Jolly good. Have some tea sent in. I may be some time.'

7

So they sent for the Dagda, ad when he came, he said; 'What have I been called for?'
'To give an advice to your son,' said Fergne, 'and to help him—'

—Lady Augusta Gregory, *Cuchulain of Muirthemne*

As he opened the door to the spartan chamber where the guest of the battalion rested, Fitzmullen-Brophy's face changed from stern warrior to jovial uncle on his best behaviour. He beamed on Wyndham so thoroughly that the ends of his moustache bristled against his cheekbones.

'Morning!' he said. 'Glad to see you're awake. Hope you're feeling better. Splendid. I'm Major Fitzmullen-Brophy. Thought we might have a word.'

Wyndham smiled politely in greeting, but worry was written plainly on his face. He made an effort to sit up, but his visitor wasn't giving him any opening to speak.

'I say, mind if I sit down? Good, good. Had breakfast? Yes? Jolly good. I've sent for some tea, what?'

The smile frozen on his face, Fitzmullen-Brophy glanced about the room while he gathered his thoughts. As was proper to a junior officer's quarters, there was practically nothing there to please the eye or comfort the body. The sole exception was an impressive crimson dressing gown – doubtless lent by Crosbie – hanging from a hook behind the door.

Wyndham had been awake for hours already. He had been feeling much better than the previous day, but had stayed in bed because he'd been told he was ill, and besides – what else was he supposed to do? The morning light spoke of a clear summer day, but the spare little room was cold, with more than a hint of damp. So he'd stayed in bed, and stared at the dingy ceiling, and fretted. The trouble he was in couldn't have been as terrible and final as he'd imagined it in his cell, but he knew that he was where he shouldn't be; that he was in disgrace. Those officers who'd showed such urgent concern last night, and this kindly gentleman sitting by his bed now, were not condemning or casting blame, but their very presence was clear proof that Wyndham was at the centre of something very wrong indeed.

The kindly gentleman was evidently not accustomed to sitting silent for very long, for he now straightened abruptly and crossed the room in two strides to stare at the window. Not out the window, but at the window. He picked a flake of paint from the inside of the frame. His voice was unnecessarily loud, but his tone was reassuring.

'Sorry about the quarters. Shocking condition. Short notice, you know. Place is too large for us most of the time. Just rattling around most of the year. Easy to overlook the odd room here and there.'

Wyndham was framing something along the lines of *Perfectly all right, I assure you*, when the Major returned at speed to the bedside chair. He leaned forward in earnestness.

'That's the problem, you see. Big old barracks, not enough men. Otherwise we'd have had you out of that cell in an instant. Or rather, you'd never have been in there at all. None of this could have happened. Dreadful business. We are most fearfully sorry, you know.'

The two men stared at each other unblinking for a long moment. Wyndham was trying to think of a reply suitably gracious but cautious, when Fitzmullen-Brophy pushed on.

'I say, I hope you weren't too badly hurt? The MO said you'd taken a rather nasty bump to the head.'

'The MO...?'

'Ah! The Medical Officer, you know. The doctor. Doctor Raftery. I believe he's been looking after you. No finer man, you know.'

There was a brief interlude when Crosbie arrived with the tea. He carried it in personally, for security reasons. If Captain Crosbie had properly limited experience in fetching tea, he was a skilled organiser and knew that the army might well ask him to do worse than carry a tea tray. He had Private Harrington, the cookhouse detail, do most of the heavy lifting, but left the man waiting a prudent distance from the door as Crosbie himself covered the last lap. The tea was delivered safely, and the two officers fussed over it for two full minutes until they felt that a creditable standard of service had been met.

When all was right, Crosbie stood for a moment by the door, rubbing his hands expectantly, straining to know how this possibly painful interview had been going thus far, but knowing better than to ask.

'You'll stay, Captain?' asked Fitzmullen-Brophy.

The adjutant could tell straight away from the address by rank that the required answer was No.

'Afraid not, Major. Duty calls, and all that sort of thing.'

'Very good, Crosbie. Oh, and I say – you couldn't arrange to have Mr Wyndham's boots seen to, could you?' He gave Crosbie a telling look, and might have risked a wink if he thought he could have got away with it. All seemed to be going smoothly enough, but it did no harm to take proper precautions. A chap could hardly run out of barracks and spread scandalous stories about the regiment if he were in his stockinged feet, now could he?

Crosbie seemed to read Fitzmullen-Brophy's mind, for he smiled instantly, if a trifle too unctuously to be quite believable.

'I'll see to it myself, sir,' he said, and he whisked Wyndham's boots from under the bed and was gone.

Fitzmullen-Brophy had an audible sip of his tea, put his cup down again, and rubbed his hands on his knees.

'Right. Very good. Now where were we? Ah yes. Well I hope you know how dreadfully sorry I am about this whole business – how very sorry we all are. Dreadful affair. You must be quite shaken. I hope you understand that the man responsible is under arrest even as we speak, and can expect to be punished very severely.'

Wyndham looked just a little startled by that, and took too large a swallow of his horrible tea.

'Please, sir. I don't think that would be strictly necessary,' he managed to splutter, and here Fitzmullen-Brophy saw the opening he'd been looking for.

'I'm afraid it will be very necessary,' he assured Wyndham, 'but of course it won't be anything you need trouble with yourself. This is a purely military matter. No magistrate's court, no having to give witness statements, nothing of that sort. Certainly, I trust, no names in the papers.'

He watched to see how that would strike home. If this Wyndham wanted to raise Cain over this matter, now was his time to say so.

He didn't say so. What he did say filled the Major's heart with an immense joy.

'It's not that, sir. Of course I don't want to have to go to court, and of course I'm very grateful to you. It's just that I don't feel that anyone should be punished for something that is really my own fault.'

'Oh come now, my dear fellow! Whatever do you mean?'

And so Wyndham told him the sorry tale.

The fight in the street had ended with curtains moving and windows opening and loud voices calling for the police, and Lynch and Moriarty had gone haring off into the night, still wild with mischief. Wyndham had stood a long moment at a loss, watching lights come on in upper rooms. He was guilty, by association if by nothing else, and that much was all he knew. One of the fight's losers, picking himself up off the road, had glared at the American, and that was enough. He'd taken to his heels.

Because he was a stranger to Saturday-night outlawry, because he was alone in this dark and unfriendly town, it was after the two soldiers that he'd run.

'That, I suppose, was foolish of me,' he confessed to Fitzmullen-Brophy. 'I should have stayed and helped the men who'd been hurt, or at least waited for the police and explained myself to them. I was too afraid. I just wasn't seeing things clearly. I didn't even have the sense to return to my hotel. It can only have been the whiskey, I suppose. I have only myself to blame for everything that happened next.'

They had waited for him down a laneway. He'd have lost them otherwise.

'Jesus, look who it isn't! The wild American himself! Are you on the run from the law, is it?' From Moriarty's tone it had been evident that this sort of escapade was all part of the night's entertainment, and that he wasn't willing to forsake the merriment yet.

'Sure this calls for a bit of a drink.'

And despite Wyndham's protests, they had taken charge of him and led him at speed down dark little streets, laughing and shushing each other as they went.

Lynch had kept a hard grip on his arm. 'Just a small little drink,' he'd been saying over again as they went. Down the narrowest and darkest of lanes, where the paving had long run out, and at the lowest door of the meanest house they'd stopped and hammered. It had been the wrong house, and they'd run again, the soldiers hiccupping with laughter amid the curses and the barking dogs.

In the end they'd somehow found the nasty little shebeen they'd sought and had stood in the street and argued with the proprietor until a bottle had been grudgingly produced and which Wyndham had been expected to pay for. That had caused further problems for, astoundingly, the rich American had run out of money.

'I have a large sum in traveller's cheques, you see,' he explained to Fitzmullen-Brophy, 'but I don't like to carry it around with me. It's more than four hundred dollars, you know, and I had only planned on taking a short stroll around the town. So all I had left in my pockets was some small change. I should have just left them all then and there, but everyone was getting angry, and I didn't know where I was. So I went through my pockets,' – he didn't like to say that Lynch roughly helped him in that task – 'and I managed to find a last shilling piece. It was some clear spirit, something they called "putcheen". I only had a taste.'

'Dirty thief.'

Lynch's mood had soured, and all the way home he'd cursed the little maggot who'd charged them three bob for a bottle of fucking turps. The same bottle went back and forth between the two soldiers, but it only left Lynch's fist with some small effort from Moriarty. The money had run out, and the drink was set to follow. The lateness of the hour had also begun to oppress them. They had missed Lights Out. They were going to be late back to barracks.

Wyndham wasn't free yet. He'd tagged along on the promise that they'd see him safe on his way, but then when they'd at last reached a main road, and all he'd really wanted now was just a direction from them, they'd fallen to a last bout of arguing and scheming. A wall might have to be climbed, and somebody would have to be 'squared' or their two names would be in the punishment book. There was no more money.

'Ah sure, look again,' Lynch had said to Wyndham, between fawning and threatening. 'Didja look in that little pocket there? Ah, come on.'

Wyndham had found that he didn't care anymore. He'd just wanted a long drink of water and a soft bed. He'd paid for that bed, just as he'd paid for mostly everything that night, so why wasn't he in it? His irritation had got the better of him at that moment, and he'd pushed Lynch away, and demanded to be pointed on the road to his hotel, and Moriarty had patted his arm soothingly and asked him to keep his blessed voice down a while.

And then he must have fallen down and hit his head.

'I'll never touch liquor again,' he said. 'That much I'm sure of.' He was trying to look wise and resigned as he said it, but his day in the cell had taken its toll, and the major could see the tremble in Wyndham's lip.

'There, there, old fellow, don't take on so.'

He was going to add, '*It was hardly your fault*,' but realised that it was very much in the regiment's interest that young Mr Wyndham here continued to believe that it was rather his own fault after all. Instead he came up with, 'We all make mistakes. A young man finding his feet in the world is naturally going to get into one or two scrapes. I could tell you stories, you know.'

But it looked like Wyndham was in no mood for stories just now.

'I just feel so very, very foolish. Yesterday – yesterday in the cell I kept on thinking how right everyone was, all the people who told me I should have stayed at home. You know that I only arrived here on Friday? Not two days away from home – two days on dry land, I mean – and I get thrown in jail.'

He held his hands against his face to hide from the shameful absurdity of his life.

'May I confide in you, Major?' he asked.

Fitzmullen-Brophy could think of nothing better, and requested that Wyndham fire away.

'It sounds like a silly thing for a grown man to admit, sir,' Wyndham began, 'but I sometimes feel that I'm not much of a grown man at all. I told myself – I convinced myself – that this trip abroad would be a final cutting of the apron strings, you know. I mean I've always known that I've led a sheltered life. I've always been a retiring sort of fellow, and I told myself that this would be a break with all that.'

'Sounds like a capital idea,' said Fitzmullen-Brophy. 'I don't quite see what the difficulty might be.'

'That's rather my point, sir. It would have been a good idea if it had been true, if this had been an honest resolution to get out in the world and stand on my own two feet.'

'And it's not?'

'I don't believe so. Not after yesterday. Oh, if you'd asked me last week or last month, I wouldn't have said so, but I was deceiving myself, you see.'

'I'm still not sure I quite follow you, old man,' said Fitzmullen-Brophy kindly.

Wyndham looked down in silence for a long moment. Perhaps it was the view of his borrowed pyjamas that forced him to speak in the end. He took a deep breath.

The games you play as a boy, he said. Games of make-believe where boys are soldiers or Robin Hoods, games where they hunt Mohawks in the forest frontier at the bottom of the garden. Some boys play with other children, having their raucous adventures and fighting their noisy battles through the streets and yards. But some boys play all by themselves, and the battlefields and the wild woods exist only for them. There is no one to intrude, to mar the illusion; so the solitary boy need not acknowledge realities, and might grow to manhood still living in his imagination rather than in the world.

His visions might change as he grew. He might see now the warriors of heroic Ireland, and he might justify his fancy by calling it scholarship, denying to all and to himself that it was in fact a consuming daydream. Although a man, he might still be something of the child, still amusing himself with the little games of his own invention, not knowing how the world can be unforgiving of such idle souls.

'I've been living in story books, Major. That's what brought me to Ireland. I was running away from my real life and chasing some stupid fantasy.'

The major sympathised, he truly did, but he was obliged to confess that he'd never been much of a one for books himself.

'Never had the brains, I'm afraid, haha.'

But he thought he saw what Wyndham meant. Didn't quite entirely agree with him though. A boy growing up alone was unhealthy – no doubt about that – but there was a lot to be said for a lively imagination, properly directed. Why, hunting your redskins in the shrubbery was just the sort of thing to give a lad an appetite for the real thing, or its nearest equivalent at any rate. Why, half the subalterns on the North-West Frontier – barely out of knee-breeches themselves – would have given up the game for lost the first time they'd met an angry tribesman, that is if they hadn't recognised the whole affair for the splendid great game they knew so well.

'No no, my dear fellow, nothing wrong with story books that tell manly stories. I don't know about these fairy stories of this Yates chap, but all those ancient Irish heroes sound just the ticket. They should teach them that sort of thing in schools.

'That and games, of course. That's where your family made their mistake, you see. Should have had you out in the fresh air all day playing games. Proper games, I mean, with a ball and teams and everything. That reminds me of a story, you know. Very apt, when you think about it. Concerns an officer of this regiment: a young chap like yourself, name of, name of... damme, I'll forget me own name next. Name of Metcalfe, that's it. Not one of your bookish types at all was young Metcalfe, but had the heart of a lion – and a most vivid imagination too.'

He leaned back in the creaking little chair and smiled at the memory.

'Imagined the whole world as a rugger pitch, you know. Fine figure of a man. Must have stood six foot two in his stockinged feet. There was talk of his being capped for Ireland, but he was sent to South Africa instead.' For a moment Fitzmullen-Brophy's gaze lost its focus. 'South Africa,' he said.

The line from Bakenkop to Bronckhorstfontein in the depths of a South African winter. Rain and more of it, and a cold you wouldn't have thought possible on the continent of Africa. The regiment had forced the Boers out of their trenches north of the Vaal. This was in June and July when Brother Boer was still fighting like a white man and not like a damned Red Indian. A steady push northward, with the two sides hardly breaking contact for more than a day. The British would force one position, push on, and then halt as they came up against another Boer line.

The battalion was as often as not split up and spread out in those days. Fitzmullen-Brophy, a newly minted major, had three companies in his care, strung out that particular day across nearly half a mile of country, huddling among the rocks and ditches as they tried to take the measure of the enemy in their trenches across the way.

Word had come that the captain of the left-hand company was down, and Fitzmullen-Brophy had gone out to see what could be done, covering the last hundred yards on his knees and elbows, with the bullets singing overhead. The company was in a shockingly exposed position and no distance at all from the Boers, who had sniped the captain, and six other men, with such ease.

Second Lieutenant Metcalfe, however, was not in the slightest bit downcast: not by the weather, nor the proximity of the enemy. Even in winter, the ruddiness of summer was still in his face and the sun was still in the golden hair that flopped out from under the peak of his cork helmet. He glowed with energy, and whereas the men were hunkered down as low as they could get, Metcalfe was jittering about on his haunches, eager to get into the game.

He explained himself to Fitzmullen-Brophy. Give him no more than thirty men, he said, and they could rush the relatively vulnerable Boer right flank, covered by the fire of the remainder of the company. He didn't put it quite that way though. Give him half the company, he said, and he could hook the ball out of this scrum. Thirty men acting as one fly half, sprinting down the open touchline on their left, going for a try. That was how he put it, and the major had seen it in his mind's eye even as it was said.

The company was in a filthy position, militarily speaking. Even Sergeant Mulcahy, that staunch man, was white-faced and hunched. Coming out from behind these rocks, bayonets fixed for a regular advance, would seem to be against all sense. But the sporting spirit, burning bright in Metcalfe, that was a different matter. If that spirit could be imbued in the men, who had waited for the referee's final whistle on many a field muddier than this, then a sudden attack stood a far better chance of success.

The attack went in, the pack surged forward, and the ball, in the end of it all, was carried over the line.

'You mean your side won, Major?' asked Wyndham, who had cottoned on that 'rugger' was some kind of ball game.

'Indeed we did. A magnificent show.'

'And Lieutenant Metcalfe?'

'Brought down by a Boer full back, I'm afraid – or at least that's how he'd have seen it.'

Brought down by a soft-nosed Mauser bullet from thirty yards out. Some distance from the body they'd found his sun helmet – a sizeable hank of his thick blond hair still stuck to the inside, and the khaki cloth turning pink in the rain.

Wyndham digested this in silence for a while. 'Play up, play up, and play the game,' he murmured. There was a tiredness, or perhaps even a shade of bitterness in his voice, but Fitzmullen-Brophy didn't notice.

'What's that, old boy?'

'A magnificent thing certainly. It's what all warriors have always wanted, isn't it? A glorious death, I mean – to die with your face toward the foe.'

'The very thing. Those legends of yours come to life, I suppose. And that's my point, you see. Nothing wrong with having an imagination – within bounds of reason, that is. Inspires a chap. I'll bet if poor Metcalfe had read books, he'd have done much the same sort of thing, only he'd have put it differently: "Come on, men! We'll have at 'em like Horatio on the bridge, and that sort of thing!" Something like that, what?'

'I think I envy him,' said Wyndham. '"Those whom the gods love die young".'

'Well I dare say there's a lot to be said for it,' said Fitzmullen-Brophy, a little nonplussed, 'but I'm not sure I'd go that far. High-flown sentiment is all very well, I'm sure, but it doesn't do to be thinking gloomy thoughts.'

He stood up with his usual suddenness. 'Look here, though: I'm so very pleased that you're feeling better. Now the doctor insists on you staying here a while longer, but we've sent for your things so you'll have your books to keep you company. I must see Captain Crosbie about one or two matters, but I'll be back in a bit and we can continue our chat, what?'

Fitzmullen-Brophy had taken a shine to this young Wyndham, for all his strange notions, but the adjutant should be notified directly that the storm had passed, and that the regiment could soldier on with unblemished record until the next Saturday night at least.

8

III 22. Ordinary thefts from civilians are left by the Act to be dealt with by the civil courts, or they may be tried by court-martial under s.41 as civil offences.

—Manual of Military Law, 1907

Strictly speaking, trying the weekend's felons was not the usual business for an adjutant, whose normal function was that of battalion secretary, but Captain Crosbie was taking personal care of the matter. Security reasons, you understand.

Such a catalogue of crime.

A sentry seduced from his watch with the dregs of a bottle of poteen; an otherwise steady man persuaded to ignore the lateness of two men returning to barracks, in return for being 'squared' with the proceeds from the sale of a stolen overcoat; a drunken affray outside a respectable public house; a corporal of the guard negligent in his duties. The list could go on for as long as a man might care to sift through King's Regulations, but none of it would weigh a feather's weight against the assault on, followed by the false imprisonment of a civilian.

What mattered here was that justice should be done, and be done solely within the regiment. More than that, it should be done right quick, so that the senior officers in command need never know about it. Justice had to be seen to be done, but not by the colonel, if that were at all possible.

Crosbie hardly needed to be told that the affair must be swept under the carpet and the carpet afterwards nailed to the floor.

The punishment would have to be severe, because the events of Saturday night had been disgraceful, but it couldn't be so harsh as to involve any authority outside the regiment, or even outside the small circle of officers in the depot. The civil police were usually content to let the military take care of its own. Thank God there had not been so much as a window broken, and no one involved in the fight outside the pub was likely to come forward. But the offences were still serious.

Crosbie faced a rather thorny legal and moral problem. First of all, there was the nature of the charge itself. Fitzmullen-Brophy had intimated that the injured civilian was content to take his coat back and go on his way, so that was all right. But if there were no complaint, no evidence, and no involvement of the civil authorities, then what on earth was to go down on the culprit's charge sheet?

If assault, robbery, and incarceration could not be mentioned, then all Lynch was guilty of was leaving barracks without permission on Sunday, just as all that could be pinned on Moriarty – if indeed, anything could be pinned on him – was returning late the night before. The American gentleman hadn't even mentioned their names.

Next was the imperative of keeping the whole business as near-as-dammit a secret from his seniors. The problem there was that, unless he assumed all the powers of Commanding Officer, he was not allowed to award any punishment more severe that seven days' confinement to barracks, and this case demanded more than that.

Crosbie thought about it and made his decision. He would take the law into his own hands. Greater than the law was justice, and greater than justice was the Regiment, and devil take the hindmost.

'Bring the first one in, Sergeant.'

Trampling on the rights of two private soldiers didn't take long. Lynch was long wedded to a life of petty crime and petty punishment. He took Crosbie's sentence in silence. Doubtless, he knew how difficult things would be made for him if he tried to stand upon strict legalities. An excessively long stint in close tack or on jankers was small beer next the more unofficial punishments that authority could dish out to an uncooperative soldier.

Crosbie made a nice little speech about how Lynch could take his long term of detention as an opportunity to reflect on his life and an attempt to mend his ways. No mention at all was made of the American gentleman, or even of his overcoat, and Lynch seemed content for it to be so.

That left Moriarty.

A soldier who had somehow worked his way from the depths of Burma to Tralee, with little enough by way of the good opinions of his superiors to help him on his way, was someone to be watched.

The accused was duly summoned and Sergeant Conway, terrible in the crimson sash of his appointment, could have been heard screaming the court procedure a mile off on a windy day. In the confines of the orderly room, it was a thing to hear.

'Company orders! Company orders, *shun*! Left *turn*! Quick *march*!' and then a short barking series of left-rights followed by a thunderous, 'Halt! Cap off!'

Moriarty cut a fine, if not particularly penitent figure. He was staring, unblinking, at the wall above Crosbie's head, but the adjutant believed he could see devilment stirring in those eyes as the charge was read out. Causing an affray in a public street. That was the sum of it. Nothing more. Did the accused's over-long moustache twitch with the hint of a smile?

'Anything to say for yourself, Moriarty?'

'Beg your pardon, sir, but they started it.'

'Indeed?'

'They insulted me, sir. They insulted the regiment, and they insulted His Majesty's service, sir.'

Too melodramatic by half, thought Crosbie.

'Did they?' he said.

Moriarty delivered his line with full dramatic intonation. 'They accused me of selling my country for a dirty shilling, sir.'

Crosbie had heard that one, or variations, before.

'Twenty-one days confined to barracks.'

It sounded little enough, but if Conway was half the provost sergeant he supposed, then a misery could be made of Moriarty's life for this next three weeks.

Crosbie stared stonily at Moriarty until the victim opened his mouth to speak, and then he cut him short. 'You may think my judgement too hard, Moriarty, but in fact I am going easy on you. If Major Worship were here you can be sure that he would not be so lenient. You are an old soldier, Moriarty, posted to the depot, and the depot is where the new recruits learn the ways of the regiment. You are setting a shameful example to them, and you are disgracing the good name of the regiment in this town.'

He went on: 'I happen to know that this brawl was witnessed by a foreign gentleman who is a personal friend of Major Fitzmullen-Brophy. You can imagine the Major's disgust on hearing of this, and you can be thankful that I – and not the CO – am dealing with this matter. Dismiss.'

And that was that. Crosbie, in wilful contravention of all legal authority, had inflicted punishment on Moriarty that might take some explaining, and had condemned Lynch to a spell of imprisonment that probably amounted to a tearing up of the Magna Carta, and none of this was to be properly documented, yet he was not sorry. With those two rogues out of circulation for so long a while there would be little chance of scandal getting out or rumours confirmed. Crosbie had overstepped the mark, but it was all for the good name of the regiment. Thrilled with his abuse of power, he lit a cigarette and drew deeply on it.

9

'…Our armies for the most part are composed of the dregs of society – sluggards, rakes, debauchees, rioters, undutiful sons, and the like…'

—Frederick the Great

When Fitzmullen-Brophy returned he found Wyndham in something of a brown study. His bags had arrived, and some small amount of unpacking had been done – at least enough to provide him with a toothbrush and something to read. It had even been considered safe now to have his boots returned, shined to a military standard, although the MO's strictures against the patient rising from his sickbed had not yet been lifted. There were a few books on the bedside locker, but Wyndham was showing no interest in them.

Fitzmullen-Brophy offered more tea – the army's answer to most problems – but Wyndham didn't show any interest in that either.

'So what are your plans now, Mr Wyndham? Once the doctor allows you to be up and about, I mean? I hope that you will come and stay with my wife and me for a few days. By way of making things up to you, I mean. Least we can do. Better than a hotel at any rate. Mightn't have much in the way of old Irish ghost stories, mind, but you can talk to the neighbours. There's a man McElligott – a most colourful fellow. Talk the hind leg off a donkey, you know. Mind you, any time I talk to him it's really just the hay and the weather going back years and years. At least he doesn't talk politics, thank God. Can't abide politics. But I'll bet he has a tale or two to tell about leprechauns and that peculiar pile of stones in the field and that. Splendid fellow. Perfect place to start your studies. That was the point of your visit, wasn't it?'

Wyndham sighed.

'You're very kind, Major, but the last few days have made me see sense, I think. I'm going to go home.'

'Oh I say! What a pity! And you've only just arrived.'

'And look at what's happened to me already. To think that I should go off into the wilds like some Irish Stanley and not have worse happen to me is absurd. The first angry farm dog I meet could run me off, or I'd fall in a ditch and break my fool neck.'

'Oh come now.'

'I don't have enough courage or horse-sense, Major. How am I supposed to gain the confidence of the plain people? Anyone who wanted could get me drunk and swindle me out of my money in seconds flat, and I'd probably say thank you.'

'You're being too hard on yourself.' Fitzmullen-Brophy thought he could hear a tearful note behind the forced humour.

'I'm going to go back home, Major. I'm going to go back to working for my Uncle Henry, and I'm probably going to turn *into* my Uncle Henry, and it's probably what I deserve.'

'Now now. It can't be as bad as all that.'

'No?'

'Of course not. You shouldn't be so discouraged at such a little thing. What you need is to climb back in the saddle, my boy. Learn to take the knocks. You'll be a better man for it.'

'I think it's too late for that, sir.'

'Nonsense! I'm sure you have a very strong character. It just needs to be exercised, you know: strengthened, given some fresh air, room to breathe, that sort of thing.'

'It's very good of you to say so, but…'

'Not at all! Look at me, man! Why, when I was a lad I don't

think I'd have said boo to a goose. Didn't get on terribly well at school either. But a few years out in the world – out in the world of men – why, it was the making of me! Made my share of mistakes, I don't mind telling you, but who doesn't, hey?'

Wyndham smiled ruefully, looking at Fitzmullen-Brophy, trying to imagine him a lost and helpless innocent. 'Somehow, Major,' he said, 'I don't believe a soldier's life would be for me. I've come to grief in Kerry. Whatever would become of me in South Africa?'

'Why, dash it, that's where you're wrong, don't you see? A young chap on his own is bound to make mistakes. That's the beauty of the army, do you see? A chap need never be alone. A fellow is protected from the worst in himself by his comrades, and he protects them in his turn. He doesn't have to agonise over anything because it's all set out for him. He has traditions and rules and whatnot. Beautiful when you think about it.

'I say – do you have the Boy Scouts in America? Why, only just this morning I was thinking about it. Character-building and comradeship and all that. The very thing.'

Wyndham confessed that he had heard something of the Boy Scouts, but believed it was too late in life to be looking to them for his salvation.

'Yes, yes. Of course. I don't mean you should *join*, of course. Silly notion. No. I mean the principle of the thing. You see it, don't you?'

'Well, I suppose I do. I can hardly deny it, really. All my enthusiasms these last few years bear it out. Those stories I was reading. The Fianna, and the Red Branch: sort of Irish knights of the Round Table. Brotherhood. Comradeship. That's always at the heart of it.'

'And there you are! It's in books!'

Wyndham laughed gently now. 'And reading books is what got me here. Henceforth, Major, I resolve to read only the morning paper and the Bible, and I'll be pretty careful with the Bible.'

'You mustn't joke, you know. I'm being quite serious. There's nothing wrong with books – within reason, that is. But character is what's important. Now, as I say, there's nothing wrong with your character, but if you don't mind my saying so, I believe it needs toughening. What you should do is join a sporting club. Team spirit is the thing you need. A fellow who's part of a team can stand on his own without fear, that's what I say.'

Wyndham could not but listen to the older man's sincerity, and take it to heart.

'Do you know, Major – I believe you might be right.'

'There you are then. A sporting club. You'll find it works wonders.'

Why not? Wyndham couldn't quite see it, but he could not doubt the major's faith. 'I'll look into it as soon as I get home,' he said.

'Oh, but you mustn't go home just yet, you know. Seeing a little of the world: that's what's so important, isn't it? It would be a bally shame to throw it all up now.'

'Which rather brings us back to my present weakness of character.'

'Now, now. I warned you about being so hard on yourself. There's no reason why you shouldn't start on something while you're here. I'm sure I could ask around and find something for you. This is the army, after all – any number of sporting chaps about.' And then he straightened in his chair. 'Oh I say…!'

His eyebrows climbed towards his scalp.

'I say!'

An angel had spoken to Fitzmullen-Brophy: an angel in a red coat. A vision had been vouchsafed him. The golden path to heaven shone bright.

'Major?'

The light of the gospel was in Fitzmullen-Brophy's face now.

'Just how long had you been planning to stay away from home, Mr Wyndham?'

'Well... I had no concrete plans, you understand, but I was vaguely thinking on perhaps six months. Home by Christmas, anyway.'

Fitzmullen-Brophy leaned forward in his chair, his hands clasped together.

'Listen to me to me now, Wyndham. I've just had the most tremendous idea.'

Wyndham would join the army. Not in a permanent way, of course, but an enlistment in the Special Reserve demanded only six months' service. Actually, the commitment was for six years, but after the initial six months only three or four weeks a year was required of the reservist. Also, Major Fitzmullen-Brophy, being a senior officer in the regiment's Special Reserve battalion, felt that there would be no difficulty in unofficially waiving, if necessary, those superfluous five-and-a-half years. Indeed. Since the Major rather thought – though he'd have to look it up, mind – that since there might be some regulation prohibiting the enlistment of foreign subjects, the whole business of enlistment would have to be somewhat unofficial in the first place.

'What it boils down to, I suppose, is that you spend only a few months as a soldier and, if the worst comes to the worst, you can buy yourself out for a few quid. Tell you what, I'll pay the money myself if it comes to that. Least I could do.'

Wyndham's mouth was slightly open throughout this involved revelation.

'I know it's rather a lot to take in, but if you think about it,' said Fitzmullen-Brophy, 'it really might be the very best thing in the world for you.'

He patted Wyndham's knee. 'I know. I'll leave you to think about it.'

And then he was gone, and Wyndham thought.

What had he done with his life?

Years hence, what would he have to look back on? He could see himself respectable, the head of a respectable family, managing a small but respectable financial institution. He saw himself in a pearl-grey suit on a summer Sunday presiding over some social affair, and sounding pompous as he admitted to having travelled somewhat in Europe, 'in my youth'. And the ensuing polite questions would be answered with what?

Pray do tell us what you did on your travels, Mr Wyndham.

What did you do with your life, Mr Wyndham? Will it make a good story? Were you the hero?

Alas no. Never that.

No. Maybe not a hero, but maybe a man.

Maybe that.

The army. Daniel Wyndham a soldier. *Private* Wyndham. He thought about the men he'd drunk with on Saturday night. Private Wyndham, with a red coat hiding a dirty shirt, smoking tobacco and spitting on the floor. No.

Private Wyndham, dressed in that subdued but manly uniform the major wore, his back straight, his chest broad: a gentleman soldier.

What would they say at home? He could picture himself six months from now, returning in that uniform, three inches taller with a row of medals on his breast, smiling indulgently at their fussing, and ignoring every blessed word. He could see himself in Uncle Henry's office, putting his booted and spurred feet on Uncle Henry's desk, and spinning yarns, and taking his whiskey neat. He saw himself in a ten-gallon hat as well, and with tigers on his buttons he'd go walking out with Emily Winters and he'd carelessly kiss her, and if she objected, why, he'd just laugh it off and go walking out with Penelope van Wyngarden.

Actually, that last part he thought he really might do.

No earthly reason why not. As for the rest? *Think sensibly, dash it* – damn it. *This is a big step you're taking.*

Of course he'd be no taller, nor would he have any medals to boast of. He wouldn't boast at all. He wouldn't need to. He'd be self-contained and self-possessed and self-reliant: the same man in outward appearance, but so much improved in all other respects.

There'd be no more daydreaming. He would live in the real world. He'd take whatever monastic vows the army required of him and he would efface himself and do his duty. He would polish those tiger buttons and wear whatever hat he was told to. He would learn to live with ordinary men. He would not become a hero, but the army would at least make a man of him.

And it was only six months.

He'd have no story like the boy Metcalfe, shot in the rain in South Africa, or the men in the dirty shirts fighting their way to Delhi, or the men of Connacht who followed their Queen Maeve to war and death; but if he grew old with no story to tell, he could at least know that he had once stepped forth and had taken his chance.

Be a man.

And now he could hardly wait for Fitzmullen-Brophy to come back.

10

When we were with Scathach, it is together we used to go to every battle, to every wild place, through every darkness and every hardship. We were heart companions; we were comrades in gatherings; we shared the one bed where we used to sleep sound sleep.

We used to practise together, in many far countries; we used to go to hard fights; we used to go through every forest together.

—Lady Augusta Gregory, *Cuchulain of Muirthemne*

Two of the junior men were in the anteroom having a smoke and a quiet conversation, but they were too deferential to rise above a polite reply to Fitzmullen-Brophy's brief good morning, nor was he particularly interested in them. A snap of agitated newspaper by the fireplace advertised what he was looking for, and there was Tummy Belcher staring at him with piggy eyes over the top of Saturday's *Times*.

Saturday's paper? It might have been last year's, or the year before's.

Major R.T. St. J. Belcher hadn't altered one whit since Fitzmullen-Brophy had last set eyes on him. Every year, Fitzmullen-Brophy found him in the same chair, at the same time, glaring at the latest outrage perpetrated by the government, or the lamentable performance of Hampshire county cricket, or the singular failure of a horse at Newmarket in which as much as five decent quid might have been invested on the soundest advice. Same old

Tummy Belcher. Not a hair different. Well, not exactly a hair, you understand. Figure of speech, of course. Possibly there was a somewhat wider expanse of pink and shiny scalp to be seen this time – but we're none of us getting any younger, you know – but it was same the old, good old Tummy Belcher and no mistake. God was in his heaven; Major Belcher had his broad rump planted in an armchair and was silently damning what it said in the papers.

How long had they known each other now? Thirty years? More? Heavens, but time flies! Fitzmullen-Brophy, barely twenty years of age and hardly a month in the regiment, and pretty damned miserable if he'd had to admit it. Very much the new boy. Not a friend in the world, it felt like. And then – oh joy! – another new bug fetched up at the mess and, his face as red as his tunic and his voice gruff with shyness, announced, 'Good morning, gentlemen. My name is Belcher.' And then, just as they'd done to Second Lieutenant Fitzmullen-Brophy the month before, not a man in the room deigned to look up and acknowledge him. Only Fitzmullen-Brophy, recognising a fellow orphan boy and a brother, had, taking his courage in both hands, extended one of them and introduced himself with an awkward grin, and after that they became friends, for what else were they to do?

That had been in Aldershot – in 1883, by God! How funny they must have looked. There was the odd photograph on various walls and mantelpieces, of course, showing stiff young men with their hair parted curiously, and an attempt to grow whiskers making them seem even more youthful, but a photograph is just a photograph, just a frozen glimpse, and our lives are not made up of frozen moments, nor do we live in the formal erect posture demanded of the photographic studio any more than we habitually sit cross-legged on the ground in the front row of any group.

Although now that you mention it, thought Fitzmullen-Brophy, perhaps there was something in the comparison between a subaltern's life and a group photograph. There you are, right at the bottom, trying to look dignified with your backside on the ground, and wondering if your flies are undone, and acutely conscious of a senior officer's boot only inches from the back of your silly neck. Ah well. An idle thought. All that was long gone, along with much of the closeness of that first friendship. Can't say it *soured*, mind, although there was a rather difficult period. It was just that a certain distance was established, and forever after maintained.

Second Lieutenant Belcher answered to the name of Thomas, it transpired, but sometime in his schooldays Tommy had become Tummy. Not that he was fat. Not really fat. But he was a stoutly built youth with a proud and solid belly for one of his tender years, and that, with the added inspiration of his surname, had rechristened him irrevocably. If the nickname had ever been meant as a hurtful jibe, any boy who had made it was long since beaten into submission, or at least understanding, by the pugnacious Belcher. He was not soft. An asset to his school's rugger team, he was further hardened by Sandhurst, although neither ordeal had managed to take much more than a scrap of meat off his frame.

So Tummy and FitzEm were best of friends, learning their trade as demanded, and hunting and dancing as allowed, when what should happen but a woman came between them.

And it wasn't just one woman, you know.

Fitzmullen-Brophy felt rather guilty about that one.

Alice Cartwright and her cousin Louisa Cartwright-Jones. Sweet girls. The sweetest girls, particularly Louisa. That's what the young Fitzmullen-Brophy had thought anyway. Thing is, though, it was Alice he'd met first, and it was Alice's undeniable charm that had captivated him right from the start. Do you know, for the life of him he couldn't remember where exactly that had been, but he distinctly recalled talking Belcher's ear off about the girl all week, silly infatuated young ass that he'd been. Anyway –

and he could remember this quite clearly indeed – when he'd met Alice again, and Belcher was there with him, her cousin Louisa was there with her, and Fitzmullen-Brophy had thought at first that this was splendid, because they all four hit it off together tremendously and, for a few weeks of that season, at every little gathering you could name, they'd made up a little party of their own – a party of two pairs.

Fitzmullen-Brophy had the happiest memories of that time. Maybe not the happiest though. Second happiest at any rate. Perhaps not as warm a memory as South Africa, mind. There'd been nothing to cloud South Africa. Nothing to stain the recollection. England in '85 might have had a balmier climate, what with there being no swarms of carnivorous flies to bother one so, nor horses dying of sunstroke all over the shop, but he had no regrets about the Transvaal the way he had about Hampshire.

Thing was – and this is what still made Fitzmullen-Brophy decry the idiocies of youth – thing was that he'd discovered that he rather liked Louisa better than he liked Alice. Now there was nothing set in stone, you understand. No promises made of the least degree. That said, it was an undoubtedly shameful and underhand thing for Fitzmullen-Brophy to switch his attentions from one cousin to the other, necessarily upsetting his supposed sweetheart and cutting out his shorter and less handsome brother officer.

It had been a damned ugly business for a little while. Belcher had kept his head, even if Fitzmullen-Brophy appeared to have forgotten his manners, but there were ugly silences and dark looks. A friendship was broken – more than one – and perhaps for good. Some chaps seemed to have taken Belcher's side. Some unkinder chaps even seemed to be mocking Fitzmullen-Brophy behind his back. Ugly business. Dashed ugly, and all his own damned fault. There's no one more pitiable than a youth who's lost all his friends.

As luck would have it, before the rift became unbridgeable, circumstances intervened. The young men were drafted overseas. The Munster Fusiliers were taking part in operations in Burma and, ruled by the sterner etiquette of active service, were called to a higher duty on the battlefield, which heeded not the love of women, and Lieutenants Belcher and Fitzmullen-Brophy were obliged to reach a hasty accommodation. It had been almost impossible, after all, in all the bustle prior to embarkation, to retain an aloofness. Thus, as the ship pulled away from the Southampton quayside, for the second and last time in their lives, Fitzmullen-Brophy had extended his hand in shy friendship, and Belcher, after the barest moment's hesitation, had taken it and gripped it firmly, saying no words. The breach had not been fatal. Fitzmullen-Brophy was indescribably relieved. Nevertheless, he never told Belcher – not then or ever after – that the evening before, when he had sought out the two girls to make decent apology, they had not only accepted it with silent grace, but had softly kissed him goodbye.

Both of them. At the very same time. One on each cheek.

He'd carried those kisses to Burma with him, and to war, and never told a soul, not even when there was drink on him.

Fitzmullen-Brophy had always believed that a hard life in a hard country was a balm to the souls of young men, and those first years he had spent out east convinced him for ever after that there are no awkwardnesses that a couple of decent chaps can't patch up between them, not when they're in real difficulties.

Women? Nothing but trouble, old boy. Who needs 'em?

Belcher had said those very words in some sweltering village on the Sittang when a native girl accidentally dropped what might well have been the last bottle of pale ale north of Rangoon. The two parched subalterns had looked in horror as the beer frothed for a moment between the floorboards. Then: 'Women? Who needs 'em?' And the two boys with their faces red and dripping under their pith helmets had collapsed in hysterical laughter.

They had rubbed along nicely ever since and, if age had not mellowed Belcher, he seemed content in his continued bachelorhood. Fitzmullen-Brophy had met Susan, of course, and had married her, and Captain Belcher had been happy to stand best man at their wedding. Years ago now. Fitzmullen-Brophy wouldn't have recalled any of it at all except that he'd been thinking thoughts about young Wyndham, and fretting over young Molly before that, and there was Tummy, the first time he'd set eyes on him in a year.

'Morning, Tummy.'

'Morning, FitzEm. Seen the paper?'

That was Tummy Belcher all over. Hasn't seen a chap all year and acts like they've been living under the same roof all the while.

'Not much in it, I suppose?' Fitzmullen-Brophy asked off-handedly.

'Damn all. Keeping up to the mark?'

'Never better.'

'And the memsahib? And the squirt?'

'Perfectly splendid. I'll tell them you were asking for them.'

'Jolly good.' And then Major Belcher would have returned to his paper and not spoken a word more until lunch, had not his friend taken a seat and sought his advice.

11

'...a younger, a weaker, and an inferior class of boy is taken for the Special Reserve.'

—Duke of Bedford, House of Lords, 1908

Major Belcher's views on the irregular enlistment of Mr Wyndham had been encouraging. The very word he'd used – 'irregular' – had been so much more heartening than 'fraudulent' or 'illegal'. His attitude was precisely what Fitzmullen-Brophy had expected, and that indeed was why his advice had been solicited in the first place.

Irregular? In some respects the very presence of Major Belcher was an irregularity in itself, as indeed was that of Fitzmullen-Brophy. The pair of them should have been promoted or retired years ago. Belcher knew this well, and suspected that his old chum knew it too, but soldiered on in hope. Every training season he'd see FitzEm come bounding in with the enthusiasm of a chap half his age, full of schemes for the betterment of the battalion, as if they might all be sent overseas on a moment's notice to the bullets and the glory and the whatnot; as if they were still young men with careers to be made; as if either of them might ever see another promotion; as if anybody cared any more.

Tummy Belcher had never been ambitious in the first place. His father had suggested the army, so to the army he had gone. He supposed that once upon he time he had vaguely expected to grow old with a chestful of medals and general's rank and a knighthood to boot, but no one had offered him any of those things, and he was not the sort to strive after them on his own account. Fact was, if a fellow spent his years of service hankering after opportunities for advancement, then more often than not he'd be condemning himself to a life of disappointment. Far better to get on with whatever work was needed and then enjoy the shooting, or the polo, if that was more your line of country.

So instead of distinction Belcher had contented himself with regimental life in the Munsters, and eventually he had wound up in Ballymullen, this lazy haven. Here FitzEm could impose his fads on the reservists for a few weeks every year and Tummy could inhabit the mess and do nothing more strenuous than play billiards, all unnoticed by the greater regiment, and certainly not by the powers in distant Dublin or Whitehall.

Concerning Wyndham? Damn the regulations, Belcher had said. A recruit was a recruit, and better a clean-limbed, well-brought-up foreigner than the normal run of guttersnipes and corner boys that blew into the regiment like dust from the street.

Once upon a time – and Belcher was sure he could even remember it – the Irish regiments had been full of farmers' boys, strong and tall. The damned nationalists and agitators had changed all that. They had decried the taking of the shilling as a betrayal of Ireland. Pernicious rot, of course, but the countrymen had stayed away, and in some of the worse years even the recruiting sergeants had been too intimidated to do their work. What was the result? Townsmen, weak in body and moral fibre equally, and not enough of them even Irish. Belcher was an Englishman himself, and proud of it, and any body of men would naturally benefit from the leadership of an Englishman, but what was the point of having Irish regiments if there weren't enough Irishmen in the ranks? Bad for the *esprit de corps*, what? And now this American chap of FitzEm's. Sign of the times. The army, along with everything else, was going to the dogs. Still and all, if FitzEm liked him, why not? So damn the regulations: a recruit was a recruit.

If Belcher had one reservation, it concerned the apparent scholarly predilections of this Wyndham character. Braininess was all very well in its place, of course. Belcher had nothing against brains, as such, but the last thing the battalion needed was a *clever* recruit. Belcher couldn't abide cleverness, especially in the ranks. A chap who reads books might well be a chap who thinks he knows better than his superiors. He'd seen them himself, you know, at Sandhurst.

Fitzmullen-Brophy however, who had come up through the militia, having repeatedly failed the entrance examination for Sandhurst, was of the firm opinion that the Special Reserve – the successor of the old Militia – was the very thing for curing a fellow of his bookishness if he be caught young, and for precluding even the merest hint of cleverness.

And so, once the doctor had pronounced him fit for the occasion and he was allowed to get dressed, he, Daniel Prentiss Wyndham, swore by Almighty God that he would be faithful and bear true allegiance to His Majesty King George the Fifth, His Heirs and Successors, and that he would, as in duty bound, honestly and faithfully defend His Majesty, His Heirs and Successors, in Person, Crown and Dignity against all enemies, and would observe and obey all orders of His Majesty, His Heirs and Successors, and of the generals and officers set over him. So help him God.

It was an understated but solemn ceremony, conducted in the unmarried officers' quarters and officiated by Major Fitzmullen-Brophy. Major Belcher and Sergeant Conway stood as godfather and best man, or at least as witnesses. The ritual was completed by Fitzmullen-Brophy fishing in his pocket for a shilling that, as he was obliged to explain to the new recruit (who thought he might be getting a tip), was the seal to the king's bargain, symbolising as it did the soldier's first pay. His actual pay, it was then added, could be expected on Friday, or possibly Friday week.

'There now,' he said. 'Welcome to the regiment.'

Straight away a sort of stiffness had come over him, because now their relationship had changed to that of officer and man. Outside of barracks, they would still be social equals, and indeed Wyndham's invitation to stay with the Fitzmullen-Brophys still stood. Indeed they would look after his luggage for him until he needed it again. But all that was for outside of barracks: a world closed to Private Wyndham for some time to come.

There had been the minimum of paperwork involved in the transformation of Wyndham from civilian to soldier. As it happened, the paper that was signed represented something rather less than the minimum, and some of the spaces on the form had been deliberately smudged or left blank. Fitzmullen-Brophy was sure he'd come up with some creative fudging when the situation might demand it and, until that day, any amount of stuff could be conveniently misfiled.

For the moment, it was easy to treat Private Wyndham as an exceptional case, because he was the only new recruit in barracks. There was always a squad or two in training at the depot, but by coincidence, the newest squad was already well advanced in its course of instruction and so would have no place for a new and unhandy man. Sergeant Conway had an idea that a couple of new recruits might be expected up from Cork tomorrow or the day after, but until then, Wyndham would be in a squad on his own.

12

How well a sword became you,
A hat with a band,
A slender foreign shoe
And a suit of yarn
Woven over the water!

—Eileen O'Connell, 'The Lament for Art O'Leary'

6. In the case to first issues to recruits at depôts, the following garments will be fitted loosely (the cardigan waistcoat being worn under the tunic):—
Dress Jackets ... ... R.H.A.
Tunics and cloth and tweed trousers ... Cavalry of the Line, R.F.A. and R.G.A.
Serge frocks ... ... Cavalry of the Line.
Tunics ... ... Infantry.

—*Clothing Regulations*, War Office, 1914

Wyndham would never have considered himself a dandy, but it had always pleased him to think that his clothes, if they didn't entirely make the man, at least advertised him as a respectable fellow, who was, whether it be true or not, comfortable in his place in the world. But he was in a new world now and, if not quite delivered naked into it, he had lost all his familiar possessions to the keeping of the Fitzmullen-Brophys, and was finding the replacement garments now issued to him to be both bewildering and disconsoling.

He had been put into the hands of a Lance Corporal Sheehan, who spoke little by way of soft words and was forever picking his nose and inspecting the results when not directly observed by higher rank. Their first stop was the quartermaster's stores, where a gruff sergeant with a shining head had piled Wyndham's arms high with all manner of rough cloth and sundry straps and brushes, and at the end, when Wyndham had his hands too full to do anything about it, he was provided with a great stiff kitbag to contain all his new treasures, and all the while the sergeant recited the list of articles issued with the speed and tonelessness of a bored priest, while his clerk scribbled it all down on yet another army form.

The smell of camphor was dizzying, what with all the scratchy cloth wedged high under his chin, and the impatience of the storemen palpable, even though in truth they had nothing else with which to busy themselves. They waited while Wyndham fumbled himself into some sort of order, and they waited again when he dropped something as Sheehan was marching him out and then dropped something else as he tried to pick up the first thing. Sheehan waited, and didn't shout or browbeat, but he didn't stoop to help either. When all was more or less secure again, Sheehan opened up with the 'left-right, left-right' barking that had accompanied Wyndham thus far and was to be the anthem of his waking life for all the long weeks ahead.

'Left-right, left-right, straight ahead of you, that building there, left-right, left-right, mind you don't drop anything. I said mind! Your blankets is slipping! That door there, right in front of you, left-right, left-right. Straighten up for Jesus's sake. And halt!

Ah Jesus, sure I'll get the blessed door, sure, and left-right, left-right, and halt! Your marching is only fucking desperate. Right. This is you. Get yourself sorted out and I'll be back in a bit.'

The cot on which Wyndham dumped his kit was no better and no worse than any of the others in the room, and he chose the one he did because just then it was in sunlight of sorts and thus there was less of a suggestion of damp. Later he'd wish he'd chosen one at the end of the row, with a corner to call his own, but for now he had plenty to be getting on with, and some wooden boards on iron trestles seemed good enough for him.

He examined his new possessions and realised that, although the names of everything had been called out as they were issued, many of these items were mysterious to him still. At least the more basic clothing was fairly self-explanatory, so taking advantage of this momentary privacy, he started to put on uniform for the first time. Of course there wasn't a mirror.

The underclothes were coarse, as he'd expected, but he hadn't signed up for comfort. The trousers and shirt were a bit of a mystery. Wyndham was a more-or-less normally proportioned young man, but he would have understood if the trousers hadn't fitted him. What surprised him was that they seemed to be the wrong shape entirely. There was a belt, though, to prevent the trousers from ballooning indecently around his waist and he was able to adjust the suspenders so that the crutch conformed to some degree to his anatomy, but it still looked and felt odd. To match the very high waist of the trousers came the very long tail of the shirt, which was a likewise coarse and voluminous garment. It could easily do for a nightshirt, but then it probably would have to. It wasn't exactly dirty, but the dingy blue-grey colour and the smell of the stores on it didn't suggest freshness either.

The tunic was just ugly, and too loose at the collar. Maybe it was meant for a more soldierly neck of corded muscle of the sort that a recruit would acquire in time.

He left the tunic aside for the time being, as it seemed to be asking too much of him.

And then there was someone at the door, and he was a poor advertisement for the way the army might make a man fill out his uniform.

The fellow's name turned out to be Twomey, and he was a small fellow, prematurely grey, and his attempt at a soldierly bearing only seemed to emphasise the shallowness of his chest and the scrawniness of his neck. He surveyed Wyndham with watery eyes and wiped his heavy moustache across the back of his hand.

'They sent me to give you a hand,' he said, and didn't seem too happy about it. Wyndham tried to be as polite and welcoming as a man in his socks can be in a room that is not quite his own. Twomey stumped in and took in the scene, and looked at Wyndham like he was an obstacle to be overcome. That was a look that Wyndham would be seeing again, but right now he thought he was a special case and thought that if whatever problem it was were addressed with directness, then all would be well.

'I'm afraid I'm not quite sure what I'm supposed to be doing with most of this, this…' and he gestured with both hands to everything that was spilled out across the cot.

'Sure I'm to give you a hand,' said Twomey. 'Didn't I say that?' And the weary impatience in his voice was already dispelling the rags of Wyndham's optimism. Nevertheless, he tried to maintain some initiative.

'I think there's been some mistake with the trousers,' he said (he knew enough not to call them pants). 'I think they may perhaps have given me the wrong size.' This wasn't really what Wyndham thought, but he needed the reassurance that he wasn't by unhappy chance wearing these simplest of garments in an utterly incorrect and unmilitary way.

Twomey gave him the once over. 'You're grand,' he said

without conviction. 'Your trousers is grand. Sure aren't you lucky to have them?' He hawked and spat in the fire bucket and sat down on the adjacent cot.

'Would you ever have such a thing as a fag on you? No? Ah sure, what harm.' But there did seem to be harm, because now the old soldier was obliged to smoke one of his own. At least it confirmed to Wyndham that a fag was indeed a cigarette, or at least a filthy brown excuse for one that Twomey was now fishing out of a tunic pocket and sticking in his face.

'So where are you from at all?

'Lowell. Lowell, Massachusetts.'

He heard the answer as if every second or third recruit through the gate was a New Englander and most of them were from better classes of places than this Lowell.

'I'm from Fermoy,' he said, as he fished out a lonely match. 'There's nothing in Fermoy. Only the army. I had the one pair of trousers on me and the arse was out of them and the knees was out of them and the father told me to go on away and join the army.'

Wyndham nodded politely, but not too politely. If he'd had anywhere else in the world to go he'd have made his excuses there and then.

'I wanted to go into the Royal Irish but I ended up in the Munsters instead.'

'Is that so?'

'The Royal Irish is in Clonmel and I have an aunt and an uncle in Clonmel. I used to have anyway. I believe the uncle is dead now.'

'I'm sorry to hear that.'

'The aunt might still be alive. I don't know.'

'I see.'

'There's nothing at all wrong with them trousers.' He paused, and sniffled deeply while he stared blankly at Wyndham's kit, not showing the least inclination to engage himself with it.

'I'll show you now how to square all of that away,' he said after a little while.

Then: 'I'll tell you a little story,' he said.

Wyndham hitched up his new trousers at the knee and sat down, indicating that Twomey please continue, although there might have been a hint of resignation or even sarcasm in his gesture.

'You want to be looking after your kit or they'll leather the head off you,' said Twomey. 'There's some of the NCOs who's awful bastards altogether if they see you and your kit is out of order. I'll tell you a story.' Twomey's eyes were moist, but all the sorrow had long since been wrung out of the man. He measured out his sentences.

'I was in South Africa, you know. South Africa's a desperate place. We were marching all over the shop. Every day we were marching and the rations was bloody miles behind us. And I'll tell you something. Do you want to know something?' He looked sadly at his dog end, which had gone out. Instead of discarding it in the fire bucket he stowed it back in his tunic pocket. There was silence.

'South Africa?' said Wyndham.

'I'll tell you something,' said Twomey. 'The clothes were falling off me. In bits they were. It was the weather they have over there. There was no replacements from the stores for bloody ages. So when the trousers fell to bits on me didn't I have to wear a blanket? "Wear a blanket, Twomey," says the sergeant. So I wore a blanket like it was a kilt.'

Wyndham nodded solemnly.

'And do you know I wasn't the only one. There was six or seven or eight of us in the company and we're marching around in these kilts only they were made out of bits of blankets.'

Wyndham was still nodding.

'They'd put you on jankers for having the smallest little bit of dirt on your uniform but they'd make you walk around in a blanket made into a kilt when they've no spare trousers in the stores. I never wanted to be in this regiment. I wanted to go into the Royal Irish.'

And then he put his hands square on his knees and stood up and took a real hard look at Wyndham's cot.

'That's all wrong,' he said. 'You have to have it all squared away properly or they'll bate the head off you. Is it Lance Corporal Sheehan that's in charge of you? He's only a bloody gossoon. He was never in South Africa. I've got more service than that bastard will ever see.' And Twomey said all this like a man who has come to the end of a long life with no hope of salvation.

In the course of a dull hour he showed Wyndham how to fold everything that had been issued to him, and he watched as Wyndham imitated him and told him he was doing it all wrong, but there was not a spark of energy in him. What Wyndham later realised was that the old soldier expected cash payment for his services, but even had he known, Wyndham only had on him the shilling that Fitzmullen-Brophy had given him, and he'd have thought it almost treasonable to part with that sacramental coin.

But at the end of it all Wyndham at least knew what a button stick was, and that the two neat little rolls of green cloth were puttees. He still didn't know what puttees were for, but he knew how they were expected to be stowed. Likewise he learned that the three hard square cushions that made up the mattress of his cot were called biscuits. 'It's because they look like biscuits,' explained Twomey, with laborious patience. And his regimental number was stamped on everything, and each article was to be displayed with the number visible, and his boots were to sit on the floor at the foot of his cot with the heels together and the toes apart at an exact degree. And this brush was for his clothes, and this for his teeth, and this for his boots, and this for his buttons. And there was a tiger on the buttons, and that, along with the

King's shilling in his pocket, kept Wyndham's soul above the damp shadows and free of the dreariness of Twomey's voice.

'Holy mother of God. It is. Christ, but I didn't believe them.'

It was Moriarty standing at the door, leaning on a broom, dressed in a suit of grubby white canvas.

'Well God bless us but look at yourself.'

There was a grin of wonderment on his face, but that wasn't all. He was undoubtedly embarrassed to be face to face with Wyndham again, but Wyndham guessed that embarrassment was not a condition that troubled Moriarty for very long.

'Hello, Private Moriarty,' said Wyndham.

Moriarty laughed at that. 'Private Moriarty! And hello yourself, Private Wilson – am I right in that?'

'It's Wyndham, and yes it is "private".'

Moriarty made no movement to come inside, nor did Wyndham offer to invite him.

'So, eh,' said Moriarty, 'how's the head?'

Believing that a hangover was being referred to, it was Wyndham's turn to be embarrassed. He tried for a rueful but worldly grin and didn't quite manage it.

'Listen,' said Moriarty, 'I'm sorry about the other night. Honest to God.' Then seeing that the American was not spitting in his eye or cursing him to hell and back, he reckoned that his little bit of contrition was enough to be getting on with, and he peered over Wyndham's shoulder to see how the mad Yank recruit was getting on.

'I'd come in only they have me on jankers after that carry-on with Lynch,' he said. 'Was that Twomey I saw coming out earlier? Christ but that man's a walking bloody disease. Did he help you with your kit? I bet it took him half the blessed day. Here – I'd better come in or they'll give me a right bloody rocket if they see us standing around nattering.'

He dodged in past Wyndham and positioned himself against the wall by the door.

'Keep an eye out there in case there's anybody coming,' he said, and rooted out his cigarettes. 'First one in bloody ages,' he said. Then, to show he was a big man, open-handed in all affairs, he offered one to Wyndham. 'You don't? Didn't think so.' The pack was already on its way back to his pocket. 'You will, though. Give it a bit of time. Bet you money.'

Then: 'Come here – you didn't give Twomey any money? No? Hah! That'll put the little gobshite in a filthy mood, serve him right. Did he tell you about South Africa? And his stupid bloody kilt? He only has the one story about South Africa and you just heard it, boy. If you ever want to get a rise out of the old fucker just call him "Jock". Go on. He deserves it.'

Moriarty's eyes drifted over the room, and the newly made-up cot. 'Jesus,' he said, 'I remember this place right enough.' Then he broke from his reverie of his own recruit days and addressed Wyndham more directly. 'Come here to me, though – you didn't really go and enlist, did you?'

Wyndham took his hands out of his pockets, the better to show off his new khaki. 'For six months,' he affirmed. 'In the reserve.'

'Whew – you're all right so. Six months? Not a bother on you. You might even enjoy yourself. But listen – is it true that old Major FitzEm talked you around to it? That's the talk anyway. He's a fierce man, isn't he?'

'I found him to be very pleasant,' said Wyndham.

'Ah but you know,' said Moriarty. 'I don't mean he's a savage or anything: just that he'd stop at nothing. A desperate fella altogether.' He peeked around the door frame and satisfied himself that the coast was clear. 'Bloody Conway,' he said. 'You'd need eyes in your arse round this place the way the fucking NCOs'd be jumping out at you.' He leaned back and pulled on his cigarette.

'Come here to me, though – what made you do it at all?'

'Enlist?' asked Wyndham. 'I'm not sure I could put it into words. I'm not sure you'd understand.'

'Do you know,' said Moriarty, 'that wouldn't surprise me, but go on anyway.'

'It's just that I think it's time I stopped leading such a sheltered life. It's time to be a man. The major said things that made me think so anyway.'

Moriarty blew smoke philosophically. 'Well so long as you're not in it for the money,' he said. Then, after another shifty glance outside, he told Wyndham how it had been for him.

'I'll tell you something. This was back when I was a young fella – only thirteen or fourteen. Back in Cork. There was this pub round our way and I'd be in there selling papers – that was my job, selling papers – and one day the soldiers came back from South Africa – this was nineteen hundred and two and the war in South Africa was just over – and there's these two fellas that started coming round to the pub. Now I don't know if you know, but there's this big barracks in Cork so you get used to seeing all kinds of soldiers all the time, but these two fellas were different.

'So I come in the one afternoon to the pub with the big load of papers under my arm, and there's these two huge fellas in khaki standing there. Mostly you'd never see the khaki because they mostly still wore the red tunic when they were at home, so that was a bit of a surprise for a start. And they were tanned almost black – let me tell you. These two big brown men with big black moustaches, and they're all in khaki, and they've got pints of porter and glasses of whiskey in front of them and each man has a girl beside him and there's a third one there as well, like in case either of the other two girls breaks down or something. Now you could have told me that these lads were the household bodyguard of the Sultan of Persia or something and I'd probably have believed you, but then one of them sees me and he wants a paper and he's speaking like a Corkman. And do you know something?

He gave me a tanner and told me to keep the change. And do you know the funny thing about it? It wasn't the money or the brown skin or the girls or any of that.'

'No?' said Wyndham.

'You'll laugh when I tell you, but it was their hats. They were wearing these big wide-brimmed hats like I'd seen on pictures of cowboys, with one side pinned up. Slouch hats, they're called, but I didn't know that then. Christ, but I thought they were the best thing I'd ever seen.'

He laughed at himself a moment.

'So I was forever hanging around that pub while those two fellas were there, and I'd be asking them questions and cadging smokes all the time, and I hell-bent on joining the army so I could be like those two. Of course the oul' fella – my father, that is,' he saw the look of confusion on Wyndham's face, '– the oul' fella only gave me a clatter when I told him I was going to take the shilling, and he was probably right too, but you know what you're like when you're only a kid. Even after those two soldiers disappeared I was thinking about the way they looked. Sure they were only a couple of old swaddies and their sunburn would have faded and their money would have run out in no time, and sure the hats went back to the stores because you never saw the like of them since. But I'd be lying awake thinking about being as glamorous as those fellas, with their stories from Africa, and the tigers on their buttons, and the slouch hats. Jesus.

'And the stupid thing was that a few years later, when I told the oul' fella to go stuff himself and went and joined the army anyway, at the back of my mind it was still about those blessed hats. Of course they were all gone by then, and say what you like, but a sun helmet just wasn't the same.'

He looked sharply at Wyndham in case there was a trace of mockery to be seen.

'You won't go around telling people about that now will you?'

he said, 'Or they'll be talking about me like Twomey and his kilt.' He laughed then, but he wasn't really joking.

Wyndham smiled reassuringly.

'Listen,' said Moriarty. 'I'd better be gone away out of here.' He picked up his sweeping brush like he meant it and checked one last time to see that no one was lying in wait for him outside.

'You go easy now, do you hear? I'll be on jankers for a fair while yet, so I don't know if we'll have a chance to talk, but sure we can have a pint the next pay day if you like.' He grinned at Wyndham's look of apprehension. 'We'll leave Lynch behind this time eh? Sure isn't he in close tack anyway? Good luck.'

And then he was slipping round the door and out. Wyndham raised his hand in half-hearted wave, and politely expressed his thanks, although for what he couldn't have said.

Privately he was still thinking what a shame it was that those magnificent hats had gone back to the stores.

13

'I shall give him a name that shall be Beaumains, that is Fairhands. And into the kitchen I shall bring him...'

...So thus he was put into the kitchen, and lay nightly as the boys of the kitchen did. And so he endured all that twelvemonth, and never displeased man nor child, but always he was meek and mild.

—Sir Thomas Mallory, *Le Morte d'Arthur*

Sergeant Duffy was the sort of man who looked as if he had to turn sideways to pass through a normal-sized doorway. He must have weighed nineteen stone, and much of that was still muscle, packed into his huge shoulders. He had boxed for the regiment in his day and been the brigade champion three years running, and was these days the immovable anchor of the tug-of-war team.

Wyndham, on first meeting him, was expecting a greeting along the lines of *Fee-Fie-Fo-Fum*, but was instead met with a welcoming smile, or at least by a further distortion of a misshapen face and the broad display of an incomplete set of teeth.

'Is it the American recruit? Christ!' he roared jovially. 'The major said you'd be along. I'm to teach you how to peel spuds, is it?'

Wyndham had sense enough to stand up straight and address the man as sergeant. Military discipline was still unlearned, but a good upbringing will stay with a boy forever.

'Ah, you're grand,' said Duffy, taking the young man by the shoulder and steering him into the great kitchen. 'There's hardly nobody in barracks until the week after next, so we're having a grand cushy life.'

The kitchen, or the cookhouse as he was to learn to call it, was reasonably warm and well lit, but there was a rankness in the air. For the rest of his days, that smell of stale grease and carbolic soap, that contrary combination of squalor and hygiene, would always be for Wyndham the very essence of the army – where visible damp on every surface was the gauge of cleanliness.

'The major's a lovely man,' said Duffy. 'He'd be into me here as soon as the training season comes around, talking about breakfasts. He's an awful man for the breakfast, but isn't he right? "Porridge, Duffy," says he. "Porridge is your only man." And by God he's right. There's some as would make you start the day on bread and scrape and nothing else – but porridge and bacon? That's how we built the Empire.'

And like it or not, Wyndham found a mug of tea thrust into his hands, for this was the great reward of cookhouse fatigue, and must not be scorned, and this was the easy, or rather the *aisy*, or possibly even the *cushy* life. After that he was indeed put in a corner with a sack of potatoes, a small knife, and a bucket, but if it took Wyndham the best part of an hour and a painful cut on the pad of his thumb to learn the fundamentals of spud bashing, Duffy deemed it an hour well spent. There were some sergeants who'd put the new recruits to scrubbing floors until the skin was off their hands and the knees were out of their good trousers, but Duffy said he reserved such punishment for bowsies as might deserve it, and not for decent men on their very first day.

As the kitchen had heated up, Duffy had divested himself of his tunic, and Wyndham noticed that sergeant's stripes had been carefully drawn on the sleeve of the man's flannel undershirt in India ink. More arresting, there was a tiger, rampant on a field of shamrocks, worked onto his brawny forearm in fading blue. Immediately above it, but probably unrelated, was a scroll bearing the name 'Lily'. The cook sergeant followed Wyndham's gaze, and seemed to appreciate the attention.

'There's a fella in town who'd do one of those for you,' he said, 'but he's stocious drunk half the time so you wouldn't want to trust him with anything too artistic.'

Hearing from the recruit no disinclination to have himself so adorned, Duffy went on.

'There'd be plenty of other fellas you'd find in Cork and Dublin and that, but sure they're only good enough for the navy. For a good army tattoo you want to be out east,' he declared. 'I wouldn't bother even with Egypt. India's your only man. Take a look at this.' And he rolled up his sleeve further to display the most shamelessly erotic image that Wyndham had ever seen. Despite himself, he looked closer. No: not just erotic, but pornographic.

'Now there's artistry for you,' said Duffy. 'Of course when I first had that done it was miles better. I didn't have the fat then, you see, so every time I flexed the big muscle there you'd see your man poking your one. Rangoon – and the whole job was only six annas, and I could have charged admission for the lads to look at it in barracks.'

He took the young man's awestruck silence as a compliment, and not wholly incorrectly either.

'Of course you'd not want the Padre to be seeing that and getting upset now,' he laughed.

'No,' agreed Wyndham in a small voice. 'No, certainly not.'

'And come here a minute till I show you something else that some people might object to.'

Wyndham braced himself while Duffy undid the apron strings at his waist, slung the apron up over his shoulder and out of the way, and pulled up his sweat-patched vest.

Even with the skin stretched by years and a spreading belly, the tattoo still had a bold clarity to it. It was a harp, the front curve of which took the shape of an unclothed female form. Not so much the classical nude, this heavy-breasted but lithe figure had more than a hint of the Hindu temple about her. Below the harp ran the legend: *I AM NEW STRUNG AND WILL BE HERD.*

'What do you think of that, wha?' asked Duffy with a wink. 'Do you know that cost me half nothing in Calcutta? Now don't go telling people that Sergeant Duffy is a rebel, now, will you?' And he winked again, more broadly yet, while adjusting his clothing to some state of decency.

Wyndham smiled along with the jest and kept his mouth shut about the spelling.

14

The objects in view in developing a soldierly spirit are to help the soldier to bear fatigue, privation, and danger cheerfully.

—*Infantry Training*, War Office, 1914

Wyndham was dog tired, but he forced himself to work anyway. He couldn't have done this a week ago. Staggering in from a day on the square, he'd have just lain down, and the three hard pads that made up the mattress on the iron bed frame might as well have been his last resting place, so loath was he to shift himself and see to his kit. And then Lance Corporal Sheehan would come in and shout and swear and bully him into putting his poor tender feet back on the floor and doing some blessed work for the love of Jesus.

Sheehan didn't need to shout so loud now. The little squad was learning that this was a pitiless world, and that exhaustion would never be accepted as an excuse for appearing on parade when a recruit's hated working suit of white canvas was anything less than white.

Wyndham leaned down to untie his boots and found that the muscles in his back would not allow him. They'd had a hard morning of it in the dank gymnasium, with the Physical Training Instructor making the recruits crucify themselves on the wall bars and then do unrealistically strenuous things in supposed imitation of the early martyrs. *And lift-two-three! And down-two-three! What's wrong with ye? And again-two-three!* Then there had been all those additional hours of square-bashing. His lower back had

had enough. It wasn't going to bend any more today. Try again after the weekend.

Wyndham grimly ignored these obstinate muscles and kept stretching until he had a grasp on his bootlaces. His fingers weren't much good for fine work these days, but they managed in the end. Then he screwed his courage to the sticking place and prised each heavy boot free. His socks were stiff but neither of them was bloodstained. He had to bend himself further to peel them off, but he did it anyway. 'And down-two-three, and off-two-three,' he grunted. He couldn't have done this a week ago.

All his short adult life he'd been doing nothing more strenuous than walking to the office when the weather was fine. Taking his Uncle Henry's physique as a warning to the sedentary, he'd also been inspired to take a stroll about town after his lunch, to stave off the day when he might be throttled by his own necktie, but that was pretty much it. Now he was up at an impossibly early hour, and spending the day being run off his feet with menial tasks and endless drill, with nothing to fuel him but the meagre preparations of Duffy's cookhouse. He had already heard the joke that if the army hanged a man and it killed him, they kept on hanging him until he got used to it.

At first Wyndham was astonished that he'd lived to see a second day of the drill square and the gymnasium, and then that subsequent days had failed to finish him off. Now, as the joke went, he was finding that he was getting used to it. He felt that the sinews, which last week were like broken rubber bands, were now replaced by taut cable, and the groaning cables in his shoulders and arms now hoisted his foot onto his lap for closer inspection.

He thought about Cook Sergeant Duffy and his rebel tattoo.

'I am new strung,' he murmured, wincing.

For all the army's concern with the care of the feet, it was scandalous how few pairs of socks they issued. In civil life – and

Wyndham was beginning to appreciate the breadth of meaning of that word 'civil' – he had owned at least one pair of socks for every day of the week. Soft socks, dry socks, clean socks; in fine wool for winter and cotton for summer, and even one pair in silk. Now he had just three pairs in thick, grey worsted. Living rough was something he had resigned himself to, but this baseness to which he'd been so suddenly reduced was too much. His civilian clothes were out of reach, and he was too new to the army to have ways of acquiring extra articles. Oh that horrible fourth morning when he had to clothe his scabbed and bruised feet, and all there was was this wool, salted and greasy! He'd have almost deserted if he'd thought his feet would carry him.

But then he had his brainwave: he would wash his own socks! Why not? There was water at hand, and soap, and Lord knows he was doing enough cleaning as it was. It was a bold step, but he was proud of himself that first night he hung his wet socks on the end of his cot.

He had reckoned without the Irish weather though, and it transpired that Lance Corporal Sheehan took a very dim view of articles of clothing being displayed in a non-regulation manner, this not being a fucking laundry. Wyndham's solution thereafter was bold, but it was successful. He slept with his socks between his mattress and his body. So tired was he on going to bed that he would fall asleep in a moment, even with the damp wool under his back, and it would be warm and dry in the morning. A week ago he could hardly even bear the feel of the blankets.

But while Wyndham humbled his soul to the washing of his wretched socks in a stone sink, others marvelled at his fastidiousness. Slattery maintained that of the three pairs of socks, one was for everyday wear, while the other was for Sundays only. He wasn't sure what the third pair was for, and wasn't going to make any dangerous assumptions either. Riordan, until the week before last, had never owned socks at all.

There was no denying that they were a coarse lot. His night with Moriarty and Lynch had given Wyndham some intimation of the soldier's ruffianly ways, but he had not imagined the rude stupidity and uncleanliness of his barrack mates. Their manners were disgusting. They farted and belched and hawked and spat and ate with their mouths open and stuck their hands down their trousers, front or back, to scratch with vigour. And compulsory washing or no: they stank.

And they were the only friends that Wyndham had in the world.

Slattery was the worst, in that he had no bodily modesty. He'd sleep in just his shirt, and stretch so extravagantly on rising that his barrack mates invariably had a view of his pale and pimply nakedness inflicted on them first thing. The cots were close together, and Slattery was unconcerned about mine and thine. At least the prospect of Slattery's dangling prick in his face provided Wyndham with that final spur to haul himself out of bed. Then there were those mornings when it wasn't dangling at all. It was all one to Slattery.

Or maybe Riordan was the worst. Never mind that he didn't know what a toothbrush was, or would diligently lick all the margarine off his bread before eating it: it was his inability to be alone or silent that would break Wyndham in the end.

'Do ye think that boot's shiny enough for Sheehan, lads? Do ye? Do ye think that's shiny enough?'

Or:

'Is that a letter you're writing, Wyndham, is it? Are you writing a letter? What are you writing, Wyndham?'

Plaintive, constant, idiotic: Riordan was a pest.

The pair of them were lost away from home, and Ballymullen was a hundred miles beyond their horizon. But they too were undergoing their transformation. They were still slovenly and base, but with their matched uniforms and haircuts, ill-fitting and brutish, there was a uniformity that had not been there a week before, and as Riordan and Slattery conformed in appearance, so their behaviour was conforming. Ugly and unhandy still, but they were on their way to being ugly and unhandy soldiers.

15

And there was poison on their clothes and on their hands and their feet, and on everything they touched.

—Lady Augusta Gregory, *Gods And Fighting Men*

What dirty eejit thought it was a good idea to set men to menial tasks while insisting that they're dressed in white, and then insisting that the same white be gleaming clean all the time?

Wyndham had recently cottoned on to the word 'eejit'.

He hadn't taken long in realising that it meant idiot, but the pronunciation made it a whole new word for him. It was an Irish word and an army word and was such a part of the vocabulary of this new life of his. He wasn't comfortable with the obscenities yet, but was practising his cussing in his more private moments, like now, when every man was too sullen and tired to do anything but see to his kit.

It could be absorbing work once you got used to it. Take boots, for instance. Polishing boots was a hateful routine at first, when the leather was new and uncooperative and the hands and mind were still learning, but already Wyndham had found the calm that transcended boredom in the hypnotic rubbing in small circular motions of a rag on a small area of toecap. A man could lose himself in that, and in the end he had a shiny boot before him, and it was a thing of beauty, especially if you had never laboured to create anything in your life before.

Every night the boot emerged from the dirt of the day a little brighter than the night before, and a step closer to perfection. In the army there was no abstract ideal of the ammunition boot

– such a boot was a real and achievable thing, and was seen on the feet of good soldiers. Wyndham would be a good soldier. His boots would be shiny and shinier yet. It had taken a while, but Wyndham was at peace now with his boots. The white canvas suit was another matter.

When the army dressed up it dressed in scarlet and dark blue with all its belts and pouches and such in gleaming white, and that was all right because it looked splendid. A man could hardly object to spending time on such an outfit when the results of rich-red coat and glossy fur busby and gleaming white accoutrements were so pleasing to the eye. For more practical wear there was khaki service dress, which was greenish-brown to blend in with the landscape and would consequently not show the dirt too much. Of course a khaki uniform should be kept clean, but it was obviously an easier matter when the more stubborn grass and mud stains were in effect self-disguising. So far then, it all made sense. But a service uniform was not, as it turned out, a working uniform, and that was where the white canvas suits came in. Canvas, certainly – but white? Why white?

Why, thought Wyndham as he scrubbed at a knee, and saw that it just wasn't good enough. Why, he asked himself as he scrubbed all over again and squinted and wondered if the grey was wet or dirt. What possessed the man, he wondered, who dreamt up this futile exercise? After this knee there was another knee, and two elbows and two cuffs and a collar and the trouser bottoms, and they were just the expected stains. It had happened that he'd worked half the night on those areas only to miss some unexplained but obvious mark on the breast that invoked the corporal's wrath on inspection.

And the wet material was uncooperative. A boot was solid and stayed on a man's hand as on a cobbler's last, but the canvas jacket and trousers flopped around and tangled themselves and wanted to trail their wet ends on the floor and get dirty all over again, even though that floor was supposed to be clean. And so your heart filled with hatred for your comrade whose turn it was to scrub the floor, even though he was right now despairing at the sight of a belt hopelessly besmirched with brass polish. And then, because you had a soul, you regretted your uncharitable anger and cursed yourself instead for being here, and the Irish weather for causing your clothes to be forever damp for morning parade, and the non-commissioned officers for their cruel ways, and then you'd see that that knee wasn't clean at all yet, and to hell with the army anyway.

You couldn't lose yourself in this sort of work. It was bad for you, and Wyndham's language, internally at least, was suffering.

Dirty eejit. Bloody fool. These were the words that went around in his head, maturing, making sure they wouldn't sound out of place when they might finally emerge to the open air. Strong words, not to be uttered lightly. Soldiers' words. Sinful words.

'Ah fuck it!' rose the despairing cry.

That was the luckless Slattery with the discoloured belt. He had only gone and made things worse, and he had thrown down belt and brush and rag and all and seemed to be on the verge of tears.

Desperate. That was another word bandied about quite a bit, but rarely in a context that made sense to Wyndham. The word always made him picture a man with his back to the wall, on the point of being overwhelmed by foes or circumstances. A soldier might not be exhibiting any obvious signs of desperation, but who knew what had driven him to join the army? Maybe he was, as so often described, a desperate man, and even a desperate man altogether. But how could the weather be desperate, and how could that be made worse by saying that it was 'only' desperate? It made as much sense as referring to a mug of tea as 'grand'.

Wyndham had been described as a grand man by an indulgent Cook Sergeant Duffy, and he'd wondered at the time if his comparatively gentle breeding had made Duffy think of him as a prince in exile, who had checked his ermine robes with left luggage at the station.

But it was all becoming more familiar and explicable now. Tomorrow their kit had to be splendid and sparkling for inspection. Tomorrow, after tonight's desperation, they would have to be indeed grand. And here was the handless Slattery with his belt all in a mess, and his boots yet to be done, so Slattery was no doubt desperate. Ah fuck it, indeed.

Daniel Wyndham hated Slattery's company, and despised the man himself, but he had a conscience and had been brought up to listen to it. If he couldn't consider Slattery a comrade in honest distress, then he could at least see him as a brute beast in pain. He wearily stood up from his cot, and took the belt up off the floor. The brass polish for the buckle reacted badly with Blanco, the khaki laminate used on the belt itself, so now the khaki was marred by a spreading white stain. When that happened there was nothing for it but to start again.

'I'll do this, Slattery, and you go see to your boots,' he said.

Slattery turned his wretched face upwards and looked speechlessly at his deliverer.

'Go on,' said Wyndham. 'Do your boots – they're only desperate.'

16

1. The instructor should be clear, firm, concise, and patient.

—*Infantry Training*, War Office, 1914

That first week seemed to last forever, but it was only a week, and before it was out Wyndham and his two comrades were joined in their mean barrack by a few more recruits so that now they formed almost a proper squad and could be drilled as such. To start with, with the new men being ignorant and Wyndham and the other two unused to such a sudden crowd, there was clumsiness that had Lance Corporal Sheehan on the verge of nervous collapse. But at least with more than three of them they didn't make quite such a mockery of the command 'form fours'.

The new men weren't as bad as Riordan and Slattery, or perhaps Wyndham's standards had been lowered. There were five of them and they were all Irish, except for Hughes, who was Welsh, but Wyndham couldn't tell the difference between their barely comprehensible accents. He'd got mostly attuned to what he supposed was the patois of this southern part of the country, and had endured many a moment of embarrassment and confusion even getting that far. And now, besides Hughes the Welshman, there was MacNeill from somewhere in Ulster (maybe), and Cassidy, Ryan, and Tobin from places he'd never heard of in his life, nor had he heard of the nearest 'big town', which was given as a point of reference and was, suspected Wyndham grumpily, the sort of place that would make Tralee seem like Paris. He was sick of Ireland. He was sick of the Irish. He hated how they were blindly ignorant of their own culture. He hated their small minds and narrow imaginations and laboured jokes. He hated the way they mangled the language and forced him to listen to it all the livelong day and halfway into the night as well. In barracks there was muttering and braying and everything in between, and none of it meaning the slightest thing, and on the square it was just the barking and roaring of the corporals, with Sheehan in particular with his harping and hectoring.

Sheehan wasn't someone you'd warm to, and wasn't the sort of person who tried to charm, but on the whole he struck Wyndham as a man without malice, who was stern only because his duty demanded it. But his voice was hard on Wyndham's ears, and there were times, with this new squad to shepherd, that he would be driven to a screaming pitch of frustration, and then he'd inflict some horrible collective punishment while he yelled himself hoarse.

There was the time that Riordan forgot his left from his right, and Slattery took Riordan's lead, and between them they bollocksed up the whole bleeding show (in Sheehan's words), and then, when the shambles was sorted out, didn't the same two diseased clowns do the very same thing again? The first time Sheehan had upbraided them, and cursed the mothers that bore them and called on some obscene god to bear witness to his suffering, but the second time he just lost his temper. He set them off running, or at least at that juddering jog-trot the army called 'doubling', and round and round the parade ground they went, their feet battering away at a hundred and eighty paces to the minute, and their caps slipping down onto their faces. Although they had not been issued with rifles, Sheehan decided that, if they had, then they should be obliged to hold them high above their heads as they ran, so up went their hands. Empty handed they were at least spared the burden, but they looked and felt absurd to be punished and seemingly ridiculed at the same time. They were usually being doubled from one place to another, and often they were being treated to this sort of thing, but today Sheehan was showing no restraint and no mercy, and whereas they might have expected to do one or two circuits of the square, here they were into their third, and Sheehan's voice was still a shrieking whine.

'Get yere fucking hands higher before I kill the fucking lot of ye!'

Cuchulain of Muirthemne would never have spoken like that, even with the battle rage upon him.

On the fourth go-round, with Sheehan's voice still calling the step like an angry metronome, Wyndham began to feel giddy. He was drenched with sweat, and that was nothing new, but his head was feeling light and his stomach perturbed. Duffy the cook sergeant had been generous that morning, and Wyndham felt the weight of porridge and tasted again the fried bread and syrupy tea of an hour past. There were lights dancing behind his eyes, and while his feet burned, his hands flapped mockingly above his head, and the back of Cassidy's shaved neck swam before him, he found himself half-lulled into a sort of nauseous hypnosis by Sheehan's harrying, for even Sheehan was now becoming too tired to do much but call out the same words over and over.

Wyndham had been hearing Sheehan's voice in his sleep for the past week, and of all the accents of Ireland, it was Sheehan's that he hated the most. And then he knew that he was going to be sick, and he tried to pull his mind away from all of this. *Think of something. Think of anything! I will arise and go now and go to Innisfree.* But the rhythm of the poem was too much at odds with the marching step. *Under the spreading chestnut tree the village smithy stands, the smith a mighty man is he with something something hands.*

'Wyndham! Get your hands up, you lazy Yank bastard! Higher!'

Should you ask me, whence these stories, whence these legends and traditions, with the odors of the forest with the dew and damp of meadows. Better.

'Left-right! Left-right! Pick them up! Riordan, you'll feel the toe of my boot in a minute!' And then it was just back to the counting and the left-rights until Riordan fell over, flat on his face. He was in the front, so the rest of them tumbled to an irregular halt rather than trample him. But Sheehan hardly missed a beat.

'Cassidy! Wyndham! Pick him up! Get him inside! At the *double*!'

And though their arms were numb and stupid, they did it anyway, and then they came back at the double and fell in like they were told, and shortly after that MacNeill was sick, so Wyndham felt that he might as well do the same now.

Why so pale and wan, proud lover? Why so pale and 'Wan, two, three, four! Ye'll clean that up, ye dirty animals! Double!'

17

The soldier should be instructed in the deeds which have made the British Army and his regiment famous.

—*Infantry Training*, War Office, 1914

Ballymullen was a barracks of modest proportions, but Wyndham's little squad almost never saw officers up close. Some day soon, it was rumoured, when they were not such a disgrace and a few more recruits had joined, they would be formed into a proper squad, or even something resembling a platoon, under the command of a proper drill instructor, but for now all visible authority was vested in the person of Lance Corporal Sheehan. Occasionally there were other non-commissioned officers in evidence, with a corporal's two or a sergeant's three chevrons displayed on the sleeve, but Wyndham's squad did everything except run and hide to escape the attention of men who were twice and even three times as powerful as Sheehan. They knew as much of the higher ranks as they did of the finer gradations of royalty.

But one day, when they were drawn up to attention after some parade-ground exercise, they found themselves under the benevolent eye of Major Fitzmullen-Brophy, who had seen them at their work and had thought to make his long-limbed way over and see how the new recruits were getting on.

It was the first time that Wyndham had set eyes on his patron since his enlistment. He noticed, as his own hard-used body quivered, that the major never seemed to stand quite still. He pushed his head a little forward as he beamed paternally on the squad, and raised himself half on tiptoe when he wasn't pacing up and down the short line they presented. He kept his hands firmly gripped behind his back, but his elbows kept twitching, as if let free he would be engaging in all manner of wild gestures. All in all, men of an agricultural upbringing were faintly reminded of the prouder sorts of barnyard fowl.

'Well done, Corporal,' the major was saying. 'Jolly well done. Shaping up well, I dare say. Coming right along, what?'

'Yessir.'

'*Jolly* good. Might have a quick word with them, Corporal. You might stand them at ease.'

'Stand at! *Ease!*' screamed Sheehan, and more or less in unison the men stamped their sore left feet to the left and braced themselves at ease with the sweat trickling down their backs.

Good show, thought Fitzmullen-Brophy. He eyed them from one end of the rank to other, not missing a thing. Men like Sheehan could concern themselves with such details as a loose button or a speck of dirt on a uniform, but an old soldier could see right into a man's heart, and weigh the man's worth. Indeed, the corporals and sergeants were necessary for putting backbone and soldierly discipline into the new men, but it was up to the old India and Africa hands to give them heart.

Splendid.

'I thought, men,' he began, 'that it would not be out of place in the midst of your training, to teach you about this corps into which you have enlisted – the regiment. Yes, quite.'

He had their close attention. He was sure of it.

'This is the Special Reserve battalion, which is to say that it is really the Kerry Militia – the proud old Kerry Militia, I should say – but it is also, the battalion, I mean, part of the greater regiment, which is the Royal Munster Fusiliers.'

He paused, and smiled at them with narrowed eyes. 'Royal Munster Fusiliers, men. It is blazoned on your buttons and badges. It is a proud name and carries proud traditions, which I trust you will all live up to.' When he was satisfied that that had sunk in he went on.

'The regiment has undergone many changes in its long history. Why, not forty years ago the two regular battalions were the 101st and 104th Regiments of Foot, and before that – before that – we were the Bengal European Fusiliers, do you see. But always – always, as no doubt you are aware – despite these official changes in name and so forth, we have been the Dirty Shirts.'

Oh, but he had them in the palm of his hand.

'Now I should say that while we take great pride in this name, I cannot stress enough the importance of hygiene and the necessity of presenting a clean and soldierly appearance, so as Lance Corporal Sheehan will no doubt tell you, we Dirty Shirts must always keep our shirts clean, eh? Haha!'

'Ha-ha!' barked Sheehan.

The squad managed an obedient chuckle at short notice.

'Now why are we known as Dirty Shirts, men? I'll tell you. India, men! India – where the regiment's origins lie. Eighteen-hundred and five, men, at the siege of Bhurtpore. Bhurtpore, men – you will see the name on the regimental colours. Eighteen-hundred and five.

'Now it so happened that during the Mahratta War, it was essential that the fortress of Bhurtpore be taken, and this task was undertaken by General Lord Lake, who was none other, as it happened, do you know, than the Duke of Wellington's commanding officer – except that he wasn't the Duke of Wellington yet, of course.'

Perhaps he had given them a little too much there, but what matter.

'Now Bhurtpore was no easy nut to crack – no, men. No indeed. And the Bengal Fusiliers – who would later, of course, become the Munster Fusiliers – were kept hard at work in their siege works. And it so happened that one day the Commander-in-

Chief – General Lord Lake, that is – was personally supervising the work and admiring the splendid efforts that the regiment was making in digging trenches and so forth. And it so happened that a party of the regiment, conscious of their muddy uniforms, apologised to the general for their uncleanliness, because you see, they had been working hard in the heat of India and had no clean change of linen in weeks. And the general told them to think nothing of it, do you see. He said, you know, that he was proud to see the men sacrifice comfort to duty. The men were looking to their duty rather than to their comforts, you see, and as such the dirty shirt was a badge of honour. And ever after General Lord Lake would ask after his "Dirty Shirts", as he called them, and the regiment has cherished the name.

'We may not be the Guards in all their finery, but we did our duty at Bhurtpore, when the Guards, devil a doubt, were too concerned with keeping their kit spotless. What I am saying to you, men, is that we can show as smart as any regiment in the army, but when it comes to the hard work we don't put on airs and graces. I like to think myself as smart as any officer in the service, but I went two months in South Africa without a change of linen, and I'll warrant that any old soldier in the regiment could say as much. Dirty Shirts do not shirk, men. Remember Bhurtpore. Eighteen-hundred and five. Carry on, Corporal Sheehan.'

He walked away, rather moved, while the usual shouting and stamping started up again behind him. The regiment would go on.

It had temporarily slipped his mind that the Bengal Europeans had suffered dreadful casualties in their initial assault on Bhurtpore, and that the fortress had not finally fallen until 1826.

But that was mere detail: the regiment would go on.

18

In the western tales is a whimsical grace, a curious extravagance.

—W.B. Yeats, *The Celtic Twilight*

It turned out that it was Wyndham who became the storyteller. He had tried once, in attempting to recapture his old enthusiasm and to convince himself that he still possessed some curiosity of intellect, to engage his barrack mates in conversation and to draw from them whatever folklore they knew, but Slattery and Riordan were both city boys and ignorant as a gatepost to boot, and it was no use asking them to recite the tales of ancient Ireland. It was as if they'd never heard of the place. More than that, discourse beyond the most primitive seemed beyond them. Neither of them could so much as structure a decent anecdote, or even tell a joke properly, and that was even after Wyndham had learned to penetrate their horrible accents. But in that gloomy barracks they all found themselves starved for entertainment, and once they had become a little used to the rigours of recruit training, and had occasion to yearn for anything besides rest, there was nothing much to do for recreation except talk. Wyndham, as an educated man, and their senior by some years, and most crucially as an American, thus was asked regularly for his opinion, and his knowledge, and in short order for tales of adventure, so that by the time the newer recruits joined, the Yank was an accepted figure of authority, at least in intellectual matters, and the spinner of thrilling yarns to boot.

The stories requested of him were not, however, the stories that interested him. He was entranced by Ireland but they wanted

America, and that to them was the Wild West. So Wyndham dredged his memory for the stories from the dime novels that had delighted him when he was twelve and were largely boring him by the time he was thirteen, and he refashioned them to suit both his own and their diverging tastes.

So they got Sheriff Fionn Mac Chumhaill (who went for the purposes of the story by the name of Wyatt Earp) who lost his heart to a Dodge City showgirl who in turn ran off with Doc Holliday, Earp's trusted right-hand man. The story was going fine until Wyndham absent-mindedly called his Fionn character Wild Bill, and was obliged to explain away his error in great haste by introducing Wild Bill Hickock as a new character weaving a wholly new strand to the old tale of Diarmuid and Gráinne.

Once on a route march he gave them the Cattle Raid of Cooley, because with cattle in the picture he thought it would be a simple business to transpose the action from Cruachan in Connacht to Abilene in Texas, where Queen Maeve was known as Amarillo Rose and Cuchalain and Ferdiad drew down on each other with six-guns in a dusty street. He had to improvise like mad in places, but discovered that the introduction of sudden gunfights or bands of whooping Apaches never went amiss. His audience appreciated action over narrative logic any day.

'Give us another of your stories there, Wyndham.'

'All right. Let me think.'

'Give us one of the ones again with the Indians.'

'No,' said Wyndham, with sudden resolve. 'No. I'm going to give you an Irish story instead – a real Irish story from the olden days.'

There was no enthusiasm voiced for this new programme, but the listeners were stuck with whatever they were given, and Wyndham was sick of making up rubbish. Today there would be no shoot-outs or scalpings. Today they would get mournful epic and high romance, and if Deirdre of the Sorrows couldn't move these simple men then to blazes with the lot of them. He waited while those who wanted to listen gathered within earshot, and for the shuffling and settling and cadging of smokes to quieten down.

He knew he had to cut the story down to what he considered were its essentials, and to leave out the odder-sounding Irish names, which he wasn't confident about pronouncing correctly anyway. So it was in the long-ago days before Saint Patrick, when Ireland was the land of champions (muted cheers) and there was a druid's prophecy that a girl would be born who would bring great woe and ruin to the Gaels, and there was the king who ignored the urgings that the child be killed at birth, so instead she was brought up in seclusion on a mountain, with no one for company but an old witch woman, and there she grew to lovely womanhood.

'What did she look like?' shouted Cassidy.

'She was the most beautiful of all the women in Ireland,' said Wyndham sternly, and tried to recapture the words as he'd read them, time and again.

And Deirdre grew straight and clean like a rush on the bog, and she was comely beyond comparison of all the women of the world, and her movements were like the swan on the wave, or the deer on the hill.

'Did she have big tits?'

Cassidy's effrontery derailed proceedings for a moment, and the guttersnipe was rebuked by Tobin.

'Would you ever mind your manners? You don't go talking about women like that. You're a bloody disgrace – what are you?'

'Would you listen to yourself? You're supposed to be a soldier now – you're not a fucking altar boy anymore.'

The issues of morality were swept aside by Ryan, who said he'd thump the pair of them if they didn't stop interrupting the story. He was a big sober man with an air of maturity that the rest respected and two fists that could break bone. 'Go on away there, Wyndham. You're grand. Go on and tell us about Deirdre.'

...Fair, comely, bright-haired; heroes will fight for her, and kings go seeking for her.

'Yes,' said Wyndham with decision. 'She had big tits.'

He had his audience then, and carried on with his story with his confidence growing and his blush fading. He was sinning, he knew, against God and decency and literary heritage, but he was a man now, and a man must get down in the dirt from time to time.

19

We don't care a rap for the Government, but we are all ready and will begin shooting as soon as Your Majesty tells us to.

—General Sir Dighton Macnaghten Probyn VC, to King George V, March 1914

On the last Sunday in July, on Bachelors Walk in Dublin, a company of the King's Own Scottish Borderers opened fire into a crowd. As was the case with most things that summer in Ireland, the factors at work were complicated. Simplified, the facts were that the troops were called out to help the police prevent the landing and distribution of arms for the nationalist Irish Volunteers. The police handled the situation ineptly and the thwarted soldiers marched home to barracks to the jeers and catcalls of an ever-increasing crowd. The soldiers had been goaded by the mob, and had been under assault from brickbats and flowerpots, but the simplest fact was that British troops had fired on unarmed Irish civilians on a Sunday evening in Dublin. The news reached Tralee with the morning papers.

There was consternation in the mess. Usually there was a strict and long-standing prohibition on talking politics in the mess. Mentioning religion, politics, or the names of ladies only led to trouble. It was an easy prohibition to observe. This was not the scandalous 18th century and no one knew any ladies of the sort that might provoke a duel. As far as religion was concerned? Well, even without the presence of a few RC officers, a chap would feel damned awkward spouting on about religion. A fellow's religion was his own affair, and possibly God's, and there was certainly no good to be had from having anything to do with it outside of Sundays.

When it came to politics, the thorny issues of the day were shied away from precisely because they were thorny, and indeed too thorny for most officers to understand. His Majesty's officers were loyalist practically by definition, and loyalist usually meant unionist, and that was that. That being that, it was wisest to leave all the grubby details to the politicos in Westminster, and that was a long way from Tralee. The gentlemen of the Muster Fusiliers had little in common with the strident sectarians. They liked to think that they stood for something simpler and nobler than Union or Home Rule. Stay loyal to your colours and your traditions and you will still be standing when all the political parties have been washed away by the tide of history. So to hell with politics: what about the cricket scores?

But today was different. Today there were three dead in Dublin, and dozens wounded, or four dead and a hundred wounded, depending on which paper you read, and a British officer had given the order to fire.

It was turning out to be a thoroughly bad year for the army in Ireland. Only last March some confounded fool in the War Office had proposed committing troops to Ulster to face down the militant unionists, and, to a man, the officers of the 3rd Cavalry Brigade stationed at the Curragh had handed in their resignations rather than comply with such an infamous order. There was more to it than that – so much more that both the Secretary of State for War and the Chief of the Imperial General Staff had been sacked – but the attitude in the mess in Ballymullen was that the cavalry, although evidently flighty and temperamental types, had had the right of it. It could be argued that the Ulstermen were in rebellion against their lawful government, or it could be argued that they were demonstrating in arms their allegiance to their monarch, but these arguments were rendered irrelevant by the army's conviction that Ulster was politics, and the army should have nothing to do with it. What had happened in Dublin on Sunday was more of the same. The army had been dragged into something that was properly a matter for the police, and now the nationalists and the agitators would be inveighing against the army, and howling about redcoated tyranny, and no doubt bringing Cromwell into it too. It was damned unfair. The army shouldn't have to put up with that sort of thing.

As heated opinions were given voice, and decent but guileless officers splashed heedlessly towards murky waters, the adjutant gave the final pronouncement. The politics of the matter were not a fit subject for further discussion. The Scottish Borderers had been landed in a disagreeable spot by the civil authorities, and while the Munster Fusiliers could doubtless have managed things better, no more need be said. Of course more *was* said, but politics were left out of it. Throughout the morning the officers hashed out the details again and again, and deplored the mismanagement and loss of life. 'Deplorable': that was a word the papers used, so the officers used it too.

Moriarty hadn't seen the papers. He was on guard at the main gate. This was a duty he felt to be somewhat beneath a soldier of his length of service, but Sergeant Conway was of the opinion that Moriarty was a slacker who needed to be reminded still that this was the army, and Private Moriarty was still in it, and should bloody well act that way.

So there was Moriarty, on a grand fine morning, gleaming with polish and sweat. The polish came with the duty. Boots were bulled and buttons bright. The discomfort came from the summer sun. It hadn't been much of a summer, and Tralee could be a breezy town, but today, just to punish Private Moriarty, the sun was splitting the stones, and slowly boiling him in his good clean kit. And then there was the hat. If there was only one thing that Moriarty could change about all of this, it would not be the sunshine or Conway's unmerciful scrutiny: it would be the blasted busby. Regulations decreed that the bloody great drum of black raccoon skin be worn for guard duties, even when guard duties were undertaken on a grand sunny day like today. It was like wearing a roll of carpet on top your head. With full ceremonial dress there was something splendid about it. You were there in scarlet and blue, wearing this big tall hat that made you look tall and fierce, and everyone was dressed alike and it was all like some brilliant fancy dress. But on guard duty you wore it with plain old khaki, and it was you all by yourself, and you looked like a bit of an eejit. From the neck down you looked like a soldier, but then you had this thing on your head that looked like it needed to be fed scraps from the butcher's to keep it happy.

So Moriarty stood there feeling aggrieved with the sweat running down into his moustache. The trick of standing sentry was to balance the body and let the mind drift, but that wasn't something he'd be allowed to do this bright morning.

Moriarty hadn't seen the papers, but rumour had been flying about the barracks. So when trouble turned up, he had a fair idea what was the cause.

Young fellas giving cheek to soldiers was just one of the things the sentry at the gate had to get used to. Small boys will give cheek to a man who isn't allowed to chase after them, and it will always be so. If the man is a figure of authority in a silly hat, then it follows that the boys will not travel any farther in their search for amusement, but will tease him and bait him for as long as they can get away with it. Another pleasant diversion for the children was their opportunity to try out whatever bad words they knew. They tended on the whole though to stop short of outright treason, and no sentry had yet heard them utter foul words against their king.

Today the boys were bigger and the language stronger and more overtly seditious. Moriarty had got a few dark looks from passers-by since he'd been on post, but in mid-morning a band of youths – old enough, by rights, to have been at work – assembled in front of the barrack gate. They were mostly, as far as Moriarty could tell, the usual sort of idlers and ugly customers who were behind most of the trouble in the town (if you didn't count the raucous soldiery), but there were a couple of fellows there who didn't look much like corner boys. They weren't quite respectable either, but it was evidently conviction rather than mischief that had brought them here. Little Fenian gurriers, thought Moriarty. Little Christian Brothers boys acting the langer. He gave them the hard stare. He'd never show fear to the likes of them.

One of them started off by calling him a British bastard. He'd almost have corrected the kid, only he'd learned from experience that in Kerry a Corkman was as bad as any foreigner, wearing the king's uniform or not.

Another one, better informed, or maybe in consideration of the oversized arms of Munster bravely adorning Moriarty's oversized hat, called him a filthy traitor. At that, Moriarty felt well within his rights to tell them all to fuck off out of it. They didn't. Now that it had been proved that they were dealing with a human being capable of speech, and not some graven image of a soldier, they were encouraged to provoke him further.

'Bastard! Murdering bastard!'

Did they know no stronger word? thought Moriarty.

'What about Bachelors Walk, ya fucker!'

Well they knew that one.

'Go on away home, or I'll tell your mammies on ye,' taunted Moriarty, but taunts were probably not what the situation was called for. These boys weren't going to leave without some sort of satisfaction.

And then one of them, a Christian Brothers boy without any doubt, actually accused Moriarty of selling his country for a dirty shilling. Moriarty was shocked at the affront. How dare the little gobshite throw that in his face, after Captain Crosbie not believing him and giving him three weeks' jankers? The bloody nerve.

And then one of the real gutties picked up a horse turd from the road and made as if to throw it. Moriarty thought of the time he'd spent getting himself all dolled up for guard duty.

'Throw that and I'll fucking kill you,' he snarled, but the boy just sneered and danced around taking aim and then fecked it at Moriarty's head. It missed, but only narrowly. Moriarty hadn't a single round of ammunition on him, but he brought up his rifle anyway and worked the bolt. The sliding rattle was a most arresting sound. Everyone either stopped dead or backed off a little, but one of the braver idealists spoke up.

'That's right! Go on and do what you did in Dublin! Traitor!'

Another working of the bolt would only prove that the rifle was empty, but Moriarty had his bayonet fixed. Seventeen inches of Sheffield steel, burnished white, wicked sharp. He assumed the 'on guard' position and put on his fiercest expression, which came naturally under the circumstances. Then by the drill book, he stamped and thrust at Young Ireland, who had sense enough to get back out of the way. Moriarty gave a tiger's roar and lunged at the next nearest boy, and then they were scattered and running up the road.

The corporal of the guard, alerted by the noise, came out as Moriarty was regaining his composure and taking his proper post again. The corporal looked at the retreating nationalists.

'Well God save fucking Ireland,' he said.

'Hear about what happened at the gate this morning?'

The news was in the mess by lunchtime.

'Some trouble, I gather?'

'Damned mob. Local ruffians. Shouted the usual seditious rot. Threw stones too, I believe. Private Moriarty was on duty. Saw them off smartly.'

'Stout fella Moriarty.'

Major Belcher from his armchair voiced his authoritative opinion: 'That's the stuff they should have given them in Dublin yesterday. Cool heads and a little restraint would have made a world of difference. The Scots were just too damned skittish. I've always said it, gentlemen. The Irishman may be wild, but put a little discipline into him and there's no finer soldier on earth.'

'Hear, hear, Tummy.'

'And I'll hazard something else. Had the Munsters been there, and had it come to shooting – God forbid – I dare say the shooting would have been a sight more effective.'

'How do you mean?'

'Why eighty or a hundred casualties but only three or four dead? Damned poor marksmanship if you ask me. Wild shooting. Smacks of panic. Typically Scotch, if you ask me.'

Some thought that Major Belcher had gone too far with that last observation. Under the circumstances it was in rather poor taste. There was no Scotsman in the mess to take offence, but it was bad form to think of keeping score when firing on civilians. And all in all, there was no getting away from the fact that this was a bad business for everybody. The incident at the Curragh in March, right or wrong, had given ammunition to the nationalists, and now there was this affair on Bachelors Walk, which was already being referred to as a massacre. The more intelligent officers could sense that the army in Ireland was in danger of being caught up in a terrible storm.

The report in that morning's *Irish Times* ran beside a piece about the deteriorating situation between Austria and Servia. The colonel, who wouldn't have known where Servia was had there not been a helpful map printed in the paper, thought that something like a little war in the Balkans would be just the sort of diversion the army could do with. One could almost envy the Austrians.

BY THE KING

A PROCLAMATION FOR CONTINUING SOLDIERS IN ARMY SERVICE

GEORGE R.I.

WHEREAS by the Army Act it is amongst other things enacted that it shall be lawful for Us in case of imminent national danger or of great emergency by Proclamation, the occasion being first communicated to Parliament, to direct from time to time that all or any persons who would otherwise be entitled in pursuance of the terms of their enlistment to be transferred to the Reserve shall continue in Army Service, and such persons shall accordingly continue in Army Service for the same period for which they might be required to serve if they had been transferred to the Reserve and called out for permanent service by a Proclamation issued by Us under the enactments relating to the Reserve:

And Whereas the present state of public affairs and the extent of the demands on Our Military Forces for the protection of the interests of the Empire do in Our opinion constitute a case of great emergency within the meaning of the said Act, and We have communicated the same to Parliament:

Now, Therefore, We do in pursuance of the said Act hereby direct that all soldiers who on or after this date would otherwise be entitled in pursuance of the terms of their enlistment to be transferred to the Reserve, shall continue in Army Service until legally discharged or transferred to the Army Reserve. And We do hereby direct the Right Honourable Herbert Henry Asquith, one of Our Principal Secretaries of State, to give all necessary directions herein accordingly.

Given at Our Court at Buckingham Palace, this Fourth day of August, in the year of our Lord One thousand nine hundred and fourteen, and in the Fifth year of Our Reign.

20

Now, Therefore, We do in pursuance of the Reserve Forces Act, 1882, hereby order that Our Army Reserve be called out on permanent service, et cetera, et cetera, et cetera…

—George RI

If the army was being mobilised, and the reserves called up and all, then it clearly meant war, and Ballymullen hadn't seen such excitement since South Africa. There were a thousand and one things to do, what with accommodation to be made for the hundreds of reservists due in over the next few days, but before any one of the mundane practicalities was undertaken, the bandmaster had seen fit to start the war in proper style, and the drums had been parading for a full hour, wearing out their drum skins and making the most magnificent din. The Munster Fusiliers would be going to war again, please God. Nothing was for certain just yet, but everyone in the barracks was cock-a-hoop. Almost everyone.

'Ah Jesus, lads,' said Moriarty.

'What's wrong with you at all?' That was Harrington, who was jumping around like he'd won at the horses.

'Do you know my enlistment is supposed to be up in October? The bloody mobilisation makes shite of that.'

'Ah you poor fellow. Are you bothered by a little bit of a war? Are you scared of the Germans?'

'The hell with you. I'll fight any bastard that looks at me funny.'

'So what's wrong with you so?' asked Harrington.

'No, listen, in fairness. I'm just saying, y'know.'

Moriarty sat down on his cot and picked up a bit of kit to clean, and threw it down again straight away. He knew what it was. Fairness indeed. He had used all the luck he had left in the world to get back from Burma, and now the gods were properly shafting him for thinking he could get away from the army scot-free. The boys who were stuck out in Burma would most likely miss the war entirely. Fairness.

'I'm just saying it's bloody rotten timing, is what I'm saying.'

'Ah God love you, you bloody fool. Are you telling me that you don't want to go to war?'

That brought in Private Balcombe. 'Who doesn't want to go to war?'

'Moriarty here is whingeing,' said Harrington. 'He's all upset about the mobilisation.'

'Call yourself a fucking soldier?' demanded Balcombe, utterly affronted, and happy to start a fight to keep him going until the Germans showed up. 'Call yourself a fucking Dirty Shirt? You some sort of fucking coward?'

'Fuck off, you, Balcombe,' said Moriarty. 'I've nothing against the war. The war's grand.' He stayed seated. He knew that a barrack-room fight could be prevented by just refusing to join in.

'If you want to know, I'm just fed up to my back teeth with the army. They've been pissing on me from a height for getting on seven years now, and just when I'm half out the door they give me a war to go to.'

'Better late than never, mate,' said Balcombe.

'Sure even if your enlistment was up,' said Harrington, 'you'd still be on the reserve for another five years. They could drag you back any time.'

'Yeah, I know, I know,' said Moriarty. 'And before you go getting yourself all bothered, Balcombe, I tell you straight that I'd re-enlist like a shot if I was out of the army and the war started.

Swear to God I would.' And all of a sudden he believed it too.

'It's just the bloody timing of it. I had the choice of joining up seven years ago and I joined up, and now I want to get out and I don't have the choice any more. Bloody army.'

'Hey! Hey! Hey, lads!' shouted Harrington to the barracks at large. 'Are ye listening to this? Moriarty here wants a nice proper invitation to the war, and none of your mobilisation proclamations.'

'Dear Moriarty,' said one of the wits in hoity-toity tones, 'May we have the honour of your presence in the war we are fighting next Saturday week. Yours affectionately, George.'

'Dress, service,' chipped in another.

'War will be fought indoors in case of rain,' added the first wit.

'That good enough for you?' said Harrington.

'You can all fuck off, the lot of you,' growled Moriarty, his face burning red.

And then in walked Lynch.

Private Lynch, brawler, drunkard, and thief, calm as you please with his hands in his pockets and a fag on the go. Private Lynch, granted a full and unconditional pardon and told to get his arse back on duty *juldi*. Nobody, it seemed, would be sitting out the mobilisation in the guardroom. The war was better than Christmas.

But barely had Lynch walked proudly through the room to his own cot, receiving the congratulations of his comrades, when there was Sergeant Conway at the door, roaring at them and asking them what the hell they thought they were doing sitting around scratching their bollocks when there was a war on, for the love of Christ.

Men were rapidly detailed off to clean this and carry that and go help the quarter blokes with the other, and threats of kit inspections in the near future. And that was mobilisation. All brushes and buckets and sheaves of paper, and anyone with a stripe on his sleeve wearing his legs out in all the rushing around, and even the officers looking like they were doing some work for once.

Mobilisation, thought Moriarty, as he sweated through his shirt, helping clear out a storeroom of all its stores. Look at the poor bastards, he thought. Slaving away like blacks and happy about it, and only because they might be going to the war. There mightn't even be a war, for all they knew. The Germans might show yellow at the last minute.

And that thought gave him a moment's anxiety, followed by surprise at his own feelings. It seemed like he'd got used to the war already, and would feel cheated if they called it off now.

Do you know what would be grand altogether? If the war could be over before the weather turned bad, and he could be back home in time to get his discharge. Then out of the army in time for Christmas, with a new medal and a pocketful of back pay. That would be the sort of war worth fighting.

He said as much to the man who was working beside him, wanting his vision to become real in the sharing. The man Moyle, a quiet sort from somewhere up the country, paused briefly, sniffed back the sweat, and gave his answer.

'We'll be grand if we're not killed. Give us a hand with them paint pots.'

21

Slán leis an uaigneas 'is slán leis an gcían;
Geal é mo chroí, agus geal í an ghrian,
Geal bheith ag filleadh go hÉirinn!
(Good-bye to loneliness and to the distant land;
Bright is my heart and bright is the sun,
Happy to be returning to Ireland!)

—'Trasna na dTonnta' (traditional)

Robinson and Dwyer were three days late, but they were here now.

Robinson stood four-square outside the barrack gate, head thrust back. He inhaled deeply through his nose, and followed it up with a thunderous belch.

'Smell that air, mate,' he said, in an unmistakeably London accent. 'Just smell it, eh? Dear old bloomin' Ireland.' He kept his feet wide apart for steadiness.

His mate Dwyer was braced with one arm up against the barrack wall as he pissed, and pissed, and pissed. 'Back to the army again, mate,' he said, shaking his head from side to side in delirious wonderment and smiling beatifically at the somewhat outraged young sentry who couldn't help but stare.

'Ah, God love you, boy,' said Dwyer to the sentry, who looked eyes front from then on.

'God bless us all,' said Robinson in happy sincerity.

The two arrivals were very much the pair. Heavy-set and

hard-handed, with huge untrimmed moustaches flourishing across their red unshaven faces. Their clothes suggested working men well set up in life, even though these suits had been slept in for a few nights already now. Robinson especially might have struck you as the type who'd normally have a thick watch chain looped across his spreading belly, but the absence was easily explained by a visit to a pawnbroker in Dublin. Each man had a pint bottle of stout sticking out of his coat pocket.

The two old soldiers had both been working as something in the wholesaler's line when the mobilisation notices went up, and they'd got their coats and walked out there and then with no more than a cheerio and were off to the post office with the papers showing that they were reservists. There was already something of a queue, so rather than stand and wait, the two men decided on a pie and a pint at The Coach & Horses, where they met a small but cheery party of Middlesex men and two sociable Argyll & Sutherland Highlanders who were all likewise giving this day of glory its proper due by drinking the health of the King and the Regiment, and paying the necessary compliments to the various other regiments as their representatives made themselves known.

They did manage to get to the post office before it closed, where the clerk issued each man with a travel warrant, five shillings in travel expenses, and two days' subsistence, calculated at one shilling and ninepence per day. All tallied up and divided, the allowance amounted to a mere four and thruppence a day, and it was absurd that the army expected a man to get by on such a sum, seeing as a single long and generous lunch hour had just accounted for most that, but Robinson and Dwyer were men of some substance, and they pocketed their king's bounty as no more than the small change it was. Truth be told, they'd both of them have been happy to fight this war for nothing. Indeed, it was pure sentiment that had kept the two of them extending their reserve service, and hang the fourpence a day that came with it. To cut that last tie with the army was to turn your back forever on India and South Africa, and all the mates who were gone. The fact was, as everyone in their Rotherhithe local had seen at one time or another, one or other of the pair would occasionally have to be bodily restrained by his mate when a few too many had been had and the siren song of re-enlistment drowned out all sense.

Well now there was no question of foolishness or enthusiasm. Their country was calling them, and they would not delay in answering. But it is a long journey from London to Tralee – practically the breadth of the United Kingdom – and a man cannot travel it on eight and six, nor even on the money in his pockets, especially when he meets a large group of Dublin Fusiliers in the bar at Paddington Station, and thereafter shares a compartment with some of them all the way to Holyhead, with nothing to do but play cards and keep the bottle going round.

The railway warrant was good for every stage of the journey from London to Tralee, but there were expenses along the way that the War Office, with their measly subsistence money, had not considered, and if Dwyer and Robinson wanted to do the thing in style, then it only made sense to visit that pawnshop on the quay in Dublin. Sure what did a man want with a watch in the army? A watch was a paltry civilian thing, which only served to remind a man that his time was not his own. You didn't need to be looking at your watch when you're killing Germans.

And then something had gone wrong, although neither man would have been clear as to what exactly, but it was clear that the Kaiser would have to wait a little for the pride of the Munsters to find themselves. There had been raucous times in Dublin, with the reservists for the Irish regiments heading west by rail and their English, Scots and Welsh counterparts going the other way by boat, so that every pub between North Wall and Kingsbridge was a scene of inebriated patriotism and riotous farewell and maudlin good fellowship, and every judy and doxie, not to mention every toucher and slacker and gouger in Dublin was taking full advantage of the soldiers and drinking their fill from the river of beer that flowed that August week. And so it was that when Robinson and Dwyer hoisted their glasses to the last party of Leinsters to leave, and thought that if they hurried they might make their train to Limerick Junction after all, they unaccountably discovered, as they found their bearings, that it was Friday, and not Thursday at all. But they were men of resource, and still had better than three bob between them, and the stout in Ireland was no more than tuppence a pint, and they reckoned that they could sleep most of the journey anyway, and a man doesn't get as thirsty when he's asleep. Railway guards and porters had been having quite a lot of practice that week in handling such customers as these well-watered old soldiers, so it was a clear run across Ireland thereafter. And when they'd been woken up in Tralee, with the bright sun cheerily winking at them through the grey clouds, they gladly parted with the last of their money, because wouldn't the army be providing for them from here on in?

Dwyer buttoned himself up, and the two men straightened their rumpled coats and squared their shoulders for this grand culmination of their odyssey. In they went, in step and with their arms swinging, but they kept their composure for only a few paces, for the first thing to befall their gaze was Sergeant Conway, and their eyes, already wet, filled with tears of joy.

Conway! And a sergeant! Bless us and save us, gawd's truth, Jesus Mary and Joseph and stone the bleeding crows. They practically fell about his neck.

He would have got them off the square and somewhere quiet if it had been up to him, but the barracks was a madhouse as it was and everyone tearing busy with the mobilisation, so he reluctantly wasted no time in marching these two beery old comrades that he hadn't seen since he was a corporal in Rawalpindi in '06 and hadn't missed one bit since – into the orderly room where an overworked Captain Crosbie would wish to put them on the books.

Oh but there were no two men happier in all of Tralee that day than Robinson and Dwyer, and even Crosbie's stiff demeanour couldn't quite wipe the smiles off their faces as they stood to attention.

The beer bottles had been spirited out of their pockets, and that was something. As a matter of fact, the depot had already processed hundreds of men that week, and a good half of them had drink taken to a greater or lesser extent, so Crosbie wasn't surprised or concerned. He had seen the full effect that those eight-and-sixpenny grants from the post office had had upon men freed for the first time in years from their domestic cares.

He'd had men laughingly declare that when their caps were on their families were covered, before suddenly clouding over, remembering that they were no longer nineteen, and asking about the separation allowance and provision for the childer. And then there were the others who would boast of being father to five – or wait a minute, sir, or is it six? – fine healthy children, and would try and count them off on their fingers and forget the names as they did so. Crosbie could expect months of angry and semi-literate correspondence from aggrieved and underpaid wives on that score. And of course there were those who didn't want to be there at all and spoke pathetically of their poor dependants or of the bad leg or the bad chest, and would have spun their tales of woe out to fill the whole day if they hadn't been dismissed forthwith to the MO who passed almost every one of them fit.

Some said nothing, but you could see that they didn't want to be back, and some the army wouldn't have wanted back if there was choice. Crosbie recognised several of the bad characters himself, or there was Conway at his elbow to mutter his recollections: 'Twenty-eight days detention in Quetta,' he'd say, or, 'Dirty in barracks and couldn't hit a barn door at ten yards on the range, sir,' or simply, 'Thief'.

And only yesterday there had been Private Williams defiantly standing in front of him. Williams who had enlisted in Liverpool, deserted in Kerry and had, apparently, been hiding down a coal mine in Renfrewshire ever since. And now they had to accept him because the King's gracious amnesty had been granted to all deserters and absconders. The regiment would not be killing the fatted calf in celebration, but they had to let him in without so much as a single hour's extra pack drill. The only thing Crosbie could say in favour of the business was that it made a welcome change from the procession of cheery drunks that had been clattering up to his desk since Wednesday.

At least these two in front of him did not address him as 'Captain, darling,' as had happened more than once.

The beer would be sweated out of them on the square. But he looked at the paunches, and the greying stubble on their chins, and knew that it would be no short time before these two could look proper in a uniform or carry full pack on a long march. And that meant there was no point yet in posting them off to 2nd Battalion in Aldershot, and that meant he was stuck with them for the time being.

II

RED LITTLE, DEAD LITTLE ARMY

'It doesn't matter what you send us. We only ask for one corporal and four men, but they must be here right at the start. You will give them to me and I promise to do my utmost to get them killed. From that moment I will be at ease since I know that England will follow them as one man!'

—Général Ferdinand Foch to General Henry Wilson (attr.)

22

Maeve looked at her, and she said: 'What are you doing here, young girl?'

'It is looking into the future for you I am,' she said, 'to see what will be your chances and your fortunes, now you are gathering the provinces of Ireland to the war for the Brown Bull of Cuailgne.'

'And why would you be doing this for me?' said Maeve.

'There is good reason for it,' she said, 'for I am a serving-maid of your own people.'

'Which of my people do you belong to?' said Maeve.

'I am Fedelm of the Sidhe, of Rath Cruachan.'

'It is well, Fedelm of the Sidhe; tell me what way you see our hosts.'

'I see crimson on them, I see red.'

—Lady Augusta Gregory, *Cuchulain of Muirthemne*

Khaki. A whole sea of khaki.

The red coats were hung up out of the way, and the quartermasters would soon be packing them in mothballs. The white canvas suits were gone too, because they were for working in barracks, and the men were off to their real work now. Service uniforms for active service, and all the pouches and belts a flat green against the green-brown clothes.

The regiment in scarlet and blue was a thing of beauty, but here was a grim and sober grandeur. The regiment was going to the war.

Rank by rank they stood proud and tall, with the old flag flying in the Atlantic breeze far above their heads.

The medals of India and South Africa, of long service and good conduct, decorated many a breast, and if there were some faces aged and yellowed by sun and sickness, there was yet a steadiness and a sternness that could not be denied, and mixed among them were the newer men, clean-faced and bright-eyed, and eager for the coming test.

Lieutenant Colonel Richard Sherlock Brasier-Creagh, Commanding Officer, 3rd (Special Reserve) Battalion, Royal Munster Fusiliers, watched over it all from the saddle of his gleaming charger, and there was a lump in his throat and a swelling in his heart.

God bless you, men, he thought.

The band finished 'St Patrick's Day' and swung straight into 'The British Grenadier'. When they finished he would make a short speech of praise and farewell.

Damme, but I wish I were going with you.

Keep it short. They'd been standing long enough already.

Lord Kenmare was there, the honorary colonel and the very picture of the finest sort of Irish gentleman. The senior Depot and Reserve officers around him – all the old men together. Was that a tremble he saw in Fitzmullen-Brophy's lip? Wouldn't be surprised. Rather felt like weeping oneself, you know. What a sight! How many of these magnificent men might not come home? How dearly might the regiment's further glories be bought? And isn't the weather splendid?

Lord Roberts should be here, you know. The King should be here.

Such hectic days, preparing for overseas, with all these old soldiers finding their feet once more and their feet finding boots, and socks, and puttees. And the lists and lists and everyone running hither and thither. But they'd done it in the end. Knew they would. Take more than this to ruffle a Munster. Professionals to a man. Gallant little Belgium need hold on just a little while longer. The Dirty Shirts are coming, and no Teutonic clockwork soldiery can withstand us when we're roused.

God! But I wish I could go with you!

What a sight.

And the smells of oils and polishes wafting, and the sound of the bass drum, now coming to a triumphant close, and the screech of the sergeant major, and the great crash of feet, and the men of the draft were at attention.

Brasier-Creagh raised his voice.

I look among you and I see your faces...

'Men! I have but a few short words to say to you. You are about to embark on a great and noble enterprise, and I have little doubt but that you will conduct yourselves with steadfastness and bravery. The German is a resolute foe, but he has not met the Irish.'

Pause.

'Remember always the proud traditions of the regiment, and remember also your homes and your families. May God go with you. God save the King.'

'Three cheers for the Colonel! Hip-hip!'

And when it was done, the sergeants took over again and with perfect obedience the men formed into column of fours, and the band playing 'Won't You Come Home To Bombay?', the draft swung out the gate and the crowd was there to cheer them on their way to the station.

Come home to Tralee, boys.

And Brasier-Creagh stood braced in salute with the old men, smiles stiff behind their moustaches and eyes glittering.

God bless you, lads.

Goodbye.

Goodbye.

'Damme, but I need a drink,' said Belcher.

Fitzmullen-Brophy blew his nose and agreed that a peg might be just the thing.

'Damned fine show, I thought,' said Belcher.

Fitzmullen-Brophy nodded, still busy with his handkerchief.

'And damned if I don't envy them, what? Damned Germans. Show them a blasted thing or two, eh?'

The mess was quiet. The waiter brought whiskey. It wasn't long before he brought more. The third time he was told to bring the damned decanter and leave it there.

23

There was anger on Finn then, and he said: 'It is a worse life than hunting to be here, without hounds, without horses, without battalions, without the shouting of armies.'

—Lady Augusta Gregory, Gods And Fighting Men

'Of course it's all railways now, you know,' said Belcher. 'Not like Burma at all. Not even like South Africa. Hardly have to put your boot to the ground, you know – or your backside in the saddle either. Motor cars and all that.'

'Quite. Quite.'

'The men have to slog along, of course – and the young warts, of course. That'll never change.'

'No.'

'But if you or I were there we'd be rolling along in a motor car.'

'I could march,' said Fitzmullen-Brophy with a hint of resentment.

'I never doubted it, old boy.'

'Fit as a man half my age, dash it.'

'Of course you are.'

'Remember Welaung?'

'Never forget it, old man.'

'Boil the size of a cricket ball on my neck and a fever of a hundred and two degrees and I damn well soldiered on.'

'Did you now? I'd quite forgotten.'

'And you could say as much, Tummy. Constitution of an ox.

Nothing ever got the better of you, did it?'

'Now that you mention it.'

'Hard service. It hardens a fellow. The young men may be young, but they're not hardened yet. You see what I mean?'

'Naturally.'

And then Fitzmullen-Brophy was on his feet, pacing dangerously around the room, waving his arms and sloshing his whiskey, addressing a wider audience.

'It was a damned mistake to leave fellows like us behind!'

'Ours not to reason why. And for God's sake, do sit down, man.'

'Rot!'

'Well sit down anyway.'

'It's nonsense! Do you know how old Johnny French is? Do you?'

'How old?'

'Oh, I don't know. Sixty, maybe. And Grierson? Met a chap who met him. Fellow is on the verge of apoplexy every time he stands up.'

'Grierson? What's he?'

'Oh, something, I expect. Corps commander – chief of staff – I don't know.'

'Well look here – you'll give *yourself* apoplexy in a minute. Sit down and have a drink. It will calm you.'

'You're a rock, Tummy. Nothing rattles you.'

And he sat down and had another drink, and between them they re-fought the war in South Africa, and marched all over Burma and the Northwest Frontier as they had in the days of their youth, and almost missed dinner, and were very late in getting to bed.

Fitzmullen-Brophy was not his usual cheery self during those days, and remained out of sorts through the week that followed mobilisation. The regular sessions in the mess with Tummy Belcher had a deal to do with that of course, but the pangs felt at the marching off of the drafts remained, and were repeated with the successive drafts, and returned most sharply when the regimental colours were sent over from Aldershot for safekeeping.

That was a moving ceremony. An escort was sent down to the station to meet the colour party from the 2nd Battalion. All attending had seen funerals with less solemnity. Fitzmullen-Brophy made sure he was there, and his heart filled with sorrow to think of his regiment going to the war without these totems to watch over them. There was no place for the colours in modern war, he knew, nor, apparently, for old soldiers like him, and they both must remain here in the sleepy depot in Tralee while the younger men went on to glory.

The next big blow was the coming of the movement orders for the 3rd Battalion, Fitzmullen-Brophy's own unit.

'Where?'

'Castletownbere, old boy. Be ready to move 8 am, Wednesday morning.'

'But-but – dash it all, Colonel – I mean to say, well, well – dash it all! Castletownbere, what?'

'Stop making such a bally fuss, FitzEm. You hardly thought they were going to send us to France, now did you? So just go and hound everyone into action and then you can go and tell your woes to Tummy Belcher if you still feel strongly about it. I'm busy.'

Major Belcher, part of the permanent staff of the depot, would be staying put for the duration, it seemed, but that didn't mean he was sitting idle either. Like the colonel of the 3rd Battalion – like everyone – he was busy, only his rock-like calm and stolid efficiency meant that he wasn't rushing about quite as much as the hare-brained youngsters. If he'd been asked he'd have told the youngsters that his years of hard campaigning had taught him that the value of timely rest was every bit as important as frenzied activity. He'd have said as much to the smooth-faced young officer he'd found one afternoon sitting in *his* chair in the mess, but he'd just spent an exhausting hour with the Quartermaster Sergeant and his accounts, and his eloquence just wasn't up to it. And thus the young pup was faced with an elderly major standing at his elbow looking dangerously like an overheating steam valve. The boy was intelligent enough not to enquire as to the major's wants, but was on his feet and off to see to his duties without even finishing his lemonade.

Confounded cheek, thought Belcher as he settled himself in the chair, ignoring the quiet smirks of some of the others in the room. The depot, it was said, did not need the colours when it had Major Belcher in his armchair.

And there, as usual, Fitzmullen-Brophy found him.

'Castletownbere, Tummy!'

'I heard.'

'But it's rot, Tummy!'

'Of course it's rot, old boy. Ever known the army to do something sensible?'

'But Castletownbere – what on earth's the point?' Fitzmullen-Brophy sat down, and just as soon stood up, making fretful gestures that only confused the waiter who hovered nearby.

'I gather,' said Belcher, 'that the navy's there. Damn all else, mind.'

'Exactly! The navy's there. My point exactly! The army goes to France to fight while the navy stays at home and keeps the Germans from invading. That's how it should be. The army fights, Tummy. We fight!'

Belcher perhaps looked momentarily uncomfortable. 'Well, strictly speaking, old man, and I don't wish to be hurtful, of course… I'm just saying what those box-wallahs in Whitehall probably think – if they *do* think that is – but strictly speaking, the 3rd Battalion mightn't actually be seen as the army as much as the county militia.'

'Rot!'

'Utter rot, of course.'

'I mean, naturally we have taken on the traditions of the county militia – and proud old traditions they are too, I'm sure – but I sincerely doubt that the Germans are going to invade Tralee.'

'Of course not.'

'And if they do, well that's why we have a navy, what?'

'Perfectly right.'

'And do you know something, Tummy? The 3rd Battalion wasn't just embodied when South Africa happened, and didn't just provide drafts for the front, but was actually posted overseas. Well, I mean to say.'

Of course Belcher knew that. Everyone in Tralee knew that. There on the 3rd Battalion's colour, midway between the tiger and the shamrock, beneath a riot of Lancastrian roses, was the blazon 'South Africa 1899–1902'. And if anybody had somehow been so blind and ignorant as to miss that, there was always Major Hugh Fitzmullen-Brophy to remind him. Indeed, the scene being played had become so familiar since the war had been declared, that if Major Belcher did not hereupon urge Major Fitzmullen-Brophy to sit down and have a drink then anyone in the mess might have thought that one of the players had forgotten his lines. Matinée performances of this show tended to be shorter, louder, and heavy on South Africa. Evening shows were more maudlin, with Burma and India coming more to the fore.

'But whatever am I to do in Castletownbere, Tummy?' asked Fitzmullen-Brophy plaintively. He had taken a seat, but not a drink.

'Don't think the hunting's up to much in that part of the world,' said Belcher, 'but you never know. There's bound to be sport of some fashion. I understand the navy has some class of a golf course. Bound to let the army play if you ask 'em nice enough.'

'Golf? *Golf*? I do wish you'd take things seriously! Golf, indeed.'

24

And it is then Cuchulain's anger came on him, the flames of the hero light began to shine about his head...

—Lady Augusta Gregory, *Cuchulain of Muirthemne*

Wyndham had joined the regiment to be of the regiment. He wanted to have his petty concerns done away with as his individuality was subsumed into the grander identity of the Royal Munster Fusiliers. He would no longer be himself – diffident, cautious, and even fearful – and would instead be a soldier, a fusilier, and a Dirty Shirt: a part of a machine whose operation would transform its parts into something stronger and purer. And thus he had accepted the hardships and, whenever his body and spirit were not utterly exhausted, appreciated them as a tempering of his soul. But he looked at his barrack mates in all their meanness, and he knew himself to be little better than they, and he saw that this was not the machine but the herd, and there was nothing noble about this herd. These khaki urchins of Lance Corporal Sheehan's squad were not the proud wild horses of the plains, but beasts bovine and slow-witted, driven from behind, and ignorantly fouling whatever they found under their feet.

The arrival of the reservists was the tipping point, when Ballymullen suddenly became a very cramped residence indeed. One afternoon, when the squad came back from the square, they discovered that they were to be amalgamated with a squad somewhat more senior in its military service to Wyndham and his mates, with quite a few of the reservists thrown in for good measure. So now all the cots in the room were not only occupied, but pushed closer together to an objectionable degree, and the senior men had taken no time in making themselves at home and finding room for themselves and their gear.

The cavaliers who were now disporting themselves in the little barrack room were making much of their extra service (be it only, in some cases, a few weeks) and in consequence their juniors found their own kit rather carelessly rearranged to make room. Neatly squared belongings were no longer squared, or in some cases to be found at all, and perfectly folded blankets were now rumpled and pulled askew. That last one was what irked Wyndham the most. He'd come in, his feet smarting like blazes, and there was the room all in a muddle and strangers blithely making free with it. Wyndham was too stunned to be outraged at first. That room was the Holy of Holies in the temple of military order and cleanliness, where carbolic soap and brass polish were the incense. Before a man attended to his person he made sure that this space was swabbed and scrubbed, and once those rituals were done to the satisfaction of higher authority, then there was at least established a piece of firm ground in the midst of this turbulent and uncertain world. It had not been easy. Sacrifices had been demanded. In the end, despairing of making their beds to perfection in time for morning inspection, the squad had taken great efforts in helping each other the night before to create cots of geometrical exactitude, and then to keep them that way, all of them slept on the floor. Sheehan had looked with favour on their offering, and nothing had been quite so bad since. But now the sanctuary was profaned.

'Sorry about the mess, chum,' said some heedless barbarian. 'We'll take this end and you lot can squeeze in down the back.' And Wyndham had dumbly accepted this and tidied up in the little barracks-in-exile down the back. What else was there to do? He was just a beast, broken to obedience.

That evening was different. The afternoon had been

exceptionally rainy; the gymnasium was found to be fully occupied, so training had been reduced to lectures indoors. As such, the men weren't so dog-tired and dispirited as before and Wyndham for one found himself rather more self-aware, and concerned with matters slightly above the primeval. He was, for this moment at least, raised a small degree above the herd. After attending to his person and his kit he pulled out one of the two books he had kept with him, and for the first time in a long time the words did not swim before his eyes or the sense of them fail to penetrate his dull brain. Indeed, he was into a second paragraph when the new barrack mates came merrily in, having been enjoying themselves in the wet canteen. One of them – none other than the veteran Robinson who had made the epic journey from London with his mate Dwyer – sat down on the foot on Wyndham's cot to unlace his boots.

'Don't mind me, old cock. Be out of your way in two shakes. Here – what's that you're reading?' He grabbed hold of the top of the book and twisted it forward onto Wyndham's chest so as to make out the cover.

'Oh, blimey – I can't read that. *Lady* Augusta. Who's this Lady Augusta then, mate? You reckon she's a looker? I wouldn't mind a Judy right now, eh?'

'Get off my cot.'

'What? Just give me a tick, mate.'

'Get the hell off my cot.'

'Here – mind who you're talking to, son.'

Robinson had one boot off and one boot on, and he was half talking to this recruit and chaffing with his pals at the same time, and all of a sudden the recruit was standing over him, tight-faced, and giving him a right earful. He had a funny way of talking, but his words were ringing clear.

'*My* cot. Get the hell off,' said Wyndham, loud enough for everyone else to hear.

'Keep your hair on,' said Robinson, rising upright, but not wanting to start anything either.

'*My* cot. *My* kit. *Our* side of the room. Understand?'

The invaders had quietened down, and were looking at how this was shaping up, gathering themselves for possible combat. And then Sheehan's squad, in the person of Cassidy, spoke up.

'Go on, Wyndham boy. Go on and tell them.'

And to his dismayed surprise his comrade turned a blazing eye on him.

'Shut up, Cassidy. Just keep your damn mouth shut and pay attention.'

For Wyndham, whose initial outburst had been just an irritated impulse, had quickly realised that if he was going to start a quarrel over something trivial, he might as well go the whole hog and address all his grievances. If it came to blows, he couldn't even cover a penny bet against these men, so he might as well go in for a pound, and go in in a righteous cause. Why just pick a fight when you can launch a crusade? Wyndham let the spirit move him.

'What I want,' said Wyndham, not at all sure if he could encapsulate what he wanted into a simple declaration, 'is for you *all* to just mind your damn manners. Please.'

Please? There was something not quite right there, but never mind. He had committed himself with *damn*.

'This is a barrack room: not a pigsty or a saloon or a bear pit! I have to live here. We all have to live here, and we should all live like civilised human beings and not like, like damned animals.'

There was so much more than that, and he couldn't frame the words. The army that he had joined should have been neither the beery hugger-mugger of the one side nor the mean spit-and-polishing of the other. None of that was faithful to Major Fitzmullen-Brophy's promise, nor to the heroes, be they of recent or ancient days. Wyndham had come in search of the warriors of old Ireland, and here they were, better for little besides slurping tea and belching in their sleep.

He wanted to shout at them, and now he had.

But he found it hard to maintain such a head of rage. He had always been a more reasonable than a passionate fellow, but his red face and voice roughened now with nervousness were good enough accompaniment to his short harangue.

He had the attention of almost everyone now, and some were asking what he was on about and some were telling him to shut up, while others were telling *them* to shut up. Sides were being taken. Men were squaring up, without knowing what for. One of the new arrivals was all for putting the green recruit in his place, which was to say flat on his back with a broken nose, and he didn't mind saying so. And then Robinson held up his hands and called for peace.

'Fair dues, boy,' he said to Wyndham. 'Say no more.' And his voice was so warm that Wyndham would have started apologising there and then, ruining it all, except that Robinson had turned to address the room at large.

'Nice and easy, lads,' he said. 'Nice and easy. Remember we're guests,' and Wyndham heard not a trace of mockery in Robinson's voice, nor saw any in his smile, nor felt anything other than a gesture of comradeship when Robinson patted him on the shoulder and left him to the unaccustomed silence he had wrought.

He went back to his book, but found no refuge there. He stared at the page, knowing that he was getting occasional looks from his barrack mates. After a little while the background muttering became normal conversation again, and it didn't take long at all for the men who'd been on the beer to grow loud and expansive. Wyndham let them. It would be Lights Out soon enough anyway. He listened. Amid the banter and bluster there were intimations of things worth listening to. These, after all, were the men who had seen active service in their day. The South Africa veterans had the greatest weight. They could brag of a real war. They could taunt the men who'd perhaps only heard the occasional whistle of a bullet up on the Northwest Frontier, but those India men were proud enough in their turn. They'd got their knees brown at any rate, they averred.

Wyndham thought about that. It seemed ridiculous to him that men should boast their manliness in the nakedness of their legs. This was hardly Sparta.

He thought of his own knees. They would never be the knees of the bronzed imperial stalwarts evoked here tonight. His knees were not heroic. He would keep them decently covered up. There was no point in trying to measure himself against men like these. Their standards might be strange to him but, for all his outburst at their swinish ways, he inwardly acknowledged them as his betters.

They had been to a war and were going now to another, and it seemed to be no more than a job of work to them.

25

The people here don't mind the war coming. They could not be worse than they are. They may as well die soldierly before God.

—W.B. Yeats, *The Celtic Twilight*

Moriarty went with the first draft out of Tralee for England. After all, marking time until his discharge as he was, he was one of the few men in the Ballymullen depot with no particular job to do, so they could easily dispense with him. He handed in his busby and his red tunic along with the rest of his kit and wangled a few extras while the quarter bloke was feeling generous or distracted – whatever. He wasn't sorry at all to be saying goodbye to the Sunday finery, but being warned for embarkation put him in bad form.

He wouldn't miss Tralee – that much was certain. He'd only been here a few months and, in a place like this, more dead than alive, that was a few months longer than a man needed. He believed himself to be the sort of lad who could get along with anyone, but he had no particular mates here. Anyway, most of the men he did knock around with were leaving with him. Harrington the smart boy was skipping to be off to war, and he could hardly keep his trap shut with the excitement. It got on Moriarty's wick. He usually preferred lively company, but now he was appreciating the qualities of duller men like Moyle.

Moyle wasn't lepping around as much, but then most people on first acquaintance thought Moyle a bit slow. Moriarty knew he was no such thing, and could be as smart in his way as Harrington, only he had the sense to be quiet about it.

Balcombe would be there, and he and Moriarty didn't care for each other at all. Moriarty always reckoned the Englishman to have too big a mouth on him and to be too ready with his fists, and Balcombe was always ragging on Moriarty for a waster and a skrimshanker.

And then of course there was Lynch. Everyone thought Moriarty and Lynch to be the best of pals, and that probably included bloody Lynch. It was hard to get the measure of a man like Lynch. You couldn't guess what was going on inside his head. Moriarty had gone out drinking with Lynch a few times because Lynch was someone who wasn't telling him all the time to shut up. Lynch was an ignorant so-and-so but he stood his round and he gave Moriarty room to speak his mind. That was a problem that Moriarty had always had about the army – fellas always at you and on top of you and talking over you. He knew the word 'camaraderie' and was all in favour of it in principle, but he only wished to have some comrades worthy of it.

And now they were all off to the war, and so far that had meant nothing except everyone flaking away nineteen to the dozen, and shoving up to make room for all the returning reservists. That was another thing – the reservists. He knew a few of them from his time out east with 1st Battalion. Out there they had been fly men, brick-red and hard with it, with jobs to do and a certain place in life. And now here they were again, diminished by their civilian clothes, and looking pale, and often poor and dirty. Beyond an initial cautious greeting Moriarty tended to keep his distance. These men were really only civilians when they walked in the barrack gate, and who had anything to say to civilians? And then, newly suited in khaki, they were strutting around and coming the old soldier, pretending that the army had never dispensed with their services years before. They larded their talk with more words in Hindustani and Afrikaans than they probably knew the meaning of, and they bored the arses off the depot men with their long-winded reminiscences and their merriment. The first lot of them weren't there more than a couple of days, but they were loud and careless and they made shite of the barracks.

And then one morning the fitter and more sober ones were formed up on the square in full field-service kit, along with Moriarty and the few of the depot men who were going to the war, and the band was walloping out all the old tunes, and the colonel and all the rest were there to give them a big send off. That was a grand affair to be sure, and Moriarty would have been lying to himself if he didn't admit to feeling a little thrill. This, after all, was what it had been about all along.

And the short march through town to the station was a proud thing too, with more flags and cheers than His Majesty's soldiery was used to meeting in Tralee, because the war was a novelty, and Munster's Own deserved a bit of applause for marching off to fight it. They hardly paused in Cork, and didn't even have a chance to get out of the train station, which disappointed Moriarty a little, seeing as it was his home town and it might have been nice to swank it around for a bit and talk big and get free drinks. By the following afternoon they were in Aldershot, to be absorbed into the regiment's 2nd Battalion.

Aldershot put Ballymullen in the cheap seats. Aldershot reminded everyone – if they needed it – that the army was off to war. The barracks were jam-packed. The quartermasters were ladling out kit like there was no tomorrow. The roads were busy with route-marching columns of men breaking in new boots, getting used to the weight of a pack again and letting their soft civilian selves run out through their pores in the August heat. The boys from Tralee were scattered to the winds, or at least were rapidly assigned to platoons and companies, with the sergeants and corporals worrying them and snapping at their heels from morning to night. As luck would have it, Moriarty found himself mucking in with a lad he knew called Whelan, only just posted over, his recruit training in Tralee not long finished. Whelan was a good-humoured fellow, and appreciated the length of Moriarty's service and the breadth of his experience. He even liked Moriarty's stories and he laughed along with Moriarty's jokes.

On their last night in England the two of them drank their last pints in the wet canteen and Moriarty, feeling better about things, explained in detail to Whelan what he should expect from this war.

'What it boils down to, boy, is that foreigners are worth nothing at all, and that goes for the Germans and French like it does for Boers and the niggers. Stick by me and sure you won't go far wrong. Will we have another? I think it's your round.'

26

...Be invariably courteous, considerate and kind. Never do anything likely to injure or destroy property and always look upon looting as a disgraceful act. You are sure to meet with a welcome and be trusted; your conduct must justify that welcome and that trust. Your duty cannot be done unless your health is sound. So keep constantly on your guard against any excesses. In this new experience you may find temptation both in wine and women. You must entirely resist both temptations, and, while treating all women with perfect courtesy, you should avoid any intimacy.

DO YOUR DUTY BRAVELY.

FEAR GOD.

HONOUR THE KING.

—Kitchener, Field Marshal

'C'mere, lads? Did any of ye read this?'

'Is that Moriarty the bloody scholar? Read what, for Christ's sake?'

'Shut up, you. Have a listen. Were you reading the thing they gave us from Kitchener?'

'I did not read it. I'll wipe me arse with it.'

'Wiping your arse with an order from a Field Marshal? Court-martial offence, boy.'

'What's it say anyway?'

'It's a guide to etiquette. A code of behaviour. It's telling ignorant gurriers like you how we're to be behaving: take your hands out of your pockets and stand up straight, you gobshite you. That kind of thing'

'Fuck off, you. Is that what it really says?'

'In so many words. Best bit's at the end. It applies particularly to dirty shaggers like yourself and Harrington. You listening, Harrington? We can't be having it off with the French girls.'

'We can't *what*? Who fucking says?'

'Kitchener says. Field Marshal *Lord* Kitchener'

'Show us that.'

'The French girls that you'd see on the postcards. The ones in the silk stockings and the frilly knickers. *Dying* for it, boy, but you can't lay a finger on them.'

'Who in the fuck does he think he is? *Lord* Kitchener. If the French girls are like they are on the postcards, he can fuck off, so he can.'

'Come here to me, boy. Listen to this. "*Your duty cannot be done unless your health is sound*".'

'Shite.'

'Remember Corporal Flanagan who went down with the clap in Rangoon?'

'The bloody clap. And the malaria. And the *delirium tremens* and all. Bloody Flanagan. I remember.'

'There you are so.'

'What became of him in the end?'

'They shipped him home strapped into his cot, raving mad, and the sweat pouring out of him all the way to Suez and his two bollocks swollen up on him like footballs and he died roaring in the lunatic asylum.'

'You're making that up.'

'Who knows what happened to him? Maybe it's true.'

'That sounds like the syph. The clap doesn't drive you mad.'

'Would you never mind him. Sure he's only making it up. Bloody Moriarty. Anyway Paris isn't Rangoon. I bet they have a better class of VD in Paris.'

'We're not going to Paris.'

'*We're not going to Paris*? Who says?'

'We're going to Belgium. Weren't you bloody listening at all?'

'After we bate the Germans they'll have to leave us go into Paris.'

27

Some talk of Alexander, and some of Hercules,
Of Hector and Lysander, and such great names as these,
But of all the world's great heroes, there's none that can compare,
With a tow, row, row, row, row, row, to the British Grenadiers.

—Traditional

'Ah lads, Doesn't this beat all?'

Everyone was too worn out to match Moriarty's enthusiasm, but the chorus of deep sighs and satisfied groans confirmed that this indeed beat all. The Munsters were halted by a stream, and Moriarty's platoon had got the prize, sheltered from the worst of the day's heat by the shade of grand big trees, and, as they'd loosened straps and belts, and rubbed their sunburnt necks with cold water, hadn't a little girl come along with two big buckets of cool buttermilk – almost too big for her to be carrying even – and let it known that this was a gift from 'Maman' for the 'soldats Anglais', and didn't she come running back after with her apron full of apples.

That was half an hour ago now, and that meant there was another whole half hour before they'd have to get moving again, and by then the sun might well have gone in a bit.

'Up on the pig's back we are, lads,' averred Moriarty, and he was right, for before the halt was up, whoever had been lighting candles to the patron saint of idle soldiery had his prayers answered in the form of a harried young lieutenant from brigade staff, who passed the word to the CO, from whom it filtered down to the companies and platoons that there was some mix-up in the order of march, and the Munsters were to stay put until they could take their place at the tail of the brigade, which, given the confusion on the road, might not be along for another hour yet.

Some of the men reacted to this joyous news by promptly putting their heads on their packs and falling dead asleep, but Moriarty, unable to find sportsmen enough to start a card school for the sort of low stakes he could afford, was content to sit on the trampled grass and smoke and watch the big parade go by.

Whelan joined him, agreeing that they were living the life of Reilly, and the two men ate their apples and smoked their fags, and revelled in the display of other mobs beside themselves slogging along.

Whelan, the high-spirited young gawm who'd passed out of Ballymullen only a few months before, enjoyed Moriarty's learned discourses on regimental history more than many another man. Now this happy youth was enjoying the war more than was decent and, freed from the load of his equipment, and allowed to sit and watch the khaki world go by, he didn't know himself.

The passing of the 1st Black Watch provoked speculation as to whether or not a kilt mightn't be so warm in this heat as the thick bulls-wool trousers and flannel long-johns of the civilised regiments, but the shining faces of the Highlanders did not seem to suggest it.

'Step out, the gallant Forty-twa! The English are behind ye!' called Moriarty, and some men took the trouble to notice him and he was advised to fuck off in accents ranging from the Glaswegian to the unmistakeably Cockney.

And then the English were indeed upon them, and not just any old English either, for the Munsters were honoured in this campaign to be brigaded with two battalions of the Guards, and now, although these men were as dusty and sweat-stained as all the rest, they marched with a certain air that told those who knew them that they could maintain that perfect rhythmic tread for uncountable hours yet, even if they were tramping over the upturned faces of innocent children.

Whelan was in too good a mood to care.

'What cheer, the Coalies?' he cried, for these stern warriors were the 1st Battalion of the Coldstream Guards, a regiment older than the army, and bodyguard to the king. They were the old Second Foot Guards, and had as their motto *Second to None*. They were not renowned for their good cheer.

It wasn't that Whelan particularly wanted to get a rise out of them, but he was ill-advised enough to break into that famous old marching song 'The British Grenadier' with too frivolous a spirit.

It was his rendering of the chorus as *Row, row, row your boat for the British Grenadiers* that proved a step too far, and before he'd got much past his first 'merrily', a shadow had fallen over him, and he squinted up, and knew his doom was upon him. The Coldstream Colour Sergeant was, of course, tall. His uniform was dusty and creased but his webbing was still arranged just so and his pack and pouches were squared so precisely that you'd have cut yourself on the corners. His moustache was twisted into miniature devil's horns. He was not amused.

'Enjoying yourself, Paddy?' he asked, with his face like one great contorted muscle.

Whelan was already embarked on a placatory 'Ah now, Sergeant,' as he struggled stiff-legged to his feet, but he was too slow. Much too slow. His back was insufficiently braced when a spray of spittle blasted his face and a voice screamed – positively *screamed* at him – to stand to fucking attention, and do up his fucking buttons, and put his fucking cap straight on his bloody head. Moriarty was already making himself scarce, and the rest of the unit, now wide awake, was keeping its distance. Some dirty bollockses, Whelan was later to remember, naming no names as he glowered at Moriarty, looked as though they'd never known him, let alone worn the same cap badge as himself, as he'd stood arraigned by the roadside.

And the long and the short of it was that Whelan was there and then obliged to shoulder his rifle and pack, and fall in with the Coalies, and march like the clappers with that bloody colour sergeant at his heels, and stand under arms through the next halt, and so on, until it was felt that he'd learned some manners.

Even his officer, the good Lieutenant O'Malley, had been unable to stand in the way of justice. As the Coldstreamer had explained – with ill-disguised disdain for a mere regiment of the Line – this man had shown disrespect to His Majesty's Guards. Even an Irish Second Lieutenant should have propriety enough not to allow such *lèse-majesté* to go unpunished.

28

'Be no utterer of falsehoods.'

—'Maxims of the Fianna', T.W. Rolleston,
Myths and Legends of the Celtic Race

Ballymullen Barracks was usually a harmonious sort of place, despite being home to two different bodies of men. The depot company was composed of real soldiers, but they had little enough reason to be proud of it, and for every old sweat with tales of the East there was a clutch of handless recruits of whom no one would care to claim parentage. Also, the depot company was merely a company and thus far outnumbered by the 3rd (Special Reserve) Battalion. The reservists saw no reason to push their weight around either because they were, if forced to admit it, only amateurs really and besides, most of them were never there except for the brief training season in the summer. On top of that, the officers were all part of the same military family, and had known each other for years, and if some might be irked at having been shunted, temporarily or otherwise, into this military *cul-de-sac*, they could content themselves with the fact that they were among Dirty Shirts. Tralee might not have had much to recommend it, but it was theirs.

Since the first week of August, that harmony had been under some strain, what with the depot processing the 'Class A' reservists and arranging drafts for the 2nd Battalion in Aldershot, and the Special Reserve mobilising in case of German invasion or a nationalist uprising, and both bodies of men competing like mad for the limited resources of accommodation. The 3rd

Battalion would shortly be on their way to defend the naval base at Castletownbere, but until then the barracks was in as close to uproar as the Royal Munster Fusiliers could allow. There was hardly room on the parade ground sometimes, it seemed, and sleeping and feeding arrangements were on the point of collapsing into catch-as-catch-can.

And that was why Fitzmullen-Brophy thought this an opportune moment to have a word with the harassed commandant of the depot.

Major Worship's office was neat and clean, except for the thin dusting of cigarette ash that settled on anything that lay on the desk for more than half an hour. The air was faintly blue with tobacco smoke but the major, if perhaps a little tired looking, appeared as neat and efficient as ever.

Fitzmullen-Brophy beamed around the door and asked if he might have a quick word, and breezed in and planted himself in a chair on the merest suggestion of Worship's acquiescence.

'Busy, I see?' Perhaps not the right thing to say, but Fitzmullen-Brophy pushed on quickly.

'Thought I might ask you a favour.' He watched Worship's eyes harden in an instant so added, 'Thought I might *do* you a favour too, as a matter of fact.'

Major Worship had known Fitzmullen-Brophy for years, on and off, and knew there was little enough guile in the man. He was, though, subject to his fads and enthusiasms, and his daily tirades in the mess against the injustice of not being sent to the war were frankly rather wearying. At times like these a genial old duffer like FitzEm could be something of a pest. So when the man proposed that he get out from under Worship's feet for a while, Worship did not look for a catch.

'Now look here, Major,' began Fitzmullen-Brophy. They were the same rank, and Worship was technically junior, but Fitzmullen-Brophy was appealing to the man as Officer in

Command, and thought that proper formalities wouldn't do any harm. 'I shan't keep you long. You know that 3rd Battalion is marching off next week, and we'll all be out of your hair, but I was rather thinking that I might lay on a little scheme that should take some of the men out of barracks for a few days.'

'Go on.'

'Well you know I've got a special interest in the young chaps doing recruit training. Well I'd like to keep an eye on them and get them away from all this irregularity. I thought a few days route marching around the county would do them a world of good. Clear up some space too, what?'

'Sounds ideal, old boy. You don't want chaps like your young American to be corrupted by the old sweats, eh? That was a neat piece of work, by the way – they should have you out recruiting for Lord Kitchener. Take 'em. Take 'em with my blessing. They're your men after all.'

'Ah. Yes. Well, some of them aren't, you see. I want to take some of the reservists too – the ones who won't be going out with the drafts until they're properly fit, you know. Fellows like Robinson and Dwyer.'

'Oh, FitzEm!' Worship bounced a pencil off the desk in sudden exasperation. 'Don't you dare mess about with my paperwork, damn it. I couldn't possibly let myself lose track of anyone at a time like this.'

'You won't notice they're gone. Honestly. I'll have them back in three days – no more than four.' And that was the first whopping big lie that Fitzmullen-Brophy had told in a very long time, and it was only his long-standing reputation for openness that kept Worship from noticing the man's stammer and reddening face.

'You see I've spoken to the Colonel and he agrees.' And that was his second blatant falsehood. 'The idea is that I take a company of the 3rd Battalion by road to Castletownbere, the new boys come with me to get their first taste of proper marching and the sweats are there to work off their bellies and put some salt into the recruits. I was thinking about some simple tactical exercises along the way. It'll do my chaps a world of good and you've got a hundred empty cots and a hundred fewer men to feed, and I'll send your chaps back by train by the end of the week, all the better for the exercise. What do you say?'

'I say you're needlessly complicating a situation that is dangerously close to complete topsy-turveydom as it is, old boy.'

'Nonsense. I'm making your life a good deal easier, I should think.'

Major Worship picked up another pencil and sucked the end of it, and then hastily exchanged it for a fresh cigarette. He frowned.

'Cooks? Transport?'

'All 3rd Battalion. I wouldn't dream of poaching anything from you at a time like this.'

'And the Colonel is happy enough with this scheme of yours?'

'He thinks it's a splendid idea.' And now Fitzmullen-Brophy was smiling firmly even though he felt his heart breaking under the unaccustomed burden of lies. Still – it was all in a good cause.

Worship made a meal out of lighting his cigarette, giving himself time to think. For the life of him he couldn't see anything *wrong* with Fitzmullen-Brophy's idea, but the irregularity of it made him suspicious. Then again, the doings of the Special Reserve had never been any of his affair, and this was a rather unprecedented set of circumstances. And he'd be getting that fussy old FitzEm out of the mess and out of Ballymullen at last, and that was surely a boon. Tummy Belcher had already departed. Gone to Dublin, apparently, to see if he still had strings worth pulling there that would find him gainful employment in this war. With Belcher and Fitzmullen-Brophy both gone the place might look less like a second-rate gentlemen's club and more like a modern army gearing up for a modern war. Fitzmullen-Brophy was sitting there on the edge of his chair, looking constipated. Let him have his little route march.

When Worship said as much, Fitzmullen-Brophy positively bounded up and was out of the office in a twinkling, his expressions of gratitude hanging in the smoky air behind him. The fellow never had any proper sense of proportion.

29

The very purpose for which Garadh was left behind with us, was it not to make fire for us and to play chess with us, because he has gone off his lustihood and his spear-throwing, and because the condition in which he is is that of old age?

—The Colloquy of the Ancients

Tummy Belcher left Tralee for Dublin with a sound breakfast inside him and a half pint of whiskey in a silver flask riding in his capacious tunic pocket. How he would fare in Dublin and beyond he knew not, but it was wise to be prepared. Somewhere in his luggage was a Webley .455 revolver, but that was only for form's sake. It was seldom the business of a field officer to fight, but his basic comforts had to be seen to if he were to remain cool and capable of making decisions.

The journey was long and lunch was abominable, and once beyond Limerick he no longer had his compartment to himself. The first couple of times some young wart had stuck his head in, and seen the crown on Belcher's cuff, and the affronted glare in Belcher's bloodshot eye, there had been a hasty apology and withdrawal, but then some damned civilian had barged in with no more than a tip of a hat, and taken a seat, and that destroyed the inviolability of the dusty little 1st class compartment. At Limerick Junction an unruly horde consisting of two artillery officers crowded in, and talked about horses all the way to Kildare. Added to the occasional rustling of the civilian's newspaper, it made for the most unholy racket. Belcher thought it a wonder that he was able to sleep through it at all.

The gunners alighted at the Curragh racetrack, where the army was busy buying up all the horses of Ireland. Terrible great lies were being told there, as horse-trading men succumbed to the temptations offered by His Majesty's hasty generosity. Forty pounds was the flat rate for a good horse and sixty for a charger and the army hadn't the time to haggle over animals that were easily worth eighty pounds, yer honour, and I couldn't part with him for a farthing less. Some owners, with only a single horse to sell, but prizing that one highly, chose to sell it twice to different purchasing officers. And all the while the young men in khaki breeches and spurred boots wandered about, dazzled by the riches on display, picking and choosing at will, and all at the army's expense.

Belcher might have enjoyed himself too, had he been younger, but he was getting too old for horses and was troubled by the piles besides. He was merely glad when the train disgorged itself of all the pink-cheeked lieutenants of cavalry and artillery who, unfortunately, were replaced by more of that stamp. Not surprising really. Impromptu horse fair or no, the Curragh was the biggest military base in the country.

Belcher's long journey ended at a hotel near Kingsbridge Station, from which it was the shortest stroll to Parkgate, which was the army's HQ in Ireland. Any strings to be pulled stretched back to here. Belcher was a mere major in an unfashionable regiment, but he had been in the army since the year dot and had knocked around quite a bit in his time and met all sorts of chaps. One of these chaps was now on the staff in Parkgate, and Belcher reckoned him the very chap to help a chap out in bringing FitzEm's clever scheme to fruition.

The chap's name was Lieutenant Colonel Hector Stewart DSO, but he was not the sort to stand on title or honour when he saw his old comrade Tummy Belcher come into the mess.

'Belcher, by God!' he positively roared, and was out of his

chair in an instant, striding forward in welcome and barking at a waiter to see about refreshment. The two men were roughly of an age, but Stewart was tall and energetic, with a shining red face that made his large even teeth look white. Besides the ribbon of the Distinguished Service Order, there was in evidence on the breast of his blue patrols a respectable two rows of coloured ribbons that bespoke many years of meritorious service across the empire. There was also a deep scar on his brow, breaking the hairline. He'd got that in the Sudan, along with his DSO. The word was that, had the wound been fatal, Stewart's action would have won him a posthumous VC instead.

The two men dined together and afterwards, once they were pleasantly warmed, but not so tight that business was forgotten, Belcher voiced his needs. Under usual circumstances talking shop in the mess was utterly out, but there was a war on, and some degree of etiquette could be waived. Indeed, with the midnight oil being burned in the various offices upstairs, it was a small matter for Stewart to summon a relevant junior staff officer, with the relevant papers to be signed. When Belcher left Dublin the next day he would be taking with him the necessary documentation allowing a detachment of the 3rd Royal Munster Fusiliers to proceed without hindrance to France. There would still be irregularities to be smoothed out, but this could be dealt with as and when the circumstances arose. Some important blanks in the paperwork had been left for Belcher to fill in himself.

'Well that was damned civil of you, Stewart, I must say,' said Belcher. 'You've saved me no end of trouble.'

'Think nothing of it, old man,' said Stewart, waving his glass about expansively. 'A fellow should be able to get some use out of a job like this. Mind you, I won't be at it for much longer – thank God.'

'Is that so?'

'Kitchener's to give me a brigade, don't y'know.'

'Well that is splendid. My congratulations. Least you deserve.'
'Kitchener hasn't forgotten the Sudan.'
'Nor has he. Good show.'
'So we might see each other out there, what? Like old times, what?'
'I could think of nothing better,' said Belcher. 'I see your glass is empty.'
'Haha! Damme, but so it is! Well here's to Kitchener.'
'And good luck to him.'
'Aye, and here's to Gordon. Gallant old Charlie Gordon.' This sentiment was delivered in a voice that would have been considered a shout by those who didn't know Stewart.

'Here's to him,' echoed Belcher, more quietly. They were almost alone in the mess. Everyone was so busy with mobilisation for one thing, and for another there was Colonel Stewart with drink in him. Stewart with his Sudanese medal and his garbled recollections. He was getting all bothered about Omdurman now. How he wished he'd been at Omdurman.

Belcher nodded, and occasionally murmured acquiescence, but never went so far as to contribute anything of his own. He hadn't been at Omdurman either. Hadn't even been in the Sudan, come to that, but he wasn't going to disappoint Stewart by mentioning it. He hadn't met Stewart until '06, he thought it was, at Lord's, in the gentlemen's lavatory, where Stewart was suffering from the effects of the June sun and perhaps a glass too many of champagne. Belcher had calmed him down, and they'd had a few drinks, and Stewart had never forgotten it, even though he forgot so much else. The sixteen years since that gruelling campaign up the Nile counted for little with Stewart, and left no firm impression on his injured memory, but he could still see, any time he closed his eyes, that burning day, and the black man with the sword, and the searing pain and the blood in his eyes. That was a day: cutting their way out of a Dervish ambush, saving the column, and there, through the blood, through it all, was that stout officer of the Munsters. What was his name? Belcher. That was it. Saved his life that day. That damn fuzzy-wuzzy would have done for him if it hadn't been for Belcher. No doubt about it.

'Kitchener's asked for me, Belcher,' he said. 'Hasn't forgotten the Sudan, you know.'

'Has he now?' said Belcher. 'Shrewd fella Kitchener. He knows his man.'

And so they kept at it for an hour or more, until Belcher confessed that he must toddle along to bed. He blessed the army for looking after its own, and finding a place for old heroes like Stewart. It couldn't last of course – not in wartime. No telling what damage a chap like that might do. He hoped that there was somebody to look after Stewart when they gave him the shove, and he hoped that the man's signature was good for anything at the end of it all. Otherwise they'd never get to France.

30

'And it would not be fitting for me to be with a man that would be cowardly... and it would be a reproach to my husband, his wife to be braver than himself.'

—Lady Augusta Gregory, *Cuchulain of Muirthemne*

Susan Fitzmullen-Brophy had, over the years, grown into the role of army wife with ease and little regret. True, she had lost her complexion to India, fought vainly against the climate for a succession of flower gardens in various dusty stations, and she had had to reconcile herself to not living in any one house with any expectation of long tenure. On the other hand, she had a happy family, and good prospects for grandchildren within a few short years, and if all was in temporary turmoil because of this war, she had seen its like before.

Hugh was different, though. He had been out of sorts for days, and had taken to coming home late with a bad head and no appetite for dinner, but that, if unusual, was no surprise to his wife. The man had little head for drink and could not be expected to keep up with the likes of old bachelors like Tummy Belcher, and he was drinking with Tummy because he was a sentimental old idiot. But then, a day or so after word came of the move to Castletownbere, something in Hugh's manner changed. He was fretting about the house more, and getting in the way of the packing. It had been decided straight away that Susan would stay in Tralee for the time being, for who knew but that this move merely portended other moves. If the war were indeed over in a few months, then there was hardly any point in looking for a house convenient to the new posting, and if (Heaven forbid!) the war went on, Hugh's battalion might be shunted all about the country. So Susan would stay put, and pack up Hugh's things, as she had for the other times he had gone on campaign, and he should busy himself with his duties and not make a nuisance of himself like that.

He wanted his field kit kept ready, and that was only to be expected. He was only going from the north of Kerry to the west of Cork, and even over bad roads that couldn't have been more than seventy miles, but he equipped himself against possible ambush by Waziri tribesmen, as he almost always did. 'Be prepared.' he quoted repeatedly, long after it had become tiresome.

She had welcomed the change in his mood that came with his sudden bright idea for marching all the way to their new station. Some of his boyishness was restored, which was certainly preferable, she thought, to the childishness he'd been exhibiting in recent days. It would do him good to get away from barracks at a time like this. Let him get out in the fresh air and feel himself useful for a change. And if it proved too much for him, and he caught a chill, or just broke down at the side of the road, then at least it should convince him that he was too old for this sort of silliness now.

But his preparations for this route march of his were bothersome in a way that just wasn't quite like him. As if she didn't know by now to put two pairs of clean socks in his haversack! In the end she sent him out to the garden, but later she found him fidgeting with her preparations, and unpacking things from his luggage to put with his marching kit, and then changing his mind, and when she found him thus, dithering in the bedroom with a cardigan waistcoat in his hands, he started to act furtively and pretended that there was nothing amiss.

Hugh Fitzmullen-Brophy was not a subtle man, and mostly Susan valued that lack in him. He also, for the most part, led a blameless life, so there was little enough cause for him ever to be furtive. Indeed, in all their years of marriage, Susan could only remember one such instance. That had been in Quetta, years ago. There was a week when he had been acting shamefaced and evasive, and although she hadn't pressed him in the least, it hadn't taken him long to confess that he had lost a hundred rupees on a horse that had possessed not a single virtue beyond the lucky name of Munster Boy. As far as she knew he had never gambled since.

And now, on their last evening together, when she thought she was on the point of losing patience with him altogether, he had come over all quiet and shy. He would be spending the night in barracks, so that he could make an early start, he said, and it was their last meal together before he marched off. She should have known from the affection with which he addressed her as 'Old stick' and reminisced about the jolly times they'd had down the years, that he was contemplating a separation rather greater than the distance between Tralee and Castletownbere.

When he left he kissed her goodbye with his usual awkwardness, and said something that tried to be hearty, but he was never the type to carry that sort of thing off very convincingly. Their daughter Molly was away staying with friends that week, so there were no witnesses to that last embrace, no cause for any embarrassment. But for all that Hugh was hopelessly sentimental he was no romantic, and certainly no great lover. He held her, not very close and not very tight admittedly, but for longer than was his wont, and then his servant Private Hennessy was opening the front gate and he quickly let her go, and beamed bashfully, and told her to be good and to look after herself.

Hennessy took the valise and a small pack, and Fitzmullen-Brophy took his blackthorn stick, and he was off with nothing more to say than the repeated goodbye that lasted the length of the short drive. When they turned out of sight into the road she heard him start to whistle. The poor man could hardly sing a note, but he could whistle a decent tune, and she instantly recognised the opening of 'The Minstrel Boy'.

The minstrel boy to the war has gone. He was certainly no minstrel, and too old to be a boy, thought Susan, but not unkindly. And thank God he was not off to the war.

And yet when the news came she found herself hardly surprised at all that that was precisely where he had gone.

31

Training in marching is begun during recruit training and must be carried out with care, especially in the case of recruits and men called up from the reserve, otherwise the training itself will result in a reduction in strength.

—*Infantry Training*, War Office, 1914

The march began well, with every man well set up on a breakfast of porridge, bacon, and fried bread, and the clouds scudding away on the westerly wind, leaving only grey rags against the pale blue. There was no band, nor any military dignitaries to see them out the gate, and Fitzmullen-Brophy refrained from making any sort of a speech. With the men fallen in in full kit he didn't even make a pretence at inspection, but grinned at them almost shyly while he shifted his weight from one foot to the other and twisted his walking stick in his gloved hands. In his eyes they weren't so much troops to be commanded as fellow conspirators in this rascally escapade. And then young Mr Fleming, a Second Lieutenant that the battalion had been happy to part with for a few days – or longer – ascertained as well as he was able that everything was present and correct, and informed Fitzmullen-Brophy, whereupon sixty-two men formed a column of fours in a manner that made them glad that no higher authority was up this early to watch them at it, and swung out, off the parade ground, out the barrack gate, and onto the main road with little enough grace but without any serious delays or collisions either. They would get the step, thought Fitzmullen-Brophy, and it would do their confidence good if they were just allowed to get on with things and muddle their own way through without NCOs bawling at them for a change. And indeed this improvised understrength company of his was in good spirits and, out on the road with no complicated parade-square evolutions to oppress them, they looked as good as any body of soldiers on the march.

Following up was Duffy the Cook Sergeant in a general service wagon that carried provisions for the march and could, *in extremis*, double as an ambulance for the fatally footsore.

The dog Bobs trailed them a little of the way out of curiosity, but lost interest in short order and returned to barracks where its food supply was guaranteed.

Fitzmullen-Brophy marched at the head of the column. His rank entitled him to a horse, and his age would have seemed to demand it, but acquiring a horse would have been too much trouble under the circumstances and besides, this was a test that Fitzmullen-Brophy had set himself. If he couldn't make this march, then he might as well retire and help Susan in the garden, because he'd be fit for nothing else in this war.

But he had few misgivings about his hardihood. After all, wasn't it for this that he had been keeping himself fit? He was more than twice the age of most of the men, but he was in his prime yet, and knew the tricks of endurance that the youngsters might envy before the morning was out. He also had the advantage of not being burdened with sixty pounds of kit, but that was a mere detail.

Wyndham was largely unaccustomed to the weight of kit and the complexity of all the straps that encased him, but it was not particularly uncomfortable yet either. He didn't know what was going on, but he had been infected by the major's undisguised excitement. Also, a change of scenery was supremely appealing. His barrack mates were there, but the drudgery and hardship of recruit drill was to be replaced by a few days under an Irish sky, with nothing to do but march along and take in the scenery. The pack was light upon his shoulders. Light also was the rifle with which he had been issued only the day before. Wyndham's squad had just embarked on drill with arms when the war had broken out and their rifles were taken away from them to give to the drafts heading overseas. Indeed, they'd had a hard enough time hanging on to what they already possessed, and many a time an unlucky or careless recruit had come off the square to find himself lightened of some important article of kit by an old soldier bound for France.

There had been other attempts to secure weapons, if only for the purposes of an hour's instruction, but Lance Corporal Sheehan's word, while loud upon the square, carried little weight in the context of a general European war. They'd tried using some timber battens, but the results were unpromising, but then there was Major Fitzmullen-Brophy working magic and requisitioning this, that and the other, and suddenly all the men warned for the route march were equipped like soldiers, and in the short time allowed Sheehan had made sure that his squad didn't completely disgrace him in handling their rifles.

So now Wyndham had an elderly Lee-Metford .303 to boast of, smelling strongly of petroleum-based preservative and leaving a faint greasy stain on his tunic. No ammunition had been issued with it, and Wyndham hadn't the faintest idea what do with it other than to present arms, shoulder arms, and order arms, although with a sudden shock he realised he'd forgotten what that last one involved. Nevertheless, he was a proud man that morning, and he knew he had been right to join the army.

They marched south, missing the town of Tralee entirely, and every one of the few people they passed on the road was a source of great interest, especially if it was somebody young and female. When they were thus lucky, the command was given 'Eyes right!'

(or left as might be) and every man snapped his head to gawk at the young lady who either blushed deeply or turned her nose in the air, depending on how the humour took her. One rosy-cheeked colleen did neither, but spat on the road, to which Sergeant Duffy, up on the wagon, called out, 'Good girl yourself!'

After a long three quarters of an hour they halted for a short spell, and every man relieved himself of the burden of breakfast's pint of sweet tea. Then they sat on their packs and jawed and smoked, and after fifteen minutes or thereabouts they were off again. The next hour was harder, with the sun well up and the men's backs soaked with sweat, but except for a few reservists who found their feet galled by new boots, they kept at it well enough.

There were still odd passers-by to chaff with, and once they were afforded a moment's hilarity when they caught up with a small herd of dairy cattle. Major Fitzmullen-Brophy was making free with his stick to bustle the cows out of his way without the company being obliged to break step or even halt, but the cows cared little about march discipline, and the simple herdsman had little respect for a fool of an old soldier leading a bigger crowd of fools, and bedamned to the lot of them. The subject of the rights of His Majesty the King in relation to Irish roads was being heatedly discussed between the major and the farmer, and someone in the ranks facetiously gave the order to fix bayonets, because things were looking dangerous, lads, and someone in authority roared at him to shut up, and then the road widened to a crossroads and the cattle turned off to the right and the Munsters carried straight on with the curse of God on them and on the whole bloody army. The last cry they heard from the farmer was something in favour of Germany, and at that a few men clamoured vainly for permission to run after the miserable old Fenian bastard and teach him a lesson. Ten minutes later the cows were long in the past and the men were amusing themselves by roaring out rebel songs.

'A Nation Once Again' had just been given a good loud encore when the second halt of the morning came.

The rest of the day was less enjoyable. The singing trailed off during their third hour on the road, and at the end of the long day it was a bedraggled lot that had to be called to attention to march the last few hundred yards into Farranfore, where they were to spend the night. Three rather shamefaced men were riding in the back of Duffy's wagon, but Fitzmullen-Brophy thought that things were going jolly well considering. He himself would be glad of a hot bath and a glass of whiskey before sitting down to a hearty dinner, but if the men were to be denied such comforts then so was he.

He didn't want to compound any of his offences by requisitioning food and shelter, but a mere five bob bought a corner of a stubble field and the use of the pump in the yard until the following morning. The men could rest themselves through the remainder of the day, Duffy could produce something nourishing, and they could all sleep together under the stars. Just like South Africa, really.

32

Warrant Officers, Non-Commissioned Officers, and Men (Dismounted).

Total Weight Carried.

A.—Clothing worn	*14 lbs. 11 ozs.*
B.—Arms	*10 lbs. 8½ ozs.*
C.—Ammunition	*7 lbs. 3 ozs.*
D.—Tools	*2 lbs. 9¼ ozs.*
E.—Accoutrements	*8 lbs. 8¼ ozs.*
F.—Articles in pack	*10 lbs. 1¼ ozs.*
G.—Rations and water	*5 lbs. 13½ ozs.*

Total   59 lbs.   6¾ ozs.

—*Field Service Manual*, Infantry Battalion (Expeditionary Force), 1914

Wyndham finally got to see Killarney and he didn't care. It was late on the afternoon of the second day and he was dead beat. Sleeping under the stars might sound manly and romantic, but it was not something to be recommended in Kerry – not even in August. A pack for a pillow and a greatcoat for a blanket did nothing to help Wyndham forget that he was sleeping in an open field of damp earth and small stones and prickling barley stubble, but he had endured his bunk in Ballymullen, and even at times had yearned for it, so he got used to a field near Farranfore and all its discomforts too.

When he woke up he was damp and shivering with the dew,

but that was the least of his problems. He discovered that he was gripped with a painful paralysis. His shoulders burned and his back ached and his legs just wouldn't work at all. He had to roll over onto his front and clumsily work himself upright using knees and elbows, but it was a very frail old man who finally found his feet, and sore, sore feet they were at that. For the sake of authenticity Major Fitzmullen-Brophy had insisted that every man sleep with his boots on, and Wyndham was thus relieved of the tricky business of bootlaces and puttees. Also, he'd had a look at his feet the evening before, and didn't think he'd quite have the stomach for it this morning.

By the time he staggered back from ablutions he wasn't so bad, but that didn't mean that he was in the whole of his health either. Breakfast did a little to set him right. The evening before he had encountered the army biscuit, which, dipped in tea or, as was the case this morning, served with bacon fat, was quite tasty. To Wyndham they were, until he was mockingly corrected, 'crackers', but even as biscuits they spoke to him of men prospecting for gold in the Yukon, or sailing around Cape Horn in a windjammer. Such thoughts helped him as he heaved his pack on again.

The men who had fallen out on the day before were declared fit to march this morning, but fit or not, no one was looking fresh. On the first stage of the march, with his muscles still stiff and his feet tender, Wyndham knew that his gear was lopsided and wearing hard on his raw shoulders. At the first halt, which came mercifully early, he fiddled with the buckles, which was no easy matter. The pack and haversack, waist belt and braces for the ammunition pouches, were all cleverly joined together in one harness that could be put on and taken off like a coat, but the brass buckles were tight upon the webbing material, a sort of heavy-duty canvas weave, which had been thickly painted with the odious Blanco. Each buckle to be adjusted had to be balanced with its twin on the other side if the harness wasn't to ride askew, and when the job was more or less done, and the whole kit strapped on again, Wyndham's fingers were sore and there was Blanco under his nails. And now he found that nothing sat right on him, and that his pack was too loose and pulling him backwards. At the second halt, which was far too long in coming, he tightened up everything to its original configuration.

It started to rain before they were on the move again. It was not a heavy rain, and soon eased to a mild drizzle that was sometimes no more than a heavy mist, but it lasted all the rest of the day, and Wyndham discovered that if there was one thing more uncomfortable than being bound all over in webbing, it was to be bound and burdened with wet webbing. They might have all been learning as much, but Wyndham cared not in the slightest for the sufferings of his comrades, and even the sing-song encouragements of the major failed to bring him out of his reverie of selfish suffering.

The rifle that had been his pride yesterday morning was a curse today, being heavy and unhandy. The long bayonet that hung from his belt together with the helve of his entrenching tool had found a way of slapping gently against the back of his thigh with each stride, and as the miles stretched on Wyndham grew to hate these filthy implements that were gradually wearing a hole in his leg. They were cowardly enemies, unwilling to attack him from the front or with any force. His pack would kill him, and was making no bones about it, but his pack was a foe against which a man might measure himself. The bayonet scabbard and entrenching tool helve were just jackals by comparison, snapping at him from behind and wearing out his spirit. Drops of water collected on the peak of his cap, and danced foolishly before his eyes, never heavy enough to fall sensibly off and out of his damn sight. His tunic collar was rough and clammy against the back of his neck, and his long flannel drawers were damp between his legs. These were the clothes he had dressed in yesterday, and slept in last night, and would no doubt sleep in again tonight, even after they had absorbed all the sweat in the world.

'Step out smartly now, men.' That was the major, with maybe not so much bounce in him today, but seemingly unstoppable all the same. Wyndham had admired the old gentleman's spirit yesterday, and had been amused by his motherly solicitude over the care of the men's feet and the state of their bowels, but now he was not so appreciative, and there were bitter thoughts in the back of Wyndham's mind that suggested that it would be better if the old fusspot just shut his big mouth or shouldered a pack himself. Step out smartly? For what?

And that was how Wyndham came into Killarney, and he was just too damn tired to wish that he'd taken the advice of whomever it was when he first got to this damn country and go here instead of Tralee. Was it beautiful? He would never remember. There was a hall where they spent the night, and there was running water to wash themselves, and the food was hot and plentiful, but that was at the end of the last half mile, which they had to march to attention, with their collars done up and their heads high and their boot heels ringing on the road in military unison. If that was Killarney than Killarney be damned.

Second Lieutenant Fleming was finding the going rather trying, but if an old man like Major Fitzmullen-Brophy could stand it, when he must have been fifty or sixty, then Fleming was blowed if he was going to cry up. Of course the major wasn't carrying a pack like everyone else or, as in the case of Fleming, a pack and two or three rifles, but all the same, it was marvellous how the old chap just kept rolling along like that. It was the major who had advised Fleming to shoulder a few of the weaker men's rifles in the course of the march. It was good form, and showed that their leaders would cheerfully share whatever burdens they placed on the men. Dashed fine chance to get to know the men too, if only by a few words here and there. Good for the soldierly spirit and invaluable to the making of a young officer. Fleming was not very intelligent, but he was obliging, and he did so very much want to be a good officer, so he did his best in offering heartening pleasantries although, given that he was new at this and they were for the most part utterly unused to dealing with officers, it was just easier for him to cheerfully relieve a couple of the more tired men of their rifles. He reckoned that if he did this enough he would come to be respected, or at least accepted, and he asked no more of the Royal Munster Fusiliers than that he be allowed to fit in.

Edward Fleming was more or less Irish, but had been born and reared in England. He was reminded of his heritage on his first day in school when he found that one of his schoolmates had used a penknife to scratch the word 'BOG' deeply into the leather of his trunk. It was a good enough trunk, and expected to last Fleming for years, so for years it lasted him, until many fellows rather assumed that Bog Fleming had crudely scratched his own name onto his luggage like the great clot he was.

He might never had formed any closer association with Ireland if he'd had much in the way of brains, but he consistently proved rotten at exams and, while to his father at least, the army might thus seem a logical career to choose, there were entrance examinations to be faced. Mr Fleming, rather than pay various crammers for however many years necessary to get the boy into one of the military academies, and then pay for an expensive military education, instead pulled the one frail string he had to hand. A talk was had with a friend of a friend, and a place was found for the lad in a reserve battalion of a not very fashionable Irish regiment. It was thought to be a happy solution. Tralee was not a place where a young man could run up serious debts or get himself into trouble, and if it did turn out that it suited him, then this was a well-proven back door into the army proper. If the whole thing proved a washout, then it would be a sight less of a waste than the fees for Sandhurst.

Fleming had been in Tralee little longer than Wyndham, but was enjoying it better. He liked the uniform and the change from school. He played a bit of hockey whenever he got the chance and he was bravely trying to grow a moustache. He hadn't made any firm friends but was good-humoured enough not to dwell on it. The place had been too sparsely populated when he'd arrived, and then when everyone had come for the annual training he was still too new to fit into the established routines. While everyone was agreeable enough, the junior officers of the Special Reserve were their own set. As with the old Kerry Militia, they tended to be young gentleman of the county who knew the same people and hunted with the same packs and had their own jokes to tell. Then the war broke on them and everyone was too busy to bother with making Fleming feel at home. He became nothing more than a sort of commissioned errand boy, being chivvied from pillar to post, or made to stand out of the way if he couldn't be useful. Then Major Fitzmullen-Brophy had found him, and taken him under his wing, and now Fleming was out on the open road with this splendid company of men and they were off to fight the Germans. The major had asked him to keep that last bit under his hat for the time being, and that was easy, since Fleming didn't really have anyone to tell it to. Of course he was pleased, and rather excited, but he had rather taken it for granted that he'd get a crack at this war sooner rather than later. I mean, he was in the army, wasn't he?

So three days into this route march and despite his sore feet and burning shoulders, it was all good fun. He was doing something useful at last, with little opportunity for making a muddle of anything, and he was beginning to get to know the men. He was learning a few more names every day, and getting always a little better at understanding the accent, which he rather felt should have come to him more naturally. He knew the slower and weaker men from helping them out so often, and the few bold souls who were not afraid to banter with an officer. In that respect, the old sweats Robinson and Dwyer were in a class of their own, and Fleming was learning, along with the rest of the column, the words to some salty old tunes, and hearing tall tales of India and South Africa, and when the weather was fine and the going easy it was a jolly rag of an outing and no mistake.

Today, a few miles out from Killarney, he fell into step beside Private Wyndham. Everybody knew who Wyndham was. He was Major Fitzmullen-Brophy's famous American recruit, who had been passing through Kerry on his travels and been persuaded to stay and join the army. What a wily old bird the major was. This Wyndham didn't look particularly special, which is to say that he wasn't the broad-shouldered tobacco-chewing desperado that some might have expected, but he was somewhat cleaner of complexion and finer-featured than his Irish and British comrades of the lower classes – most of the time, that is. Just now his face was red and sweating like everyone else's, but he remembered his manners and could exchange perfectly civil words with Fleming for a quarter of a mile or thereabouts. In truth, the conversation made both men feel rather awkward, and even a little lonely. They were social equals, both somewhat out of their element, but it was clear that even if their difference in military rank could be ignored, they had really nothing at all in common. Wyndham was some years out of school, and had never been to the sort of school that Fleming had known. Wyndham had no taste for sports or games. Wyndham, it transpired, was even carrying two books in his pack. Fancy that! Fleming had closed his last book the moment he'd heard that he needn't be swotting for Sandhurst, and he had every confidence – so far justified – that he'd never have to open another one as long as he lived.

'Sure you don't need me to carry your rifle then, Wyndham?'

'No, sir. Thank you very much. I believe I can manage.'

'Jolly good. I expect I'll just see about giving Riordan back his then.'

'Yes, sir.'

'Yes, well – carry on, and that sort of thing, Wyndham,'

'Thank you, sir.'

And he was just about to drop back and start getting to know someone else when Fitzmullen-Brophy signalled an unexpected halt.

'Oh, I say. We're halting. I believe the major wants to say something.'

Fitzmullen-Brophy had been running this over in his mind for miles and days now, and he still wasn't sure what he should say, but the farther they got from Killarney, the clearer it became that they were heading steadily away from their supposed destination. So either Fitzmullen-Brophy had to endure a certain amount of covert mockery for not being able to read a signpost, still less a map, or he admitted a deception that would have to come out sooner or later anyway. He was a forthright sort of fellow, and it suited him to face a problem head on, to tell the truth and shame the devil. So here, with yet another turning off to the west being ignored, and a good, dry-ish open space by the roadside for the men to gather round, he set the stage, planted one booted foot upon a tussock, and made his speech.

'You may smoke,' he said. That was always a good opener.

'Now first, men, let me say how very pleased I am with the way you are all shaping up. Old sweats and new recruits alike – you are all putting up a splendid show.' He beamed to show that he meant it, and gathered his thoughts for what was coming next, for he was not here to congratulate them.

'What I mean to say, though, is that we face more hard marching in the days and weeks ahead, and harder marching too, I'll warrant.' He looked to see frowns among his audience.

'That is correct, men: I said weeks. Now you may have thought that the march to Castletownbere will hardly take so long, but some of you more familiar with the country hereabouts may have guessed that we are not on the road to Castletownbere. Indeed not. My intention is to keep on marching until we reach Macroom, by which time I trust that your stamina will have been improved by as much as route-marching can improve it. From Macroom we will be taking the train, not to give you all a rest – a well-deserved rest, I might add – but because time is of the utmost importance. We cannot delay any further. I should clarify that the train will not be carrying us to Castletownbere but to Cork, where Major Belcher is even now arranging our passage to France.

'Yes, men – to France. And we must hurry ourselves, for the Germans are not dawdling.'

He studied the faces of his men, but not one of them displayed any intelligence.

'Men, I should explain matters to you. I confess that I contemplated deceiving you as to our true purpose, and by covering up falsehoods with yet more falsehoods, but that would hardly be worthy of the task we are setting ourselves. I confess that I have misled our commanding officer in Tralee, who yet believes us to be on the road to Castletownbere where most of us are to take up duties, which, in my opinion, can be performed perfectly adequately by the navy. Our commanding officer is naturally bound to obey all orders issuing from the War Office, but I, men, am too old a soldier to worry about pieces of paper when I scent gunpowder in the air, what? This is a fighting regiment, and by Jove I mean to fight!

'Now let me say that I do not subvert orders lightly, but I believe in the very depths of my soul that I am obeying the spirit of our orders. We are at war, and we are soldiers, and what we are doing is merely the cutting of some red tape. I expect that

I shall be in a great deal of trouble when we are found out, but my conscience is clear and, more than that, I shall be glad that in the hour of need I was not twiddling my thumbs in some out-of-the-way safe haven, but marching towards the sound of the guns, hey?'

He hadn't realised it yet, but he was gesturing emphatically with his stick by now.

'Now some of you men are destined for the front anyway, so it should be all one how you get there. To you special reservists, though, who have enlisted for home service only, I want to say what a perfectly splendid opportunity is being given you. There are those of you, I know, who enlisted without any thought of ever having to serve on the battlefield, and it may be that you are apprehensive, but let me say that active service is a boon not vouchsafed to every soldier. Nothing better, don't you know? Now it may be that this will be a long war, possibly even lasting into next year, in which case the 3rd Battalion will undoubtedly be called to serve overseas. Such was the case in the South African war. So what I mean to say is that if it's a long war you'll be going anyway, but if it turns out to be a brief affair, well a few months from now, when the other chaps come home, you'll be kicking yourselves for not getting into it – but of course you won't have to be kicking yourself because we're cutting a few corners and getting in early, do you see?'

He still wasn't getting quite the reaction he wanted. He simplified.

'Men, do you want to clean your buttons in Tralee while other men march off to fight?'

'No, sir!' shouted Fleming, with eager sincerity. Good man Fleming.

'Do you want to sit idle in whatever hole in the corner the War Office sends us to while other men are adding to the regiment's laurels?'

'No, sir!' and that was Robinson and Dwyer in loud chorus, with a few more hesitant contributions from less forward men.

'There's a war being fought in France, men – not in Castletownbere – and you've shown me these past few days that you're fit to fight it. I say let the navy guard our coasts, what? And let the good old 3rd Battalion of the Royal Munster Fusiliers show the Germans what we can do!'

That got a cheer, of sorts. Many were still unsure as to what the major was about, but they were looking forward to making the last part of their journey by train.

They swung into Macroom like khaki kings. They were travel-stained and weary, but they were proud of the long march they had made, and pleased at the smiles and cheers they met. The major's praise and encouragement were loud in their ears and they were off to the war and the weather was grand. There were some who, with the sun shining and they after doing so well, were of the opinion that they deserved a pint of beer at the very least, but Fitzmullen-Brophy was wise to the ways of foolish young soldiers and vicious old sweats who could have drunk the town dry and themselves insensible in no time. So he kept a close eye on them while they made themselves respectable in the hospitality of one of the greater landowners of the district, and as they washed and brushed themselves as well as they might, Sergeant Duffy prepared the only reward they would be getting.

Duffy was coming with them to Cork and beyond, but the GS wagon containing all the cook's gear, given the irregularity of their journey, could not. Duffy was going because, as he explained to Fitzmullen-Brophy, he was, like the major, too old to be getting into too much trouble. Sure wasn't he near the end of his twenty-one years, and what harm would it do him if they took away his stripes? He'd never get another chance for going to war again, and besides, the lads needed to be fed, because there might be damn all that the French knew about cooking.

Fitzmullen-Brophy needed a sergeant, and he admired pig-headed loyalty, so it was decided that Duffy would stay on and the wagon could go back with the men who would be going no further. There were two men who had bad feet that weren't getting any better and the more senior was put in charge. With them would go a special reservist who was altogether the wrong sort – an Irishman who was not eager for a fight – and another who was a mere boy and wasn't sure at all if his mother would allow him to go off to France like that.

And then there was Hennessy, the major's servant, and his defection was gall to the major's heart. Hennessy wasn't your classic type of officer's servant, who had faithfully followed his master down all the years, from one campaign to the next, uncomplainingly organising bed and board in the most trying of circumstances, finding hot water even where the bullets flew, and in the end fading away in some peacetime billet, still 'doing' for his 'bloke' when both were grey and forgotten. Hennessy was a depot man, assigned to Fitzmullen-Brophy when Fitzmullen-Brophy was performing his duties. He had been to South Africa, and if the army wanted to send him to France – even at this hour of his life – he'd go, but only in conformance with lawful orders. Besides, he'd been in Tralee too long, and after the days of marching his feet were at him. He would not go on. Fitzmullen-Brophy was rather disgusted with the man. It was a betrayal of the holy bond between officer and orderly and it set a jolly bad example to the men. A man with South Africa ribbons crying off a perfectly decent chance to get into the war, indeed. When the wagon departed, with its cargo of weaklings and backsliders, Fitzmullen-Brophy found something to keep him busy elsewhere.

But before they went, and Duffy still had full possession of his pots and pans and a great store of government food, along with all sorts of extras that had been scrounged along the road, a last supper was decided on. It was a stew that would have anchored a battleship in a gale and was a joy to hungry men out in the open air. Following it was a pudding containing all the flour, suet, and currants a man could wish for, and called 'duff' as all such confections were. It was a long time before it sank in with Wyndham and others not used to army English that such puddings were not named in honour of their Cook Sergeant. To wash it all down there was tea that tasted of stew, but Dwyer and Robinson, along with others of the old sweats, had conjured up bottles of beer out of thin air, and the major, in the interests of fairness and discipline, dug into his own pockets for lemonade for everyone else. He was careful though to send his most innocent young recruits to the pub to fetch it, with Wyndham in charge of the money and the change.

After that the train journey to Cork was a treat and a lark. Everyone was nice to the soldiers and here they got the send off they felt they'd missed in Tralee. It wasn't as if the girls were hanging off of them, and the old women weeping and the bands playing, but there were a few packets of cigarettes thrust on them and, when it was made plain that these were Irish troops, a few holy medals and rosaries came their way too. Wyndham was more than a little embarrassed by the gift of a miraculous medal, with the Virgin enamelled in blue on it. He obviously didn't hold with Papist superstition, but he was hardly going to offend anyone – and particularly not the Virgin Mary – by casually discarding it. Not when he was off to war. He managed to swap it with a boy named Sweeney for a boiled sweet, although Sweeney was a decent soul and would doubtless have offered him the sweet for nothing.

Wyndham, crammed in against the window of the third-class carriage, thankfully on the shaded side, sucked pleasurably on the sticky acid drop and reflected yet again on the amazing fact that he was indeed off to war. He hadn't been out of his clothes in days – and probably smelled every bit as bad as the men crowded up around him – and he was off to the war, with an old crone in a shawl having called down the blessings of the saints on him and a policeman having stood to attention and saluted him. It was all a mad dream, and there was no use in trying to question or make sense of a dream. This sunny, smoky, smelly train would rattle him to Cork and he'd rest his feet until then, and if he didn't wake up, and the dream went on, he'd just keep on following the major to see what happened next.

He had sent his mother a picture postcard from Killarney. As far as his family was concerned he had been staying with a nice old couple called Fitzmullen-Brophy, and he must have been leading quite a dull life in Ireland because he had very little else to say. Now, with the devil in him, he contemplated mailing another card from Cork, casually mentioning that he was finally leaving Ireland and taking that trip to France. Of course that wouldn't do, and he had every intention of writing his sister a long and truthful explanation of the whole business, and letting her filter it as she thought timely to their mother. The thing was, though, that Wyndham wasn't at all sure if he could even formulate a long and truthful explanation as to what he had done, nor could he encompass what he was proposing to do. He was going to a war. He was going to France to fight against the Germans. He, an American, was going to go to France with some Irish soldiers under a British flag to fight the Germans for invading Belgium.

That made no sense, or at least none that could be summarised on a postcard.

The journey wasn't long but the train was very slow, and the stupid chatter died down soon enough and the carriage was quiet with men dozing or enjoying in peace this first ease that most of them had known since mobilisation was proclaimed. Wyndham watched the fields and trees go by, but every time he let his eyes close, then and later that night, it wasn't those fields he saw, but the slower-moving fields of the last few days. The days on the road had been pain and sweat and bother, but he would never remember the tender feet in hard boots or the pack straps sawing through his shoulders. He saw Ireland on those days the way he had always hoped to see it, and now on the rocking train he was already lost in those cold mornings and the stony road climbing through rough fields under a changing sky.

33

Then the three pushed out their currach from the beautiful clear-bayed shore of Ireland... And the currach did not neglect that order, but it sailed forward over the green-sided waves and deep places till it came to its harbour in the east of the world.

—Lady Augusta Gregory, *Gods And Fighting Men*

When Belcher and Fitzmullen-Brophy had cooked up this scheme back in the mess in Tralee, it was the grandeur and boldness of it that caught them so that, even though they were both, if you want to put it that way, organisers by profession, there were some details that escaped them. Time was of the essence, after all, so they accepted that a certain amount of muddling through would have to stand in for careful planning. So bamboozling their way from Tralee to Cork without attracting the attentions of the Provost Marshal was the one stage of the operation that had been most clearly thought out. Things got a bit vaguer after that. But Belcher knew chaps, and Belcher, for all his gruff ways, had a knack of getting to know chaps. In Cork Belcher had bought drinks, and made connections, and leaned on men of junior rank where necessary. Be loud and in a hurry and people tend to speed you on you way.

By the time Fitzmullen-Brophy assembled his cheerful band on the platform, there was Belcher to bustle them onto another platform to wait for another train.

'Devil of a business standing here where everyone can see us.' Belcher was glaring around at everyone in the hope that they'd keep their distance. 'I say,' he said, 'Couldn't you have done something to make the men less shabby? Look like they've been dragged through a damned hedge backwards.'

'Oh I don't know about that, old man. Considering.'

'And you look half done in yourself too.'

Fitzmullen-Brophy was offended. 'I don't know about that at all. I feel quite splendid. Tip-top form. *Really* fit, you know.'

'Hmph. If you say so. But we'll attract attention. Barracks is only up the hill, you know, and that chit I got from old Dotty Stewart in Parkgate isn't quite working the magic we'd hoped. Some brass hat comes by and sees a scruffy lot like this and next thing you know he's asking damn fool questions like who we are and where we're going. Already ran into Halliday of the East Kents. And O'Connor from the Rifles cornered me last night after dinner. Asked me what I was up to and took ten bob off me at billiards, the dog.'

'We must be careful with our money, old boy,' said Fitzmullen-Brophy. 'It will be a while before we can look to the army for the care and feeding of the men, you know.'

'For shame, FitzEm! Damn rifleman challenges you to a game and you back down because you're afraid to lose ten shillings? Hardly becomes a Munster Fusilier, you know. Think of the regiment, man.'

'You're right. Of course you're right – but we're at war, you know, and I think there are some niceties that need to be packed away with the colours and the regimental silver and that. Couldn't you have told O'Connor that you'd injured your hand or something?'

'And turn down what might have been a jolly decent game of billiards? Don't be a fool, man. Besides, I needed to sound him out about what's happening in the wider world outside Tralee and our chances of slipping away to France and so forth.'

'Any good?'

'Damn all, I'm afraid. And the man's a positive sharp at the table too. Lucky to get away only ten bob down. Ah. I believe this is our train, thank God. About damn time.'

Fitzmullen-Brophy called to his lieutenant. 'Mr Fleming! Our train!'

'Very good, sir – Sarn't Duffy! This is our train. Have the men fall in, please.'

'Yessir, and you aren't to say "please" to me, begging your pardon, sir.'

'What? Oh, right. Very good. Thank you, Sergeant.'

The only sort of sergeant Duffy had ever been was a cook sergeant, but after more than twenty years in the army he had a fair recollection for the parade ground commands. Boarding the train was not a complex manoeuvre, and they'd done it once today already, so they didn't disgrace themselves too badly.

The journey to France was a lengthy exercise in chicanery, bluff, and misdirection. Belcher flaunted his bogus orders wherever he thought he could get away with it, and shouted in the face of scepticism and suspicion. In that season of frantic patriotism it was easy to overlook fudged paperwork and to smooth the path of truculent officers who were, when all was said and done, heading in the right direction, off to give the Kaiser what for.

Nevertheless, the men spent days hidden in anonymous sheds, crammed into spaces below decks, unfed, unwashed, like fugitive criminals or contraband cargo.

When they finally did arrive in France it was by way of a roomy old private yacht, owned by a retired naval officer, who landed them some fair distance out of their way.

They landed under the largest Union Jack that could be found aboard, lest this mob of dirty Irish soldiery be mistaken for a Prussian invasion force, and the Munsters staggered ashore, cramped and nauseous, unclean and sour-smelling, with their buttons dull.

While the bedraggled men dressed their ranks on the quayside,

Fitzmullen-Brophy proclaimed to the people of France the arrival of their allies. The people of France in this case were represented by a hastily organised deputation made up of an official in a tricolour sash, a couple of self-important hangers-on, and the parish priest, all escorted by two elderly soldiers in antique uniforms that, next to the businesslike khaki of the Munsters, betokened something of the comic opera.

Fitzmullen-Brophy wished them a good day, declared himself enchanted, and then his French vocabulary failed him.

Private Wyndham, as an educated man, and thus presumably conversant in French, was at Fitzmullen-Brophy's elbow to interpret, and prompted by the major, he too wished them a good day, and explained that here were Brittanic soldiers come to fight the Germans. He and the major then conferred briefly before unanimously wishing long life to France and coming to the salute. Slightly too late, the rest of the unit crashed to attention behind them. The man in the sash, who obviously did not exercise his love of public speaking as much as he'd have liked, replied with sonorous dignity and fine declamatory gestures, but kept it brief all the same. The finer points were not quite grasped by his audience, but they caught the gist of it. All was well.

'Tell him that we'd very much like somewhere we can have a wash and brush-up and something to eat,' said Fitzmullen-Brophy in an aside to Wyndham, and Wyndham, who had in his time rehearsed talking to hotel staff, made a decent attempt at it. He was hampered not only by his inadequate French, but by the fact that, this being the coast of Brittany, his hosts weren't hugely comfortable with the language either. Nevertheless, language differences aside, a Breton was a Frenchman – especially in that August of 1914 – and providing these Englishmen with a few bodily comforts was the least they could do if these Englishmen were shedding their blood for France.

And soon enough, as the food and wine went round, when it was revealed that these Englishmen with tigers on their buttons were in fact Irish, and hardly Protestant at all, the generous welcome afforded to them became a wild celebration that almost made up for the grim days and nights of the journey.

34

They're taking a trip on the Continong
With their rifles and their bayonets bright...

—'Where are the Lads of the Village Tonight?'
R.P. Weston and H. Datewski

This wayward element of the 3rd Royal Munster Fusiliers was, hardly more than a week after their break from Tralee, coming to operate as a cohesive, if not entirely efficient unit. In command there was the partnership of the two majors, with Belcher providing the solidity and Fitzmullen-Brophy the energy. Beneath them there was Lieutenant Fleming, learning the arts of leadership, and obeyed as much for his agreeable nature as for the single pip upon his cuff. Sergeant Duffy was the power behind Fleming's throne, such as it was – such as either of them were – and a few of the more promising old sweats were acting lance corporals (unpaid). Wyndham, the world traveller and man of many nations, found himself elevated to the position of clerk, secretary, and most of all interpreter for Major Fitzmullen-Brophy. So far he was enjoying himself.

Only a few days in France and he hardly recognised himself, nor could he remember any time in his life that had so unexpectedly suited him. The open-air life and the physical tiredness that precluded any more complex concerns had a lot to do with this, but the rest of it was down to France. The passage of this bold band of fusiliers through northern France was little short of idyllic. Welcomes were uniformly enthusiastic, bordering on the rapturous, and no man set out hungry in the morning or went altogether sober to his rest at night. And all the while the weather remained splendid.

Their course was slow, though, and roundabout. The meticulous staff officers who had planned for the landing of a British Army in France had never made provision for the likes of Fitzmullen-Brophy's lot, so while the locals were prodigiously forthcoming with food and shelter, getting anywhere by rail was not a straightforward affair. All the young manhood of France was on the move, crammed into trains, and the next trains along after those, and keeping every railway line in France busy almost, but not quite, to the point of overload and collapse. So the Munsters hopped short lifts where they could, sometimes in the goods wagons that all the armies of Europe were coming to know, but more often in the second and third class carriages of infrequent and interrupted civilian services on minor branch lines that never took them quite where they needed to be, but at least were always moving them generally eastward.

Much of any given day was spent marching between one rural railway station and another. Troop trains rattled by, and French and Irish cheered and saluted each other. Away from any railway line there were civilians to hail and womenfolk to compliment. The Catholic majority also made a point of ostentatiously blessing themselves at any church or wayside shrine to curry favour with the natives. No man could yet make the credible boast that his good behaviour had earned him the physical affections of a mademoiselle, but the French weren't locking up their daughters when the dirty soldiery marched into their village either.

So only a few days in France and Wyndham had been kissed by so many girls that he was hardly blushing any more. He was accustomed to having wine with his dinner. His face was tanned, and his hair was growing back to a more natural and respectable length. His knees were turning brown too, ever since Fitzmullen-Brophy, sensible of the summer's heat, had bestowed a dispensation of active service and authorised the men to cut off their trouser legs at the knee. It was more daring a fashion than the French of these parts were used to, and increased the Munsters' appeal, as if their curiosity value wasn't enough already.

Along with the rakishly exposed knees there was the bared throat, because in this weather tunics were never buttoned much above the waist. Indeed few of the men even had sufficient tunic buttons anymore, because they were very free with souvenirs for the children they met every day, and often too they bestowed buttons and badges on pretty young things by way of love tokens. 'Fierce as a tiger, darling,' as Robinson always said, as he pulled a girl onto his lap to give her a good close view of the regimental device: an Irish Bengal tiger with a cockney accent and a roguish wink.

They came surprisingly close to Paris on their travels, being shunted one day into a marshalling yard not many kilometres north of the city. There was much wild speculation among the soldiers sprawled in the straw of the wagons as to the delights of that sinful metropolis, and Wyndham thought of the assurances he had made to his family so long ago about the dull propriety of his planned European jaunt. What did he need with Paris now? It was enough to be out tramping the roads like this – a khaki-clad Bohemian. He had drunk French wine and been kissed by French girls. He slept in his clothes and washed in horse troughs and he carried a rifle on his shoulder. He didn't really believe that Major Fitzmullen-Brophy would actually march them to this war: it was too unreal. But now they were most of the way there and the war was still going on and it occurred to Wyndham that, untrained recruit and foreign national though he was, there might yet be the possibility that he would be facing personal danger sometime soon, and that he should really let his family know where he was, just in case.

And then, before dark, and before anyone had decided to hop

on a southbound train and chance it, they wangled the means to get moving northward. A French military official who had something to do with the railways marked them down on his clipboard as the 3rd Battalion of the Royal Munster Fusiliers and found the means to move them along before a regiment of Algerian light infantry descended on him.

The 3rd Battalion of the Royal Munster Fusiliers: that was what Fitzmullen-Brophy settled on when the weary eyes of the French officer fell on him and asked, through Wyndham, just who he might be. He could have said that his command constituted drafts for the 2nd Battalion, but he had been in sole charge of these men for so long now that he was feeling more proprietorial than was prudent. He had led them across three countries, with no resources but their own to rely on. They had no lines of communication, no commissariat, and they acted on orders from no higher authority. They were like those freewheeling mounted infantry units, Boer and British, that had criss-crossed the veldt, fighting the war as they'd found it, in those happy golden years.

So the major had been proud to let the Frenchman know that this was an independent command that he was taking to the war. He had said it was the 3rd Battalion, but in his mind these men were something better, something braver.

In his mind they were the Fitzmullen-Brophy Commando.

Tummy Belcher did not believe in travelling light, even on campaign.

'Discomfort is all well and good for the young men,' he maintained. 'Toughens them up, what? But an old boy like me knows that one must look after oneself while one can. I'll start pigging it when needs be, but until that day, dammit, I mean to have clean linen and decent food and drink.'

So the old campaigner had supplied himself with plenty of shirts and socks and underclothes, and a sleeping bag along with extra blankets, and some collapsible camp furniture, and a small hamper of the better sort of preserved food, and a case of whiskey that came prudently with a lock. A small handcart had to be found to carry it all. Major Belcher tended not to march when he could help it, but preferred to join them at the end of any given day, catching up usually by hired pony and trap. Furthermore, until they actually found themselves in a trench, and the winds of war had blown down all the houses in France, Major Belcher was determined to sleep every night in a bed and eat all his meals off a table, and he would be damned if those meals were deficient in the number of courses.

'Damn all point in going to war on an empty stomach. Be eating rice and dead mule and lucky to get it any day now.' And he would cite some dreadful privation from wars gone by to prove his point and then shout at the waiter to refill his glass. Where there was no waiter, or even any hostelry to be easily found, it was Belcher's habit to walk straight up, Fitzmullen-Brophy in tow, to the cleanest looking house in the vicinity and merely state his requirements in his most English schoolroom French.

'*Bonn*-jure, madam. Noo-soms officeers Brittanick,' he would begin, and then, if it was morning, say, demand eggs (*uhfs*, what?) and bacon (what's bacon, dammit? – oh, never mind), *sill voo play*, and, as quickly as possible because their train would be leaving soon, *mercee*. And the lady of the house would consider the two English oddities dressed in their mustard-coloured golfing suits, and usually conclude that the line of least resistance was to feed the old gentlemen and get them on their way quickly. She would usually decline payment too, on the grounds that the stout gentleman never offered any and his lanky companion fussed and muddled with small change in a currency that was always beyond one or other of them. It was simpler to be generous and patriotic. It was war, after all.

The way east and then north showed them ever more evidence

of the oncoming war. There were soldiers everywhere now. The French looked so colourful in their red and blue, but there was something amateur and slapdash about them, at least as far as their British allies saw it. Unlike foreigners, the British did everything with a proper soldierly precision, even if they didn't cut much of a dash in their drab uniforms. There were traffic jams on roads and railways, and during a halt enforced by one such obstruction, the Munsters were treated to an exhibition both of martial colour and of the strains imposed on the *Entente Cordiale*. A gaunt French officer of engineers and a leathery lieutenant colonel in a kilt were arguing to the extent that each man's face, burned and yellowed by long imperial service, was now darkening to purple. Perhaps they fought over right of way at the crossing, or maybe it was some long-remembered and deeply resented violation of the Auld Alliance, but for want of any other common tongue, the two were reduced to blackguarding each other in broken Arabic amid the crowd of soldiery and the stalled transport. The many bystanders could have stood and watched it all day.

Along with the diversions and entertainments there were worries. The two majors were becoming increasingly aware that they were coming ever closer to a confrontation with higher authority. There was the hope, which had seemed very real back in the mess in Tralee, that they would merely arrive at 2nd Battalion and be treated to a stern reprimand from the CO, which they would accept with all humility before being welcomed into the fold and letting the war wash away all sins. So far though, they were seeing no friendly faces. Indeed, so far, the only senior officer to have paid them any attention was a red-tabbed maniac driven to instant frenzy at the sight of the Munsters' mutilated uniforms. Their trousers had been shortened with jackknives for the most part, and unhandily hemmed, so that some soldiers were looking quite ragged and all were guilty of the destruction of government property. He strode across the road towards them, spitting venom and demanding who in hell they were, and was making things very uncomfortable, but Belcher had faced up to worse in his time. He was travelling with them that day on a donkey he'd acquired in the morning, and, being higher off the ground than Fitzmullen-Brophy, was assumed to be in charge. He quoted chapter and verse about shorts being permissible in hot weather (damned fool had had a touch of sun himself, he thought), and he steadfastly stood his ground while he was damned for his slackness and his men were condemned as a horde of blasted Hottentots. The rant ended when some men of the Warwicks passed with their entrenching tool carriers suspiciously empty of entrenching tools. Here, up towards the Belgian frontier, with the war close and thus soon to be over, more cumbersome items like entrenching tools and greatcoats could be had by picking them up off the verges of the road. No man would be wanting his greatcoat in this heat, and no man was likely to be fined for losing equipment when he'd just finished putting the kibosh on the Germans.

The Munsters continued without further molestation, but Belcher and Fitzmullen-Brophy were uneasy that they were leaving behind them a bad-tempered staff colonel who might be wondering why a body of Munster Fusiliers was roaming loose, some distance from any parent formation. And too often now, as they neared the British Expeditionary Force's designated area of concentration, they found themselves having to introduce and explain themselves to all sorts of khaki officials with lists and clipboards and questions. The paperwork Belcher had wangled in Dublin was occasionally waved under staff-wallahs' noses, and while no one had yet to question it particularly, it wasn't being accepted as some sort of royal warrant or magic ticket either.

They overreached themselves in the end. The third week of August was drawing to a close and the military situation on the road to Maubeuge was appearing more hectic with every mile. Belcher's donkey had proven unsatisfactory after only a day, and he damned the wily Frog farmer who had squeezed the equivalent of two pounds ten out of him. Where was his blasted patriotism? Did he want the Germans to win the war? And now for want of anything better, Belcher had decided on a mule and, emboldened by their long run of luck as much as he was embittered by the whole donkey business, he was just going to requisition one from the Army Service Corps. An army mule was just the thing for carrying a well-set gentleman the last leg of the journey – better than any damned French donkey at any rate – and the ASC possessed such a wealth of them that they would easily part with one.

It turned out to be not so easy however. Had it just been the corporal in charge, Belcher would have signed a chit or pushed his weight around as need be, with a small bribe to be considered as a last resort, but the mule lines were under the eye of a young lieutenant who was too new and inflexible in his job to merely part with one of his beasts. Belcher was trying the soft approach, which involved the friendly offer of a bottle of whiskey, when Fitzmullen-Brophy, who was standing by fidgeting, grabbed his sleeve and directed his attention to where a motor car had been obliged to stop nearby.

'I say, Tummy! Look there! That couldn't be O'Meagher, could it?'

Belcher squinted and damned himself if it wasn't after all.

Lieutenant Colonel J.K. O'Meagher was the first Munster Fusilier they had set eyes on since leaving Tralee, and he was a very important Munster Fusilier indeed. He was, in fact, none other than the commanding officer of the 2nd Battalion, which was to say that he was the regiment's most senior representative in the entire Expeditionary Force. Right now he was hunched in the back seat of the car, looking decidedly out of sorts.

The two majors couldn't help but cross over to him.

'I say, Colonel! Is that you, sir? Well damme, how do you do, Colonel? It's Belcher – from the depot.'

O'Meagher looked up from under the shadow of his cap. 'And Fitzmullen-Brophy. How do, FitzEm?'

'Splendid, Colonel – just splendid. And delighted to see you, of course. What news of the war? We've brought drafts from home.'

O'Meagher sniffed and stared down the road, as if he had expended all the effort he was willing to in looking at the two majors. 'The war? Nothing but a blasted great mare's nest so far.' There was a glum pause, then: 'I expect something will happen shortly. Not my affair any more, I'm afraid.'

'Not your affair, sir?'

'Being sent home, gentlemen. Just not up to it, I'm afraid.'

'Oh *bad luck*, sir,' said Fitzmullen-Brophy. And it was. It undoubtedly was. There was a pause, which the majors were unwilling to fill with questions that might possibly be tactless. Finally, with the traffic still not moving, O'Meagher went on.

'Bringing drafts, are you? Regiment's up around Le Cateau by now. Charrier has command. I'd better be getting on. Best of luck to you both, now.'

But the car still did not move off, and the majors stood there for a few seconds before they touched their caps in considerate salute, and said, 'And to you, Colonel,' and walked off themselves.

They had much to think of all of a sudden. There was some speculation as to why O'Meagher had been given the shove, but it really didn't matter whether it was illness or incompetence or scandal that removed him. What was more of the moment was that the CO of the Munsters had been relieved, and that his replacement was still only a major like themselves. Of course neither man suggested rushing north to assume command. They knew they both had seniority on this Major Charrier, but they also knew that the army just didn't work that way.

But all the same there was the glimmering of a dream. Neither of the two men saw himself as ambitious, but they heard duty calling, and each man felt that the call was for him alone. Belcher had never sought distinction, but that was now, perhaps, the very quality that suited him for command. He was steady and dependable, after all. He thought not of promotion but of the regiment. If everything went to pot in a hurry it would take an unflappable sort of fellow like him to see everything right in the end.

In Fitzmullen-Brophy's ears the bugles were sounding. It was for this that he had been keeping himself ready all these years – keeping himself fit. This was a situation calling for energy and resolve. There were too many plodders running this army. They needed to be shown what an old South Africa hand could do in command of a crack battalion – and it *would* be a crack battalion with a man like him in charge. And it would be him. He had several months' seniority on Tummy, didn't he?

But they both knew Charrier from his hitch in command at Tralee. He was an efficient sort, and unlikely to hand over gratefully to the first couple of old warhorses to come through the door. The battalion was Charrier's show now, and no two ways about it, but that did not disguise the fact that the Munster Fusiliers were already down one senior officer before a shot had been fired.

'They'll need us, Tummy.'

'They will, FitzEm, and devil a doubt.'

'Better get back and see about that mule.'

'Mule be buggered. We'll need a motor car.'

And that was their downfall.

The plan, such as it was, was for Tummy Belcher to speed north and stake his claim to high office in 2nd Battalion, with (ideally) an unofficial joint-second-in-command for himself and Fitzmullen-Brophy, or – failing that – senior advisory positions as majors emeritus and stand-in company commanders. These were all details, though, that could be hammered out as and when. What was imperative was that an officer of the regiment be on hand directly, so as to forestall any meddling by the higher-ups and to prepare a place for the men who would be foot-slogging up the road to join in the fun as soon as they could. It seemed only sensible that Belcher should be the one to travel at speed and in style. Marching was for younger men, after all. Fitzmullen-Brophy wasn't exactly younger, but he did have his heart set on finishing this journey as he'd started it, at the head of his men, and while he wouldn't have said so out loud to Belcher, they were *his* men,

It wasn't just Wyndham or young Lieutenant Fleming that he had enticed into joining the great adventure: most of the men following him would still be undergoing recruit training, or wasting their lives in the west of Ireland if he hadn't rescued them. Indeed, much as he wanted to get into this war, he knew he wouldn't care to have to relinquish command of this happy band and have their particular identity, and even his own, submerged into the army.

Now, acquiring a mule in an army well supplied with mules should not have proved too great an obstacle for a determined officer of long service, wise in the chicaneries of indents and requisitions, but motor transport was an entirely different matter. For a start, motor cars were few and far between, and those that did race by in clouds of dust were always occupied by red-tabbed officers sitting imperiously behind and attending, no doubt, to the brain and sinews of this great European war. Then, when the majors made hasty and emphatic enquiries, they eventually discovered that these few vehicles were technically not even army property, but had been provided by the patriotic enthusiasts of the Royal Automobile Club, who had even gone so far as to volunteer their services as drivers. Learning this wasn't hugely helpful. They'd had vague hopes of finding a large motorcar park, with a body of obedient army drivers in attendance. After casting about for some time in all the bustle, they did strike it lucky and glimpsed a car parked on the shaded side of a barn, but instead of an unquestioning other rank to salute and do their bidding, they found a cheery civilian with his cap on backwards and a pair of goggles hung about his neck. There were also some Army Service Corps types brewing tea hard by, while one of them fiddled with an exposed engine of a motor lorry and the rest pretended not to see the approaching officers. No doubt the whole caravan could be bullied into mobility if one were willing to expend the energy, but for the moment it suggested some gypsy encampment that would be here for a good while yet. But it was the man with the motor car that interested the two majors. He was clearing the dust from his throat with a mug of tea while his cooling engine ticked and pinged beside him.

'I say! Anything I can help you fellows with?' he asked.

They did not care to have their military rank so blithely disregarded, and Belcher would gladly have exploded at this frivolous lout with his 'you fellows', only Fitzmullen-Brophy, conscious of their possible role as supplicants and mindful of his manners, elbowed his comrade aside and took over before Belcher could do anything to offend. And it was clear to the eagle-eyed Fitzmullen-Brophy that this motor car chap was a civilian, what with his tweed suit worn with a rather loud tie, with a non-regulation leather coat draped across the car's front seat.

'I say. Yes. How do you do?' said Fitzmullen-Brophy. 'Splendid weather we're having, what?'

'Oh rather!' said the motorist.

'This your, ah, vehicle, yes?'

'And isn't she just a beauty, though? Two-cylinder, eighteen-horsepower Riley, and do you know I must have been averaging a hundred and fifty miles a day in her this past week, or a hundred and fifty kilometres anyway – they're the same thing, aren't they? – and she hasn't given me the least bit of trouble. She's a pip.'

'A pip, eh?' said Fitzmullen-Brophy. 'Quite so, I'm sure. Now we were wondering how one might go about engaging her, or rather you, I mean both the machine and a driver, I mean, to take this officer to Le Cateau, or somewhere thereabouts at any rate.'

'Fearfully sorry, old chap,' said the civilian, flinging out the dregs of his tea and handing the mug back to its owners, 'but unless one of you happens to be a Captain Pomeroy of the General Staff, then I'm very much afraid it can't be done.'

Fitzmullen-Brophy was opening and closing his mouth as he sought for something to say, but Belcher was having none of it. A mere captain? To ride in a motor car when a major must somehow shift for himself? And all this at the whim of some pipsqueak civilian? Outrageous. He pushed to the fore and declared, 'Captain Pomeroy is clearly not present. Doubtless the exigencies of war have kept him from your arranged rendezvous. I, on the other hand, require a means of transport directly. You will kindly convey me to Le Cateau forthwith.'

The civilian was impressed but not cowed. Indeed he grinned at Belcher as if the major were merely some crotchety uncle. 'I say – steady on,' he said, holding up his hands in placation. 'I mean I can hardly be expected to just drop this Pomeroy chap on your say-so, what? I mean I don't even know who you are.'

'My name is Belcher,' said Belcher. 'Major. Royal Munster Fusiliers. I am not at liberty to reveal anything more. Now you may not realise it, but this is a theatre of war and I am fully empowered to commandeer this vehicle should I deem it necessary.'

'But of course that would hardly be necessary,' cut in Fitzmullen-Brophy.

The civilian looked displeased, and looked like the sort of

chap who'd put up his fists then and there in defence of his two-cylinder, eighteen-horsepower Riley if it came down to it, but Fitzmullen-Brophy's encouraging smile warmed his innocent heart. Also, he was an Englishman at his country's service and he knew that two majors outranked one absent captain.

'Tell you what,' he said. 'Play fair and I'll run you up to Le Cateau in an hour – but no farther, mind. Traffic's the very devil on the way back.'

'Stout fella,' said Fitzmullen-Brophy. 'We couldn't ask for more.'

'My pleasure. Who did you say you were?'

'Munster Fusiliers.'

'Well begorrah, eh?'

'Quite.'

35

'Those are the champions that did deceit and falsehood among the Sidhe... yet they will not be killed, nor will they kill any one. It is to work out their own destruction they are come.'

—Lady Augusta Gregory, *Cuchulain of Muirthemne*

'Major Belcher? Of the Munsters?'

'Of the Royal Munster Fusiliers,' corrected Belcher, giving this young staff officer the best of his disapproving gaze. Belcher might be for the high jump, but that was no reason to let standards slip. Let some pup forget basic etiquette and you've pretty much handed the game to the Germans.

'Yes, well, Major, the provost marshal will see you now.'

Belcher heaved himself out of the little bentwood chair and followed the staff-wallah down a narrow hallway. The painful interview was to take place in a schoolroom, which was appropriate enough in a way. Belcher reflected that it was the master's study where he'd usually got his canings.

Fitzmullen-Brophy was already there, sitting to one side and looking uncomfortable. Like Belcher he had been relieved of his sword and his pistol, which at least allowed the two men the small pleasure of imagining themselves dangerous, rather than merely naughty. At the teacher's desk sat a humourless colonel. *Looks like a flogger*, thought Belcher, but knew that here was a man who could theoretically have him hanged if it came down to it.

'Sit down, Major,' said this military chief of police. No '*please*'. Of course not.

'I intend to get this foolishness out of the way as quickly as possible, so you will do me the kindness of not speaking, and certainly not of demanding any sort of rights under law. There is enough tomfoolery as it is.'

So that's how it's to be, thought Belcher. No-nonsense type clearly, this beak.

'Although the complaint against you is different in substance to that weighed against Major Fitzmullen-Brophy, I consider them to be of the same essence and will dispense with both of them at the same time. Understood?'

Belcher nodded. No point aggravating things by speaking.

'You, Major Belcher, attempted by false pretences to take possession of a motor car, which was at the exclusive disposal of the general staff. Your attempt at browbeating and hoodwinking the driver of this vehicle to go along with your little scheme having almost succeeded, you were interrupted by one Captain Pomeroy, aide to General Murray, to whom the motor car in question had been officially allocated. That's "officially", Major. Damn thing wasn't a taxi.'

The man spoke without hesitation or reference to notes. Belcher had to admire his style.

'There followed an altercation of a most ungentlemanly nature, which was – and this is rather more pertinent – of potential detriment to the smooth functioning of our lines of communication. Do you understand that, Major Belcher? There is a war on. We are under quite enough strain without our staff captains being waylaid by sightseers.'

Belcher bristled at that.

'Sightseers, Major.' The provost marshal laid the tip of a forefinger on the desk, and that was all the emphasis a man like that needed to make.

'Your presence in France is completely unauthorised. You have no orders. You are in the way. You are a walking impediment to the prosecution of this campaign.

'And that,' he went on, 'is where I might return to Major Fitzmullen-Brophy.'

Belcher heard the suggestion of a nervous shuffle from that quarter of the room. Man never could keep still, he thought.

'The matter of Major Fitzmullen-Brophy,' said the provost marshal, 'is perhaps equally serious and equally imbecilic. While Major Fitzmullen-Brophy is the instigator and chief perpetrator of this idiotic affair, it appears that you, Major Belcher, have aided and abetted him at every turn, which I must say speaks very badly of an officer of your age and experience. Together you have conspired to appropriate some sixty men from the regimental depot in Ireland and spirit them, without one scrap of permission, all the way to France.'

Belcher opened his mouth in token of protest, but the provost marshal forestalled him.

'Were you about to refer to this particular document, Major?' He held up Exhibit A. 'This nonsensical farrago signed in Dublin some two weeks back by one Colonel Stewart? This particular document, which, deceitfully obtained, was supposed to allow you to pass dry-shod through the stormy waters of army bureaucracy? This piece of paper which might perhaps only have been of actual value had a ha'penny stamp been affixed to it?'

Belcher closed his mouth.

'Captain Pomeroy was not impressed by this piece of paper, Major, and neither am I.

'What might impress me, if I wasn't so damn busy with things that actually matter, is the sheer damned barefaced effrontery of it all. Do the pair of you think that you can just steal a platoon and go off wandering like that? Heavens above, gentlemen, but am I to understand that many of these men of yours have not even completed their recruit training? Do you think we can just accommodate you and your little private army? This war is not for amateurs, gentlemen, and I have the time neither to be answering frantic signals from Ireland nor for pandering to the whims of officers who should damn well know better.

'You're a damn disgrace, the pair of you, and worse than that you are a waste of my precious time. As such there will be no formal proceedings brought against either of you, but you are to be sent home forthwith, and you can each expect so great a black mark on your respective records that maybe the Kerry Militia will have you but the army never will.'

He stared at the two of them, daring them to question his judgement even for the smallest instant.

Fitzmullen-Brophy spoke up. 'What about my men, sir?'

The provost marshal, who had been perfectly contained, looked for a moment as though violence might be done. He hissed at Fitzmullen-Brophy through clenched teeth. 'They are not your men, Major, and not your concern.'

'With respect, sir,' said Fitzmullen-Brophy with quiet dignity, 'I wish this case to be referred to a higher authority.'

The provost marshal's eyes blazed. 'Your request is denied, Major. Higher authority has considerably more important things to occupy its attention.'

Belcher, agreeably surprised at his old comrade's show of steel, decided that if he was in for a penny he might as well go in for a pound. He squinted at the provost marshal's ribbons and badges and tried to guess at where the man had served and with whom. Belcher had been in Tralee too long to know the players in the army game these days, but he knew that the man at the very top was an Irish cavalryman, and he took a wild gamble.

'We wish to see Field Marshal French,' he said resolutely.

'Do you indeed?' said the provost marshal, turning to Belcher with interest.

'At once, if possible,' affirmed Belcher.

'You know the field marshal?'

'Served with him in South Africa, don't you know.' And that, in a way, was very broadly true. For one wild moment, Belcher was on the brink of inventing reminiscences of how 'Tummy' Belcher and 'Johnny' French had fought the Boers shoulder to shoulder, but he thought the better of it.

'Then it might dismay you to hear,' said the provost marshal, 'that Sir John did not appear to recognise your name when he happened to speak to me earlier today. He was kind enough, in the midst of all his more pressing business, to ask briefly after the affairs of this office, and I did briefly apprise him of your case.'

'And?' said Belcher.

'The exact words he used were "blithering idiots". Dismissed, gentlemen.'

Belcher and Fitzmullen-Brophy were given back their swords and revolvers, which made them both feel more ineffectual than before. They had evidently been deemed harmless, or even ridiculous. Anyway, it was impossible to wear a sword while riding in a motor car. For they got their motor car too in the end, if not the one that had got them into these difficulties. GHQ wanted these troublesome old men out of their sight without delay, so the two majors left Le Cateau in disgrace but in style. They travelled without escort. No one reckoned them worth the bother.

The driver was under orders to take them directly to Amiens, where they would be out of everyone's way and where they could arrange their own damn transport back home. The driver, though, was another civilian, and military orders meant little enough to him, so when Belcher demanded that they stop somewhere to pick up all his baggage, the man had no objections.

GHQ had wanted the disgraced majors gone in a hurry, but there are always delays. The degradation in the schoolroom had been on a Friday, but a free car couldn't be found until late Saturday, and what with the war and what have you, it was Sunday afternoon before the majors tracked down their lost sheep.

The Fitzmullen-Brophy Commando was no longer where they'd left it. The men had been marched back the way they had come to wherever was not so inconvenient, and there they were waiting. Waiting for precisely what, they did not know, but they were soldiers, and waiting in ignorance was the most natural thing in the world for them. Second Lieutenant Fleming had been left in charge because he seemed a biddable sort, and no initiative was required of him. Accommodation was a barn and food was a sack full of tins without labels.

'What do you reckon's in them, Sergeant?' asked Riordan, as Duffy took possession of the rations.

Duffy held up each one and peered suspiciously, looking in vain for markings on the tarnished and pitted metal. 'Could be anything, lad,' he said. 'I reckon this stuff is left over from the Crimea. Mr Fleming, sir? Permission to go out on the scrounge?'

'Um, I'm really not quite sure, Sergeant. I rather think we're supposed to stay put for the time being.'

'Ah, sure, I wouldn't be long at all, sir, unless you want old tinned donkey for dinner.'

Fleming didn't have to think long about it. 'Carry on, Sergeant,' he said.

Duffy was amiably chatting in English and Hindustani to a French housewife at her front door, when Fitzmullen-Brophy spotted him.

'Sergeant Duffy! I say! Driver, stop!' He was half out of his seat as the driver pulled over to the verge, and then he toppled forward as the brakes came on, caught himself, fell backward in the seat again, and then fumbled for an age with the door handle.

'Duffy – where is Lieutenant Fleming? Where are the rest of the men?'

He twisted the door handle the right way and almost tripped himself on the running board in his haste to get out. Duffy gave him and Belcher a cheerful salute, told him that there was nothing to worry about, and asked if he might have perhaps two bob in francs to buy some vegetables from the good lady of the house.

'The lads is in the barn in the field beyond there, sir, and if Mr Fleming isn't with them you'll find him in the house with the blue door. And did you find the battalion at all, sir?'

'Afraid not, Duffy.'

He elaborated somewhat to Fleming when he found him near the barn, but didn't want to upset the poor youth with too much detail. Fleming took it in without undue difficulty.

'Oh I say, sir. Bad luck,' he said, and was unable to express himself any better than that. Fitzmullen-Brophy wasn't up to saying much more either. He beheaded a dandelion with his stick, but his heart wasn't in it. After an uncomfortable silence he said, 'I suppose I should say something to the men.'

'Of course, sir,' said Fleming. 'I believe they'd like that. Dashed disappointed to be losing you of course. Bally shame.'

Fleming struggled for a moment, and added: 'It was a jolly good scheme, sir.'

'Thank you, Fleming,' said Fitzmullen-Brophy. 'Good of you to say so.'

To give proper vent to the feelings of his heart, or because he had run out of other things to do, Fleming followed the major's example and kicked the head off another dandelion.

The men took the news much as Fleming had, and cried shame on headquarters. One man even stood up to protest that, if Major Fitzmullen-Brophy was going home, then the rest of them should have nothing to do with fighting their bloody old war for them. Several voices gave assent, and Fitzmullen-Brophy had to calm them down, his voice thickening with emotion. All of them, he pleaded, were soldiers of the king, and were bound to do their duty, however hard that might be. He was sure that, whatever befell them, they would conduct themselves in a manner that gave credit to the regiment and to their country. He blew his nose hard and thanked them for their good conduct, and wished them the very best of luck.

Wyndham took it all in with the most profound sense of anti-climax. He had, as they grew ever closer to the war, accepted that he would be in it. He had come to terms with the probability of mortal danger. He had finally let his family know where he was. And now Fitzmullen-Brophy, their Moses, would no longer be leading them, and although it had not been made at all plain what would happen to them, they were most certainly not marching north any longer, which meant that they might instead be about to go backwards, or even follow their crestfallen commander home.

They cheered Fitzmullen-Brophy as he turned to go, and he turned quickly lest they see him weaken, and Fleming shyly accompanied him back towards the car. Belcher had been left there brooding, unwilling to face the men or talk to anyone. But now they met him, puffing towards them at speed and waving his stick with uncharacteristic energy.

'Tummy! Whatever is wrong?' said Fitzmullen-Brophy, momentarily surprised out of his despondency.

Red-faced and pop-eyed, Belcher bustled up to them, and wheezed out the news that would change everything, he said.

'Damned great battle, FitzEm! Heard it from some signals-wallah passing by. Whole damn expeditionary force fighting up beyond Maubeuge.'

'And?'

'Looks a bit dicey, they're saying.'

And straight away Fitzmullen-Brophy saw his fortunes change again. Of course the army needed him – it always had. But what made up his mind was the certainty that, with the war suddenly wide awake and roaring, the army would surely now be too busy to keep an eye on an errant band of fusiliers.

'Tummy,' he said, 'I think you had better tell the driver that we will be staying put, if it's all the same to him. Meanwhile I think we should relocate to some quarters where the authorities will have great difficulty in finding us. I say we sit tight and wait and see.'

Oh, but they had gravely underestimated Hugh Fitzmullen-Brophy when they let him go free.

36

The size of the plain, the number of the host,
Colours glisten with pure glory,
A fair stream of silver, cloths of gold,
Afford a welcome with all abundance.

—The Voyage of Bran

The brigadier general surveyed the landscape with dissatisfaction.

'There's a canal right across the middle of the damn battlefield – a bloody great canal.'

'Yes, sir.'

'And houses – whole bloody rows and terraces of them.'

'Yes, sir.'

'And slag heaps and pit heads and all sorts of other nonsense – just there, where we're supposed to be fighting a battle.'

'Yes, sir.'

'The whole damn place looks like bloody Derbyshire – the uglier parts at least.'

'Now that you mention it, sir…' But the brigade major thought better of continuing while his superior was in full flow. The brigadier general was not the explosive sort but his temper tended to be eased in little jets of high-pressure sarcasm, which were almost invisible until you realised that they'd seared one's skin off. Stand at a safe distance, don't do anything foolish, and everything should be all right in a minute.

'So my point is – *if* you can see what I'm getting at – is seeing as we actually *have* Derbyshire, and the Black Country and such, would somebody kindly tell me why the thundering blazes the army does all its training on Salisbury Plain?'

'Ah, yes, sir. Quite.'

'Bloody nonsense.'

'Absolutely, sir.'

'War Office is filled with blasted halfwits.'

'Sir.'

'Well if anyone raises a fuss about having trenches dug through his damned Brussels sprouts, then place the bugger under arrest.'

'Yes, sir.'

'Blasted Belgians.'

And thus the stage was set for the battle of Mons – the greatest battle the British Army had fought since Waterloo. As it happened, the fact that the field of Waterloo was nearby was not lost on any of the British soldiers who had a scrap of education or who had taken time to read the blazons on their regimental colours. The intervening nineteenth century had given to the men in khaki a very different landscape to the one fought over by Wellington's redcoats and, as had just been pointed out, that posed problems.

The Saturday that was the eve of the fight was spent, as the irascible general, along with the commanders of all the other brigades and divisions in the corps had decreed, digging trenches through kitchen gardens and other stretches of ground that the Duke of Wellington would never have chosen for a battlefield. Then on the Sunday morning, with the weather still dull and uninviting, the German guns opened the battle. It was Napoleon's Grand Battery, but with high explosive this time, and it had the defenders wishing that they'd spent their Saturday digging deeper. The men who had been in South Africa had known what it was like to be under fire, but the intensity of this bombardment outdid anything the Boers had ever brought down on them.

The shells screamed in and exploded in angry black clouds, making the earth shake and the air reverberate, and flinging clods of debris every which way. The first salvo came in a little after dawn and pious civilians on their way to church hurried on, or hurried back, depending on how they valued their souls or their bodies. It was two hours before the initial cannonade tailed off, and by then there was almost nobody to be seen out of doors or above ground.

And then, just at the time that decent folk might have been sitting down to a Sunday breakfast, their souls uplifted by morning service, the German infantry made their first appearance. It was nothing like that other Sunday ninety-nine years earlier, when the Prussian great-grandfathers of these men had been Britain's allies, and when the blue-coated enemy had paraded in brave array before pushing in fearsome columns across the shallow valley with the battle flags fluttering bravely over all. The Kaiser's men flew no colours, and only had they not been moving in their masses in a late summer morn, they would have been almost invisible.

They were dressed in a greenish grey – the German equivalent of khaki – and even their fine ornate helmets of leather and brass were hidden under drab cloth. In the grey sunlight not even their bayonets glittered.

The shelling eased off and died and the British officers stood on the parapets of their trenches, or sat in the saddle farther back, and focused their field glasses and estimated ranges. The British had as many as eighty thousand fighting men stretched along the line of the canal or in reserve close behind. They were outgunned and seriously outnumbered, but they held a sound defensive position. The old soldiers had their skill and experience to trust to and the younger men didn't yet know enough to be daunted by the odds or to believe themselves mortal. The new quick-firing guns of the artillery were to be fired in anger for the first time.

Each infantryman with his rifle and his hundred and fifty rounds was about to know the excitement of aiming at a moving living target. The great test was upon them all.

'Range! Eight hundred!' The call went up and down the line.

Eight-hundred yards. More than ten times the effective range of a musket of Bonaparte's day, but today it was no impossibility. Sights were adjusted accordingly. Rifles were rested on parapets, with five-round clips set out alongside by men most confident of their skill and speed. Eight-hundred yards – four times the range at which they'd won their marksmanship badges, but they could do it if asked.

The Germans came on. There were no drums and colours, but there were bugles and officers on horseback, waving with their swords. And the first rounds of British 18-pounder shrapnel whistled and burst in white smoke over the German lines. The range was six-hundred yards now. *Look to your front.*

The Germans were not arrayed in solid blocks as on the battlefields of the previous age, but as the range closed they still appeared a formidable crowd, filling the fields, slowing pouring across the land, an uncountable host. Officers suddenly dry-throated raised their voices for the words of command.

It was set to be the biggest engagement fought by the British since Waterloo, but the Royal Munster Fusiliers were not there.

37

Macmorris: *It is no time to discourse, so Chrish save me: the day is hot, and the weather, and the wars, and the king, and the dukes: it is no time for discourse. The town is beseeched, and the trumpet call us to the breach; and we talk, and, be Chrish, do nothing: 'tis shame for us all: so God sa' me, 'tis shame to stand still; it is shame, by my hand: and there is throats to be cut, and works to be done; and there is nothing done, so Chrish sa' me, la!*

—Shakespeare, *Henry V*, Act iii, Sc 2.

The Munsters were miles back, billeted in and around a village right on the Belgian border. Indeed, it provided some quiet amusement for many to stroll a little forward into Belgium and then back a bit into France. Moriarty named it the Grand Tour, but after he had made it and laughed over it, he disdained it in other men as somewhat passé. He had been to Rangoon, hadn't he, and up-country from there, hadn't he? A little wander from this little hamlet of Vieux Reng in France to the equally insignificant Grand Reng on the other side of the frontier was nothing at all to an old soldier who'd seen the empire. Besides, they'd had enough walking to last them a long time, what with having had the feet marched off them the past couple of days to get here.

Young Whelan was having another crack at the Grand Tour though. He strolled over to where his section were sprawled about, his hands in his pockets. 'Shove over for me there, lads,' he said. 'I'm just after walking all the way from Belgium.'

Nobody laughed, but Whelan didn't mind at all.

'You've grand energy there, boy,' said Moriarty, 'but you'd need to save it.' He was affecting the manner of the old soldier among these young fellas of the 2nd Battalion, half of whom had never left Aldershot until a week or two ago. Thus to him the long march to Belgium had been a *trek*, where a stream might be forded at a *drift*, and any village passed was a *dorp*. He had never been next, nigh or near South Africa, but he casually identified himself with the old sweats anyway – and why not?

This present dorp wasn't a bad place at all, and the natives were still generous even with the entire British Expeditionary Force gathering here, so bully-beef stew was amply supplemented by cheese and fruits and fresh bread. There was beer and wine to be had too, no matter how watchful an eye was kept by the officers and sergeants, but after the exertions of the march, little enough was needed to put a man into a deep sleep, without any uproariousness on the way. So Saturday night had been quiet, and the Royal Munster Fusiliers had slept like babes in the scattering of barns and sheds allotted to them, safe from the rain.

Now this morning, with the church bells ringing for Sunday mass, word had come that it wasn't going to be much of a lazy day at all, and the Munsters had bolted their breakfasts and stood to their arms, only to find idleness forced upon them as the morning lengthened. The officers were scurrying hither and yon, but the men had nothing to do but sit around in sections and platoons, watching the comings and goings, guessing at events, and waiting for their turn. A brief drizzle set them grousing, but then they heard the guns.

'Jesus, lads – it's started.'

And men clambered to their feet and craned their necks, and in ones and twos made their way to any bit of high ground, until almost the whole battalion was moving northward without orders. The officers were so engrossed in what was happening towards

Mons that it was a while before they even noticed what was going on around them, and with some irritation the men were ordered back.

'Have them dig trenches along the line of that lane,' suggested a testy major.

'I believe that's private property, sir.'

The major actually hesitated, before deciding that war was war.

'Get them digging anyway – but don't break down any walls or fences. Just keep them busy.'

'What's a reng?' asked Whelan.

'A what? A reng? I don't know. I give up.' Moriarty had hacked his way down about two foot, and nobody seemed to be expecting more of him, so he was sitting with his feet in the newly made trench, letting the sweat dry, and having a fag. Whelan was prattling away.

'I asked Mr O'Malley. The names of the villages like – Grand Reng and Vee-ucks Reng. He says it's French and that one means old and the other means big. So it means big reng and old reng, but he doesn't know what a reng is.'

'Just shows you that them big schools don't teach you everything.' Moriarty was watching the senior officers, glued to their field glasses. The guns hadn't let up. He spat out a shred of tobacco and turned to Whelan.

'But aren't you some sort of eejit to be talking to officers like that? What's a reng – Jesus.'

'But do you know what it is?'

'I'll be honest with you – I've forgotten.'

There were dispatch riders on the road – men red-faced and running, urgent men on gleaming horses, men on bicycles pedalling hard – but none came near the Munsters, or paused to answer their calls for information. But the guns told them that there was fighting up towards the canal, and it was not slackening.

The men were wondering, and the sergeants were ill at ease, and the officers were all in a lather of nervous impatience. They weren't by any means the only unit being held in reserve, but no one could help thinking that this was some slight upon the regiment.

'The whole of 1st Brigade is in reserve,' explained Sergeant Major McEvoy, reassuring himself as much as anyone within earshot. It was a special day indeed when a senior NCO could speak almost as an ordinary man to other men. 'It's not a real battle if they're leaving us out of it. The Coalies and the Jocks and the Black Watch and us – they'd never leave us out if it was a real fight.'

'That's a lot of artillery if they're just shouting the odds at each other, Sarn't Major.'

'They'll call us when they need us. That's what the reserve is all about, son. If the mobs up in front of us make a hames of it then it's up to us to save the day, and if they don't do so badly then we're here to deliver the knock-out punch to the Germans.'

'What do you think will happen, Sarn't Major?'

'I'd say we'll be moving forward soon enough, and you can thank your lucky stars you won't have to be fighting from that wretched little scratch of a trench.'

The day was brightening up but smoke was beginning to drift across the mean industrial suburbs. Up at the canal waves of German infantry were moving forward and being beaten back, leaving more and more bodies on the ground with each attempt. The British weren't having it their own way, however. For every shell the Royal Artillery sent at the Germans, a dozen came back, bursting all along the British line and showering the British gun positions with shrapnel. Out in the open as they were, the gunners and the horses suffered accordingly. For the infantry in their shallow trenches it wasn't so bad, but all along the line, where the parapets were littered with empty cartridge clips and feet slipped on the scattering of expended brass, there were also to be seen the fluttering tapes and bloody wads of field dressings. There were bodies crumpled at the bottom of trenches or neatly laid out for collection behind the firing line.

Some unlucky regiments, placed uncomfortably forward and facing the brunt of the German attacks, took a frightful mauling. In the Middlesex and the Royal Irish the casualties were climbing into the hundreds. The regimental aid posts were working flat out, and any man capable of walking was better off walking, back to wherever someone not so beset could have a look at him.

The Munsters saw a few of these coming their way – unfortunate to have been hit or fortunate to be out of the fight, none dared say yet. Moriarty, eaten with curiosity, was one of the many who clamoured forward to hear news of the battle.

'What ho, the Diehards,' he said to a Middlesex man, forcing a cigarette on him. The man, bandaged and grimy, took the smoke in his good hand. 'Good man, Paddy.'

'What's it like up there, mate?' Moriarty asked eagerly. He had given up his usual nonchalance.

The Englishman flashed a dazed grin, 'Hot enough, mate,' he said. 'But we're giving the bastards a right good seeing to.'

And that was as much as they heard from anyone. It was hot enough, but the Germans were getting a right fucking pasting and no mistake. The officers of the Munsters, who were trying to make sense of the matter from an observation point on top of a slag heap (which the old South Africa hands called a *koppie*), did manage to waylay a young cavalry subaltern, who only stopped because he thought they were someone else. He told them a hairraising tale of an unending and unstoppable flood of Germans, supported by a brutal weight of firepower. He spoke of a doomed last stand of the Royal Fusiliers in defence of a railway bridge, and of a line bending dangerously and already perhaps outflanked. The gentlemen of the Munsters judged him a high-strung, even hysterical type, letting the side down, but all the same they itched to know for themselves what was really happening at Mons. Surely the order sending them forward was on its way. They smoked cigarette after cigarette and spoke tersely when they had to speak at all, lest their emotions get the better of them. The older men remembered the Black Week in 1899 when the Irish won the only laurels to be picked up from those stricken fields. The younger men looked at the ribbons of South Africa on the older men's breasts. Why weren't the Munsters being let play their part again? 1st Brigade of 1st Division in I Corps and last into the fight, if they ever got into the fight.

In the end the waiting got too much, or at least it must have got too much for Brigade HQ, for the order came to move forward a thousand yards. This brought them no appreciable distance closer to the battle, but it gave everyone something to do, and relieved the various battalion commanders of the temptation of just pitching in to the fight off their own bat. There was no undue haste. With two Guards regiments represented in the brigade, the Munsters were being very correct in all their movements.

The villagers watched them move up, taking it as a good sign that the action was moving away from them, but so nervous all the same. Some children skipped along with the troops, pleading as always for souvenirs, but their mothers called them back and shoved them indoors. Last to go was one happy urchin wearing a necklace of British tunic buttons – all lions and unicorns, tigers and lambs, elephants and sphinxes, and all to be polished up every night as diligently as any recruit would do it. The little girl stood in the street, cheering the English and calling through a gapped-tooth smile for the blood and entrails of the Boche.

The tentative advance of the Munsters and 1st Brigade appeared to be part of a general push to the front. The action was still a long way away, but all eyes were wide open in expectation of meeting Germans around the next bend in the road.

'Should we fix bayonets, Sergeant?'

'You should do nothing except what you're bloody told to do. Look to your front and keep your big yap shut.'

More wounded coming back. More ambulances and ammunition wagons going forward. Cavalry squadrons stood ready wherever there were open fields. Only their officers were in the saddle, but every man was standing by his horse's head, waiting for the call that would put boot to stirrup.

'Jesus, lads. Start a fox across that field and in a second you'd see the biggest cavalry charge in history.'

They halted far too soon, and occupied trenches just dug and now vacated by the Royal Sussex.

'Fierce generous of you to do a bit of digging for us.'

Or: 'Call this a trench, boys? The line's as crooked as a quartermaster's accounts.'

'Yeah? Well you can sit here and straighten it while we go and see off the Germans for you.'

And the Sussex men moved forward with a cheerio, and the Munsters settled down into the shallow scrapes that were no better or worse than the ones they'd just left, or any others that were dug across this landscape this day. They found comfortable firing positions, and squinted down their rifles, adjusting the sights with finicky professionalism. Corporals and sergeants barked and snapped, and junior officers strode up and down the line, speaking in unnecessarily loud tones. In short order, with the Germans still making no appearance, everyone grew fractious again.

'What in the name of Christ are they keeping us here for?'

'Take it easy. They'll send us up soon enough – isn't that right, Sergeant?'

'Right enough. Wait for the word.'

'Permission to get a brew on, Sergeant?'

'Better not. Better not. Sure there wouldn't be time to drink it.'

Moriarty checked his ammunition, straightening the cartridges in the clips, wiping flecks of dust from them, and buttoning them up in his pouches again. Nothing to do but fiddle and fret.

'Here, Whelan. Do you know who those fellas were? The Royal Sussex?'

'What? Who?'

'The call them the Orange Lilies.'

'Go 'way! They're Orangemen?'

'They were once upon a time.'

'Jesus – and they seemed decent enough.'

'I keep telling you, boy – you've got to watch yourself. There's all sorts of gurriers allowed into the army.'

The afternoon passed, with the senior officers in continual and purposeless conference and their juniors looking on anxiously. Twice more the battalion was roused out of position and sent forward, and each time they thought that this was it. The press of wagons and horses grew thicker, and the staff officers and runners were so frequent that they were almost tripping each other up. The Munsters interrogated every man they met with a bandage on display, and some told of annihilation and some of easy victory, but everyone spoke of the grey waves of the enemy that were always to be seen, framed clear as day in the foresight guard, and nothing to do except pull the trigger.

'Honest, mates – it didn't seem rightly fair. Rapid independent until I went through all my right-hand pouches and I'll warrant I hit with every shot. Couldn't miss, lads, and the bastards just kept on coming.'

One Irish Rifleman, grateful for a swig of water and a smoke, averred that if he hadn't caught the nick off a shrapnel bullet up in the shoulder, the same shoulder would be banjaxed anyway from the recoil, and the hands would almost be burned off him, his rifle got so hot. 'And the bastards just kept on coming.'

And the day lengthened and the line was still holding. Half the British guns were knocked out, and the machine-guns too, but so long as men with rifles kept their heads and kept their ground the line held. The Boers had taught them to shoot straight and to shoot fast, and the Germans had blundered onto a battlefield that was more like a firing range to some. The line held, and the Germans withdrew. For the few British battalions that had been pounded almost to ruin, it was a miraculous release. For others it was no more than the army's due. And for those units like the Royal Munster Fusiliers there was a heartfelt dissatisfaction that they had not been given their chance. They could only hope that when it came time to mount an advance tomorrow, they, as fresh troops, would be given the place of honour. They would drive the Germans on the points of their bayonets and show those mobs that had done no more today than musketry drill what real fighting was about. Today they had just held off the Germans. Tomorrow there would be a victory.

But in the early hours of Monday the order came to retreat.

38

Name: P. A. Charrier

Rank: Major (R. M. Fus)

Occupation: **Gentleman**

General Return of the Officers, Non-Commissioned Officers, Privates and Others, who were Quartered in the Military Barrack of Ballymullen Tralee on the Night of Sunday, the 2nd of April, 1911, and of those who arrived on Monday, the 3rd of April, who were not enumerated elsewhere.

—*Census of Ireland*, 1911

If a man must go before his time, then he could do worse than Paul Charrier. He was forty-five when he died and he left behind a wife and five children, but had he been given the time to reflect, he might have thought that no day could ever match his last. Had he lived, and had he been granted less final circumstances in which to demonstrate his ability – circumstances, that is, which did not kill him and wipe out his entire command – he would most likely have gone far. He held the rank of major when he died, as he had for nearly five years already, but had just been advanced to the command of his battalion, the war having proved him more suited to the task than his colonel. Had he lived just a few weeks longer, then, he'd have been confirmed in his rank of commanding officer, and had he lived to see the expansion of the army in the following year he'd have been in command of a brigade before the summer of 1915 was out, with divisional command following hard on the heels of that. He would have been a general, and directed his part of the war from a château behind the lines, and the younger men, not knowing him as his Munsters could have known him, would not have cared about some deed of bravery done when the war was just begun. Charrier, with his thick neck and impassive nature would have fitted in too well amidst the generals who demanded the same mix of coolness and aggression from the men they directed in their doomed multitudes to the front. History would not have been kind to him if he'd lived.

But Paul Charrier was killed cleanly by a bullet on a bright day in late summer, when the land was still green. There was cavalry on the field that day, and the guns were to the fore, as they had been at Waterloo, or any other battle from olden times. If there was any barbed wire it amounted to no more than a few strands fixed by a farmer to border his field. Paul Charrier wore a sword that day, and fought his battalion across open country, with no higher authority to trouble him. No officer could have wished for better.

He died on the road that ran south to the village of Étreux. With his French parentage he would have been one of the few Munster officers not to pronounce it 'Etrucks'. French parentage or not, his name was pronounced to rhyme with 'barrier', for it would have been utterly absurd for an Indian-born British boy to have been burdened with a name like Pole Sharriay. No. Major Charrier was pleased to be able to speak French like a native, but he was a proud Briton, and on this day, more than anything, he was a Munster.

As an old South Africa hand he was wearing what suited him, and what suited him was his sun helmet rather than the regulation service cap. No one was going to tell an acting CO that he was improperly dressed – not at times like these. The helmet was adorned with the hackle of the regiment, a spray of green and white feathers, advertising that here was the man in charge. He likely didn't need it. Command sat easy on him.

With the exception of his headgear he was very correct. He had taken the time to shave that morning because not to do so was unthinkable. His boots were a little dusty, but his tie was straight and his gloves were buttoned. It was another hot day, but the Dirty Shirts would have to know it far hotter before they'd deign to loosen their standards.

The day began at Fésmy. For most men it began too early, but for the Munsters this was the day when they would be given the chance to prove themselves. Fésmy was an undistinguished village south of the Belgian border, but it was large enough to serve as a temporary headquarters. Just up the road was the crossroads of Haut Rêve, and south across the Sambre-Oise canal was the village of Oisy. From Oisy the main road led to Étreux. From the village where Charrier had woken up from his very brief sleep to the roadside where he was killed that evening was less than four miles as the crow flies. Today was Thursday. Many of the troops now dragging themselves to their feet in and around Fésmy had been marching hard since the previous Saturday, so as not to miss Sunday's battle. Sleep had been scarce and the weather remained mercilessly sunny and warm. No one had a notion of when or where the retreat would stop. Sometimes units were halted at night, but just as often they stopped only when the road ahead became too congested. Sometimes, then, they were allowed to fall out by the roadside and sleep until it became possible to move, and just as often they had to stand dumbly in all their equipment, waiting for the order to start them moving again. The Munsters, in reserve at Mons, were not quite fresh, but had not been as badly punished by the days of retreat. For this reason they were chosen as rearguard. Charrier was given two guns of the Royal Field Artillery, with a troop of hussars by way of a cavalry screen. Some Coldstreamers would hold their position on the road out of Haut Rêve for a while too, but this would be the Munsters' day, and Paul Charrier's day.

He was a large man in his prime and rather heavy set, and as the day warmed and the action with it, Charriers face was seen to be flushed, with the sweat softening his shirt collar and beading in his businesslike moustache. But no one could say that they'd seen the major in the least way flustered. Why should he have been? He was in his element. This was like a field day on the Curragh, but with deadly purpose.

He was tasked with covering the retreat of General Haig's I Corps, with holding off the Germans for as long as it took for a comfortable gap of eight miles to open between the retreating British and the advancing Germans. Eight miles. Making allowance for minor delays, that meant that the Munsters would be expected to hold their ground for three hours after the last British unit slogged out of Fésmy. If the Germans arrived in any strength during those hours Charrier would have a fight on his hands. Two guns, a few hussars, and a battalion of the Munster Fusiliers against German First Army. Let them come.

Everyone in the battalion was up and busy from an early hour, and the men taking up their positions around Fésmy saw the increasingly weary army trail through, heading south. In happier circumstances they'd have catcalled at mobs less fortunate than themselves – told them to step out smartly, or reminded them that they were going the wrong way – but there was something sobering at the sight of the unravelling army. Even the spectacle of a colonel, dead asleep, taking a sudden spill out of the saddle, elicited no derision. The haggard Connaught Rangers stumbled in a little after dawn, fell flat out on the earth the instant they were halted, and lay like the dead for three hours until painfully roused.

It was getting on for nine, and the Connacht men were not long gone, when the first German cavalry arrived. The Royal Munster Fusiliers were about to get into the war.

39

122. The reconnoitring patrols in the front line are usually followed by stronger detachments, to furnish reliefs for the patrols and to drive the enemy's reconnoitring troops from the field. In certain circumstances full information can only be gained by an attack, for which it may even be necessary to employ a force of all arms.

—Felddienst Ordnung, 1908

It was the first time anyone had seen the Germans. The officers with their glasses were the only ones to get a decent view, but everywhere along the line eager men were craning their necks and peering through the cover, chattering excitedly to each other.

'Uhlans, lads! See the big long lances on them!'

The Germans were only a patrol, and they could see what was facing them. They dismounted and fanned out a little, at what they reckoned was out of range.

Captain Jervis commanding D Company stood on top of a low wall and fixed the German patrol with his binoculars. 'Range five hundred, Sarn't Major?' he said.

'Yes, sir. Five hundred near enough.'

'My compliments to Lieutenant Deane-Drake, and tell him to give them a volley.'

Maybe everyone was too excited, or maybe the range was too long. The German horseman fell to the ground all right, but there were obviously enough of them alive to return fire. The Munsters had felt the kick of a rifle many times, but only the older men had heard the sound of a bullet as it smacked through the air just above their heads. This was the war.

Several shots passed close to Captain Jervis, with one of them punching into the plaster of a wall only a few feet from his head. He lowered his binoculars and stepped down to ground level, but with no show of haste. He saw the tense faces and the bright eyes of his men; some of them grinning, none of them blinking. He felt the same way. This was the grand moment. But he was afraid too – of making a mistake, of losing men unnecessarily, of disgracing himself. Even down here in cover he felt he was in a very exposed position. His company was at the apex of the angular roadblock around Fésmy. Behind him was the battalion and before him was no one but the enemy. If he failed in some way then the whole defence might disintegrate in an instant. With a moment's conscious effort he ignored his fears and took comfort in the orders he had been given. Hold until ordered to withdraw. Simplicity itself.

Like everyone else, Moriarty had been thrilled to see the horsemen in grey, and that surprised him. He'd only ever been shot at before by wily natives sniping unexpectedly from cover, and that sort of thing was no good at all for a man's nerves. But seeing the enemy like this, out in the open and behaving like proper soldiers and – and this was undoubtedly cheering – in such small numbers, that, as it turned out, had been the very thing to dispel the jitters. His had not been the platoon chosen to open the war, but that first volley had been a marvellous thing, and now Moriarty and all the men around him were arranging their clips of ammunition on the bank in front of them, eager for their own moment.

It didn't come for a long while. The Germans kept their distance, although more of them did seem to be appearing as the morning wore on. After an hour or more there was the sound of heavy firing off to their right rear, and that caused a little bit of consternation, until the officers broadcast the reassurance that it was merely another company coming under pressure, but that they had the situation well in hand. Moriarty, along with the rest of the battalion holding positions around Fésmy, might have felt the strain somewhat as the noise of battle continued away behind them, and their minds might have conjured up images of angry Germans with their long steel lances breaking through and coming up the road at their rear, but they were not kept waiting long. The enemy to their front seemed to have made their minds up, and the fire directed on them from around eleven-ish was far more considerable than those first unconvincing shots from a few cavalry carbines.

Starting from almost nothing, the air was soon filled with angry metal. The bullets buzzed and hummed overhead, whickered through the foliage and whined off stones and tree trunks. It was still only August, but the leaves were falling, and little bits of twig were showering down too on the Munsters' heads. And soon after that they heard for the first time the approaching whistle of an incoming shell, and that was when Moriarty first felt the giddy excitement in his breast turn to fear. It might have been outright panic if the corporals and the sergeants hadn't been there, roaring on as if there was still something routine about all of this. Moriarty found himself almost paralysed, his hands loath to do their work, and he was disgusted with himself. He concentrated on the unnecessary arrangement of cartridge clips, willing his hand steady. He jumped when a cluster of leaves landed on the back of his neck and stuck halfway inside his collar, and he cursed a blue streak as he beat it away, with Whelan laughing at him fit to break his arse.

'Fucking eejit,' said Moriarty. 'Fuck's sake.' But he saw that Whelan's hilarity was just the nerves too.

'Look to your fucking front, the pair of you!' shouted the corporal.

They did, and that made it easier. Nobody was getting hit, not that they could see at least, and it was funny how fast you could just get used to things. The Germans weren't rushing them yet, although grey shapes could be seen moving tentatively forward. The order was given for independent firing, and that made them all feel a lot better, even though the shelling became more intense and accurate.

In the middle of it all, with seemingly everyone shooting away like blazes at targets they couldn't quite see, the cooks came up. The D Company cook was a humourless sort, and had little flair for cookery either, but he was dogged and punctual and, as the men were witnessing, surprisingly brave. The German bullets were flying down the road, and the cookers were coming up, and cooks with big dixies of tea and stew were trying to do their work with their sergeant bawling at them and they trying to keep low and out of the way. Those who took a moment to appreciate the scene found it wonderfully comical.

'Go easy now and don't be spilling that tay!'

'What's your hurry, lads?'

'Send this back, boy – this isn't what I ordered at all!'

D Company's stew was the same as ever, and there were bits in it, but for those who still had any sort of appetite it was as good as any picnic.

40

'Am holding Fésmy village, being attacked by force of all arms. Getting on well.'

—Message from Major P.A. Charrier 2/RMF to General F. I. Maxse GOC
1st (Guards) Brigade, 27th August 1914

A little after noon and the rain suddenly came bucketing down, which was good and refreshing at first, but damned uncomfortable in no time, with gear becoming heavy and buckles uncooperative. The poor visibility also aided the Germans.

They had the measure of the situation now, and had arrived in sufficient numbers as to bring sufficient fire down to keep the Munsters busy and at the same time make a determined attack on Fésmy. Moriarty and his mates never knew it, but for a little while the Germans were right in behind them, and it was only a sharp counterattack by C Company that cleared them out of the village again. It wasn't enough to see off the Germans for good, though, and the attackers kept on trying. One enterprising officer sent in his men under cover of a herd of cattle driven before them.

'They're coming again!'

'That's cows, you big fool.'

'There's Germans in among the cows! Can you not see them. You blind eejit?'

'Christ, but you're right. The dirty bastards.'

The 2nd Battalion of the Royal Munster Fusiliers had never been presented with a better target than this but, while most brought their rifles to their shoulders and gleefully let fly, some reservations were voiced amid the rapid fire.

'My uncle has a small dairy herd. 'Twould break his heart to see the waste,' said one Kerryman, expertly thumbing in a fresh clip and getting on with his work.

'My father has four acres and it's all rock and bog,' said one of his mates, his speech punctuated by the rhythm of his rifle. 'He never had any cows at all. Fuck the farmers. They're always complaining.'

'It ain't right shooting cows,' said one Englishman.

'What's the matter? You're no farmer's boy.'

'And you was never in India, son. You go kick a cow that gets in your way in India and you'll get what for and no bloody mistake.' He was upright and half kneeling on the bank, his rifle aimed and rock steady, but not firing. 'Do harm to the bleeding cows and the blacks is up in arms and it's bloody pack drill for you – I see you, you bastard – gotcha!' The bolt snapped forward and a shape in a spiked helmet dropped from view.

Every man there could land fifteen rounds onto a distant target in under a minute. The fifteen was the bare minimum and the regulation target was considerably smaller than a cow, so it wasn't long at all before the ground in front of the Munsters was blocked with carcasses. The man whose uncle had a small dairy herd was doing a sorrowful calculation of the damage in pounds and shillings when a German bullet caught him. There was a frantic quarter minute in which equipment was wrenched aside and clothing pulled open with slippery fingers, but they'd hardly worked out how to tie on a dressing when the man was dead. Not long after that the order to withdraw came through.

That order had originated with Major Charrier. He was responding to the heavy pressure the Germans were exerting on his small force, but he had no intention of cutting out altogether. The companies would fall back to a less exposed position in Fésmy and continue the fight. There would be no retreat until the order came from Brigade. It was thus unfortunate that the messenger bringing that order took a wrong turning on the narrow country roads and nearly ran into a German cavalry patrol. He didn't fancy his chances against three lancers when he'd only a bicycle under him, so he dragged himself and the bike into a hedge and kept very still for more than an hour. There was the sound of heavy firing off to the right somewhere, and that was probably the Coalies or the Dirty Shirts he'd been sent to find, but it was also a bloody big lot of Germans. He was a brave enough young fellow, and the war was still something of a game to everybody, so when he reckoned himself safe he got back on the road and pedalled hard towards the sound of the guns. He never did find the Munsters though.

By the time it occurred to Charrier that the necessary order might indeed have been held up, it was largely too late to do anything about it. There were masses of Germans coming in from the north and from the east, and Charrier had his platoons and companies performing the slow leapfrog of a fighting withdrawal. The textbooks would say that such a manoeuvre is just about the most difficult thing that can be done, but Major Charrier never displayed the slightest doubt or hesitation, even as men he had known and commanded for months and years were falling in their ones and twos before his eyes.

The enemy was closing in, the air was filled with killing metal, and there was blood splashing on the ground, but the battalion was being handled with all the assured competence of a well-run training exercise.

Not everything went according to plan, but then nothing ever does. Some men wanted to stay, and 'have one more crack at them, sir'. The cook sergeant was enticed out of the line of march by the sight of an unclaimed pig in a yard, and that at least added some comedy to the dangerous afternoon. Then, at a crossroads by the canal bridge near the village of Oisy, it was discovered that B Company was missing, and various messengers were sent off to find them. The delay caused by this was probably the one single thing that would get them all killed.

They'd had their dinners brought up to them in the day, but there was no one to give them tea come the evening. You couldn't say the cooks were rattled – not rattled, mind you – but everything was a sight more urgent and making tea among the bullets just wouldn't be as funny as before. By six o'clock it was clear to everyone that they were bent on merely getting the hell out now, and any fighting was just an attempt to keep the retirement going in good order. The Munster Fusiliers were not going to win the war today.

There was still plenty of light when they left Oisy behind and there was a fine straight road open in front of them. That meant, of course, that the Germans could pursue at speed down the same road and harry them for hours yet until dark came on. Charrier's men had kept this fight going for around nine hours and three miles so far, but there would be ever more Germans arriving, while the gap between the Munsters and their parent brigade was widening all the time.

But there was plenty of fight left in Paul Charrier yet.

All up and down the column the order rang out to get off the road, to get into the ditches and keep moving for Christ's sake. Moriarty wondered what was going on. The roadside ditch was dry enough but it made for unhandy going. He wasn't bothered about that for long though. At the south end of that fine straight stretch Charrier had set up his two machine-guns and now the air between Moriarty and his mate Whelan in the file on the opposite side of the road was hissing with bullets. Up ahead could be heard the wonderful racket of two Vickers guns going full blast. That was about a thousand rounds a minute between them, all telling the Germans that this road was closed, thank you. Moriarty hunched his shoulders in and hoped to Jesus that he didn't miss his footing and go tumbling out onto the road, but he didn't and neither did anyone else. Everyone who wasn't in a tearing hurry when they reached the end of the road, half a mile on, was grinning at each other. It was a grand thing.

The reason there was another delay here and they all weren't belting off south again soon became apparent. The Germans had cut them off.

41

No other claim to a memorial near Étreux is likely to be advanced – certainly nothing which would not take second place to the Munsters.

—Historical Section, Committee for Imperial Defence, 7th June 1919

The guns of the Royal Field Artillery were magnificent. Usually the Munsters viewed the artillery as an idle bunch of bastards who went by on horseback or sitting up on the limber, rattling along cool as you please and doing nothing but raising dust for the poor weary infantry to choke on. But today the gunners were fair rushed off their feet. They'd started the day up by Fésmy, sending shrapnel shot at the German batteries as fast as they could load, and when the German guns found them in their turn and the deadly little bullets started showering down among them, the British gunners stayed hard at it, loading and firing and sweating like the clappers until the order came for them to withdraw. Then somehow a gun and a hard-working gun crew became a tidy vehicle with four wheels and six horses, and with the other gun and the ammunition wagon became part of a caravan that thundered off south in an urgent but orderly fashion. Then south of Oisy they unlimbered so smartly that you'd think there was nothing to handling an 18-pounder field piece and a small herd of horses in the constrained space of a country lane and a kitchen garden.

Yes, the guns were a credit to the army, and it was a great shame for everyone on the British side that day that there were only two of them. Then, in the early evening, and just north of the village of Étreux, a German high-explosive round found its mark and there was only one.

Moriarty saw it happen. He'd just gathered that the houses ahead were occupied by the Germans, and everybody was busy getting off the road and finding cover. The day had been too long altogether. Giving the Germans a bloody nose was what this rearguard business had been all about. Shoot off a clip or two, duck down behind the ditch, and fall back while the going was good. If you or none of your mates got hit it was exhilarating and close to being fun, but they'd been at it nine hours now and would have been happy to be somewhere else entirely. And now the road out was blocked, and the whistling of incoming shells seemed to be coming from a different direction entirely. There were just too many bloody Germans, and that was the truth of it. Moriarty was just finding the strength to start grousing about it all when their own two guns came up at the gallop. That's the stuff lads, he thought. Put a couple of rounds into those houses down the road and we can be on our way and out of this bloody pigsty.

And then there was a thunderous crack and the lead gun team was all over the road, with torn-up men and screaming horses and bits of timber and horse tack thrown about among the blood splashes. Moriarty stared blankly for a moment, and then turned away before he could dwell too much on the terrible lot of horse guts that were usually crammed into your typical horse.

For Major Charrier the day's tactical problems had become of a sudden very simple and very tough. The battalion had to punch through the German line and on to Étreux and the road south. That was all there was to it.

The German centre appeared to be a house on the west side of the road, some two hundred yards distant. There was firing coming from windows and from loopholes knocked in the walls. That would have to go. Charrier lowered his glasses, mopped his face with his handkerchief, and set about organising a frontal assault over open ground.

Moriarty was glad that his platoon wasn't chosen for that show. The attack went forward but barely made it half way. Charrier, who had led the attack in person, came back unscathed, but not many came back with him. He gathered some more men and tried again, and this time when he came back he was holding tightly to his arm just below the elbow and the blood was dripping out at the cuff of his tunic. That was when Moriarty began to feel properly frightened. The sweat was drying clammily on him and he was hungry and weary, and here was the CO stumped, and the battalion with him.

The battalion had run out of options, but no one was giving up yet. Moriarty found himself giving covering fire to the succeeding attacks, and that was just grand by him. He watched as twice a party of Munsters pushed so close to the German-held house that the officers were using their revolvers, but the Germans held on. And more Germans were still coming on up from behind, or from the front, as was technically the case, and the Munsters were being unwillingly herded into these few houses and fields astride the road outside Étreux.

Company Sergeant Major McEvoy, who'd being doing no end of herding himself this past week, and probably needed a rest more than most, gathered his wits one more time. Courage he still had in plenty, but he'd been the last into his blankets and the first up and about since before they'd left Aldershot. There was the company commander to be kept on the straight and narrow, and all the subalterns to be prevented from running astray, not to mind the more than two hundred men accounted for in all the lists and reports and nominal rolls with which his pockets were stuffed. He could have done with a five-minute sit down and a mug of strong tea and a fag, but another attack had just failed and reinforcements had to be brought up, and the road was alive with skipping bullets and shrapnel balls. The men were jaded tired and no doubt beginning to feel the breeze too. Discipline would hold a good while longer but, failing a brew-up and a smoke, spirit was what was needed now.

Moriarty watched as McEvoy, who never moved slowly, trotted up the bullet-swept road and came back down at a run a couple of minutes later. Behind him, crouching, came the reinforcements he had organised. The men holding back the Germans to the north now knew that if they couldn't push through to the south then it would all end here. This was it.

CSM McEvoy, taking charge even though there were officers present, led the way, shouting, 'Come on, boys! The Irish never lost a Friday's battle yet!'

Maybe so, but as it happened, today was only Thursday, and the German bullets took their toll.

42

The action is likely to become a classical example of the performance of its functions by a rearguard… The survivors were warmly congratulated by the Germans on the fine fight they had made.

—Historical Section, Committee for Imperial Defence, 7th June 1919

Major Charrier was hit a second time, leading another attempted breakout, but he wouldn't let that stop him, and he kept on his feet, directing operations and handling his battalion while still exhibiting some measure of calm. He died cleanly in the end, from a single bullet and (as a surviving officer so considerately wrote to his widow) with his face toward the enemy. By the time Charrier was killed, there was hardly a battalion worthy of the name left to command. Most of the 2nd Munsters were still alive, but they were scattered across the fields in ones and twos and half platoons and broken companies, some trying to push through to the south, some still trying to hold off the German advance from the north, and a great many lying crumpled in ditches, beneath hedges and in the lee of walls. The wounded gritted their teeth against the shivering, and watched the blood seep through their inadequate dressings. There was precious little praying, and even rather less cursing than might have been expected. The place was beginning to look like a real battlefield. There was the wrecked British gun – a centrepiece surrounded by dead horses, and the buildings roundabout had been set on fire by the shelling. The ground glittered with broken glass and spent cartridge casings. In the morning everyone had been well spread out and well hidden, but the bodies of those no longer living and those not yet dead were easily seen now, neatly laid out on the side of the road by their mates, or sprawled or huddled as fortune had found them.

The light was beginning to fail when as much of the battalion as could be gathered into one command fell back to the cover of a walled orchard. The fit men were no more than would constitute a well-found company, but there was no officer on his feet above the rank of lieutenant, so it was a lieutenant who took charge. They'd lost all hope of getting away, but the rules of the game as they understood it insisted that they should continue to make a fight of it until the end.

Little by little their comrades who had not made it to the orchard were accounted for by the Germans, and as that happened, the fight, which had run from the isolated positions outside Fésmy, down the miles of road across the canal and through Oisy, found its focus at last, here beneath the apple trees at Étreux. The Germans had two machine-guns in position firing into the orchard, and now were able to bring up two more, until nothing could be heard above the terrible percussive racket. The Munsters took up what positions they could, and returned fire into the gloom, but too many an intrepid marksman was cut down too soon, and the beautiful British musketry so amply demonstrated in the morning was reduced to a scattering of nervous potshots.

The end came when the ammunition ran out. The machine-gun officer having been killed, his sergeant performed the duty of smashing the guns. There were still some dependable sergeants around. There were only four unwounded officers. There had been nearly thirty on the battalion strength in the morning. There wasn't even a quarter of the battalion capable of getting to their feet and surrendering when the time came. Francis Moriarty was not among them.

Truth be told, Moriarty had never even known that a last stand was being made in the orchard. He had gone along on one of the attempts to hook out of it to the left somewhere, and by some miracle it had worked. It was Captain Jervis who was leading, and he was doing it so well that it looked as if they might somehow pull it off. He had the best part of D Company with him, along with various odds and sods, and they went south, in alternate waves, towards what they hoped was the German flank, using the lie of the land to good advantage and attracting little hostile attention. No haste. No panic.

Ahead was an arrow-straight line of hedge, which proved on second glance to be masking a railway cutting. That's where the Germans would be. The men assembled in a dip in the ground, peering through the long grass, and acknowledging the breathless instructions of their superiors.

'Fix bayonets.'

They were going to rush the last fifty or however many yards to that hedge and get stuck into whatever Germans were there. That was the plan. Moriarty was badly scared, but he'd been scared for hours now and it was too late to do anything about it. When the captain blew his whistle he'd stand up like everybody else. That was one good thing you could say about the army. They made it very easy for a fella to blindly obey. Moriarty turned to look at the other faces, and most looked the way he felt. You couldn't tell the heroes from the cowards. They all had that pale nervous fixity of expression. One man was chewing his moustache as if it was the last nourishment he'd ever see, and then by chance he turned and caught Moriarty's eye, and Moriarty saw that it was Lynch.

Lynch's face lit up. 'Howya, Francie boy! Didja kill many Germans at all?'

'A fair few, boy – a fair few,' Moriarty automatically lied in reply. He was certain he'd hit one or two earlier on, but it would be too fussy to say it like that.

'Get a few more now, wha?' and Lynch jabbed his bayonet forward a few times in excited dumb show. And then they were off.

Captain Jervis had lost his whistle so they went forward at his shout, and it wasn't fifty yards but more like eighty. The range made no difference to the Germans, who opened fire the moment the Munsters broke cover. Lynch took a bullet in the face that knocked him over. Moriarty stumbled in avoiding him and fell so hard the wind was knocked out of him. By the time he raised his head it was almost all over. His surviving comrades were covering the last few yards to the hedge, and then there was just the captain and one man he didn't recognise, and then it was just the captain, futilely emptying his revolver at the enemy.

They took him alive, because it hadn't yet occurred to anyone that they didn't have to.

By then Moriarty was frantically crawling through the grass towards cover. He'd had a brief glance at Lynch, and was pretty sure he was dead, but probably wouldn't have stopped even had the man been obviously breathing. He made it to a hedge, and pushed his way through it, and kept on crawling, praying to the Blessed Virgin in a string of obscenities, and waiting for a German bullet to catch him in the backside. Another hedge and a wall later and he stopped to rest for a spell, and it was only then that he thought to ease whatever it was that was gripping his windpipe, and he found that it was the sling of his rifle. He was briefly amazed and oddly proud that he still had his rifle with him. Sure if he'd kept a grip on it, then it was clear that he still had his wits about him and hadn't been panicked at all.

43

128. All cavalry commanders are responsible that touch once established with the enemy is never lost by night or by day.

—*Felddienst Ordnung*, 1908

It was nearly dark and Moriarty hadn't a clue where he was, so he found what he hoped was some decent cover in the corner of a field and waited – waited for the moon to come out and light his way home, or for the Germans to go away, or for someone to come along and win the war before things got any worse. Mostly he just needed some time to rest, because he was knackered tired and his nerves were jangled to bits. Before doing anything else, he sparked up a fag, and held his cap down over his face in the hope that the light wouldn't give him away. It was the perfect cigarette, and if he could, he wouldn't have minded crawling into that smoky little space inside his hat and staying there until dawn, and damn the Germans.

He hadn't many cigarettes left at all. He didn't have much in the way of food or water on him either. Water wouldn't be much of a problem, he thought. After all, the country around here was more like Wexford than Burma. He had a little tea and sugar with him, but he doubted he'd be in any position for a quick brew up. For food there was just his emergency tin of bully beef and the few biscuits that came with it. There would be fruit on the trees to supplement that though, and if there were Germans about, or angry French for that matter, then it would hardly be the first time Moriarty had slocked apples out of an orchard without being seen. For the real bare-faced thieving though, you needed someone like Lynch. Lynch would steal the sugar out of your tea, and he wouldn't even be in want of sugar. Lynch could have walked all the way to bleeding Paris and arrived wearing a top hat and with his pockets crammed with silver spoons, the dirty gurrier.

Moriarty wouldn't have felt sad for the loss of Lynch, but he was feeling very alone, and for all that Lynch was a Dubliner and a bowsie with it, he had also been a Dirty Shirt and a mate, and didn't deserve to get himself shot in the face in some field in France – unless it was in Belgium. And that went for all the other poor mugs in the battalion too. He'd known a few of them since years back, and had only been lumped in with the others a few weeks ago, but it was a rotten shame that today should have been their lot.

He saw that his rifle needed cleaning. There was a clod of mud and grass stuck to the foresight, but the insides were what really wanted attention. He had somehow held onto the rifle out of the same pitiless conditioning that demanded that the weapon be scrupulously cleaned after every firing. That meant boiling water and oily rags or the sergeant would take the head off you. Moriarty had seen Hawes, his platoon sergeant, get shot, and he reckoned that CSM McEvoy, if he was still alive at all, had worse things to be worrying about than some cordite residue baked into the barrel of Moriarty's rifle. Well here's to McEvoy, and to poor old Sergeant Hawes with the bullet in him, and to the boys of the old battalion. Rest easy, lads, wherever you are. Francis Moriarty wishes you well, but he's glad he's away out of it.

He woke up. It was properly night now and he could make out what he took to be camp fires burning in the fields beyond, so he took the last swig of his water bottle, gathered himself, and pushed through the hedge behind him, looking for a way out and a way south. He couldn't tell where he was going, or what time it was, but he crossed a railway line at one point and reckoned that that was the line they'd been trying to cross when the Germans stopped them, and that meant he was headed the right way. When dawn came it first appeared over to his left, and Moriarty was well pleased with himself. Navigating cross country in the dark and slipping past the German Army while he was about it? There was nothing you could teach this old soldier.

His complacency died a sudden death when he heard the horses, and he was into the weeds in an instant, his heart thundering. He had been going down a little winding lane with grass growing down the middle, but the horses' hooves were ringing on metalled road, so he thanked Christ the bastards weren't right on top of him. He wondered for a moment if the horsemen weren't German after all, or if they were even cavalry, but then he heard a voice giving what was undoubtedly an order, and it wasn't speaking English and it probably wasn't French either. Somebody, as it quickly turned out, was being detailed off to check the laneway. Moriarty tried to back himself as much into the overgrown verge as he could, with his rifle gripped determinedly in his hands as the Germans approached.

There were two of them, and they didn't look very dangerous at all. They looked tired, and their horses looked tired. They carried tubular steel lances, which in their hands looked more ungainly than fearsome. The grey cloth covers on their spiked helmets had shrunk in the rain, pulling back to reveal a gleam of leather and brass at the peak. The one who found Moriarty looked too old to be any harm at all. He was most likely a reservist, unlucky to be dragged back to the colours just at the end of his term of service, and the weeks gone by had made him haggard and even quite elderly, what with the grey in his moustache and the dust that covered him. He had been riding half asleep when suddenly he was looking at a rifle pointing at him out of the long grass, and a khaki-clad soldier, grim-faced, at the other end of it.

Moriarty didn't even know if he had a round up the spout, nor had he any idea as to what he was going to do next, but the old fella in front of him wasn't giving him any trouble just yet. The other one, younger and sunburnt, had gone a little bit ahead, and he stopped and turned in the saddle, but he seemed at a loss too. And there they all sat, the three of them – two on their horses and one with his backside on the ground by the side of the lane. No one made a sound, and all that could be heard was the buzzing of a couple of wasps and the fading hoofbeats from the main road.

Since Sunday the Germans had been aware of the speed and accuracy of British rifle fire, and yesterday they had been reminded of it by those Englishmen (or so they termed them) who'd held up a whole division for a day and inflicted horrible casualties, and had turned out in the end to be a mere battalion strong, and here was one of them, rifle at the ready, at point blank range, and they with only their great useless lances in their hands.

Moriarty sensed his little advantage, and before it might occur to the two troopers that the man on the ground was in a ridiculous position, he gestured up the lane with the muzzle of his rifle, and kept his face as hard as he might. *Walk on there, lads. Keep going. Give me any bother at all and I'll kill the pair of ye.* And to his astonishment, they gently put their heels to their horses, and passed on up the lane in silence.

44

He halted not from that headlong course until he left neither plain, nor field, nor bare mountain, nor bog, nor thicket, nor marsh, nor hill, nor hollow, nor dense-sheltering wood.

—The Frenzy of Suibhne

Moriarty had been halfway round the world and back, but the two days he spent trying to rejoin the retreating British Army easily counted for the longest journey he'd made in his whole life. By the time he'd escaped from the ruin of the Munsters at Étreux he reckoned that the rest of the army had a full day's head start on him, and with the Germans on their heels they'd be moving as fast as they could. There were a whole big lot of them, though, and that meant that when they were spotted by German cavalry they could keep on marching, and let their rearguard cavalry exchange a few shots if it came to it. They certainly wouldn't all have to run and hide under a hedge, which was something that Moriarty was obliged to do every time he heard hoofbeats on the road. That was another thing: the army was using the roads, which, as Moriarty knew from the wringing journey up to Mons, were mostly arrow-straight. He couldn't afford the luxury of the main roads now, and was wary even of the winding lanes, so all in all he was travelling a slower and more roundabout route than the men he so desperately wanted to catch up with.

His sense of direction wasn't up to much, but the sun kept on shining so he always had a notion of which way was south. When dark came he found a good road heading where he wanted to be so he chanced it. He felt he was making good time until he heard sounds that might have been Germans, and legged it into the fields. After that it wasn't long before he lost his way and was forced to stop until dawn. He wished he'd paid a bit more attention on the road up. Then the signposts might be a bit of use to him. As it was, all he knew was that Paris was in the right direction, and he wasn't finding any signposts pointing to Paris.

He was wary about approaching houses, but sometimes he'd turn a corner and be in someone's yard, or if he saw the house in good time he'd be faced with the choice between a long detour or the possibility of hospitality and refreshment. This was hardly deserted country, but people tended to bolt their doors at the appearance of a foreign soldier. If the armies hadn't been up this road then the locals would have had no opportunity as of yet to tell British greenish-brown from German greenish-grey, and anyone who might have been conversant with the English language did not seem to recognise it when it was plaintively shouted in a Cork accent.

Then there were the farm dogs. Moriarty was a city boy and he hated farmers and their dogs and the nasty territorial temperament that both shared. One particular beast came out from under a fence with speedy fury and tried to rip the arse off him, and Moriarty had to be handy with his rifle butt. He never met the dog's owner, and was in no mood to either. Thereafter, whenever his approach set a dog barking his throat tightened and his heart was set hammering.

Only twice was he given succour by his French allies, and that was a grand thing altogether. He got the impression from one old doll that he could have stayed for as long as he liked and even inherited her farm when she died, but he was nervous about staying in the one place. In his mind he kept on seeing those German horsemen with their long lances, and as soon as his belly and his haversack were full, and his feet bathed and not quite so sore, he was on his way again, out the back way and over the wall into the fields.

He walked all the way through Friday and Saturday, but he didn't know or care what day it was. The relief of getting alive out of Étreux had long since worn off, and most of his self-confidence with it. The periodic frights and alarms were wearing him down, and there was no lonelier soldier in all of France. He'd been in the army seven years and this was the first time he didn't have someone to talk to. He'd left his chums in Rangoon, and in Tralee, and now in Étreux. He'd left them and now there was no one to go back to. The Munster Fusiliers were all gone, and maybe the whole army was gone now, and there was just him, an orphan who couldn't even speak the language. Private Francis Moriarty, the last of the Dirty Shirts, tramping the roads with stubble on his face and his buttons dull. A sorry relict of a once proud regiment.

It was late in the day and the sun was level in his eyes, so that meant he was going the wrong way. But that was the way the path was going and he just didn't have it in him any more to strike out across country. He'd follow this path to what looked like a gap in the hedge up ahead, and then maybe he'd be able to see what was what. There were little flies darting around his head, so what with the annoyance they gave him he wasn't keeping as sharp a lookout as he should have been. He came to the gap, and beyond there was the road again, and square in the middle of the road was a horseman. Moriarty squinted, stupefied with tiredness and surprise, and couldn't see a lance in the horseman's hand. The man was the neatest, cleanest human being that he had seen since the retreat began. With his precisely wound puttees and his still-glossy leather, and the neat red cover to his still-stiffened cap, the horseman's appearance was crisper even than the Coldstream Guards with whom the Munsters had been brigaded. He was a military policeman, and British.

'Who are you, soldier?' he asked Moriarty, as if the fusilier were just another soldier, instead of a man who had walked alone out of the land of the dead.

'Munster Fusiliers,' Moriarty answered, with a voice that belonged to a man he'd forgotten.

'Two hundred yards beyond the crossroads,' said the redcap. 'You'll find them somewhere on your left.'

'Find who?' said Moriarty.

'The Munsters,' said the redcap tersely. 'And you'd best hurry along.'

'What?' said Moriarty.

The redcap pointed. 'Crossroads. Keep going straight on two hundred yards. Field on your left. Got that? And put some *juldi* into it. You'll be moving out directly.' And then he was talking to some ragged bunch of Gloucesters who were suddenly crowding up behind Moriarty, telling them where to find their battalion and to keep on moving, smartly now.

And Moriarty looked at them and saw more soldiers coming up along the road behind them, and he peered down the road beyond the redcap's horse and he saw in the reddening light more men yet, scattered along the verge, or trudging along, and he could see horses and guns and ambulances too, and here was the whole army it seemed, and he had found them. He walked to the crossroads, and saw men in all the fields about, and he went on a hundred yards, two, hurrying now, and looking at the men he passed. Their faces were all the same – blank and grimy – but Moriarty wasn't really seeing their faces. And then there it was: the grenade still flaming on the front of a cap, a brass badge not yet given away as a souvenir. He could hardly have made out any detail, but he knew that there was a tiger on that badge, and on the buttons, because that was Whelan grinning at him.

'Jesus! Well would you look who it isn't!' said Whelan with delight.

Moriarty flopped down beside him. He wanted to say something offhand and clever. He wanted to break down and weep on Whelan's shoulder.

'You'd never have a fag on you?' he asked.

45

Boots, ankle, Pairs 1, Approx. weight: 4 lbs
Socks when taken off should be stretched, well shaken, and placed on the opposite feet when next worn. Where the socks fit over the tender parts of the feet they should be greased inside.

—Field Service Pocket Book, 1914

On the day before the Munsters were destroyed at Étreux, II Corps fought a battle at Le Cateau, long since vacated by Sir John French's headquarters. The battle was fought in defiance of orders, but the corps commander knew that if he did not halt the retreat for a while at least, and allow the formations under his command to regain some sort of cohesion, then the corps was in grave danger of disintegrating just from straggling. In effect, then, the Battle of Le Cateau was fought by men who were too tired to march, and found it marginally easier to fight. Eight thousand of them were lost that day, but II Corps escaped annihilation and the German advance was momentarily halted. For the survivors, the retreat recommenced that very night. They had fought the battle as they had fought three days earlier at Mons, which is to say that they had waited in their shallow trenches for the enemy to come at them, but that hardly constituted a rest. So, a forced march up to Mons last week, a battle on Sunday, a harried retreat, another battle on the Wednesday, and the retreat keeping on for another week more. And through it all the weather remained glorious.

It was too hot for anything, but the men marched. They dumped their packs, with or without orders. They left behind spades and entrenching tools and greatcoats. Being given so little time to sleep they abandoned blankets too. Khaki serge was often subjected to radical alteration with jack knives, with sleeves and trouser legs cut away and tunics sometimes discarded altogether. Men who had lost their caps wore handkerchiefs, knotted at all four corners, on their heads, so that some units with their bared knees and chests gave the impression of a brutish seaside outing gone horribly wrong.

Sensible men knew better than to take their boots off when the rare chance was presented them. Feet momentarily freed from stiff leather swelled up, and after that a man had to cut away the seams of his boots to get them on again. Many, of course, could not march at all. The older men, grown soft on reserve, were marching in new boots, not three weeks out of stores, and hardly pliable or moulded to the shape of the foot yet. Men staggered along as they could, perhaps mercifully numb to the pain, and where they could not, they could be seen forlorn on the roadside, lost to the army and to themselves. Some were lucky enough to find space in an ambulance, but luck was relative when a man was in such pitiable shape that his socks had to be removed under general anaesthetic.

With the entire British Expeditionary Force thrown into reverse, things that usually came forward, like the rations, were now going backward, and away from the men they were meant for. Some units subsisted throughout the retreat on whatever they carried on them, but iron rations tended to be carried in packs and when packs were dumped it was by men who were beyond caring about the contents. If a man kept his tobacco on him, then the diet of nothing beyond a few biscuits didn't hurt quite as much. The army was generous with its tobacco, but the ration scale had been drawn up in consideration of an army of pipe smokers. They were still somewhat behindhand when it came to this new fad for cigarette smoking. Thus, when men were lucky to come across supplies of tobacco, they seldom had any papers in which to roll it.

For those who were awake enough to see them, the roads south abounded in riches. The Army Service Corps, pushed ahead by the retreat and unable to bring the supplies to the fighting men, had left quantities of food for the hungry soldiers to help themselves to. Army biscuit was indestructible, but tinned beef did not respond well to being left in the sun for hours or even days.

'Oh Jesus, but that's disgusting,' said Moriarty,

He had peeled open a tin only to have pink salted meat, warm and liquid, spill out over his hand and part of the way inside his sleeve.

'Oh Christ, but that's only horrible. I'm not eating that.'

'What's gone wrong with it?' asked Whelan.

'Sure all the fat has only gone and melted in the sun,' said Moriarty. He tipped the tin and let the mess dribble out and splash on the paving. 'Aw, look at that. I'm not eating that.'

'Open another one,' said Whelan. 'maybe it's just that one that's gone bad.'

'Sure they've all been lying out in the sun,' said Moriarty, but he picked up another tin anyway. It was the same as the first.

'Here you two!' shouted a sergeant. 'Hurry along now.'

Whelan, who had not enjoyed the brief French hospitality afforded to Moriarty on his way to rejoin the army, thought he'd chance the pink mess, and with a grimace he held the lip of the can to his mouth and slurped. He wiped his chin on his cuff.

'It's not as bad as it looks,' he said, but not very convincingly. 'Salty as bejesus, mind. Is there any water?'

Moriarty scanned the impromptu supply dump. 'Not that I can see,' he said.

'Ah bollocks. Now he tells me.'

The army-issue water bottle carried a quart, but that didn't go far in weather like this. In India or Africa a strict water discipline would be enforced, but everyone was too tired and too scattered to worry about such niceties, and sure wasn't a grand green country like this bound to have plenty of water? But unless there was a well directly by the roadside, then the answer to that question seemed to be no. No man was going to leave the line of march to look for water. He feared losing touch with his comrades, or his officer feared losing yet another man who, once out of sight, might well succumb to the temptation to sleep. So you hoped for a village with a pump or a fountain, and you hoped to get there soon, and if that didn't happen you prayed for a river or stream. In any case, when you found whatever you found, you elbowed your way into a press and, cheek by jowl with horses and mules and men, you sucked in as much as you could, and never gave a thought to the risks of dysentery or what have you.

The sergeant shouted at them again to hurry up, but he didn't put any heart in it, and he might well have left them and forgotten them after that if they hadn't stumbled and trotted to catch up. They didn't particularly know this sergeant. He hadn't even been in their company. Until the other day he was just one of the busy NCOs who'd been hustling the newly expanded battalion into some sort of order fit for active service. Now he was practically the second in command. In charge was Lieutenant Musgrave, and him they didn't know either. He was a twenty-two-year-old platoon commander and a decent enough sort as far as anyone could tell. From the ranks he appeared to be just another of those almost indistinguishable young men of good family that Sandhurst stamped out in lots every year. Now, to all intents and purposes, Lieutenant Musgrave commanded the Royal Munster Fusiliers.

It was not a command, though. Musgrave had merely inherited the name and the relics of the battalion. He and his men were no more the Munster Fusiliers than sailors clinging to a raft were the ship that had foundered. The Munsters were gone – dead in the orchard in Étreux. True, there was a 1st Battalion out in Burma still, and the various reserve elements in Ireland wearing the tiger on their buttons, but to the men who had come to fight in France, 2nd Battalion had been the regiment and the world. And now that was gone. Not reduced, but gone.

When the straggled handfuls of escapees of Étreux collected themselves on the day after the fight, their numbers were so few and their battalion organisation so shattered that the Munsters were, without a second thought from higher command, struck off the order of battle. If the 1st Brigade of the 1st Division of I Corps was again called upon to fight, the Munsters would not march with them. Musgrave and his men were now classed as 'army troops', as opposed to troops integral to any brigade or division or corps. They were to be no more than a collection of odd-job men for whom the army might find work – if ever, that was, this retreat ended and a sufficient level of organisation could be imposed. Until then they were assigned, in the mind of the general staff, to the army's growing heap of broken bits and spare parts.

When Moriarty found Whelan and the rest, he thought for a moment that he'd found his way home, but he quickly learned that all he'd found was another band of orphans as lost as himself. Besides the lad Whelan, the only one of his mates to have made it this far was Moyle. The other depot men who'd come with him from Tralee were all gone.

'Even Harrington?' asked Moriarty, even though he'd never liked Harrington or his smart mouth too much.

'He was wounded not long after we crossed the canal. It wasn't too bad, but there was no way of getting him out of there. The Germans'll have him now.'

'Balcombe was still fighting fit when last I saw him,' said Moyle. 'He's a tough bastard. He might traipse in yet like yourself, Moriarty.'

'That's right,' said Whelan. 'Sure we thought you were a goner for certain yourself and here you are and not a bother on you.'

'What about Lynch?' asked Moyle. 'There's another tough fella for you.'

'Not tough enough,' Moriarty told them. 'He was down in the grass with a big red hole in his face when I saw him last.'

'Ah God rest him,' said Moyle philosophically. 'There's a fucker I wouldn't have thought you'd have been able to kill at all.'

And more names were recalled, and after they were called to their feet, and formed up and marched off, the three of them stuck together in the column, and each man spoke of what he remembered of the fight at Étreux, and what he himself had done. But as the day wore out, and night brought no halt, the conversation trailed off.

When the next day came, no man wanted to speak much. They were given no more than a couple of hours just after dawn, and though everyone slept like the dead, no one felt the better for it. Everything hurt so much worse when a man was tired. Every sense was dulled except pain. Every chafing strap and every rub of coarse cloth against sunburnt skin weakened a man's spirit further. The air was heavy with the road's dust, and the little flies swarmed about the men's faces. The roads were paved with stone setts, which gave no comfort to the feet. After a while it felt as if each step was hammering the hot little hobnails upwards into the tender sole of the foot. They took whatever roads they were told, and sometimes they were halted without being told why, and were forced to stand waiting for the road to be cleared of whatever it was causing the delay. Sometimes they were obliged to take long detours without reason, and sometimes they even had to retrace their steps. There was no rest, no water, no cheer.

The next day was worse, and the day after that worse yet. It was only discipline that was keeping them going, or maybe just habit. Moriarty saw a sergeant major of another regiment march by. The man had his unsheathed bayonet tucked upside-down into his belt, with the hilt held tight under the belt buckle and the point right under the man's chin. It was clear that any time the sergeant major's head drooped he'd get a sharp reminder to get his chin up. There was professionalism for you, thought Moriarty. There was regimental pride. Then again, he reflected some time later, he might have dreamed up the whole spectacle.

Men were imagining all sorts after a few days without sleep.

'Ah look at that,' said Moyle one time, his face all lit up.

'Look at what?' asked Moriarty, for diversion if nothing else. He raised his tired eyes to follow Moyle's gaze.

'Ah isn't that grand,' said Moyle. 'Isn't that lovely.' But he never said what it was he was seeing.

There was a pronounced camber on the French roads, to allow water to run off quickly, and Moriarty's particular hallucination was that he was not walking along a road at all, but along the curved top of a very high wall, and it was all he could do to keep his balance.

Whelan jostled into him and he nearly fell. 'Keep in, keep in, for the love of Christ,' he said to Whelan, and sidestepped unsteadily into the centre of the road. If Whelan even heard him he didn't show it. The boy's legs were still working but he seemed dead asleep.

While the men on the roads could only see the road, or the visions that crowded their exhausted minds, the picture on the map was clearer – less nightmarish, but just as alarming.

What happened was that three large German armies had rolled down on one medium-sized French Army, to the left of which was the rather small British Expeditionary Force. The British could boast that they had held their ground at Mons, which was true enough, but there was the implication that they could be holding that ground still if French Fifth Army had not fallen back, exposing the British flank and compelling a general retreat. The fact was that the four-and-a-bit divisions of the BEF, even while they were being steadily reinforced, could hardly have stood for long against the fourteen divisions of German First Army, no matter how wickedly skilful the British Tommy was with his rifle. They had to go back or be swamped.

But a retreat is something more easily said than done. There is the simple problem, for instance, of roads, and how a division on the march – even one that's been knocked about a bit – will take up near on fifteen miles of road. Add to that the ideal eight miles that were desired between the retreating British and the advancing Germans, and then look at a map of northern France just to see exactly how much road space is available. The Germans were not going to stand back and allow their enemies to arrange themselves into fifteen-mile-long columns of march, nor did the map present any neat system of parallel roads running due south. Roads branched and converged and wandered in between, and all of them had to be made use of if the army was to hold together. Keeping the retreat moving and not turning into collapse; keeping the army functioning as an army: these were the concerns that ensured that the staff officers, like the marching men, had to go without sleep. In the confusion that was always on the point of dissolving into chaos, it was lucky chance that reunited Moriarty with his mates, and no wonder at all that Fitzmullen-Brophy and his men never did manage to find their parent regiment.

And above the tangled logistical concerns there was strategy, for the British could not allow themselves to lose contact with the French, lest the allies be separately overwhelmed and destroyed in detail. And above strategy came politics, because if the British were fighting for the survival of the army and for national honour, the French were fighting for France, in the most immediate sense. A British disintegration, or even disengagement, would open the German way to Paris.

And all these problems came to rest on the shoulders of Field Marshal Sir John Denton Pinkstone French, commanding British Expeditionary Force. Sir John was a small man with a love of horses and a taste for tall women. Even at the age of sixty-one he retained the reputation for being an improvident, womanising Irishman, and it was all justified, except possibly the Irish bit, since despite his proud Irish ancestry he had been born and bred in England. He had done well in the Sudan and then made his name in South Africa, when the army discovered that it needed more cavalry than it actually had. Any cavalry commander who didn't muck things up too horribly was bound to have his career advanced. By 1914 he possessed the supreme qualification of seniority and, with the few men even more senior being too old or too grand, the job of taking the army to France was given to him.

And now he was watching that army fall apart. His headquarters in those days were in a succession of oppressively hot rooms in requisitioned buildings, each one further south than the last, where he sweated in his shirtsleeves and absorbed reports of sacrificial rearguard actions, misfortunes, and downright blunders. The 2nd Munsters were far from being the only unit to have been lost on the retreat. And potentially worse than the various battalions and squadrons and batteries struck off the order of battle, there had been the shocking case of two infantry colonels who had been caught in the act of shamefully yielding up their weary battalions to the enemy. Energetic and timely intervention by an aggressive cavalry officer had prevented the surrender, but the high command dreaded that this might be a symptom of a rot in the heart of the army. To some it looked as if the rot might even have infected the field marshal.

The losses of Mons and Le Cateau weighed heavily on him. As the retreat continued he found himself less and less able to exercise control over his army. When he saw units reduced to less than half their strength by straggling, he gave the stragglers up as lost forever and thus saw his force dwindling towards extinction. And all the while, as Paris drew nearer, his allies were pressuring him to turn and fight, for the British to play their vital part in a battle where every last man would be counted. Johnny French was in his true element on the hunting field (and perhaps, as his detractors might have had it, in the divorce courts). Strategy and politics were overwhelming him. Relations with Général Joseph Jacques Césaire Joffre strained with immense difficulty across the linguistic gap. Général Joffre had never seen any reason to learn English, and Sir John, although he had lived in France once upon a time for the sole purpose of learning the language, had evidently thought that any accent other than an English one was suitable only for foreigners. In an atmosphere of misunderstanding and mistrust it hardly helped that the English general was an Irishman called French.

But Whitehall leaned on him and Kitchener sent strong communications to stiffen him. Reassurances were earnestly made to Britain's allies that Britain would stand firm. Unconvinced, but respectful of his superiors, Sir John finally agreed to halt the retreat and turn around.

By then it was too late. The British had retreated too far south to play a decisive role in the great battle that developed in early September. Maybe that was no bad thing: something like half a million men fell in less than a week's fighting on the Marne. But that battle turned the tide of the war. The halt of the BEF on the Seine also gave the stragglers time to catch up and for the army to pull itself together again.

And that was how, in the end, Fitzmullen-Brophy's commando rejoined the Munster Fusiliers.

46

For certain I am Suibhne Geilt,
One who sleeps under the shelter of a rag.

—The Frenzy of Suibhne

The Fitzmullen-Brophy Commando didn't have to lie low for very long. To prevent the men from being taken away from them, or possibly even sent home, a rapid change of address was thought necessary, but the billets in which they were quartered were already paid for by the army, whereas the two majors were low on cash by now and leery of making high-handed requisitions that would only attract the army's attention. This matter was still being debated when the army found them, but all the army did was tell them to stay put.

The word didn't even come from an officer of rank – at least not directly. What happened was that a messenger cycled up, asked for a Lieutenant Fleming, and handed over a communication that said, in effect, that the undersigned officer was too damn busy just now to worry about any vagabond Munsters, but they should make themselves ready to move all the same. Everything was in a state of flux of a sudden, and the Munsters had evidently slipped to the bottom of a long list of priorities. Of the Majors Belcher and Fitzmullen-Brophy, not a mention was made, neither then or thereafter. They had been dismissed from the minds of the gods at GHQ.

So they decided to hold on where they were and trust to luck, while news of the battle in Belgium was eagerly sought. Events were moving too fast for newspapers to record, and the village could not boast a single telephone, so they ended up doing precisely as they were told. They kept their gear packed and ready, and they sat around waiting. Belcher stayed mostly in the house the majors had chosen as a billet. He alternated between dozing and counting the hours to his next meal. Fitzmullen-Brophy tried not to fidget, and when that didn't work, he strode fruitlessly about the vicinity, never out of sight of the road, and always ready to hail any passing soldier, French or British, who might know what was afoot. He conducted an overly fussy inspection of the men, and throughout the day stuck his nose into the barn from time to time until they were sick of the sight of him. They slept, or pretended to be asleep when he appeared. In between they got Wyndham to tell them stories.

Fleming was at an utterly loose end. Mooching probably constituted conduct unbecoming an officer and a gentleman, but he mooched anyway. He didn't quite have the imagination to be bored, but he didn't enjoy feeling so bally useless.

On Monday night, and still no news, Dwyer and Robinson sneaked out to a local estaminet and got drunk, which in itself wasn't too great a sin. They were old soldiers with an astonishing head for drink and the unconscious good sense to know when enough was enough. But a few of the younger men went with them, and drank French wine like it was beer, even though a couple of them shouldn't even have been drinking beer. They were in disgusting condition the next morning, and relations with the locals were a little strained. With everyone on edge about the German invasion, they were not feeling warm about drunken English brutes loose in the street. Someone had been insulted. A window had been broken. Fitzmullen-Brophy went to soothe and mollify, while Fleming had his first experience of company orders, presided over by Belcher. Pack drill didn't seem like a clever punishment if a man might be called upon to march soon, and forfeiture of pay made little sense if no one was being paid, nor proper pay records being kept, but Tummy Belcher was a traditionalist when it came to discipline. Thus the offenders, pitifully sick, were set to drilling in full kit, poorer by a shilling a day for the next week.

By Tuesday afternoon the rest of the men were scattered around the locality in twos and threes, seeing what they could see and seeing what they could scrounge. Fleming had the devil of a time getting them together again when the word finally came. Pick up. Fall in. Move out.

'Retreat?' demanded Belcher.

'Apparently,' said Fitzmullen-Brophy, equally perplexed and indignant.

'Are we to believe that we've lost the battle?'

'Not from what I heard. Our fellows did splendidly. It was the French that let us down. Flank's in the air, you know. No option but to fall back.'

'Blasted Frogs.'

'Quite.'

'Still, you know – it's always the way.'

'How's that, old man?'

'We always lose the opening round of any war.'

'Why now that you mention it, Tummy, I believe you're dead right. South Africa. Made an awful mess of that at the start.'

'Exactly. Same in the Crimea. Same against Napoleon. Same in the Sudan, for that matter. Let Gordon get killed.'

'True, true,' said Fitzmullen-Brophy, frowning. 'Why is that, I wonder? Not Gordon, of course. The other thing.'

'British character, old boy. We're a placid sort of race – not some gaggle of impulsive foreigners. Takes a deal to provoke us. The other side always gets to land a few punches while we're coming up to scratch. But we always thrash 'em in the end, what?'

'Right you are, Tummy.'

'Take your German. Been positively twitching to start this war for Lord knows how long. Drilling endlessly in Potsdam and gnashing his teeth at us. And what have we been doing? Idling. Just toddling along. The amateur tradition, FitzEm. We're the gentlemen and they're the players, forever practising. And now the game's begun we have to get warmed up, get our eye in, and watch the score mount in their favour while we do it, eh?'

'Precisely.'

'But we'll thrash 'em in the end. You mark my words.'

He said as much later on, when the two old friends parted company. Belcher would not be joining in the retreat – at least not on his feet. The canny old soldier was already learning the tricks of this newfangled sort of war. Instead of trying to bully motorists into taking him where he needed to go, he merely flagged down a passing motor lorry, jovially enquired where it might be bound, and asked if he might be given a lift. This one was going south, and that was good enough for him. He had his gear hefted into the back and heaved himself up into the cab, wrapped in his greatcoat, and with his flask handy. He extended his hand to Fitzmullen-Brophy and wished him the best of luck. It was an uncommonly sentimental gesture from the man.

'See you whenever the retreat stops, FitzEm.'

'Yes. One wonders where that might be.'

'Corunna,' said Belcher, and then barked with laughter. 'Corunna! And even if that's where we end up we'll still give them a damned good hiding! Goodbye, FitzEm, and good luck. Drive on, driver.'

Fitzmullen-Brophy's men were swept up in the forward edge of the retreat, so although they marched, and marched hard for days on end, they were spared the worst of it. Not for them the jams and confusion, or the fear of German cavalry at their backs. Furthermore, they were well rested when the retreat began, and never having made it up to Belgium in the first place, they had something of a comfortable head start and less distance to travel. A few men did drop out, and a deal of kit was surreptitiously dropped along the road, but the men who finally fell out when the halt came on the banks of the Seine were, in their commander's view, better men for the experience. Their faces were brown and the soles of their feet hardened to leather. Some of the younger men were looking older, and consequently more manly and soldier-like. When it came to the deficiencies of uniform, their rather shabby appearance was not nearly as bad as some. They may not have fired a single shot between them yet, but they looked like men on active service.

Fitzmullen-Brophy was proud of them. He was quite pleased with himself too, even though he had been unable, in the end, to finish the retreat on foot. Two days into it he had been presented with a horse. There were a lot of officers' chargers going spare because a lot of officers who had gone to Mons would not be coming back. Majors, and particularly majors of Fitzmullen-Brophy's vintage, rode, so some sergeant placed in charge of spare mounts, and not caring for the responsibility, simply offered Fitzmullen-Brophy a horse with as little fuss as he would have made in giving up his seat on the bus to the old boy. Fitzmullen-Brophy was a little hurt to be thought weak, but a horse like that was well in keeping with his dignity and, if he were to be honest with himself, he was feeling just a little run down. Once in the saddle he realised how close to the end of his endurance he had been. At the next halt he had to be lifted down, and once they were safely across the Seine he was put to bed and didn't wake up for a night and half a day.

Somewhere Johnny French was having a screaming match with Kitchener's and Joffre's representatives over the desperate and urgent need to commit the BEF to battle, but at the same moment all that concerned Fitzmullen-Brophy was that he was still pleasurably dizzy from so much sleep, and was enjoying a quantity of jolly decent coffee, even it was, for some unaccountable reason, served in a bowl.

Wyndham, who had arranged the quarters and established a good relationship with Madame, had fallen into the role of major's orderly. He had been so roughened by his experiences these last weeks and months that now he did not think it in the least way servile or demeaning to concern himself with another man's laundry. The major's shirts needed attending to, and that was just another of the necessary facts of this new open-air life, like latrine pits and stiff socks.

Fitzmullen-Brophy didn't care to see his American protégé acting as a mere officer's servant – that was no task for a gentleman volunteer – but he did see the benefit of having someone to talk to Madame in her own language and see to the provision of clean linen. But a clean shirt did not make the man, and Madame did not quite understand gentlemen's collars.

'Wyndham,' said Fitzmullen-Brophy, 'I believe I will go and visit the barber. Tell Mister Fleming that I will come looking for him in an hour, and you might as well tell the men that there will be a kit inspection at…' – he cast about for his watch, 'Oh I don't know – say just before teatime.'

'Very good, sir.'

'And I really should find out what the general situation is too – with the war and whatnot. I dare say the higher-ups won't be troubling us any more about our irregularities. Need every man they can get now, I'll warrant. All hands to the pumps and all that sort of thing.'

He buckled on his belt and straightened his cap. His Sam Browne could certainly do with a polish, but that wasn't Wyndham's job.

'Capital coffee. My compliments to Madame.'

He found a post office and wrote a brief note home to his wife, and the postmistress helpfully directed him to where he thought he wanted to go, although 'coiffeur' sounded rather too foppish for his requirements. He didn't want to come out with his moustache curled, or him reeking of scent like some Frenchified pimp. One heard stories about foreigners, you know. Thank heavens the place, when he found it, was discreet and civilised, and indeed already patronised by several British officers.

After he'd been attended to in a manner that would almost have done credit to an English establishment, Fitzmullen-Brophy saw that an officer having his boots cleaned was dozing under a newspaper and that the paper was *The Daily Sketch*, and apparently not very old. He would never have dreamed of doing such a thing at home, but this was war, and he touched the officer on the sleeve and asked if he might have a look. The voice underneath the paper rumbled that it was a damned rag and only good enough for keeping off the sun, so please do, and there was a rustling disturbance of newsprint and emerging from it was none other than Tummy Belcher.

'Tummy!'

Belcher squinted. 'FitzEm. Fancy meeting you here. Keeping well, I hope?'

'All the better for seeing you, old boy! This is perfectly splendid! What have you been up to?'

'Making myself useful, matter of fact. Lines of communication. Kept damnably busy, I can tell you.'

'All hands to the pumps, old fellow.'

'Too true. Not a permanent job, thank God. Chuck it in a minute when the regiment turns up.'

'Any news of the regiment, Tummy? We haven't heard a bally thing in an age.'

Belcher shifted in his chair so he was more or less upright and looking his old comrade in the eye.

'Bad news, I'm afraid,' he said.

Somewhere to the north the engineers were blowing the bridges across the Marne, and the rearguard were staggering on through the last heart-scalding miles of the retreat. In the pleasant little barbershop on the Seine, Fitzmullen-Brophy felt the clouds of war blotting out the sun that had been brightening his soul.

'Gone?' he said, with such emotion that the white-jacketed Frenchman who come to attend to his boots looked up in polite inquiry. 'The whole battalion?'

'Near as dammit,' affirmed Belcher sadly. 'Or so I gather. The usual odds and ends came out all right. A few cooks and transport men and so forth. Fighting men, though? Hardly any, I'm afraid. A hundred perhaps? Maybe more. I expect that there are more that will turn up in time, but HQ has given the whole show up as lost. Battalion's gone. Army troops for the time being. Or corps troops. Same thing really.'

He could see that Fitzmullen-Brophy was taking the news as a bereavement, which was only proper, one supposed, so long as a fellow didn't get hysterics or some such. The thing to do in these situations was to keep talking. Murmur the correct sentiments. Soften the blow. Pour on the balm, or whatever it is one does with balm.

But for all that, Fitzmullen-Brophy was bereft. He was a British officer and a Munster Fusilier. He was facing up to the practicalities. The battalion was gone, but there was a remnant, and those few men represented the battalion's legacy, with Fitzmullen-Brophy as the next of kin and thus sole beneficiary. To inherit command as a consequence of such calamity was a rotten way of getting what one wanted, but this wasn't a bequest that could be turned down either. The important thing now was to ensure that some uncaring outsider wasn't made caretaker of the surviving Munsters. That should not present too great a problem. The army was desperately short of everything, particularly officers, and when it came to the matter of the copybook blotted on the road to Le Cateau, Belcher rather thought that he had smoothed things out quite a bit.

Belcher's years in Tralee had distanced him from the other players in the army game, but the enforced intimacies and casual collisions of the past few weeks had done much to remedy that. Indeed, Belcher reflected that he'd have had to attend every hunt and race meeting the length and breadth of the United Kingdom to meet a wider and richer assortment of His Majesty's officers. But here? Couldn't help running into familiar faces at every turn, he told Fitzmullen-Brophy.

'Remember old Beano Hetherington?' he asked.

Fitzmullen-Brophy searched his memory a moment. 'Yorkshire Light Infantry, wasn't he? And a wicked spin-bowler as I recall.'

'Not that good a bowler, but a keen sportsman all the same,' said Belcher. 'He's in the Adjutant General's branch now, but not the sort to be hidebound by petty regulation. Not much he wouldn't do for an old Dirty Shirt in distress. I don't think we need to worry any more about that unpleasantness with the provost marshal.'

'Well thank heavens for that. Well done, Tummy.'

'And remember Auntie Anstruther?'

'Old Auntie! Why I haven't seen him since Bloemfontein in '01. He here too?'

'In the QMG, old boy. Got me my present job, don't you know. At the very least he'll turn a blind eye to the few requisitions we might need to make good any equipment deficiencies. Have you seen the state of some of the men trailing in? Shocking poor show.'

'I'll send you round a list of the few things we might want. Jolly well done indeed,' said Fitzmullen-Brophy. That was the ticket. That was the old army stuff. Officers finding their feet, staying calm in the face of disaster, and making good the damage.

Men like Tummy and all the old India and Africa hands. Men like himself for that matter. That was why they were going to win this war.

First things first though – finding the poor broken 2nd Battalion was something that needed to be attended to right away.

'Look here, Tummy – you don't happen to know where they might have fetched up?'

'Hard to say, old man. Could take some finding in all this ballyhoo. I'll come with you, of course. I should be able to get us a car.'

And he was as good as his word. Fitzmullen-Brophy hastened back to his billet to put young Fleming in the know, and he had hardly done that when Belcher pulled up in the back of an imposing Rolls-Royce touring car.

'All above board,' he assured. 'Just need to have the contraption back by tonight. Hop in.'

So with the two majors seated in comfortable state in the back, and Wyndham riding up front beside the driver, they set out along the byroads of the Seine in search of the wreckage of the Munster Fusiliers.

The British Expeditionary Force was scattered all over, but wherever one looked, it presented no more than a sorry sight. Enough units had held together, and maintained enough discipline, that this was still an army, but the majors could not help but reflect that it looked more like a rabble. Soldiers were sparked out asleep in haystacks and under trees, and anywhere that wasn't too unyielding or too in the way. Unshaven, dirty, and so often ragged, they looked like heavily armed tramps for the most part, but what dismayed the majors was the attitude of some of the troops still awake.

'Did you see that? Did you?' demanded Belcher. 'That idle beggar saw us, I tell you! He looked directly at us and he didn't salute! He did not salute, damn it!'

'Oh leave it be, Tummy.'

'No, sir! That's the second time it's happened. I will not tolerate slackness, FitzEm. Driver, stop!'

'Drive on, driver. It's too late to go back now, Tummy. I do sympathise, but we really don't have the time.'

Wyndham was relieved that Fitzmullen-Brophy had his way. The soldiers that gave sullen looks and refrained from saluting still had rifles. Let Major Belcher grumble all he likes, he thought, but please don't pick fights with men who have just marched two hundred miles and have their collars open. He had marched many of those same miles himself, and he knew that if some choleric officer, well-fed and shiny, descended from the great height of his expensive automobile to tell him to smarten himself up, he would feel aggrieved. If he'd gone through what some of these men had endured, that grievance against well-upholstered authority might justifiably manifest itself as something that looked like the French Revolution. So drive on, Major. Pretend you didn't see anything.

In the midst of dissolution there were still traces of order. In contrast to the rest of the ragamuffin army that disposed of itself wherever it halted, here in one field that might have been on the Salisbury Plain for its neatness, there were pitched lines of bell tents, gleaming white. They only found it because the driver was looking for a place to turn. A somewhat dishevelled staff captain with a brassard on his sleeve and a clipboard under his arm was coming out of the field into the lane, correctly closing the gate behind him because one always closes gates behind one in the country.

'I say! Captain!' hailed Fitzmullen-Brophy.

The man looked up as if he had been slapped. His face was drawn and his eyes red-rimmed. He blinked at the major and his little motoring party. He saluted, but the correctness of the salute was at odds with the furious look on his face. Slapped and laughed at.

'Yes?' he rasped. Just give him one reason – just one.

Fitzmullen-Brophy had been dealing with over-strained chaps all afternoon, so he kept his voice soothing, but this fellow really did seem in need of a lie-down – in some nice private hospital for preference.

'I was wondering if you might know where we'd find the Second Munsters,' said Fitzmullen-Brophy, with his gentlest and friendliest smile.

'Second Munsters, Major?' said the staff-wallah, his voice cracking with what sounded like outrage. 'Why *yes*. Matter of fact, Major, you should find them in those tents there,' and he whipped out his clipboard and rattled out any further information the major might find helpful, '…along with various elements of the 2nd South Staffords, 2nd Worcesters, and 1st King's Liverpool, sir.' His cheek was twitching all the while, and a line of spittle was beginning to run from the corner of his mouth. Fitzmullen-Brophy tactfully ignored it.

'Why that is fortunate, what? Very kind of you, Captain. Much obliged.'

'Why not at all, Major,' said the man with bitter sarcasm. 'And might it be too much to request you gentlemen to close the blasted gate behind you?' And with that he snapped to attention and held a quivering salute for a good five seconds longer than was proper or comfortable, before turning on a wobbly heel and stalking off at speed. Belcher took in this blackly comic turn with an astonished look, while Fitzmullen-Brophy nudged him in the ribs, repeating, 'Let it go, Tummy.'

The army's standard circular tent was designed to shelter fifteen men at a time in no particular comfort, and if everyone was on the thin side and too tired to care, then you could probably squeeze as many as twenty inside. The sleepers were arrayed in radial fashion with their feet toward the tent pole. Clothing and personal effects doubled as pillows, and boots, if they were taken off at all, were usually placed in the centre where many a wise old soldier used them for basic sanitation. A man who pissed in his boots was spared from negotiating sleeping comrades and guy ropes in the dark, and he enjoyed the added benefit of boots made supple by what was euphemistically referred to as the 'sweet pea' method.

So that was the smell that greeted Wyndham as he poked his head through each tent flap – chamber pots and feet and the combined breath of fifteen or more men who hadn't cleaned their teeth or themselves in weeks, and all of it warmed by the sun beating down on the canvas. No wonder everyone smoked tobacco in this army, he thought. If he had a cigarette to hand he'd have started the habit there and then just to mask the smell.

He held his breath and peered through the shade at badges. He wouldn't have known any of the men of 2nd Battalion at the best of times, and here in the dim light the faces were indistinct under hair and dirt, and either gaunt or puffy with extreme fatigue. So he looked for the bursting grenade instead, although he knew too well how this campaign had dealt with buttons and cap badges. He caught a glimpse of brass under one man's head. The first time that happened he was at a loss as to how to go about getting a closer look, but by the third tent he just reached in, and pushed the man's head to one side, murmuring, 'I beg your pardon, mate.' It sounded wrong, but out of all the military vocabulary of British and Irish troops, 'mate' was universal and inoffensive, and Wyndham was making himself accustomed to its use. The man groaned as his cap was pulled out from under him, but that was all. The badge was a Staffordshire knot, and the cap was returned with no more gentleness than was necessary.

Fitzmullen-Brophy was going down another line of tents, and positively tiptoeing. Belcher, as usual, stayed in the car.

He thought it improper for an officer to wake sleeping soldiers. It wasn't any fastidiousness on his part, or a precious regard for his rank, but he felt that a man was put at a disadvantage if he was woken up by someone he was expected to salute. Bad form. What if he'd a bad head on him? Man just woken up might say something prejudicial to discipline. Wouldn't do.

With his paternal instinct it was Fitzmullen-Brophy who recognised his own, and he looked smilingly down on them in silence as they snored and farted in oblivious promiscuity on the tent floor. He held up one hand to signal his find, although he could have shouted for all he was worth, and called up the drums and bugles too if he wanted much of a chance of waking them. Wyndham caught the gesture and abandoned his own search. A dirty figure coming out of another tent saw it too. He was dressed in his underclothes and still three parts asleep, and he padded across the beaten grass in his grimy bare feet, one hand rubbing his bearded jaw and the other scratching his backside. He looked at Fitzmullen-Brophy as though he knew him from somewhere, and then he looked at Wyndham with the same expression. Wyndham would have had to go over and inspect the identity discs hanging on a greasy string around the man's neck if he wanted to put a name to him, but then the disgraceful spectre in filthy flannel spoke.

'Private Wyndham?' it asked, with a slack grin.

'Private Moriarty!' said Wyndham.

'So you found this Lieutenant Musgrave under a hedge along with another fifty-odd orphan babes and now you and your chum want to adopt them, correct?'

'I'm not sure I care for the way you put it, Beano old man, but that is pretty much the size of it,' admitted Belcher, a little testily. He was rather surprised that good old Hetherington, who'd always been such a sporting chap back in India, had become quite pernickity in his old age. Promotion had evidently hardened his arteries and dulled his spirit of adventure. All that Belcher wanted was *carte blanche* in the matter of taking command of what was left of the battalion, and here was his one-time comrade in arms looking as though he was making difficulties.

'Look, Tummy,' said Hetherington, 'I'll do what I can about that unpleasantness with the PM at GHQ, but don't think they've forgotten that you and Fitzmullen-Brophy should be back in Ireland by now, and keeping a damned low profile while you're there.'

'But that's bloody rot and you know it, man. They might have had a point a couple of weeks ago, but sending experienced officers home now is downright absurd. Have you seen the state of the army? Have you? Fellows not saluting, you know. Saw it myself. Never saw the like.'

'And you're proposing I should have a few of them shot?' Since joining the staff of the Adjutant General, Hetherington had become touchy about anyone else having views on discipline.

Belcher didn't notice the trace of sarcasm. 'Wouldn't do some of 'em any harm.' he said. 'But what I mean to say is that you shouldn't be turning away officers when more officers are exactly what you need. This Musgrave fellow seems to be the right sort – family from Tipperary, I believe, father in the Church – but he has too damn much on his shoulders and he's half played-out after this past fortnight.'

'All right then, Tummy – I'll tell you what. You do not – most emphatically *not* – get command of the battalion, and the same goes for Fitzmullen-Brophy. Clear? For a start you're just too damned unofficial and for another thing there isn't a battalion any more. The two of you can take charge of Musgrave's little party and you can tack on the lot you brought from Ireland. There's another remnant of the Munsters alive and well up towards Savigny, I believe, and you can jolly well keep your paws off them.'

'Can't say fairer than that, old man.'

'And another thing: anyone arrives to take over – and I don't care if he's a colonel from Tralee or a runny-nosed clerk from GHQ – *anyone* – and you damn well obey orders. Not your battalion. Not your show. Be sure to tell Fitzmullen-Brophy.'

Belcher grinned. 'Very white of you, Beano. Much obliged.'

'Remind me,' he said to Fitzmullen-Brophy outside, 'to send good old Beano a dozen of whiskey.'

'We've got it, Tummy? We've got it?'

Belcher took an appreciative sniff, catching the first coolness of autumn in the air. 'Pretty much, FitzEm. Up to a point at least.'

'Oh well done, old fellow! Jolly well done!'

'Nothing to it, old boy,' said Belcher, with no small degree of satisfaction. 'Now let's whip this unit into shape and go and fight the war, what?'

The war. The brief respite in the fields by the Seine was over far too soon. Hardly had the BEF halted than it was turned around and marched to the Marne where the Germans and the French were throwing every last man they had into the battle that must surely decide everything. In a struggle of this scale the British force amounted to little more than a drop in the bucket, but France was pleading for that very drop. The men in khaki were still in poor condition, but their short rest had done them some good, and the prospect of finally getting a crack at the enemy was putting heart into them.

Few were as heartened as Major Hugh Fitzmullen-Brophy, who was finally leading men into battle. His command was barely more than the size of a company as companies had been when last he took the field, and barely more than half the size of companies as they were instituted now, but he didn't care a fig. He was a man who had met his destiny. He was leading the Munsters to war and they were going to show the Germans what was what. Belcher drifted rearwards somewhat, which was all to the good, as it would have been awkward having two majors in charge of so small a unit, and there was the added benefit of Belcher's skills in acquiring all manner of useful things in his unofficial employment in the lines of communication. Before they marched, the grosser deficiencies in clothing had been addressed, and if they were still a woefully shabby lot, they would not be left naked to the autumn wind.

So the army marched north. No one had quite recovered from the hurts and privations of the retreat yet, but this was not such a hardship. There was none of the nerve-jangling exhaustion and the feeling of being driven from behind. No one was likely to feel an uhlan's lance in his back. Also, the march was slower and more considered. The Germans were somewhere just ahead, and units advanced with caution and stayed in close touch with each other. The Germans were somewhere just ahead, but – and for the first time since the retreat began – there was singing in the ranks. Their French allies sang stirring songs about the day of glory and the Sambre and Meuse. The British roared out the music-hall favourites of the day, and often they did not even rise to such cultural heights. When they were being creative they sang dirty ditties to the tune of well-known hymns. Mostly they sang of one man who went to mow. It was a sign of good morale, if undoubtedly monotonous, but that first morning the Munsters kept that song going until as many as twenty men (and their dog) had gone to mow a meadow, and only then did they get sick of it.

The next day was the red-letter day. They came upon a troop of cavalry, tired and grubby like all the rest of the army, but full of good news and grinning like cats who'd got the cream. Almost every man had, hanging from his saddle, a German helmet.

Fitzmullen-Brophy hailed their officer, who answered loud enough for everyone to hear. The Germans had turned tail!

This troop had seen it with their own eyes. The whole advance had just turned around and fallen back northwards, back across the Marne, and these men had been nipping at their heels.

'Fox killed in the open!' called the young cavalry officer, and hoisted a pickelhaube on the point of his sword for all to see. The Munsters raised a lusty cheer. Clearly the Germans didn't have the bottom for this war. That was foreigners all over, averred the older men who had seen the world. They didn't have the powers of endurance of the Briton – or the Irishman for that matter.

'So step out smartly, men,' called Fitzmullen-Brophy as the cavalry trotted on. 'We've got to catch them before they run all the way back to Berlin!' And the Munsters cheered again.

Another hard march, but then the war would be won.

47

They will boast a victory over a king or a chief of the reavers; and they will afterwards escape though wounded. Woe to him who shall wreak the destruction...

Great are the signs: destruction of life: sating of ravens: feeding of crows, strife of slaughter: wetting of sword-edge, shields with broken bosses in hours after sundown.

—The Destruction of Dá Derga's Hostel

It was probably too early to be crying Tally Ho. The cheery cavalrymen that met the Munsters might have had much to be pleased about, but many another squadron was engaged in desperate dismounted actions at various points between the Seine and the Marne. In truth, the news of a German retreat was premature. What was happening was a redeployment of the German armies to oppose the energetic counterthrusts of the French. The Germans who had been seen pulling back northwards were doing so because the British were considered a beaten enemy and very much a secondary threat. Not only were the Germans so far not repulsed, but they were dealing with the French counterthrusts in a spirited fashion.

But the overall French plan must have been a very sound one, because it was succeeding despite the failure of its individual parts. The French hit the Germans flank and centre, and as these attacks were beaten back, the Germans found themselves pushing in different directions, so that the German First Army was fighting its way westwards while the Second Army was pushing on to the south, with a sizeable gap growing between the two formations. It was into this gap that the resurgent British force was to be driven like a sharp wedge.

Before this could happen, though, and the German armies could be sundered, a cool-headed senior German staff officer saw the impending danger and called for the over-extended armies to fall back across the Marne and consolidate lest they suffer dismemberment and annihilation. Some would criticise this decision as being too cool-headed by half, when what was needed was impetuousness and drive, but that was all for later. In the second week of September the Germans pulled back. They were denied Paris, but in turn they denied the Allies a decisive victory.

For the most part, then, the advancing British were marching into a vacuum. There were tenaciously defended river crossings, and cleverly dug-in German machine-guns to hold up any attempted pursuit, but the bulk of the British forces found themselves advancing onto the biggest battlefield in history without making contact with the enemy. Somewhere to the rear of the tentative British advance Fitzmullen-Brophy's men could hear the guns, but that was all. What they saw clearly was the desolation left by the battle.

There were the scenes that everyone expected. They crossed bridges where the old stone arches were gone, and replaced by stout timbers placed according to the most modern principles of military engineering. There were wrecked and abandoned German wagons, and once they passed a French battery standing untended, with a straggling row of new graves alongside and the bloating bodies of horses attracting what looked like all the flies in that part of France. There were a few houses burned out, or with their roofs broken in and all the windows shattered, but the battle had been on such an enormous scale that there were wide swathes in which nothing much had happened or, at least, where no picturesque evidence had been left behind. They were just ordinary fields and roads, with bits of wreckage here and there. Wyndham had been expecting tattered colours fluttering in the smoky air, and the gallant dead artfully arranged around a gun with a broken wheel. The reality was more mundane and somehow, sometimes, more fearful. He never saw a single body, but he would catch sight of an unsettling number of crows attending to something lying in a field, and once he saw what was undoubtedly blood splashed across the timbers of a wagon. There were spent rifle cartridges of a foreign manufacture that the men picked up off the road and inspected with interest. The air often smelled bad. More distasteful than that smell of corruption was the fact that all this destruction was so clearly imposed on a perfectly everyday world. The ruin was horrible, but there was so much that survived all around it, and the obvious contrast was disquieting. That dismembered horse was lying in someone's front garden. Those were someone's good curtains flapping in a broken window. And the rubbish of war was rarely abandoned military gear but common household items. There was broken crockery everywhere, and broken furniture. Instead of looking glorious and tragic, the aftermath of battle looked messy and squalid, and that was worse. You could celebrate or mourn a tragedy, but a mess had to be cleaned up somehow. In condemnation of it all, the word 'Hun' was gaining currency.

'Prussian frightfulness, men,' declared Fitzmullen-Brophy, surveying yet another ransacked hamlet through narrowed eyes. 'Your German, as you can see, not only has no sense of decency, but is a damned poor loser to boot. Wanton destruction is meat and drink to him and women and children are his prey.' And he thumped his clenched fist on the pommel of his saddle and startled his horse.

'Bastards,' said Robinson in solidarity, forgetting that he had only that morning been augmenting his kit with underclothes filched from a washing line. 'But we'll sort them out, Major.

We'll bloody well give them what for. See if we don't, sir.'

'Good man, Robinson. Wyndham? Be so good as to tell Lieutenant Musgrave that we shall halt at that crucifix up there. And tell him to watch out for broken glass.'

Broken glass: that was another more noticeable feature of the German withdrawal across the Marne. Every bottle of wine in France had been looted, and the evidence lay along the sides of the road in uninterrupted glittering lines. When the men halted they all had a careful look at the grass before they settled down for a rest. Robinson peered at some intact bottles before irritably kicking them into the weeds. 'Empties,' he said. 'All bloody empties. Bastards.'

'You shouldn't be using bad language here,' chided Sweeney, inveigled out of Tralee a month before, and evidently a pious lad still. He said it quietly because he was afraid of the old sweats, but he said it forcefully enough all the same, because he would have been ashamed of himself to allow an Englishman to be cursing away in the shadow of a roadside Calvary. Robinson took it in good humour. In his long years serving in a southern Irish regiment he had encountered such an attitude before.

'Sorry, mate,' he said to the offended lad and then, winking up at his crucified saviour, 'Sorry to you too, old cock.'

Dwyer guffawed, as did Moriarty and many of the sweats within earshot, but a few took umbrage all the same. They wouldn't have called themselves Holy Joes like the young fellow there, but Robinson's carry-on was just asking for bad luck.

Then Whelan surprised everyone by saying that he wished he could go and see the padre. This was the same Whelan who was embracing the life of a soldier with a big bear hug. Whelan who wanted nothing more in his life than a proper moustache and a fund of stories to tell. Whelan who would not think himself a man until he had VD and malaria and a broken nose to go with the good-conduct chevrons on his sleeve. Whelan wanted to be as carefree as Robinson and Dwyer and as cute and worldly-wise as Moriarty. And here he was admitting that he really should go to confession.

'Ah, come off it, boy,' said Moriarty, dismayed that a youth to whose upbringing he was attending should exhibit such waywardness.

But Whelan had been at Étreux, and seen the perfect battalion he'd joined in Aldershot broken in but a single day. He was still only nineteen, but he had looked in the face of death and the censure and mockery of his comrades were of small concern next to that. His immortal soul was riding in an all too evidently mortal body, and if the two were to be separated suddenly, he felt he wanted the soul to be made fit for inspection. He didn't explain himself very well, but most of his audience had shared his upbringing, and they followed him without difficulty. Moriarty saw their sympathy with Whelan's position, but didn't want to back down.

He didn't not believe in God, but in joining the army he had rejected his old civilian life, and listening to the parish priest and saying the rosary of an evening were all part of that. The rejection had been complete. Moriarty was a Christian in so much as he wasn't a heathen, and he was a Catholic only because he wasn't a Protestant. He was a Dirty Shirt, a Munster Fusilier, a soldier. A soldier did not live in a state of grace, and it was unreasonable to expect him to die in one. Whelan was letting the side down by falling back on values that were not military.

'Listen,' he said. 'The padre is only going to make you say novenas and get you all worried. You got out of Etroo because you've got luck, and that's all a man needs. And I'll tell you something else, pal: you've fought your battle. The Germans are bate. A few more weeks and we've won. You've fought your battle and you're still here, and you don't need the padre filling you up with visions of hell fire. You're lucky. Stop worrying.'

Whelan didn't seem convinced, but he said no more on the matter. Robinson piped up again to lighten the mood by telling the story of a dissolute sergeant who converted to Methodism. The same sergeant took to believing so strongly in the dictates of his conscience that he went so far as to question King's Regulations (except that this was way back when it was Queen's Regulations). What happened? They had to get the man back on the drink in the end.

As an encore, Robinson was retailing the one about the Jew in the Gordon Highlanders, and was building to a rather obvious punchline about kilts and circumcision when the order came for them to fall in.

'Oh to hell with it. Anyway, Ikey says, "And I bet you've never seen nothing like this neither, missus!" No? I'll tell it better next time. Give us a song someone, but for Christ's sake don't make it a hymn.'

Someone struck up 'Tipperary' but no one knew anything more than the chorus, so after singing that twice they went back to the one man who went to mow. It was easy to remember the words for that one.

They had some excitement in the afternoon. Somewhere up ahead someone had run into a German rearguard position. The first anybody knew about it was the hard pattering of machine-gun bullets on the road. A second or so later they heard the burst of firing, and only then did it occur to everyone to take cover. Fitzmullen-Brophy sent Lieutenant Musgrave to climb a tree and report on the situation. The major would have joined him but was beginning to doubt his ability to shin up a tree and maintain any dignity. He hadn't seen any Germans yet in this war.

Even with field glasses Musgrave could only, with difficulty, make out a few scattered figures in the far distance whom he took to be British. The Germans were invisible, and it was highly unlikely that they'd even seen the Munsters, let alone been aiming at them.

With nothing else to do for the time being, the men were ordered to go to ground in a smart and soldierly manner. It was good practice, even though the chances of this presaging a German counterattack were negligible. So the men were finding cover and lighting up and, at a sufficiently discreet distance from the officers, having a bit of a nose around to see what could be picked up in the buildings roundabout. There wasn't much. The drink was all gone and any food was rotten, so unless you wanted to be carrying pieces of furniture along with you it all made for poor looting. One man had made it his speciality to prise bricks out of fireplaces, because he knew that somewhere in France there was an old man or woman who kept a cash box hidden in just such a place. So far he had nothing to show for his efforts but a blunted end to his bayonet. It was his mate, idly rooting round in the rubbish of the back yard, who made the discovery. It was the smell that alerted him. There was a dead German soldier half buried under a collapsed outhouse – the first German the Munsters had encountered since Étreux.

Almost everyone came and had a look – even some of the men who'd been at Étreux.

'Look at the boots on him,' said someone. 'Your feet would only be rattling around in them.'

'They're half worn out too. There's a fella that's been doing his share of marching and all.'

'God rest him,' said Moyle.

'What? Fuck off you, with your God rest him!'

'God rest him, I said, and fuck off yourself.'

Before another theological argument could kick off, Lieutenant Musgrave arrived and shooed them all away. If Mister Musgrave wanted to insist on the enemy dead being shown some respect, then that was all right. He had been at Étreux. He could do what he liked. Just so long as no one was going to start saying a prayer for the departed.

A gun came galloping by, summoned to deal with the machine-gun nest up ahead, but when it went into action they couldn't get a decent view of that either. At last they were given the go-ahead to move off again, and as they formed up on the road, Moriarty surreptitiously dropped something into a fold on Whelan's pack.

'Hang on – you've got something on your gear there,' he said, and when Whelan turned around there was Moriarty holding up a spent German bullet.

'Jesus,' said Whelan in wonderment. 'And I never even felt it land.'

'What did I tell you, boy?' said Moriarty grinning, 'You're just lucky, so you are.'

48

...A heart without envy, without hatred, a heart hard in earning victory.

—Lady Augusta Gregory, *Gods And Fighting Men*

Lieutenant Noel Musgrave had indeed been found under a hedge by Fitzmullen-Brophy. That was how one slept on this campaign. Unroll your valise (if you still have one), climb inside as if it were a sleeping bag, and do it all under a hedge that will keep you out of the weather and out of everyone's way. Not that anyone slept for very long, of course or, as had been the case in the terrible days after Étreux, slept at all. But after he and the few men he had with him made it to the comparative safety of the rest of the army, and it was clear that they wouldn't be much use as a rearguard any more, things became less fraught. Musgrave just did as he was told and kept marching south, trying his best to hang on to the few men he'd brought out of Étreux with him.

He was three years in the army and had just received his promotion to full lieutenant when the war broke out. The step was automatic, and had nothing to do with merit. He wasn't a bad officer by any means, but all his soldiering so far had been done as part of a peacetime battalion in England. Taking charge of a disaster was a lot to ask of him. That was why he was so relieved to be woken up one afternoon by Fitzmullen-Brophy. He didn't know the man, but he saw a major's crown on the cuff and a fusilier badge on the cap, and he knew he had made it safe home. The major's appointment might be unofficial, and even unauthorised, but if he wanted to take over then Musgrave was only too happy to let him.

Musgrave had never met the man before, nor Major Belcher either, but he knew both types well. There were officers who accepted that the army carried on as well as it was going to, and merely asked where a man's family came from and where he had hunted, and tended to let nature take its course thereafter. Major Belcher was clearly of that stamp. To an officer like Belcher, any man who had been accepted to wear lieutenant's pips in the regiment was evidently the right sort, and until he committed some alarming error should just be allowed to get on with things.

Major Fitzmullen-Brophy was the other type. If Musgrave had been naturally irritable, or a man of too independent a spirit, he might have characterised Fitzmullen-Brophy as a meddler. He asked where Musgrave's people came from, but his next question was not about hunting, or even school or cricket, but about stew. Senior officers, if they took an interest in their work, always had a fad. Some might obsess about standards in drill, or work themselves up over such details as the exact shade of khaki of an officer's tie. In his time Musgrave had encountered a colonel who had a fad about the sun, and never permitted any man to go about uncovered, even in Wiltshire. Then there was the other colonel who occupied half his life with persuading men to turn from drink to cocoa, and the major who took too uncomfortably close an interest in the sexual habits of his juniors – not that many of them had any sexual habits at all yet. Fitzmullen-Brophy's fad, or at least his chief fad, was evidently diet.

The remnant that had followed Musgrave out of Étreux had not been the remnant that included the battalion cooks. So what were the men eating? Bully beef and biscuit? No no. That just would not do. Now that the emergency was over the men should get something filling and nutritious, and did Musgrave know how to produce a stew under such circumstances for so many men? Aha, there was a knack to it you see. Many young officers never thought to learn such tricks, but when the major was in South

Africa he had learned the value – the inestimable value, mark you – of being able to do without the cooks and their cumbersome supply train.

And of course Musgrave knew the best way of building a fire? No? Tut tut, Lieutenant.

Not that Fitzmullen-Brophy's disapproval was ever harsh. Indeed, the man welcomed opportunities to lecture Musgrave, and anyone else, on this, that and everything. After paying attention to the state of the men's stomachs and bowels, he enjoyed through the days following to test Musgrave's knowledge of such things as knots and tents and the care of horses' feet. One never knew when one might need to know such things.

'Be prepared, Musgrave,' said Fitzmullen-Brophy. 'That's my motto. Be prepared.'

Musgrave rather liked the old major, and was glad to have him, but he did rather wish that the old busybody might just belt up from time to time.

What made it all easier was Lieutenant Fleming or, more correctly, Second Lieutenant Fleming. Nothing gave a young man self-confidence like having a deferential junior. Above him there was Fitzmullen-Brophy quizzing him on Things Every Junior Officer Should Know, but by way of counterbalance, there was Fleming, who was more his own age, but agreeably respectful, and with just enough brains to shut up and keep out of everyone's way. Fleming wasn't a regular officer, of course, and had this been the mess in Aldershot, an officer like Musgrave would naturally have kept his distance from a militiaman like Fleming. Of course the days of freezing a chap out or cutting him dead were over, thank God, but it just didn't do to let Special Reserve officers think they were as good as regulars. Here in the field, and with Fleming's single pip to Musgrave's two, it was a much happier relationship.

Neither man would have had anyone to talk to if not for the

other. Fleming was eager to please without being any sort of a crawler, and after two nights of sleeping under the same hedge and two mornings of washing out of the same canvas bucket, their relationship had reached a cordiality that allowed Musgrave to address Fleming as 'Bog', but kept Fleming from being over-familiar with Musgrave, who had never been blessed with a nickname anyway. In short, Fleming was revealing himself to be a decent sort, and Musgrave asked no more of any man.

Special Reserve or not, give a chap like Bog Fleming a year or two and he might make a perfectly decent officer.

49

The armies will reach the following lines: Third Army, Thuizy (exclusive) – Suippes (exclusive); Fourth Army, Suippes (inclusive) – Ste. Menehould (exclusive); Fifth Army, Ste. Menehould (inclusive) and to the east.

The lines so reached will be fortified and defended.

—Helmuth von Moltke, General Order, 11 September 1914

Musgrave was killed on the north bank of the Aisne.

They had crossed the river on the girders of a half-demolished railway bridge two days before, with the rain whipping them. Hobnails slipped on wet steel as Fitzmullen-Brophy, obliged to go on foot again, earnestly exhorted them to be careful and not to look down. Wyndham looked down. There was no other way to go about it. He felt the wind pushing him and saw the water moving below, but he made it safe across, and so did everyone else. There were other bridges and better bridges, but the army was in something of a hurry, and the little band of Munster Fusiliers were being moved forward in case reinforcements were needed urgently.

With everyone across the river they were, as should not have surprised anyone used to the army, instructed to wait, and then to move along to somewhere else, and then to wait again. Belcher had been able to re-equip the men to a small degree, but there were not enough greatcoats and waterproof groundsheets to go round, and Wyndham's knees were still open to the air. There might have been shelter if they'd been allowed to look for it, but the order had been given to stand by, and it was an order that was repeated by way of occasional staff officers. They made themselves as comfortable as they might, sheltering against a bank, and they watched the war go by.

The pursuit of the beaten foe had ended. The Germans had fallen back so far but here on the slopes above the Aisne, with their guns ranged on all the crossings, they had halted and dug in. The British had forced those crossings at a cost, and pushed on up those slopes, but what they met was a solidly entrenched and almost continuous line. At Mons, and in all the rearguard actions during the retreat, the British infantrymen had hunkered down and squinted through the sights of their rifles, and the German footsoldiers, with their bayonets held in front of them, had been obliged to advance across the open fields. Now it was the other way round, and the British advance had been stopped dead for the time being.

That, of course, was not good enough for high command. They had won this war on the Marne and were damned if they were going to have their victory spoiled here a week later. If the Germans were allowed to make a stand here then they could get their wind and their balance back. They had to be pushed out. They had to be kept on the run.

But the Munsters watched in the rain as the stretchers were carried down the hill. The Germans were not allowing themselves to be evicted from the heights. It was a grimly fascinating sight for men unused to it. The wounded were most often the victims of gunshot and shrapnel, and the wounds were unnerving rather than terrible to look at. Blood was black-red against grey-white skin. Clothes were black in the rain, and every man was spattered knee-high with pale mud.

Troops bereft of their regiments could easily be forgotten when it came to feeding, but corps troops, like Fitzmullen-Brophy's men, were, if orphaned, at least closer to the supply bases, so

Sergeant Duffy had little trouble in organising tea and bully-beef sandwiches for everyone. Wyndham held his wad of bread and meat close under his chin, the wet skirts of his greatcoat slapping against his knees.

'Do you think it hurts, Wyndham? Do you think it hurts getting shot?'

That was Riordan. Wyndham had come to live with Riordan's pointless questioning the way he was coming to accept all the discomforts and indignities of army life. There was even something to value in being considered an oracle and a man in the know, even if it was only by some idiot like Riordan. He still wasn't going to look Riordan in the face when the man was eating though.

'I expect it does,' he said placidly. 'I imagine it hurts quite a lot, Riordan.'

'I wouldn't want to be shot,' said Riordan, giving it some thought while he chewed. 'Jesus no.'

'Please close your mouth when you're eating.'

'What? How do I do that?' Riordan was not being in any way sarcastic. 'How would I get the food in if I had my mouth closed?'

'I'm sure you'll figure out something,' Wyndham replied, too quietly to be heard over the slurping of tea.

They spent all night there against that bank, but in the morning they were moved on in haste. The sun had come back out at least. Where they halted seemed to be nearer to the enemy, because they could hear crackles of musketry and bursts of machine-gun fire much more clearly than before. If you stood up and craned your head you could see the shrapnel shells bursting above a ridge. The traffic in troops going forward and casualties coming back was busier. Coming on for noon, and everyone's stomachs giving out, a battery of 18-pounders unlimbered nearby and started firing over their heads. When the vital order came Fitzmullen-Brophy was unable to hear it, and the staff-wallah from Corps HQ had to make himself understood by shouts and gesticulations and emphatic references to the rough sketch map he carried.

Watching all of this, and seeing Fitzmullen-Brophy nod in understanding, and with Musgrave and Fleming then nodding in their turn, and all of them looking so very serious, the men gathered that something was up and a thrill ran through the ranks. Was this it? Was this it at last? They moved on uphill to where some other units were forming up, and with the noise not as terrible, Fitzmullen-Brophy announced that they were being held in reserve for an attack being made by the brigade and should make themselves ready to move forward in support at a moment's notice.

Despite having been expecting something like this since yesterday, and indeed since last month, Wyndham was dumbfounded by the news, but everyone was just obeying, and he found he was too. Lieutenant Musgrave looked grave but competent as he directed the men to take up position alongside a bend in the road. And then a shell came screaming in and he was dead. He must have heard it, because he was turning and looking for cover, but there was no cover, and then the blast had knocked him down and the little shrapnel bullets had torn into him, and he was dead.

50

...Seven men,

Six men,

Five men,

Four men,

Three men,

Two men,

One man,

And his dog,

Went to mow a meadow.

—Traditional

Lieutenant Musgrave was dead. So was Private Slattery. The Welshman Hughes and another man named Boyle, whom Wyndham didn't know, were wounded. One of the wounded men was stunned, but sitting upright, and the other was howling on the ground, but the two dead men were clearly dead. Musgrave's body had been knocked down and rolled over, and when they got to him he was crumpled and twisted in no natural fashion. A puncture wound was very visible in his back, and when they moved him they found two more. Slattery's body was in even worse state.

This was the same Slattery that Wyndham had unwillingly slept next to all those nights in Ballymullen – the loathsome creature that had been the first living thing he had seen on so many mornings. Private Slattery, ignorant and crude. Slattery, whose Christian name Wyndham had never known, if the poor disgusting thing had ever even been acknowledged a Christian. Here he was in a field in France with his skull shattered and his brains leaking out. Wyndham was put in mind of a soft-boiled egg that had been given a good rap with something a little sharper than a spoon. Slattery's eyes were open, and no more intelligent than they had been in life.

Wyndham was thinking these thoughts, and the men around him were still staring down at the bodies, when Fitzmullen-Brophy came up at a fair clip, waving his stick and bawling at them to take cover. They had to be chivvied towards the edge of the field like sheep, so stupefied were they by the suddenness of it all. That one shell must have been a wild shot, because they were fortunate to be spared further visitations for the time being. Fitzmullen-Brophy guessed that it might even have been a British shell falling short. He had known that to happen before. Damned bad luck on Musgrave. He'd been the right sort. Only known him a few days, but knew that the young fellow played a straight bat. And now, he realised with some dismay, he'd have to write to Musgrave's parents. That was an aspect of war that he had never missed in the years of peace. There was nothing to do about that now though. Important not to dwell on such things, and that went double for the men. Keep them moving. Keep them busy.

They advanced further up the slope, keeping low. Fitzmullen-Brophy kept on telling them to spread out, to open up the formation, but the men's instinct was to bunch together. They were lucky that no other shell came over. They saw a few bursting here and there, and they heard many more booming beyond the immediate ridge line, but that was all. They presently came to a laneway, slightly sunk into the side of the hill, and there the wounded were being tended to and there the brigade commander was trying to make sense of the attack.

'Take cover behind the crest,' he told Fitzmullen-Brophy. 'Dig in and wait for my order.'

The exact line of the crest wasn't obvious, so Fitzmullen-Brophy kept them moving forward until he heard the distinct crack of a bullet passing close by. He couldn't see where it might have come from, but here he halted. The soil was firm, and the tools were not ideal for digging. Wyndham, along with the rawer recruits from Tralee, had had no practice at this sort of work and the few of them who had done any labouring in civil life were unused to the short-handled mattock that the army issued for these purposes.

Wyndham had other concerns too. He still didn't know how his rifle worked. There had been an attempt at musketry drill weeks before, when they were wending their pleasant way across Normandy, but among that small body there were three different models of rifle, which made uniform instruction impractical. The drill hadn't got so far as actually allowing anyone to fire a live round. And then there was the uncomfortable fact that Wyndham still hadn't any ammunition, live or not. The 2nd Battalion men and the old sweats had their pouches bulging, and had added to this with cotton bandoliers of cartridge clips, but Wyndham must have been running errands for the major when those had been issued, and he'd been a little too diffident to ask for one from these men when he was so obviously a novice. His obsolete rifle was merely a token of his status as a soldier, and a tool for drill, and another thing to be kept clean. Employing it as a weapon was still a long way away. But any minute now he might be required to start killing Germans with it.

Fitzmullen-Brophy was preparing for that eventuality rather more thoroughly. He had left his sword with his horse (he'd never found much use for either in South Africa) and relied on his stick as a badge of office and his trusty old revolver for the more practical work. He thought of it as trusty because it was a robust and reliable piece, although, had he thought about it, he'd never had to rely on it much. He'd fired it from time to time, and even fired it at the enemy, but he'd never been certain he'd actually hit anyone. Still, it fired a reassuringly large bullet, designed to fell the sort of determined rapscallions encountered on the Northwest Frontier, who were usually just too brave to lie down when shot with anything of a smaller calibre. The regulations required that an officer carried twelve such bullets on his person, but Fitzmullen-Brophy had an extra packet of cartridges in one of the side pockets of his tunic. Be prepared.

Moriarty and the other survivors of Étreux had dug fast and deep, and their own ammunition was already arranged as suited each man best. All along the short line every man who smoked was smoking hard.

The noise from in front grew loud and urgent, and it wasn't long before a messenger came sprinting up with the order to move up. Fitzmullen-Brophy was not in the leastways glad that Musgrave had been hit, but it had been the idea that the younger man would be leading any advance on the enemy. Now it was Fitzmullen-Brophy's task, and Fitzmullen-Brophy's hour. The moment of the great test was at hand. He stood up. He wished he had a bugler. It probably wouldn't have been appropriate, but he'd have liked a bugler all the same. Even though everyone in his small command was within earshot of his voice, he blew his whistle and waved the men out of their little trenches. He realised that he hadn't given the order to fix bayonets, but that could wait. This was not an attack just yet. This was just a move forward by a few hundred yards to a new line. The line was supposed to be at the edge of a field to the right of a copse, and maybe trenches had been dug there and maybe they hadn't. Fitzmullen-Brophy kept a sharp eye out as they breasted the rise.

Beyond there was just more landscape. They could see no battle at all. There was a suggestion of drifting smoke on the opposite hill, but nothing else. Not a single man or horse was to be seen. Fitzmullen-Brophy hoped that he had identified the right stand of trees to mark his objective, and he hailed Fleming and indicated the direction. The German machine-gunner probably had his eye on them already, but Fitzmullen-Brophy's waving arm seemed to act as a starting signal to him. The range was long, and the Munsters never heard the firing, but in a few seconds of their coming over the crest of the hill the bullets were skipping among them.

This was when Riordan found out what it was like to be shot. Something kicked him on the shin and down he fell. As Wyndham had predicted, it hurt a great deal, but most of that came later. The terror of it was sufficient for the time being. The man who was directly behind Riordan fell down on top of him, with an impossibly neat little bullet hole almost dead centre in his forehead. Moving left from them, as the German machine-gunner would have seen it, three out of the next five men fell. The rest of that initial burst missed altogether or thumped into the turf in front of the men's feet.

The men who had been under fire before were running fast for cover at the bottom of the field, but others, who had never heard the sound of machine-gun fire directed at them, and the range being what it was, didn't hear it for two-thirds of a second after it had happened and were slower off the mark. Too slow. One of them was hit before he had the sense to move and another, the message sinking in just a little too late, was caught before he could find shelter.

Not every man thought too slowly or too much of himself. Robinson was halfway to cover when he saw that one of the men down was his mate Dwyer. He turned and, assessing the situation in an instant, and appreciating that Dwyer was a fine hefty man, he grabbed hold of whomever was nearest to give him some help. It happened to be Whelan, who had given no thought to stopping for anyone. He was seeing the breakout from Étreux all over again when a big hand caught him by a webbing strap and almost jerked him off his feet. Robinson wasn't letting go, so back Whelan went with him at the run. Dwyer was gripping his thigh with both hands and cursing a blue streak.

'Ah Jesus, Charlie mate,' he said. 'It's bad. It's bad.'

'Hold on, Jim mate. I'll have you out of there in a tick.'

Whelan later declared that it was the longest bloody tick of his life. Somehow they got Dwyer onto Robinson's shoulders, and that should have been that, but as Robinson was lumbering his way down to the hedge and cover he roared at Whelan for having his hands empty.

'Do some fucking work, son! See to that lad over there. He's still kicking. Quick now!'

The lad was Riordan. Whelan didn't give a toss for any kid from Ballymullen, but Robinson roared with righteous authority and, scared as he was, Whelan was no coward. He stood frozen for a second, and afterwards could not even remember whether the bullets had been going by or not. Then he put himself in motion and did as he was told.

He thought how convenient it was that soldiers were covered in straps. With one hand still holding onto his rifle, he laid hold of one of Riordan's webbing braces and simply started dragging. He had the strength of ten men that day, he reckoned, because he made it the length of that field before the Germans had time to kill him, and he pulling the howling and whimpering Riordan along every inch of the way.

The other wounded would have to make shift for themselves for the time being. By the time anyone considered their plight, it was from the safety of the hedge. From there it seemed an awfully long way back for a fellow to go to aid a man who might be dead anyway.

Robinson's effort was a case in point. The bullet that had

broken the big bone in Dwyer's thigh had torn open the big artery there too. Even with a rifle sling squeezed around his leg, Dwyer was losing blood fast. His eyes were wide with fright and he was breathing too quickly, but presently that slowed and then stopped altogether. Robinson, his tunic sheeted with blood, closed his friend's eyes and cursed sorrowfully until Fitzmullen-Brophy came up and put a hand on his shoulder. There were South African ribbons on Dwyer's breast, and that was worth a great deal to the major.

'Bad luck, Robinson,' he said. 'Damned bad luck. Nothing you could do.'

Robinson wiped his moustache on his cuff and nodded silently, not looking up.

The other casualties would have to wait. Fleming dutifully volunteered to go and fetch them in, but the moment he ventured out he attracted fire. It broke Fitzmullen-Brophy's heart, and he was seriously thinking of making an attempt on his own, when a captain of the Berkshires appeared, tumbling through the hedge with bullets following him.

'Afternoon, sir,' he said, somewhat out of breath. 'You our reinforcements?'

'Second Munsters,' said Fitzmullen-Brophy. 'Yes, I believe we are.'

'Then I'm afraid you're in rather the wrong place, sir. We need you over there, about fifty yards left of that farmhouse. You see it?'

Fitzmullen-Brophy could, but insisted that he had wounded out in the open.

The Berkshire man peered up the slope. 'Oh I say, sir. You didn't come over there did you? Bad show. You should have come up by the lane. But I'm sorry, sir. Can't be helped, I'm afraid. I'm to tell you that you that you are to advance to our position right away and cover our attack. Very sorry, sir.'

And thus, obedient above all, the Munsters left their fallen where they were, and ran after the Berkshire captain. A man called Hodge was hit on the way, and so was one of the two men in the unit named Horgan.

The destination was a line composed of shallow trenches, a length of boundary wall, and a good deep ditch. The ditch was battalion headquarters for the Berkshires.

'Glad to see you, Major,' said their CO. He was the usual middle-aged businesslike sort: calm in the midst of a battle, and still rather dapper, even in a ditch. 'You're the reinforcements from Brigade?'

'That's right,' said Fitzmullen-Brophy, his heart hammering from the run.

'Is this all there are of you?'

'Afraid so.'

'Damn. Still – can't be helped. What I need, Major, is for you to hold this line for the time being. Fritz knows we're here, which is rather a bind, so keep your heads down. All goes well and you'll be following us forward in quarter of an hour or so, but whatever happens it is imperative that you hold this line. Clear?'

'Clear, Colonel, and the best of luck to you.'

'And to you, Major – *Finlay*!' he called for his second-in-command. 'B and C Companies will advance! A and D will follow at an interval of one minute!'

And the orders were relayed rapidly up and down the line. Whistles blew, and men rose up from the grass and moved forward with their bayonets fixed. The Munsters slotted themselves into the positions just vacated, uttering encouragement and good wishes to the departing men.

A machine-gun opened up somewhere ahead, and then another one over to the right.

The Munsters watched the Berkshires fall. Fitzmullen-Brophy wasn't having it. He was damned if he would stand by and be a spectator to the deaths of good and brave men. He pulled out his field glasses and tracked across the landscape.

'Anyone see anything?' he called. 'Anyone see that bally machine-gun?'

'Sir, do you see that bit of a shed above on the right? I think one of them's in among the bushes there below that.'

That was Sergeant Harris. Good man, Harris. Came out of Étreux with Musgrave and the rest. Fitzmullen-Brophy found the spot indicated, and caught a spark of muzzle flash. That indeed might be it. Now to show friend Fritz what the army had learned in South Africa.

'Moyle?' he called.

Private Moyle was a quiet type, and a steady type. Moyle was also one of the men who wore the crossed rifles on his sleeve – the badge of a marksman first class. The man came up smartly and crouched beside the major. Fitzmullen-Brophy pointed out the suspect spot and asked Moyle's opinion.

'I'd say you could be right, sir,' said Moyle with deliberation. 'And I'd say it's a good six hundred yards, and maybe more like six hundred and fifty.'

'Well see what you can do about it anyhow, eh Moyle? Good man.'

The British service rifle, the Short Magazine Lee-Enfield .303 inch, was in many respects a troublesome piece of work. It had been redesigned several times over the years, but the specimen in Moyle's hands was still recognisable as a close cousin to the rifle Fitzmullen-Brophy remembered from South Africa, and it retained many of that weapon's besetting sins. It was a fussy rifle, with too many moving parts that made it intolerant of clumsy handling. It kicked harder than a modern rifle should, and had been known to break the collarbones, and even the jaws, of careless recruits. The propellant in the cartridges burned too hot and the residue was too harmful to the steel of the barrel, so constant cleaning was necessary. The cartridges themselves had an irritating tendency to catch against each other, leading to stoppages. But the army persevered with the Lee-Enfield because, when it worked smoothly, those cartridges could be fed through the action at a phenomenal rate, as the Germans had learned at Mons and at every rearguard action along the road to the Marne. Moreover, the good gunsmiths of Birmingham had provided the rifle with sights adjustable to 2,000 yards. Now although it was a fact that few men could even see a target that far away, the gunsmiths averred that a bullet fired from their rifle was still airborne, still travelling on a predictable course, and still lethal more than a mile downrange.

Now the fact was that, in this modern age, most of the better rifles (and the German rifle was very clearly one of the better ones) could do as much, and would even boast the somewhat greater distance of 2,000 metres. But those rifles were in the hands of men who knew not South Africa.

Brother Boer, in the saddle before he could walk, and practically born with a rifle in his hands, could pick the eyes out of a sparrow at half a mile, and could (and did) work much destruction on British troops in the open. A proposed solution was for the British soldier to emulate the Boer. If the British rifle was deadly accurate at long range, why was its bearer not trained to fire at long range? When the army came home from the veldt it embarked on a feverish campaign of musketry reforms, sending men out on the ranges until they could damn well shoot straight. Marksmanship was all the rage. On the principle that a horse can be led to water but not made to drink, the army appealed to the soldier's mercenary inclinations and brought out his latent excellence with cash inducements. With an extra sixpence a day dangled before him the average British soldier became something of a crack shot. Sixpence was three pints of the cheaper beer, after all. Thus, with the leisure of peacetime at their disposal, a great many men had worked hard at winning that proficiency pay. By the time this war had rolled around, a man could be ashamed of himself for being classed as a mere second-class shot, and the marksman's badge was commonplace. And these men could not just shoot straight – they could shoot exceedingly fast too.

At Mons the army got back the full value of all of those sixpences.

Fully a third of the men who had come out of Étreux wore the crossed rifles, but Moyle had been singled out for the addition of a small star that advertised him as the best shot in his company. If Moyle said that the putative German machine-gun position was 650 yards off, it was no guess. Squinting at ranges was part of the qualification. Rather than relay the information up the chain of command and back down again, Fitzmullen-Brophy told Moyle to call the target himself. On his instruction all the regulars adjusted their sights and took careful aim. At Moyle's 'Fire!' they let loose, and that made them feel much better. They fired off a second volley, and a third, and it was then made clear that while they hadn't hit the German machine-gunner, they had agitated him considerably, because suddenly the greenery about the Munsters' heads was being chewed up by bullets. The next command should have been, 'Rapid, independent, fire!' but Moyle's version was 'Flake away,' and they did.

The machine-gun kept at them, but they knew that even if they weren't hitting it, it wasn't hitting the Berkshires. Other guns must have been though, because Fitzmullen-Brophy could make out a scattering of bodies to his front, and all the way along the Berkshires' line of advance. Couldn't be helped. To tell the truth, even though he and his men were just potting at the enemy from cover, the whole business was exhilarating. After the past weeks in some sort of military limbo, the Munsters were back in the war, well found in ammunition and confident of their ability to pay the Germans back for Étreux. And they must have been a right annoyance to the Germans because, after five minutes of flaking away from behind cover, the Munsters attracted the attention of the German artillery.

The shell that killed Lieutenant Musgrave had been shrapnel, which is to say a round bursting in the air and using a small explosive charge to shower little spherical bullets down on its target. A high explosive round was different. This was a parcel of TNT in a steel casing, which slammed into the ground and exploded in a savage black cloud of chemical smoke and earth and lethal steel shards.

The first German shell landed short, giving everyone a clear view of what was in store for them. It might almost have been deliberately aimed there by way of a threat. The next shot was long, but nearer, and everyone felt the blast. Wyndham was deafened. He was huddled in the headquarters ditch and stayed that way long after the little pieces of debris had stopped pattering onto his shoulders. It wasn't that he was scared: the experience was too stupefying for an emotion as small as fear.

He became aware of a hand shaking him and a voice shouting. He opened his eyes with effort and looked up into the face of the medical officer of the Berkshires, who had stayed behind with a few men when his battalion went forward.

'Are you hit?' the MO shouted, for the second or third time.

Wyndham shook his head.

'Then go and find out who is, and be quick about it,' the MO told him.

The Berkshires had stretcher-bearers of their own, but they were busy far out in front, doing what they could for their comrades among the flying lead. Wyndham obediently stood up on unsure legs and set off, but turned around after a two steps to retrieve his rifle.

'Never mind that, man. You'll need both hands if there are any casualties. Hurry now.'

And Wyndham set off again, steadying himself against the side of the ditch and minding where he put his feet. He was climbing out to ground level when someone grabbed his ankle from below and pulled him back down. It was one of the MO's assistants. 'Listen, lad!' he shouted.

Listen? Listen for what?

Of course, shaken and with his ears ringing, he hadn't paid any attention to the screaming approach of the third shell. The first two had nicely bracketed the British position. This one fell pretty much on target. It was the end of the world all over again, although the Berkshire men sheltering in the ditch took it rather better than Wyndham did.

'Right,' said the man who had hauled Wyndham back. 'That wasn't so bad. Up you get now, and for Christ's sake keep low.'

Again Wyndham did as he was told, and scrambled up to be mildly surprised that nothing much was changed at ground level. There was smoke, and a sharp smell in the air from the explosion, but the world was still there.

Had anybody been hit? What was he supposed to do about it if there had? Bind up wounds with his handkerchief? It was all he had. The little packet of first field dressing was another of those things with which he had never been issued. He crawled along, looking for Major Fitzmullen-Brophy, looking for guidance, looking for company. Two more shells came over before he found the major, but both were misses as far as he could tell. The major and Lieutenant Fleming were crouched in the lee of a wall, and Fitzmullen-Brophy was expressing his desire to push on forward. Better to be out of here and closer to the enemy. Better by far.

He was about to give the order when he spotted a runner sprinting back towards him. The man dived through the hedge and tumbled into the headquarters ditch, from where he was directed to the commander of the Munsters. Breathless and rattled as he was, he straightened his cap and saluted Fitzmullen-Brophy. Proper form, even though he was keeping so low as to almost be on all fours.

'Word from the colonel, sir,' he panted. 'You're to hold this position, if you please, sir.'

And he presented a page torn from a notebook, which elaborated very slightly on this message. The Berkshires' attack had stalled for the time being and there was the possibility of a German counterattack. Hold firm. Wait for further orders. Blast.

'Tell the colonel he can count on us,' said Fitzmullen-Brophy, disappointed but resolute. 'Hurry along as soon as you've got your breath back. Good man.'

He looked down and saw Wyndham, who was trying not to appear as though he were cowering.

'Pass the word along, Wyndham. We're staying put. Tell everyone to strengthen their positions.'

The cannier men hardly needed to be told, and were already hacking away with their entrenching tools, working like demons against the arrival of the next German shell. The men who'd come from Ballymullen – Wyndham's comrades – were slower, nor was their eye for ground or instinct for bullet-dodging as good as those who had survived Étreux. Maybe that was what killed Cassidy, Ryan, and Tobin. Maybe it was just luck. But one minute they were there, digging and scraping, getting in each other's way, and then they were gone. They could have kept a sharper ear out for the incoming shell. They could have dived for cover faster. Or maybe it made no difference. One moment Wyndham was scampering towards them, trying to stop his cap from slipping down over his eyes, and the next he was knocked flat, and three of his barrack mates were gone.

The smell this time wasn't just burnt chemicals. A fair length of Cassidy was spread out from the point of impact and tangled in the low branches of an adjacent tree, and the stink was worse than the worst latrine smell that Wyndham had ever endured. The wretched obscenity that was the rest of Cassidy still had most of Cassidy's face. The carcass lying nearby might have been Ryan or it might have been Tobin. There was nothing recognisable of the third man to be seen.

Wyndham crawled a little closer, not believing what he was seeing, and then he crawled backwards until he backed up against some shelter. There he stayed, curled up numb and white, while the battle, if that's what this was, went on.

The Berkshires started to come back presently. The first few staggered in with hastily bandaged wounds, and then there were the stretcher cases. Last of all were the withered companies, leapfrogging back in good order, but still losing a man here, a man there. As was fitting, the commanding officer was last of all. He returned in haste, but it was a dignified haste. Nevertheless, there was no hiding the fact that he was shaken by the last half hour.

'Bad business,' he confessed to Fitzmullen-Brophy.

'Blighters are dug in too damn well. Couldn't get close. Had two companies badly cut up trying. Locke of C Company managed it, but it wasn't enough. Didn't see it myself, but he wasn't able to hold off a counterattack and I couldn't get any reinforcements up to him. Brave fellow. Still up there. Must write to his father. Only one officer left in C.'

Fitzmullen-Brophy nodded in grave sympathy. 'Jolly fine effort all the same. Just say the word, Colonel, and my men will have a crack at it,' he said.

'Good of you to offer, Major. Expected nothing less. But it's no use. Word from Brigade – no lodgement established in the German line anywhere at all. We must just hang on here until reinforcements come up, and if they've sent us you, then I don't suppose any more will be coming. Damn.'

'Just tell me where you want us,' said Fitzmullen-Brophy. 'We've been firing away at their machine-guns, but we could do with one or two of our own.'

'So could we. Lost them both weeks ago, and the machine-gun officer with them. Got bracketed by a German battery. Blasted Huns always seem to have more artillery than we do.'

That certainly seemed to be the case here. They could see the British shrapnel detonating above the German positions, but it seemed so ineffectual next to the German high explosive that thundered down among them. There was more to the British line than the position held by the Berkshires and the Munsters, so at least the attentions of the German guns were mercifully dispersed. A few shells fell dangerously close, but the men had been digging deep, and many were thus spared who would otherwise have been smashed and pulped like the three recruits from Ballymullen.

The Berkshires had their chaplain with them, and while he had spent most of his time in the headquarters ditch with the medical officer, he occasionally did the rounds among his dwindling flock. He came to the Munsters, and his reception was greeted with respectful deference from some and a few cheeky grins from others. Moriarty was one of the latter.

'You're in the wrong parish there, Padre,' he said, because if you couldn't pull an officer's leg in the middle of a battle then what was the use of battles?

'All Roman Catholics here I suppose?' said the chaplain, and sat down beside Moriarty in his little trench.

'All sinners anyway, sir. There'll be a few Protestants to be found, I reckon, if you look carefully in all the holes. I reckon it'd be worth the effort, mind – I'd say some of them would be feeling very religious this minute.'

The chaplain laughed politely, and gave Moriarty a cigarette, and went on his way. Sweeney was just plain embarrassed to be approached by an Anglican, and looked away rather than endanger his soul at this moment by engaging with one. He wouldn't even take the offered cigarette. That would have been like taking the soup from Protestant missionaries during the Famine.

Whelan acknowledged the man as he would any officer, but privately he thought it very unfair that when he felt most in need of a chaplain, the only one around would be the wrong sort altogether. Jesus! What if he got killed and this man buried him? Where would that leave him?

Wyndham was surprised out of his numbness enough to receive the chaplain as one should receive a visiting clergyman, except that tea served in the good china wasn't really an option. He thanked the man for his kind attentions, and exchanged what amounted to small talk. He even took the cigarette, out of good manners, and even allowed the padre to light it for him.

'I don't usually,' he said.

'Dreadful habit,' said the chaplain with a gentle smile, 'but I find it works wonders for my nerves.'

The well-spoken Munster Fusilier was clearly in need of something for his nerves, because both match and cigarette had to be steadied with both hands. Indeed the young man gave the impression that he'd forgotten how to smoke.

It was a decent Turkish blend, and the novelty and the sharpness of it gave Wyndham something to think about besides his plight. It never occurred to him to inhale.

There came a tense moment in late afternoon, when they were 'stood to' to prepare for an expected German counterattack. Where this expectation came from was never found out, nor did any attack materialise, but for half an hour they lined the parapet with rifles at the ready, some hoping for a chance to get back at the enemy, and some hoping only to be allowed to live through this day. Runners came and went, and it was a diversion – if a rather mean-spirited one – to watch them cross open ground. They never did see the one who arrived towards evening, though. This one brought the order for the Berkshires to hold and for the Munsters to retire.

They waited until it was properly dark and then, after handshakes between the officers, Fitzmullen-Brophy led his men, stiff-legged after being cramped so long in their trenches, out of the line and over the hill to the rear. He insisted that they follow the route they had taken in, although it had proved so dangerous in daylight. He was damned if he was going to leave any wounded unattended through the night. They went back and forth across that field several times, not smoking, and not even talking above a whisper, although the Germans were half a mile away. They couldn't find the men they'd left on the way in. Fitzmullen-Brophy concluded that they had been picked up by roving stretcher parties during the day, but all the way back he was nagged by the painful doubt that they'd been searching the wrong field.

III

CONTEMPTIBLES

All of this is now like the fragment of a dream, and the troops who marched and sang are many of them on the further side of the boundary; but still the memory remains, though the rows and ranks of men are gone...

—Mrs Victor Rickard, *The Story of the Munsters*

51

...There was many a sword and shield left broken, and many a dead body lying on the ground, and many a fighting man left with a foolish smile on his face.

—Lady Augusta Gregory, Gods And Fighting Men

On the Marne the Germans lost their chance of an early victory. The French and British lost theirs on the Aisne.

The German positions proved too strong for the Allies to push them out, so the Allies moved left and attempted to hook them out instead. That didn't work either. Seeing the possibility of taking Paris before winter reappear, the Germans tried a flanking movement of their own, but the debilitated armies of their enemies still had the wherewithal to foil them. Instead of there being any sort of a breakthrough, the line merely extended west and then north as flanking move countered flanking move. At the English Channel they ran out of room to manoeuvre.

Armies raced to the sea, but there were still plenty of men left to man the trenches dug along the Aisne, and along every mile of front yet fought over. On the Allied side, those men were mostly French. France had bled that autumn, but France had the whole adult male population to put into uniform, whereas the United Kingdom only had the British Army, what little of it was left. The British Expeditionary Force had suffered terrible casualties on the Aisne – more than in all the fighting of the campaign so far.

The 2nd Royal Munster Fusiliers remained as army troops for the rest of September – odd-job men, fatherless and motherless still. They tried to rebuild the battalion, but their attempts were so often set back by repeated demands on their manpower. Drafts would come from home, and platoons and companies would be organised, and then the call would come for urgent reinforcement in a threatened sector, and the casualty lists would be drawn up and the process of reconstruction would have to start all over again.

Fitzmullen-Brophy's party was luckier than most. They endured two more adventures like their day in the line with the Berkshires, but they got off lightly both times. Despite there now being a new colonel to command the battalion – if there ever was going to be a battalion – they led a semi-independent existence, answering to Brigade and Division as much as to anyone else.

Major Hugh Fitzmullen-Brophy was wearied by the exertions he endured, and disheartened by the losses he witnessed, but he was glad that there was no more talk for the time being of sending him home. He still thought of himself as fit, but he was reminded too often that he was not a young man any more. He felt a stiffness in his joints that had never troubled him before, and the coming of autumn gave him a cold in his chest that took its time in going. He felt rather ashamed to have to resort to Tummy Belcher's whiskey and to have to write to Susan for winter woollens. He had worn such things many times before, but that wasn't the point: these weren't the hills up by the Afghan border, nor was it winter yet. And another thing: the war shouldn't have lasted this long. It wasn't that he felt personally culpable for the failure of the army to beat the Germans by now, but as he watched the new men come in from Tralee, there was no hiding the rashness of his scheme to get into the war so fast. The men he'd brought with him would have had ample time to finish their recruit training if he'd allowed things to take their proper course. And maybe Cassidy, Ryan, and Tobin might still be alive because of it.

He tried to push such thoughts to the back of his mind, but he had never been callous enough an officer for that.

Lieutenant Edward Fleming was getting along well. He still knew precious little about commanding a platoon, but the evolutions of the parade ground and the pitfalls of the officers' mess were a long way away. His stock with the men, and with himself, had risen considerably when he got his chance of bringing in a wounded man under fire. The wounded man turned out to be dead, but that was a small point. A bullet had nicked Fleming's arm but he hadn't reported sick. On top of it all, his moustache was beginning to look pretty good at last. All in all, it wasn't turning out to be such a bad war, and he was immensely grateful to the major for bringing him along.

Sergeant Cornelius Duffy went back to cooking, but he stayed on as sort of a platoon sergeant all the same. He wasn't going to leave the major alone.

Private Charlie Robinson kept his good humour after his mate Dwyer died, but as soon as they were out of the line he got drunk, and he stayed drunk as much as possible thereafter. No one knew quite how he managed it, and no one took him to task over it either. Lieutenant Fleming was still too shy to challenge him and Major Fitzmullen-Brophy was too indulgent to punish an old South Africa hand. Also there was the fact that Robinson remained a good soldier.

Private Francis Moriarty, after seven years in the ranks, was offered a lance corporal's stripe but he turned it down. A man who accepted a promotion like that was only letting on that he was a cut above his mates. He'd be there with a single stripe on his sleeve with no friends and the sergeants still pissing on him from a height. No thank you. Private Joseph Moyle was offered the same, and he took it, which made Moriarty change his mind, but it was too late. It rankled all the more when he worked out that the offered promotion came on the day that, had there been no war, he would have gained his discharge from the army.

Private Timothy Whelan finally found a chaplain, attached to the Connaught Rangers, to hear his confession. Whelan was a month shy of his twentieth birthday, and since August he had killed or mortally wounded eight men, but when he knelt down before the priest he spoke of a churn of milk that he and his mates had stolen from the back of a house up near Maubeuge, and when they had drunk what they wanted out of it they left the rest to spoil in the sun. Whelan was absolved of his theft, but he was not made easy in his soul. What he couldn't tell the padre was that a man in the South Irish Horse had shown him some dirty postcards, and Whelan was utterly determined to acquire a set of his own as soon as ever he could.

Private Patrick Riordan was the first of them to make it home. The bullet wound to his shin was severe but clean. He was evacuated to a hospital in Le Havre, and thence to England. He was back in Ireland by the end of the year, walking around with a stick and drinking whatever people were buying him. It was a grand life. He was not sent overseas again because he was only a Special Reservist who had never finished his recruit training in the first place.

Private Daniel Wyndham wound up in hospital too.

52

I shall go after the heroes, ay, into the clay…

—Egan O'Rahilly, 'Last Lines'

Hôpital de Sacre Coeur,
Paris

October 10th

Dear Sarah,

Although it will not surprise you that there is rather more truth to be told, you should know that everything in the letter I wrote Mother is true all the same. I have not been wounded. The reason I have been in hospital is down to a swelling of the knee caused by my accidentally kneeling on a rusty nail. Honestly. I have not been shot. I might say that I have not been in any danger, but that would be a lie. This is a war, and a just war at that, and if it is necessary for me to be placed in harm's way then I will not shirk.
France is a beautiful and splendid country and worth fighting for. I am far from being the only American that thinks so. Indeed, I was taken to Paris by a member of an American volunteer ambulance unit that was formed in Paris when war broke out. If my driver is in any way typical of the volunteers

then I can declare they are all fine fellows, and risking far greater dangers than I.

Recognising me for a fellow expatriate, he went out of his way to take me to Paris, as he maintained I would receive far better attention here than in one of the British base hospitals, and as far as I can tell, he was right. Everyone has been very attentive and very kind. It was quite comical how I started out as un pauvre Anglais, *before becoming* un pauvre Irlandais, *until at last graduating to* un pauvre Americain. *By the time I was declared* un brave Americain *it was evident that I was well on my way to recovery, and I was discharged earlier today.*

I have seen very little of Paris, and most of that from a hospital window, but it is a very fine city. I can assure you (and Mother, of course) that there is none of the immorality or frivolity that concerns her so much. The French people are utterly dedicated to this war, and it is a very noble thing to see.

I am very sorry to be causing you such concern, and I am very sorry for having deceived you, but if I read your letters correctly, sister, I do believe you are secretly rather proud of what I am doing.

I will be returning to the front as soon as I find out what train I am to catch, but you needn't fret for me too much. As things stand I am not so much a soldier as a sort of secretary to Major Fitzmullen-Brophy, who is a kind man and a very fine gentleman. Furthermore, what with winter coming on, I can't imagine there will be much more fighting. People are talking of a peace settlement before Christmas, but if the war does start up again next spring I should be out of it, as my enlistment runs out in December.

With things more settled at the front the mail should be more regular and your letters won't be piling up any place.

Thank you for your encouraging words, and please do tell Emily Winters that she may write me.

All my love,

Daniel.

P. S. Do you think it proper that I write Penelope Van Wyngarden? If so, could you (tactfully) ask her if I may?

D

He was going to cross out that last bit, and had his pen poised so long that the ink was in danger of drying on the nib, but in the end he left it as written. Two lines blotted out would only deface the letter and raise suspicions beside. Anyway, he reminded himself, he was in Paris, and at war, and Massachusetts was far away. His sister's disapproval really shouldn't concern him the way it used to.

Paris. Here he was at last, and under circumstances unguessed at too. He was not the studious American tourist who had left home in the summer. Now he was the brave British soldier, receiving looks both admiring and sympathetic from passers-by – some of them female and disconcertingly fetching. Of course he was getting some scandalised and disapproving looks too. That was on account of his trousers, which were the same ones that had been cut down to shorts and indifferently hemmed back in August. The waiter in this pleasant café had looked askance at his bare knees when Wyndham had come in, but the waiter had seen Scottish Highlanders before this, and this customer, if underdressed, at least wasn't wearing a skirt.

Wyndham at least had the dignity of a bandage on one exposed knee, but reminded himself to look out for an understanding quartermaster at the first opportunity. Before that, before he left Paris, he had a whole shopping list to run through. A man who was shot tended to be invalided out with no more than a cheerio from his mates, but a man who succumbs to the swelling of the knee over two days, and is publicly offered to be evacuated to Paris, tends to receive any number of requests for little luxuries.

So before he dealt with the challenges of the Gare du Nord in wartime, Wyndham would have to track down pipe tobacco and handkerchiefs for the major, and chocolate and socks and reading material in English for whoever happened to be on hand when he was helped into the ambulance. He had no idea where to start. He didn't want to disappoint anyone in his unit, but he felt that he'd have to go absent without leave if he spent all the time necessary in trying to please everyone. Then there were his own comforts to be taken into consideration. He wanted a haircut and he wanted underclothes that weren't government issue. Did he even have money for half of this?

He addressed the letter to his sister and signalled the waiter. The time had come.

'Bear up,' he muttered to himself. 'Remember the Aisne.'

The waiter looked like a man of the world. He should know where to acquire those dirty postcards for Whelan.

A good soldier should never be found wanting of a good billet. That's how Tummy Belcher had always managed to spend every night of the war so far indoors. He could not own to any fixed abode, but wherever Fitzmullen-Brophy's detachment of the Munsters happened to be sent, there was Belcher, somewhere to their rear, with a roof over his head and space to stow his extensive kit. There was more than that even. Belcher justified his existence by taking charge of the stores and the rations and the lines of communication, such as they were, and somehow, with every move, he found the transport to shift the ever-growing stock of necessaries that he hoarded. Belcher had an eye for a bargain and had picked up all sorts in all sorts of places, and his instinctive feel for army morality kept his various acquisitions just the right side of larceny. He also, of course, knew chaps all over, and bartered favours and whiskey for blankets and tinned beef and waterproofs and whatnot. His role of unofficial quartermaster and adjutant was tolerated by the new colonel when he arrived, and soon appreciated too. It wasn't just the whiskey that was delivered to him one morning either. The new colonel feared officers of a certain age and an independent and intractable spirit, but he quickly recognised Belcher's usefulness. No doubt a time would come when the scattered detachments of the 2nd Munsters would be brought together again as a battalion, and order and the rule of law would have to be imposed on awkward characters like Belcher and Fitzmullen-Brophy, but for now Belcher was free to run his little khaki fiefdom.

At the moment, this was centred on an outbuilding of a farm near Armentières, and it was here that Wyndham arrived on a dull October day. Belcher thought well of Wyndham. He admired the young man's spirit. Joining the army had been an obvious mark in his favour, but following FitzEm to the war like that showed pluck, and rare pluck for a foreigner. Belcher's regard for Wyndham didn't mean that he was on hand to welcome the American back, of course. Wyndham may have been a gentleman, but he was still an other rank. Nevertheless, the word was that Wyndham could reclothe himself from Belcher's stores as he pleased, and no paperwork needed, and Wyndham, feeling the cold, was only too happy to accept this generosity.

The smell of mothballs brought back memories of his first day in Ballymullen, but the stores here were nothing like what the depot had boasted. This place looked like a small second-hand shop, or an uninspired jumble sale. An English corporal was in charge. Wyndham recognised the face, and knew that his name was Thompson, but the corporal's stripes were new.

'Major gave them to me on probation, you might say. He wants an NCO in charge and gave me the job when I come out of hospital. Nothing much the matter with me but my feet's buggered, so it's a cushy job in the rear for me.'

'I've just come from hospital myself,' said Wyndham.

'Yeah, I know,' said Thompson. 'Paris, right? Lucky sod. All I got was a bleeding hospital tent behind the lines. How long did you get?'

'Two weeks.'

'Two weeks? You won't know the place, son.'

Wyndham had had no end of trouble finding his way to Armentières, and he confessed that he'd never known the place at all.

'You know what I mean, mate. The company, the unit, whatever you call it. It's all changed, isn't it? Here – you don't mind if I sit down a minute. Like I say, the feet is in a right state.'

He settled himself and lit up a fag and talked about the comings and the goings and the doings of the unit.

'We've been bloody here, there, and everywhere. Few chaps has got hit, and quite a few more has got sick – like me and you, for instance – and there's a whole lot of new faces too. Reservists come in from Tralee. Old sweats the lot of them. Some of them are right old men who've been sweated on the square since the war begun, and others are the idle buggers who only answered their call up when they'd settled their affairs at home. You know – get the spuds in, send the missus off to her sister, find someone to mind the shop – that sort of thing.

'Some of them are all right, but some of them is coming the old soldier like you wouldn't bloody credit. "When I was in Egypt", "When I was in South Africa", "We didn't do it that way when I was in bloody India holding Kitchener's bloody hand, sir". That sort of thing. Useless bloody shower. You can bet your arse I'm glad I got these stripes, so I don't have to put up with all that shite.

'Here – don't you mind me going on like this. I've bloody nobody to talk to the whole bloody day. Anyway – major says you're to get the deluxe service, my lucky lad, so what can I do you for?'

To Wyndham's consternation there were no trousers.

'First thing I ran out of, mate. It's the weather, isn't it? But don't worry – I think we can make you decent. Hang on.' Thompson rummaged for a moment, reconstructing as he spoke a trade route running from the horse artillery through an old chum of Major Belcher's. Finally: 'Here we are. Try these.'

Not trousers but breeches. Snug at the knee, reinforced at the seat, and not ballooning around the backside like what Wyndham was used to either. He was captivated at first sight.

'Only got two pairs,' said Thompson, 'so one of them had better fit you.' But that first pair fitted just fine and, for the first time since the day he'd had put on khaki, Wyndham longed for a full-length mirror.

As he went about the laborious business of wrapping his puttees and lacing his boots again, Thompson rooted out a groundsheet and a blanket and a cardigan waistcoat.

'I already have one of those,' said Wyndham, referring to the cardigan.

'Take another. Wear both of them at the same time too, or if you can do without one you can swap it for anything you want. Same with socks. I'm giving you three pairs there.'

'You're very kind, but I managed to buy socks in Paris.'

'Take these anyway. Worth their weight in gold in the trenches. Trust me. You should see the state of my feet.'

Wyndham took them. It was a strange new world indeed when the stores were just handing out kit for free, where a corporal was being friendly and not standing on his rank, and when the government was issuing apparel that made a man look and feel like a man.

'Anything else?' asked Thompson, as Wyndham did his best to stow everything.

Wyndham's eyes tracked along the goods, his mind filled with new possibilities.

'I don't suppose you'd have such a thing as a slouch hat?' he asked.

No, there were no slouch hats, but Wyndham wasn't too disappointed. He was properly dressed and, as he quickly discovered, a sight better dressed than most. The summer fashions of mutilated uniform had largely disappeared, but Wyndham, with his original cap still largely in its original condition, immediately stood out as an elegant new arrival. Caps were evidently being worn floppy and shapeless at the front that autumn. The wire stiffener that gave a flat circular top to the cap had been bent all out of shape or, more commonly, removed altogether. The resultant softer crown was more comfortable and looked less like a cap from a distance. With German snipers not a hundred yards from the front-line trenches, that second consideration was the clincher.

Men who had lost their caps were wearing a most unmilitary piece of headgear. This was the 'comforter cap', universally known as the cap comforter, because of the backwards way kit was described in the quartermasters' lists. It was little more than a tube of knitted wool like an extra-large sock. The sort of kind heart that provides knitwear for poor soldiers designed it as to be worn under the cap or around the neck on cold nights. It was never intended to be worn as a substitute for the cap, yet Wyndham was seeing them everywhere.

Even French troops were beginning to look shabby, with the brave reds and blues covered or replaced with duller cloth, or mostly just darkened with grime and lightly spread all over with mud. At least there was something proud and martial to see in the new arrivals from India. The costumes, like everything else, were still khaki, but undoubtedly exotic. The men that Wyndham saw in turbans, although formidable-looking soldiers, were stamping their feet and blowing on their hands when not engaged in work. Brown skin had a distinctly greyish tinge on some men, and running noses and chattering teeth were part of the picture. Hardly surprising: the Lahore Division had exchanged the Punjab in August for Flanders in October.

Finding anywhere was next to impossible. Armentières was marked on maps. It was served by road and rail. Getting there should not have posed too many problems once one had worked out that you asked for 'Armeteers' when seeking directions from an English speaker. But half the roads were in German hands, and all the others were clogged with military traffic, with most of the drivers not knowing their destination and simply following the wagon or the man in front. There were still refugees too. The war had swept over the district in a few days in August but since it had come back it was giving the impression that it was here to stay. Some dogged farmers persisted in their work, but the prospects for 1915 were unfavourable.

Even the locals who had stayed would have been hard put to help a lost Tommy find his unit. Bar the absence of a few trees and the partial destruction of a few buildings, the landscape was as it had always been, but the names were changing. The British adaptation of French and Flemish tended to be careless, and sometimes the original place name was ignored altogether. Sometimes, indeed, names had to be found for features that had never needed them before, with previously unconsidered rises in the ground marked and emphasised on artillery maps, and trenches and command posts acquiring what amounted to postal addresses. It had become a parochial world far more insular than the departing peasantry had known. Men in the line knew their own trench, and everything visible from the parapet. Officers and runners knew a little more, and everybody was familiar with the nearest hamlet that served as a rest area, and the nearest little town behind that which might as well have been the capital city of this newly staked-out country.

Belcher's storehouse was located at a place once known only after its owner, the family Lefévre. It was now Three Poplar Farm. The trees were in fact elms, but the army did not officially recognise elms. Also, there were only two of them left, and the blast that had brought down the third had left one of the survivors looking pretty shaky. From there Wyndham had to find his way to another location known since two weeks ago as Sutherland Farm, but the Argyll & Sutherlands had moved on and the premises tended to be marked on sketch maps now as the Piggery. It lay somewhere between Ploegsteert ('Plug Street') and Touquet ('Tucket', but try asking for Tookey or even Tokay). No main roads led there, and the little lanes were deep in mud. Closer to the front the lanes were eschewed in favour of paths that had the sole virtue (if even that) of being hidden from direct German observation.

Every track was in use by men and mules, and every depression and the lee of every bank was home to a field kitchen, a dressing station, or a supply dump, yet no one had much of an idea as to where to find the Munster Fusiliers. Wyndham was wondering if he'd ever find the place before dark, and was wondering whether turning back to the relative comforts of Armentières might constitute desertion. A party of signallers helped him out in the end, and were even so good as to give him a mug of tea while they argued among themselves where Wyndham needed to go and the best way of getting there without getting shot.

It turned out to be no more than two hundred yards, but that was as the crow flies and not as the front wends. The Piggery, which Fitzmullen-Brophy really wanted to be named something more heroic or patriotic, still smelt very strongly of pigs, but it had a roof and was convenient for the front line. The yard was indifferently cobbled, but at least the dungheap had been shovelled away somewhere downwind. The back door opened onto a dank little space, which led to a narrow cut that turned left into a waterlogged ditch, overhung with weeds and partly floored and reinforced with brushwood and hay, and that ditch was the support line. A brisk trot across eighty yards or so of overgrown pasture led to the front line.

It was a journey that no one liked to make, but Fitzmullen-Brophy chose to make it anyway, at least once a day, just to keep on good terms with the perfectly decent bunch of riflemen who were holding the front. He shared the Piggery with the commanding officer and the headquarters element of the rifle battalion and would have been ashamed to watch his opposite number go out into danger every morning while he stayed indoors himself.

A communication trench was being dug between front and support lines, but the ground was wet and heavy and progress was slow. Tomorrow the two units would switch places, or at least that was the plan, unless Corps HQ thought yet again to yank the Munsters out of the line and shuttle them off somewhere else.

There was little enough to be found in the Piggery, but Sweeney was there, sitting on an upturned bucket and patiently boiling water in a mess tin held over a candle flame.

'For the major's tea,' he explained. 'It won't be ready for ages, but there's nothing else to be doing. Are you back so?'

'I'm back,' admitted Wyndham.

'You're looking well,' said Sweeney.

'Thank you.'

'You won't be wanting your old job back – will you though?' asked Sweeney.

'What do you mean?'

'You know – doing for Major Fitzmullen-Brophy.'

'What do you mean "doing"?' asked Wyndham.

'You know – looking after him and that. Officer's servant like.'

'I was never the major's servant,' said Wyndham with patient dignity. 'I merely assisted him where necessary.'

'So you're grand so. You won't mind, like. Only it's a right cushy number. Sure the man has hardly any kit and there's no point trying to keep it too clean out here. And it keeps me out of the wet too.'

'Well enjoy it, Sweeney. You're very welcome to it.'

'Ah thanks. The major gave me it because I've never fired my musketry course. Better I'm out of the line, he says.'

'The major around?'

'He's off having a nose around the other trenches I think. Mister Fleming's about though. Don't know where, mind.'

'I suppose I should report to somebody,' said Wyndham. 'Sergeant Harris here?'

Sweeney put on his funeral face. 'Ah no – Sergeant Harris only got himself killed there, day before yesterday. A sniper did it.'

Wyndham had hardly known the sergeant for more than a fortnight, and had had little enough to do with him then, but he knew how to react to the news of a death.

'I'm so sorry,' he said.

'God rest the poor man,' said Sweeney. He observed a decent interval of silence, and then added, 'Sergeant Duffy's in charge now.'

'I'll go look for Sergeant Duffy then. Mind yourself, Sweeney.'

'Mind yourself, Wyndham. You're looking very well.'

'Thank you.'

'Well look at the cut of yourself,' said Moriarty, playing mine host in his corner of the trench. He was one of the ones with a slovenly knitted cap pulled over hair that wanted cutting. His moustache was straggling all over his face too.

'Are you a cut above us now, with your fancy cavalry togs and all?' he said.

'How are you, Moriarty? I'm glad to see you well.'

'Nothing can kill me, boy,' Moriarty laughed, and then hurriedly touched the wooden stock of his rifle, vexed at his own foolish boast. 'Well nothing except a Hun bullet or a shell or the consumption or something, of course.'

Wyndham smiled. 'I brought you chocolate,' he said.

Moriarty was touchingly surprised. 'Jesus,' he said, 'You are better than the rest of us. Sit down there a bit and we'll have some. Mind your good clothes, though.'

They sat, and companionably stuffed their faces. Moriarty was terrified lest someone come upon them and he be obliged to share. He finished quickly. 'So tell us about Paris, then,' he said.

Wyndham swallowed and thought.

'Paris,' he said finally, a wistful look coming across his face.

'Go on – Paris.'

Wyndham thought about the hospital ward, and the café and a rapid search around windy streets and small shops before the train left.

'Paris,' he said. 'It's everything you've imagined.' And his eyes misted and a shadow of a smile played across his face.

'Well go on, for the love of God,' said Moriarty. 'Tell us about it. Tell us about the girls.'

'The girls,' said Wyndham, 'are the most beautiful I've ever seen.'

He let that settle in for a moment and went on, 'If I live through this war, Moriarty, I will go back to Paris, and I will sit in the gardens of the Palais Royale and watch the young ladies go by, and I will ask for nothing more from life.'

'Go on – really?'

'No. Not really. I don't suppose I could do it.'

'Why not?'

'They wouldn't let me.'

'What do you mean. What do you mean they wouldn't let you? Who?'

'The girls. They don't allow you just to sit there. They won't let you alone. They see a man in uniform and they have to come up and thank him for what he's doing for France.'

'Get away.'

'And then they ask if there's something they can do – you know – to repay you for your efforts and your sacrifice and all.'

'Ah you're messing. You're making this up.'

'You know what I think, Moriarty? I don't think it's patriotism or gratitude that moves them.'

'No?'

'I think they're just bored. All the men are away at the war, you see. Why else would they go up to a total stranger and ask him to go to a café with them, or to the theatre – or even home with them?'

'You're making this up. You have to be making this up.'

'It's a very beautiful city, Moriarty. You really should go there. The picture galleries are the finest in the world outside of Italy, so they say.'

'Bollocks to the blessed picture galleries. Go back to the girls there. Do they really throw themselves at fellas like that?'

'They're very lonely, Moriarty – and very bored. One feels very sorry for them, you know.'

'And these aren't brassers or prossies or the like?'

'Private Moriarty, I am ashamed. These are respectable ladies. Respectable by Paris standards, at least.'

And then he took the opportunity to gaze into the middle distance and sigh contentedly.

'And so very beautiful,' he added after a while.

Moriarty had seen nothing but the mud walls of a trench in a wet field on the Belgian border for days past. He was hungry for entertainment and not amused by Wyndham's silent reveries.

'So what did you *do*, Wyndham? For the love of Christ!'

'I fear I am being indiscreet.'

'Indiscreet my arse. What happened next?'

'And here's Lance Corporal Moyle! How are you, Lance Corporal? I've brought chocolate.'

'Ah good man yourself, Wyndham,' said Moyle, accepting the offer. 'I heard you were back. You should go and find Mr Fleming and let him know.'

And Wyndham heaved himself up and slapped the mud from his seat and was on his way to do Moyle's bidding, but Moriarty stopped him.

'Ah come on now,' he said. 'You can't leave a fella hanging like that. Moyle, you dirty eejit, what did you have to go butting in for? We were just getting to the good bits.'

'You mind how you go talking to the non-commissioned officers, you,' said Moyle.

But Moriarty ignored him. Wyndham was already on his way.

'You'll finish the story later, will you?' Moriarty called plaintively. But Wyndham was already gone.

'I'll only kill him if he never tells me what happened next,' muttered Moriarty, to himself as much as to Moyle.

But Wyndham had no idea what happened next. He had never told a dirty story in his life, and was very hazy as to the ingredients that made up one. Still, if he had the gumption to negotiate the purchase of erotic photographs with a complete stranger, then he should be able to invent something juicy before he faced Moriarty again. Juicy – but necessarily vague.

53

'Gentlemen, examine this ground carefully. It is going to be a battlefield; you will have a part to play upon it.'

—Napoleon at the field of Austerlitz

Fitzmullen-Brophy wandered alone. The fields were wet and neglected and empty. Except for the crows there was no wildlife at all. There were men enough, but they kept silent and out of sight – creatures too fearful to come out by day. Traces of them could be glimpsed: the careful raising of a sentry's head; the furtive movement of a man leaving the trenches on some errand; the drift of woodsmoke marking some optimist's attempt to cook something palatable out of army rations. Sometimes there were shots too. Mostly they were distant and random, but once or twice they came close to Fitzmullen-Brophy, and one was most certainly aimed at him, and would most certainly have hit him if he had not just that second ducked his head to avoid catching a bramble.

He tramped these melancholy fields because he liked to get out in the fresh air. As soon as the wearisome business of army paperwork was out of the way – and he'd never had a head for that sort of thing – he would wrap up well and take his stick and be gone for as long as he could get away with. He visited the men in the line, of course, and then paid his respects to the neighbouring units. Seeing as that necessitated climbing out into the open, and that hadn't got him killed yet, he had resolved to stay in the open as much as possible. The Piggery was dank and unpleasant and the trenches were unhealthy for a man trying to shake off a head cold. It was almost impossible to keep one's feet dry. Besides, it was bad practice for an officer to be around the men for more than was necessary. It made them uneasy.

And naturally these daily jaunts behind the front line were not merely for exercise or pleasure. Far from it. A soldier who has seen the Northwest Frontier or the Transvaal knows better than anyone else the value of an eye for country. Fitzmullen-Brophy was coming to know every fold and hollow of these fields, imagining how he would move his men across them, or how the Hun might come at him. And it was not just the land behind the British line that he explored, but sometimes, where there were still trees and hedges for cover, he had ventured forward of the line. This was not some peculiar eccentricity either: the commanding officer of the rifle battalion had made the reconnaissance with him on more than one occasion. An officer did not sit passively in a trench, waiting for the enemy to decide his fate, and a British officer did not let the enemy tell him where he might or might not go. No man's land was a convenient term, but the conviction was that British ground extended right up to the German wire.

Fitzmullen-Brophy had tripped on that very wire one night, and had very nearly come a cropper, only his companion had caught onto his arm before he fell. He was not in the leastways embarrassed about that, but the wire itself bothered him. As entanglements went it didn't amount to much, and in daylight would have been an inconsiderable obstacle, but it was wrong that the Germans should have more of it than his own side. He was proud of the British Army, and the smallness of the army added to his pride. A small professional force, well trained and well led, had met the largest army on the continent of Europe and bloodied their nose for them. How? Professionalism. Stick-to-it-iveness. Sound military instinct. Yet here were the blasted Germans, who were supposed to be attacking, remembering to bring rolls of barbed wire to the war, while the British had hardly enough for a strand or two. It was a rum business, and reflected poorly on the British organisation. Someone had *not been prepared.*

Of course there was so much to do all over, and so few men with which to do it. The trenches should have been deeper and more extensive, but with battalions at half strength and less it was all they could do to man the thinly stretched line as it was. Linking one platoon's trench to another's was often too much to ask, let alone digging proper communication trenches. At the present, all work was concentrated in keeping the trenches from falling in or flooding, and the battle against water would certainly have been given up for lost if there had been anything else to occupy the men.

Fitzmullen-Brophy was reminded of the poor drainage in the area when, keeping in the cover of a hedge, he rounded a corner and saw that the puddle of a few days ago had become more of a pond. It was hardly too deep to splash through, but he had no appetite for a soaking. The alternative was to break cover and detour through the open, where any wide-awake Hun could pot at him, but Fitzmullen-Brophy's contempt for the enemy was as great this day as his distaste for wet socks. He was dashed if he'd allow the blasted Germans to oblige him to crawl through water. He gathered his wits and made a run for it. Nothing happened. No shot rang out, and that made him feel immensely bucked. The Boches didn't deserve to win this war if they kept such a poor lookout.

Making it to a sheltered pathway, he started to think, not for the first time, what a fine country this was after all, even in this colourless autumn. He would like to come back here after the war – in the summertime ideally. He could bring his grandson, or however many grandchildren Molly saw fit to bless him with, and they could see where their old Grandpa had fought the Great War.

Made it all worthwhile, really.

He took to whistling 'As I Roved Out One Morning' as he

walked, and as he came back towards the Munsters' position he heard through the bushes someone join in the chorus.

'Who goes there, Major?' said the voice, after a few bars.

'A friend, O'Leary,' said Fitzmullen-Brophy. His whistling had partly been good spirits, and partly a way of alerting the sentry who might not otherwise have been so alert, and the sentry knew it, and Fitzmullen-Brophy knew that he knew it. It didn't matter. The Germans were hardly going to come at them from this angle. But it pleased him that an officer could share a joke with his men, and that a man could join in a tune with an officer. That was something the Prussians would never have. They could impose the discipline but never nurture the easy spirit of proper soldiers.

Let them come. The Munsters would be more than a match for them.

54

…We are of the one country and the one soil, and we will give our bodies and our lives for your sake.

—Lady Augusta Gregory, *Gods And Fighting Men*

Wyndham was in very good odour with the company on his return. He couldn't bring gifts for everyone, but his chocolates and cigarettes were judiciously bestowed. On top of that, he found that the status of the surviving recruits from Tralee had risen in his absence. He may have been useless and handless still, not knowing a rifle from a button stick as far as the regulars were concerned, but he had been with them at the Aisne, and that was more than could be said for the replacements who'd been drifting in. Half of those fellas were only mouth, and they were all full of excuses as to why they'd missed the first month of the war. Drilling in Aldershot? The war was in France, mate.

So the Yank was all right. He didn't come the old soldier and he was open-handed and he told good stories. The ones about Paris weren't very convincing, and were sparse on details, but the ones he got out of books were all right. They weren't for everyone, but Wyndham had a small audience who were glad of the diversion, and could be grumpy when they didn't get it.

Wyndham was appointed company clerk, which meant that he never had to find out what happened to his rifle after he'd been invalided out of the line. It also meant that he had a billet in one corner of the Piggery, and was spared the tedious and endless tasks of maintaining the trenches. Any man not on sentry-go or without a specific job spent half his life with a shovel in his hand shovelling muck out of the bottom of the trench onto the parapet, but there was always more muck at the end of it. The only saving grace about this life was the shortage of shovels. The alternative to shovelling was the collection of materials for providing walls and floor to the trenches and for vainly trying to keep the water levels down. Wyndham was lucky to be out of all that.

It was surprising how quickly it all became routine. The days here went by so slowly that Wyndham's return was for a few hours the talk of the trenches, but was old news by teatime, when the chocolate was all gone. By the next day he might never have been away, and by the day after that he was so well settled in that he'd almost forgotten it himself.

His official duties were light. He took the daily nominal roll from Duffy and compiled the company diary for Fleming. Duffy was conscientious with lists but his handwriting was atrocious, and it was too much to expect Fleming to compose a paragraph detailing the weather and the minor doings of the unit. The young lieutenant had, after all, turned his back on academia. After that there was whatever paperwork came up the line from Brigade, and from their distant parent, the battalion. Wyndham had little idea as to the proper forms for this sort of bureaucracy, but neither did Fitzmullen-Brophy for the most part. So much of it too was irrelevant to the point of fantasy. Writing a return for the number of socks in store was something that exercised Wyndham's conscience for some hours, causing him to wonder whether he should include his Parisian stock in the total, and if any of his comrades had similar caches of unauthorised socks hidden in their haversacks. In the end, on Duffy's authoritative advice, he counted the number of men in the unit and halved the total, in the hope that higher authority might take pity on the poor sockless Munsters.

But another signal from the rear demanded to know how many men had been inoculated against typhoid and were proficient in shorthand. Wyndham actually conducted a brief survey on that one, but time was short and answers were frivolous and insincere. He again appealed to Duffy, but the sergeant merely took the flimsy piece of government paper and headed in the direction of the latrine.

Fitzmullen-Brophy didn't care one way or another. He simply wanted waterproofs and a stockpile of ammunition, and since he could only have the latter, he would glance briefly at whatever Wyndham handed him and irritably sign it before demanding that Wyndham send out another requisition for gumboots and ground sheets. And with such attitudes to provide example, Wyndham learned his way around military bureaucracy.

His life wasn't free of travails though. He was detailed with bringing up the rations in the evenings, and that was no easy matter. He and Duffy, and whoever else was needed, would set off after dark, stumbling through the wet fields, with nothing between them and some stray German bullet. The muddy pathways made for hard going but they didn't dare stray off them for fear of getting lost. The ration dump wasn't too far in the rear, and there was usually hot tea to be had, but there was always too the fruitless argument between the storeman and Sergeant Duffy, the connoisseur of army food. It wasn't that Duffy was on the lookout for extras like everyone else: what he repeatedly took issue with was the quality of the stock, and he would make a great show of unwrapping and inspecting things by the light of a hurricane lamp. All he got out of it was the rancour and ill will of the storeman, who was there to dole out what was there, and not to humour any bloody Irish epicure. Then there would be the slippery journey back, carrying sackfuls of tins or great clumsy cans of drinking water, with the cold of the night meeting the sweat of the body.

The mail tended to come up with the rations, and its distribution was Wyndham's job too. It was this duty above all that made him an accepted and even popular member of the company. He was the Yank who brought good things, and if there was no letter or parcel from home today, there was always news of the outside world, be that world the supply dump behind the lines, or Company HQ in the Piggery, or even the goings-on in the next trench, for some of the positions were so exposed that the soldiers manning them could not be relieved without a major reorganisation of the line. A man would crawl out of his trench by night to draw rations for his section, and Wyndham would crawl in during the morning as a messenger from civilisation.

And if he didn't have much in the way of news, and the lads had time on their hands, then that's when they'd be wanting one of his stories.

This was the usual way of it.

There was nowhere to sit, so they stood, ankle-deep in brown water, and there was nothing to do, so they listened to Wyndham. He had most of the stories in his head, but many verses and favourite quotations filled the water-stained notebook he now pulled from his tunic pocket.

The Milesians were invading Ireland, and Amergin the druid was the first to place his foot upon dry land, bursting into song as he did so, and here Wyndham gave it to them verbatim.

> *'I am the wind that blows upon the sea;*
> *I am the ocean wave;*
> *I am the murmur of the surges;*
> *I am seven battalions;*
> *I am a strong bull;*
> *I am an eagle on a rock;*
> *I am a ray of the sun;*
> *I am the most beautiful of herbs;*
> *I am a courageous wild boar;*
> *I am a salmon in the water;*

I am a lake upon a plain;
I am a cunning artist;
I am a gigantic, sword-wielding champion;
I can shift my shape like a god.'

Wyndham saw the looks on the faces of his audience and thought it best to cut the whole thing short. He waited silently as the notices came in.

'What in the name of God?'

'Jesus!'

That was the initial reaction, but O'Leary was only half joking when he said, 'I dunno, lads. That's powerful stuff. I'd have to hear the tune, though.'

That got a bit of a chuckle.

'I am the waft from the latrine bucket,' said Moriarty.

That got a laugh.

'I am the chats in your long johns,' contributed Whelan. Others were more serious.

'What's that about seven battalions? Was that a lot in those days?'

'No point saying so if it wasn't.'

'Fair enough, but seven? "I am a brigade and a bit, I am an understrength division?" I don't see it.'

'Seven like in the Bible. The deadly sins and that. It's one of those numbers.'

Something had struck a chord in Moyle. 'Think of it though, lads. Ye're all lined up on the strand, and them Milesian bastards is coming towards ye, and the fella in the front, instead of shouting orders, starts spouting that class of stuff? I don't know now. It might put the wind up you.'

'Sure give it a lash yourself and see what happens,' someone gleefully suggested.

Moyle grinned and shrugged. He stood with his face to the

parapet, threw his arms wide, and called towards the German line.

'D'ye hear me?

'I am the wind up your back;

'I am the bayonet up your jacksie.'

That raised a cheer. He paused to think for a moment and then continued, louder.

'I am the gap in your wire;

'I am the sights set at two hundred;

'I am ten rounds rapid.'

Another pause, as they egged him on, Then:

'I am the tot in the tay!'

They roared approval. He pushed on, letting the spirit move him.

'I am the jam on the biscuit!

'I am the wax on Lord Kitchener's moustache!

'I am the badge on the RSM's sleeve!

He took a deep breath.

'I am the tiger on the buttons!

'I am the collar on the dirty shirt!'

They clapped him on the shoulders and howled and laughed. A few of them bobbed their grinning heads above the parapet to see what mischief they'd made among the ranks of the enemy, but there was no response.

55

Fragrant branch, thou didst promise me that thou hadst for me love –

And sure the flower of all Munster is Little Dark Rose!

—'Roisín Dubh' (traditional, translated by Patrick Pearse)

It had all started with a cap on the end of a stick, waved about above the parapet to attract a sniper's attention and to provide some innocent amusement, but service caps were too precious a commodity to be used as bullet-lures, and the shapeless woollen cap comforter, it was pointed out, looked like 'any old thing'. And so a sandbag was stuffed to the shape and size of a human head, and a short crosspiece was added to the stick to make a proper scarecrow of the thing, and another sandbag was added by way of shoulders for this dummy.

Whether the sniper was genuinely fooled, or perhaps because he was possessed of the sporting spirit and wanted to show a polite appreciation of their efforts, he shot the makeshift cap clean off the sandbag head. And so the dummy was considered to be a regular decoy, and a military resource, and not just the product of some bored swaddies feck-arsing around.

And then one morning it was found completely transformed.

It was only to be expected that someone would draw a face on it, so it was no surprise even to see that the eyes had enormously exaggerated eyelashes carefully done in charcoal, and that there were cupid's-bow lips rendered in boot polish. Further efforts with sandbags, however, had added a full figure below the point where any sniper might have been expected to see it. The new-made body was generously stuffed above, and cinched tight below, to present an hourglass figure that made the dummy the star attraction of the whole company front before the morning was out.

'Her name's Rosie,' said Moriarty, and many of the old Ballymullen hands thought this was the gassest thing. They well remembered, or let on that they did, the début performance of Major Fitzmullen-Brophy on his return from India to Kerry. Moriarty told the story anyway.

'You know what he's like with his physical training and his fitness and that. Well he's hardly there a day or two and he has the whole depot company out one morning like we were all recruits. They had to put a stop to him in the end, but that morning weren't we all lined up in our drawers on the parade ground shivering and coughing and groaning and all, and out comes the major, and he's beaming from ear to ear – sure you know yourself – and he's got these short pants on with his knees in the wind, and the same knees are bouncing up to his chin the way he's running out to us. Christ! – but I'd a bad head on me that day, and I thought just the sight of the major was going to finish me off. And he's there doing this deep breathing with his two arms away out from his sides, and these deep knee bends to make him look all bow-legged like he wants the jacks bad, and he's making us all do the same, and – Jesus, lads – you should have heard the coughing out of us.

'"Now, now, men," says he, "I shouldn't be hearing all that coughing out of ye. A high level of fitness is one of the first duties of any soldier." And he says, "Look at me, men. I'm forty-nine years old, but I'm as fit as any man half my age," he says. And he's telling us all about his daily exercises that keep him so fit. "I'd be up at six," he says, "Summer or winter; rain, sleet, or snow. And I'd run the whole way round the barracks and the fields and the ranges twice. Then," says he, "I'll finish up with a cold bath and feel rosy all over." And I swear to God that someone in the rear rank goes, "Ah sure poor Rosie! God love the poor wee girl!"

And that was the end of that particular parade.'

A long time later, it occurred to Wyndham that Moriarty had only been posted to the depot company a few months before he himself had joined the regiment, and that Fitzmullen-Brophy had already been several years in Tralee by then. But in darker times he always had before him that cold morning in the trenches at Armentières, and the men recalling Fitzmullen-Brophy's ridiculous PT parade and wiping the tears of laughter from their grimy faces.

He could never remember what became of Rosie.

56

The winter is creeping in, the summer is gone. High and cold the wind, low the sun, cries are about us… The ferns are reddened and their shape is hidden; the cry of the wild goose is heard; the cold has caught the wings of the birds; it is the time of ice-frost, hard, unhappy.

—Lady Augusta Gregory, *Gods And Fighting Men*

Wyndham was liked and trusted within the unit, but no one man could be trusted with the rum. The stuff came up in cumbersome two-gallon stoneware jugs, and each jug not just carried, but positively escorted. The arrangement put Wyndham in mind of the Wells Fargo stage, and he had no doubt that, should the ration party be ambushed, they would be quick on the trigger in defence of the rum jar. It was only ever one jug at a time, because two gallons of strong rum would do the company for several days unless Major Fitzmullen-Brophy were notably heavy-handed with the ration, and that he most certainly was not. He had nothing against drinking *as such*, and thought that it could be a fine thing *in moderation*, but in his eyes there was a whole world between a man taking a pint or two of ale in good company, preferably in the context of a jolly sing-song, and a young soldier being introduced and habituated to spirits.

He would not go so far as to impose teetotalism on his men, but he really did think that an issue of cocoa would be far preferable to the demon rum. As it was, he had forbidden its issue to soldiers under the age of twenty-one, but Tummy Belcher declared this was nonsense and got his old chum the MO to back him up when he paid the unit a visit. Seeing as rum was to be issued on medical advice, Fitzmullen-Brophy resentfully ordered that it be issued like medicine, which is to say with a tablespoon. Soldiers who had reached the age of maturity had the paltry sixteenth of a pint served to them in a little tin measure, which they had to drink then and there under the eye of an officer to prevent hoarding. The younger men had to stand still and slurp their rum off a spoon, held by the stern major or by Lieutenant Fleming. Private Wyndham held the rum jar and Sergeant Duffy supervised the delicate business of pouring. It was all very solemn, and was the centrepiece of the morning ritual that was the dawn 'stand to'.

Every morning in the shivery pre-dawn the men stood to their arms, which is to say they lined the parapet, rifles ready, and peered out into the dark until it was bright enough to see properly. If the Hun did not attack in that hour or so of poor visibility, then he'd lost his best chance for the day. Afterwards, in the cold first hour of morning, with water being boiled for tea, the rum procession would proceed along the line in sacramental majesty. In the unconnected outposts where the rum party were obliged to climb out of the trenches and move short distances in the open, there was much anxiety about a sniper's bullet shattering the rum jar, but so far all had been well, with officers, men, and rum all getting through safely. Fitzmullen-Brophy would have hated to admit it, but it seemed that the German could sometimes be a sportsman.

The ration having been served out, the rum jar was entrusted to the care of Sergeant Duffy, who kept it in a padlocked box concealed somewhere in back of the Piggery. Its location was not precisely known to anyone, and any attempt to go rooting for it would have aroused instant suspicion. Duffy was a sober man, but Wyndham knew that a second water bottle in the sergeant's possession did not contain water, and that this off-the-books rum, besides keeping the chill out of Duffy's chest, was doled out in small amounts to particular friends. There were some old soldiers, Duffy confided, as would only die without the drink to keep them going, and sure the tiny wee ration was nothing to a man who'd had to drink the cholera and the dysentery out of his system in his time.

This secret and unauthorised bottle was entrusted to Wyndham one night. Duffy knew his man, and knew him to be one who would not betray a sacred trust. No one man could be trusted with the rum, but maybe one abstemious American could be responsible for just a little rum for just a little time. Wyndham wasn't quite teetotal, but he had, out of misplaced politeness, turned down his tot the first time it was issued to him, and had thus been marked down as an abstainer ever since. He did have a sip of the stuff once afterwards, but the concentrated spirit put him in mind of a fire in a sugar refinery. An acquired taste, evidently.

It was a wretched night, with rain after a day of rain, and off on the left of the line there was an outpost that would be half flooded, with the men stuck there all day and in no hope of relief until the next night.

'Poor old Robinson will be feeling bad,' said Duffy. 'I don't think he'll be able for this class of war much longer. He's too old for it and he's not used to the cold climate either. He'd be grand in India, but the damp here can't be doing him any good. And then there's poor old Dwyer getting killed, God be good to him.'

So Wyndham was the man to carry the rum of mercy to Robinson.

'Only for Christ's sake don't give it to him, or he'll have the whole bottle off you. Give it to Moyle. Moyle's in charge of that section, and he's not the sort to be bullied by Robinson. Let Moyle have a drop too. No one else, mind. And have one yourself if you get too wet on the way. But only a drop. No one else. Do you hear me?'

'Yes, Sergeant.'
'And wrap up well.'
'Yes, Sergeant.'

Wyndham, wearing pretty much all the clothing he possessed, turned up the collar of his greatcoat, pulled a sandbag around him by way of a shawl, and splashed his way along the trenches in the dark. Going across in the open would have been quicker and probably dryer, but there was no light at all to travel by. When he came to the end of one section of trench, a sentry gave him the direction: 'It's twenty yards straight that way. And if you run into the fence you've gone wrong. If you get lost altogether you can sit tight and wait for morning or you can sing out and someone will guide you back in – but don't be shouting too loudly. Understand?'

'I think so.'

'And the password is "Dolly Gray". Got that?'

Wyndham had missed the popular tunes of the South African War. 'Dolly what?' he asked.

'Dolly Gray – she's the major's bit on the side. Good luck now.'

He could have stood up straight and walked and no one would have seen him, but instinct drove him to crouch, and a stumble on the uneven ground forced him to his hands and knees. It occurred to him that he was as likely to meet a British bullet as a German on a night like this. The skirts of his greatcoat dragged and tripped him, and he realised why few men in the front line wore them, or if they wore them they hacked them short. The rain had eased off but the tall grass was soaking and all the taller vegetation was dripping. He was just about giving himself up for lost when a voice, quiet but clear, spoke from close by.

'Who goes there?'

'Dolly Gray.'

It was a password that was giving much innocent merriment all along the line that night, and of the available answers, the man of Moyle's section chose: 'Pass, Dolly, and be recognised.'

Wyndham crawled forward, and the voice said, 'Mind yourself,' and then his hand went down on empty air and his face went down into the weeds and he was momentarily in danger of falling head first into the trench, and then he went wrong in righting himself and fell head first into the trench anyway.

'I said "Mind",' said the voice reproachfully. 'Are you all right?'

'I think so.'

'Who is it? Is it Wyndham?'

'It is.'

'Sure I'd know the voice anywhere. What is it you want?'

'I'm looking for Lance Corporal Moyle,' said Wyndham.

'Ah sure you needn't bother with that "lance corporal" stuff – you'll only be giving him notions.'

'Shut up, you,' said Moyle out of the darkness. 'Are you all right there, Wyndham? Did you get wet at all?'

Wyndham had landed on all fours in several inches of cold muddy water and was soaked to the elbows. His legs had been wet enough already, but that didn't make it any less unpleasant.

'I'm all right,' he said and squelched forward to where he heard Moyle.

'Mind yourself,' said the sentry, and Wyndham felt the ground fall away beneath him again and suddenly he was knee-deep in water and would have pitched over into it if the trench hadn't been so narrow or if Moyle hadn't been there to steady him. He heard a reproving sigh from the sentry, who had made his post in the shallowest and driest part of the trench.

Wyndham did his best to ignore the wet feeling that was spreading steadily through his underclothes and, unable to see who might be listening, tried to intimate to Moyle that he had been made a part of the rum conspiracy.

'Sergeant Duffy sent me,' he said. 'With something for Robinson.'

'Come along this way,' said Moyle, evidently party to the plot.

The moon was beginning to come through the clouds, and Wyndham could see a few of the men that made up this command.

There was a man sitting on a box, his chin on his chest, and another man upright and leaning against the trench wall, but somehow still asleep. Around a corner, in a little *cul-de-sac*, there was Robinson, visible only by the tip of his cigarette, glowing orange where he crouched well below the parapet.

'Here you go, Robinson,' said Moyle. 'Duffy sent the bold American with a drop of comfort for you. Give us your mug, old son.'

The voice behind the cigarette end was rasping but friendly.

'Well come on in, my boys, and make yourselves at home. I'd put the kettle on only I ain't got no bleeding kettle.'

'How are you, Robinson?' asked Wyndham.

'All the better for your visit, Wyndham my lad. I do confess I was beginning to feel the effects of the damp, but now here you are to put all that to rights. And you can tell Duffy I said he's a good 'un and a proper bleeding gentleman.'

He held out his mug and his hand was rock steady. Moyle measured out a generous but not excessive wallop, and after Robinson had swallowed half of it in a gulp, Wyndham surprised himself by asking if Moyle would care for one himself. He didn't say, 'Sergeant Duffy told me to tell you...' – he offered Moyle a belt like they were a couple of travelling salesmen getting convivial in a railroad car. To his further surprise, Moyle declined.

'I would but I won't,' he said, and left it at that. Then, 'Are you right, so?'

'Ah – yes. Yes, that's everything, I think.'

'Grand. I'll show you the easier way to get back so. Are you right there, Robinson?'

'Right as rain, mate.'

'I'll show Wyndham how to get back.'

'God bless you, Wyndham.'

'And you, Robinson.'

'Come on along,' said Moyle to Wyndham, and they went.

The outpost consisted of no more than two short trenches making up an uneven T, but even so Wyndham nearly lost his sense of direction. So when Moyle said, 'Up we get,' and hauled himself up and out, Wyndham just took the whole business on trust and followed him.

'You don't want to do this when it's pitch dark,' Moyle said quietly, 'or you'd get lost entirely, but this way is dryer. Longer, mind – but dryer.'

They were crouched in the lee of a hummock, with the ground falling away back towards where Wyndham thought the Munsters' position was. What moonlight as was showed inky-black hollows that might have been a pathway of sorts.

'Can you see where you are?' asked Moyle.

Wyndham thought he could, and said so.

'I'll go with you a bit of the way all the same. Give me a bit of a stretch of the legs.'

The crept on until they reached a tree and Moyle said that it was safe to stand up from here.

'Safe enough, anyway. Don't light a fag or anything though.'

Moyle stretched until he stood spread-eagled in air, and he rolled his head around a few times for good measure.

'You get stiff,' he said. 'Been in that blessed trench since yesterday night, and we'll be there all tomorrow too, and you can hardly move at all in the daylight.

'I'll walk a little of the way with you.' he said. 'Do me good. They're not going to get up to any mischief while I'm gone, and if the Germans attack there'd be damn all I could do about it if I was there.'

'Right,' he said shortly after. 'This is as far as I go.'

In truth, they had come no distance, but it didn't matter. Wyndham recognised the stand of trees they had reached and could find his way home without trouble. He said so to Moyle.

Moyle slapped the trunk of one of the trees. 'Mountain Ash,' he said. 'Rowan. They're the ones will keep the ghosts away. Either that or they let the fairies in. I forget.'

Wyndham's ears perked up. He'd been among the Irish since June and this was probably the first time anyone had brought up a genuine Irish folk superstition.

'Tell me more,' he said, all thoughts of his blankets in the Piggery fleeing away.

'Ah, you know,' said Moyle.

As the silence lengthened to indicate that Wyndham did not know, Moyle went on.

'It's just the stuff that you'd be hearing growing up.'

'What sort of stuff?' asked Wyndham.

'Ah, you know. The stuff that the old people would be saying.'

'Go on,' said Wyndham, with earnest patience. It was like trying to land a fish that might not have been securely hooked.

'You know,' said Moyle. 'Leaving milk out for the fairies and that.'

'People leave milk out for the fairies?'

'Some people. Sometimes.'

Wyndham was afraid to ask any more questions, but after a while Moyle went on anyway.

'I'm not saying that people really believe in it all, mind. It would just be the sort of carry-on that had always been the way. I mean there are stories, you know. There'd be things that everyone knows, like you don't go cutting wood around a fairy fort. That's one everyone knows.'

They do? thought Wyndham.

'But there's many a farmer who'd go and gather wood there if he thought no one could see him and he wanted the bit of timber.'

Wyndham was brimming with questions, but he settled for asking, 'Fairy fort?' He'd come across the like in his reading, and envisioned turreted castles that shimmered in the misty air, where mortals went only on foolish or gallant errand.

'Fairy forts or fairy rings,' said Moyle. 'That's what people would call them. It might only be a little bit of a mound or a few big stones in a field. They're all over the place. Been there forever. People say the fairies made them. I don't know one way or the other, but it's bad luck to be interfering with them.' Moyle paused again, and surveyed the vicinity as if looking for a handy mound or a ring of stones that would provide him with an example of what he was talking about. Certainly, if he was watching for signs of German infiltration he didn't look too concerned.

'I see,' said Wyndham, as the pause lengthened.

'Oh there's all sorts of stories. If you build your house on the path between two fairy rings you're only asking for trouble. Now I say that if there's fairy rings all over the place you'd be hard pressed to find a place that's not on the line between two of them. Sure that only stands to reason.'

'I see,' said Wyndham again.

'It's all old cod,' said Moyle, 'but it's been that way forever so people haven't done away with it yet – all the fairies and leprechauns and the banshee washing your shroud and that. My Uncle Peter swore one night he saw the banshee washing his shroud in the river.'

'Is that so?'

'My uncle Peter McCarthy. An awful old fool. Desperate man for the drink, and wandered in his head even when he wasn't drunk. He heard a fox and thought it was the banshee. Did you ever hear a vixen screech?'

'I don't think so.'

'It's a very eerie sound. It would make the hairs on the back of your neck stand up. Especially if you hear it close by. If you were a bit fanciful it might put you in mind of a woman screaming, but whatever it sounds like, you can take it from me that a vixen doesn't look anything like a woman doing her washing. Not even in the dark. That tells you what sort of a character my Uncle Peter was, right enough.'

Moyle gave a little derisive snort, and stopped again, as if he'd got to the punchline.

To get him started again Wyndham asked, 'How did he know it was his shroud?'

'That's what it always is. If you see the banshee it's always your shroud that she's washing.'

'Ah.'

There was silence again until Wyndham asked what became of Uncle Peter.

'Ah, he's still alive, but I haven't seen him in years and years. I imagine he's still mad, and probably madder now. He'd be the man to talk to about the rowan trees.'

Wyndham found himself wondering what would have become of him if, on first landing in Ireland, he had encountered Uncle Peter McCarthy instead of Private Francis Moriarty.

'It's very easy,' said Moyle, 'to be reminded of that class of thing when you're out here.' He waved an arm to encompass this dark landscape straddling the Belgian-French border.

'It can give you a very eerie feeling. I know that the Hun is only just over there and he'd kill you as soon as look at you, but you can't help thinking of all the things that Uncle Peter and the old ones would be on about. You'd see things in the shadows that aren't right. That's why I don't mind this trench as much as the others. I like having the trees. They're lucky.'

'You're sure?'

'Sure enough. Rowan trees are lucky.'

'I'll remember.'

Moyle shuffled his feet. 'The cold is desperate though. The wet gets into your bones.'

Wyndham nodded.

'But you could say that about any trench,' said Moyle.

'Will you take that drop of rum, Lance Corporal?' Wyndham asked.

'I'm grand, mate,' said Moyle, 'And you needn't mind about calling me "lance corporal" when it's just the two of us.'

'Well thank you, Moyle, and good night.'

'Safe home, Wyndham.'

57

In their lonely struggle, hidden away from the sight of others, they drew on the past; it was as if the dead of their race had spoken to them and awaited them.

—Charles Carrington (Lord Moran), 1/5th Royal Warwickshire,
An Anatomy of Courage

The Munsters were taken out of the line and put back in again two days later, into the same place. It was as it had always been. The line was still that poor straggling thing. The trenches were still not joined up, nor were the defences of any depth or complexity because it was all the woefully understrength battalions could do to man what they had. And while the trenches did not grow deeper or stronger, they grew steadily wetter, and men were kept busy enough fighting off the wet that they could spare little thought, in the usual run of things, for fighting the Germans.

The Germans still confined their activities to a little daylight sniping, and only the oldest inhabitants could remember when the artillery had last made its presence felt. The British guns were few, and ammunition had run low, for no one had reckoned on the war lasting this long or the intensity of shellfire being so great. In a few months the armies of Europe had almost emptied their magazines.

The Germans were husbanding what was left of their ammunition too, even though they had rather more than the British. Also, having come with the intention of blasting their way through the fortified zones of France and Belgium, the German ammunition was better suited for smashing down trenches. The

British, with the lessons of South Africa in mind, had imagined a war of the wide-open spaces, with men and horses manoeuvring in the open, and had designed their artillery accordingly. While the Germans leaned more towards high explosive, the British had invested in shrapnel. It had paid dividends in August and September, but wasn't much use to them now, unless the Germans came out of their trenches and attacked again.

And the Germans must. They could hardly get to Paris before Christmas now, but here on the outermost end of the Allied flank they still had a chance of prising the last corner of Belgium from their enemies' grip. Those few Flemish acres were of little use to anybody who did not call them home, but they provided an avenue for a renewed German advance, if such a thing were feasible, or if not, the loss of them to the Allies would put them at a severe disadvantage for when the war would properly start again in the spring.

So it was for this last effort that the Germans had been saving their ammunition and their manpower. The focus of the effort, when it came, was the Belgian town of Ypres. With its walls and cathedral and imposing municipal buildings, it had been reckoned a city, but the modern age had largely passed it by, so it had never grown much beyond its narrow medieval confines, and had thus been overtaken in size by the industrial towns. There was a railway though, and like all towns Ypres was a crossroads, and that was what made it worth fighting for. If the British and French were pushed out of this town, they would be obliged to fall back, not just as far as they had been pushed, but all the way to the next road and rail junction, or otherwise they could not supply an army in the field nor hold a sustainable line. The next town back might well be St. Omer, which was where British GHQ had set up shop, and if St. Omer fell the BEF would have to reorganise itself, somewhere farther and less conveniently to the rear, with the Channel ports at their back. Of course, if the Germans could take, or sufficiently threaten, Calais and Boulogne, it would be well worth their efforts. The British lines of communication would have to be rebuilt much farther to the west, if indeed the British chose to go to that trouble. Maybe they might even give up the game for a bad lot and leave the French to fight the war by themselves. Britain had ostensibly come in to save Belgium. If Ypres fell, and the last corner of Belgium with it, what was the point of fighting on? So the Germans had to take Ypres. Thus the new colonel explained matters when he came on a visit to Fitzmullen-Brophy. The new colonel, being a man of education, pronounced it Eepray, which was of interest to Fitzmullen-Brophy, as he had seen the name written down but had no idea how it was spoken. Purists favoured Eeps, but the wits had instantly and lastingly christened it Wipers.

The Munster Fusiliers were still scattered all over, but the new colonel was doing his best to keep his eye on them, so every once in a while he would come squelching up the line from Armentières, his unforgiving eye peering into everything. The eye went with his rat-trap mouth and his close-clipped black moustache. He gave every impression of being a capable man. He was, in short, the very sort of commander that the Munsters needed in this hour of crisis. He was also younger than Fitzmullen-Brophy, but then so many colonels were these days, and Fitzmullen-Brophy had already had a few years to get used to it.

'The Hun has to take Ypres, FitzEm,' he said, as they took whiskey-laden tea in the Piggery. 'And he has to do it before winter sets in. GHQ is expecting the main effort to fall well to the north of here, but you can bet however much you like that he will be attacking all along the line in order to keep us busy. You've got the Rifles in front of you and the Bedfords over on your right and that's pretty much it. There's nothing behind. You don't hold them here and the line's broken.'

'You can count on us, sir.'

'I know I can, FitzEm. I'll be sending you some new drafts tomorrow. Not many, but it's all I can spare. You'll need more wire too – all you can get. Trouble is, everyone else needs it too. I had a word with Belcher. He might have a chum somewhere who can help, but we can't depend on it.'

'Tummy won't let us down, sir.'

'Well if he can charm up a few batteries of 18-pounders too, I'll put him in for a bally DSO.'

'We will do splendidly as we are, sir.'

'Well said,' said the new colonel, and he drained his mug in a decisive manner and put on his cap. He had come to put heart into the men, for it was all he could do, and it was good to see that old Fitzmullen-Brophy had heart enough to spare. He'd need it. Too much line to hold: not enough men, not enough artillery support, and not a single machine-gun to bless themselves with.

'The very best of luck to you, FitzEm,' he said as he departed the Piggery.

'Thank you, sir. And you needn't worry about us, you know,' said Fitzmullen-Brophy.

'Good man,' said the new colonel, and after a last piercing look around him he was gone, with his silently obedient adjutant in tow.

The little yard of the Piggery was crowded. Stores were piled up wherever there was space, with the usual rubbish of an army accumulating wherever it was authorised to do so. The adjutant of the rifle battalion was there, consulting a list, with a couple of signallers from the same unit seeing to something technical. Sweeney was cleaning the tea mugs in a bucket of soapy cold water. Wyndham stood by, waiting on the major.

Fitzmullen-Brophy stood, watching the new colonel depart, and feeling the weight of what had been laid on him. He wore a knitted scarf these days instead of collar and tie, but he remained every inch the soldier. He thought of fights he had known. On the Northwest Frontier the terrain had favoured the enemy, and it was the enemy too who had the advantage of numbers, but the British Army had never really risked defeat, nor could such a defeat have lost India.

There had been thin times in South Africa, but the Boers could never have won, and all a man risked there was his life. If the Germans swept down on them here, and could not be held, then the line would break and the whole army plunged into terrible jeopardy. But there was more to it than that. The Munsters were his now. There was a new colonel, but he was far away. The Munster Fusiliers belonged to Fitzmullen-Brophy, and that was a sacred trust. They had done magnificently at Étreux, and gone down gloriously, but he owed them better than another Étreux.

He thought of the fights he had known and the odds he had faced, and where that brought insufficient comfort he looked back to the fights of the days before that. The Regiment. The regiment had fought, and kept their colours, and had come home again. He thought of the men who had marched from Dagshai to Delhi, sweating their white shirts black. Their names were lost, but their deeds were remembered. What had the odds been at Delhi? And did the Dirty Shirts pause for a moment to weigh them before they stormed the breach?

And Bhurtpore – when they came back after that decisive repulse, and built anew their siege works over the bleached bones of their own dead – did they look over their shoulders, back down the road to Agra, and think of safety? No. Nor did they think of it at Plassey, when they followed Clive into the heart of Bengal's army – three thousand men against fifty thousand.

Plassey, Condore, Gujerat – those were the battle honours of the regiment, embroidered on the colours as a memorial to the men who were more than men, to the men who were the regiment.

Bhurtpore, Ferozeshah, Delhi.

A hundred days under the walls of Delhi, outnumbered three to one, and all at the hottest time of the year.

Lucknow. Afghanistan. Burma.

He'd known Burma himself, of course.

South Africa.

They fought, they died, and they gained their immortality thereby.

'No, Colonel,' he said to himself, 'I believe we will do splendidly as we are.'

58

Many a heart that now beats high,
In slumber cold at night shall lie,

—Thomas Moore, 'Before the Battle'

The new drafts were the usual lot. They may have been good men and right men, but until they could prove it, they were only strangers. The officers were glad of them though. Fitzmullen-Brophy had an extra twenty-two men to reinforce his position. Lieutenant Fleming, on the other hand, was even more pleased. He finally had a junior.

The twenty-two men had been led to the Munster trenches by an officer. His name was Garvey, and like Fleming he was only a Second Lieutenant, but he was without doubt Fleming's inferior. Fleming never sought to inquire the date of Garvey's commission – it didn't matter. Garvey had come from the 4th Battalion. The 3rd, in which Fleming held his commission, and in which Wyndham had enlisted, was no more than the old county militia under another name, and that name was Special Reserve. The 4th was another unit of the same type, but it couldn't call itself 'special'. It was the old South Cork Militia redesignated 'Extra Reserve'. Not so special at all. Just a social club for young enthusiasts who got together at weekends and played soldiers in Kinsale. Naturally Fleming would look down on the junior battalion, and out here, where experience counted for so much, Fleming had it and Garvey did not.

Bully for Garvey that he'd volunteered for foreign service so readily, but where had he been at the Aisne or on the Race to the

Sea? Not that Fleming intended to lord it over the youngster, but seeing as he'd stood at the major's right hand since August, it was obvious that he was the senior lieutenant and that Garvey must accept his place at the bottom of the pecking order. And by way of a bonus, Fleming realised all of a sudden that there was the chance that the new lieutenant might turn out to be a decent chap, which meant that the two of them could be pals, and that would be perfectly wonderful.

Among the new arrivals there was also a sergeant, and Duffy wasn't too pleased about that.

'Look at him, sir,' he said to Fitzmullen-Brophy. 'Methuselah Murphy. He was old when I was young. He should never have been sent out here.'

The sergeant's name was in fact Hegarty, but he was indeed very old. His face was yellow and his moustache pure white, and besides the two ribbons for South Africa he wore the medal of the Burmese campaign, in which Fitzmullen-Brophy had fought in his youth, and which had been fought to a conclusion more than twenty-five years earlier.

'Sure how did he even get past the MO? How was he even still on the reserve?' asked Duffy.

Fitzmullen-Brophy was not going to let a contemporary of his be condemned for decrepitude.

'Needn't be much past forty, you know, Duffy. Still hale, I don't doubt. Don't let appearances deceive.'

'I'd say he's rotten with the malaria, sir. We should send him back now.'

'Nonsense. We need NCOs and his experience will prove invaluable.'

Duffy sighed.

'I suppose it's better he is a sergeant then, sir, because if I put him to filling sandbags, sure his old heart would give out on him.'

'That's enough of that, Duffy. Carry on.'

Filling sandbags had become the prime task. Parapets were being raised and thickened, and this sector of the line was in the process of being transformed into a chain of ramshackle earthen redoubts. Even Wyndham and Sweeney were roped into it, and Wyndham, who thought he'd been toughened by this war, had hands so racked and blistered that when he put down the shovel he had trouble picking up the pen.

By day the Munsters shovelled, and by night they wired. A few rolls of barbed wire had come up – maybe not enough to stop a German attack, but certainly enough to give almost everybody a taste of how frustrating and frightening it was to have to stake out barbed wire in the dark. It was an uncooperative article, and there wasn't so much of it that they could just uncoil it, secure it, and get back to the trenches. No: the ground had to be surveyed, and the stakes had to be driven just so, and the wire had to be stretched out exactly to get the most out of what there was. Feet got tangled. Hands and clothing got torn. Whelan got a horrible scratch across his face when a coiled end whipped at him. And of course the Germans could hear them.

They lost three men to snipers in one night, and one of the three died on the stretcher before he'd been got out of the line. Everyone was as nervous as cats. They muffled the mallets with rags, but that meant that the hammering, instead of being silent, now sounded like muffled mallets, and opportunistic bullets still came singing out of the dark. Thank God it was dark, or none of them would have stood a chance. There was thick cloud by day, and it stayed by night to block out the moon. The Germans sent up flares from time to time, but they were only signal rockets and failed to illuminate no man's land. They were more than enough to put the wind up the wiring parties, though.

If a rocket went up, the drill was to freeze rather than throw oneself down. An immobile man, so the thinking ran, was invisible in the negligible light, whereas any movement would be spotted. Whelan had been paying out wire, backing clumsily along, when the alarm was hissed, and he froze there, almost doubled over as he was. He knew in a moment that he couldn't hold that posture and unwillingly sank to his knees. He closed his eyes at the thought of a sniper's bullet, and stayed that way, unable even to remember a prayer to say silently. And then a voice said, 'Right. Off we go,' and he opened his eyes and had no idea any more what direction he was facing. He stood up shakily, stumbled, reached out to steady himself, and snagged a bit of wire that leapt up and lashed him across the face.

He cried out, and was urgently shushed and bundled back to the trench where Duffy had a look at him.

'You're grand,' he said, and wiped Whelan's face with a wet cloth and gave him a swig of rum. In truth it didn't look so bad at all, but the next day, with the cuts scabbing and darkening, Whelan was an ugly sight. A medical orderly arrived that day. He put some antiseptic ointment on Whelan's face and that was that. The orderly came in charge of a four-man stretcher party sent by the new colonel. It proved to be a thoughtful gift.

The day after that the German attack began.

59

But at last the men of Lochlann came against Ireland…
And Finn and the battalions of the Fianna went out against them, and drove them back.

—Lady Augusta Gregory, *Gods And Fighting Men*

The first shells were remarkably accurate. They came howling out of the pre-dawn dark and thumped to earth so near the Piggery that when they detonated a moment later they pitched Wyndham out of bed.

It wasn't really a bed at all. Wyndham slept on a narrow shelf, which his weight threatened to tear from its aged brackets. Thus it was propped and braced from below by two stout sticks, which Sweeney was always in danger of dislodging. Sweeney slept directly beneath on a bed of sacking. He didn't mind. It was only right that Wyndham should have the shelf because he was a sort of a gentleman after all. The explosion brought the shelf and Wyndham down on top of Sweeney, and parts of the roof down onto them both. Mornings at the front were always hard, waking with frozen feet to another shivering day. But this awakening was like the last trump. By the time he had gathered an idea of where he was he was rolled onto his back on the wet floor with little pieces of the roof falling in his face and blanketed arms and legs flailing blindly in the dark beside him.

For a man who'd had it even worse, Sweeney seemed to be taking it better, because the voice Wyndham heard was Sweeney's.

'Are you all right there, Wyndham?'

It showed remarkable courtesy from a fellow woken by a

comrade falling on top of him in an artillery bombardment. Without thinking for a moment whether he was all right, Wyndham responded with automatic politeness.

'Yes, thank you, Sweeney. And you?'

There was the scrape of Sweeney pushing off the fallen shelf and gathering himself.

'I got a bit of a bang on the nose, I think, but I'll be grand. Are they shelling us?'

'I think so.'

They might have stayed there as they were, there on the floor, until the war was over, but a commotion was beginning on the other side of the rough partition that separated officers from other ranks. A match was struck, and there was the sound of boots scuffling on the floor. They heard Fitzmullen-Brophy asking after Fleming, and Fleming replying, shakily enough, that everything was perfectly all right. There the niceties ended and the battle began.

Fitzmullen-Brophy started moving fast and talking loud. He stuck his head around the partition, into the tiny space where Wyndham and Sweeney were still sitting stunned, saw that they were unhurt, and briskly told them to be up and about, and as they sorted themselves out they could hear him taking stock of the other residents.

Every man slept in his boots, so rising was a short and uncomplicated affair, but even as Wyndham was rooting in his wrecked accommodation for a few essentials of kit, a second salvo came over. They were awake to hear this one coming, and were huddled on the floor when it arrived. Four German howitzer shells exploded in ragged unison, sending an awesome tremor through the ground and bringing down another shower from the roof, but these shells landed farther away from them, up towards the front-line trenches. This bombardment was no idle spite. This was the prelude to something.

Fitzmullen-Brophy was on his feet faster than any of the others.

'Stand to,' he said, and was out the door, buckling on his revolver as he went. Everyone bustled out after him.

All along the line the Munsters were clinging to the sides of the trench like shipwrecked men washed up on the rocks. In the very few places that weren't knee-deep in water the men were hunkered down and balled up, with their hands over their heads. A few shelters had been dug out of the sides of the trench, but they could barely hold off the rain. One of them had come down on its huddled occupants, and it was lucky that it had been such a poor excuse for a dugout, because both men had been quickly disinterred by their mates before they could suffocate. Other such holes had been hurriedly forsaken before they collapsed too.

There was still no light, save for the dull orange hearts of the explosions, but no one was going to put his head up to take a look at that. It was hard to tell at what point the distinct salvoes merged into an irregular but steady pounding that moved up and down the line and back again, sometimes falling on the front and sometimes on the rear. Through it all, Duffy managed to make tea and supervise its distribution. Wyndham drank his gratefully but was horrified to learn that he was expected to carry a dixie of the stuff over open ground to one of the outposts.

'There's nothing to it, son,' said Duffy. 'They can't see you and they're hitting nothing anyway. Have a wee belt of this.' And he thrust his bottle to Wyndham's mouth and, for the first time since his first night in Tralee, Wyndham partook of hard liquor. This wasn't just a taste, like the one that had acquainted him with army rum – this was a hearty swig, so generous that he had to wipe the excess off his chin. He gulped it down without it killing him. It certainly took the chill away.

'Good man. Now off you go.'

And off Wyndham went, slithering on the sides of the trench, slipping in the wet grass, the big covered tin sloshing and thumping against his leg as he ran, and then he was safe, or as safe as anyone, and receiving the welcomes of the grateful men in the outpost. The return journey was easier, and he certainly felt braver this time. He even had the presence of mind to take in his surroundings. The eastern sky was grey now, and over in the distance, where the Bedfords were holding the line, he saw eruptions of earth and smoke that boomed in his ears a moment later. From this distance, and after the hour he'd just been through, it looked almost harmless.

They were the last shells to fall. Wyndham climbed back into his own trench as men were uncurling and finding themselves, straining their ears for the whistling roar that had somehow ceased. There was a tightness in every man's chest still, but that could soon be lightened with tea and rum. Fitzmullen-Brophy left Duffy to see to that, even though he doubted they'd be given any time for breakfast, or much time for anything at all.

'Anybody hit?' he called out.

One man was dead, and very dead at that. The two men nearest to him had been wounded by debris that might have been loose stones or shards of the shell casing, but might just as well have been pieces of their mate. The stretcher party got busy.

Fitzmullen-Brophy pulled himself out of the trench and stood tall in the growing morning light, his field glasses up to his eyes. He wasn't there long. A bare half minute after the shelling stopped the machine-guns manned by the riflemen in the front-line trenches opened up.

'This is it, men! Here they come! Range two-fifty! Wait for my order!' Then, in more conversational tones, he said to Fleming: 'Poor show, Bog. They should have come at us the instant their guns ceased firing. Should have kept our heads down longer.'

Fleming had been rattled by the alarms of the morning, but to share the major's professional confidences like this fortified his soul, and to be addressed by his nickname for the first time, here at the moment of battle – why that was simply the best thing.

The view from the parapet, without the benefit of field glasses, was not up to much, and the men stared through their rifle sights in vain. Some men noticed that they were trembling, but that was only the cold, or maybe the battering from all the shelling. They'd be all right in a minute. There was nothing wrong with their nerves at all. Give them something to shoot at and they'd be grand.

'Hold your fire, men! Hold! Wait for my order!'

For the first time they could clearly make out the position of the front-line trenches because the men of the forward battalion were manning their parapet, and their heads and shoulders could be seen. The Munsters ran the risk of firing on their own side if they were over-eager. Their job was support. Wait for it.

And then they saw the Germans, or shapes that could only be the Germans. Not much like Mons, nor even Étreux. Just scattered figures in the bad light coming in and out of view. Three signal rockets went up from the British line. That was the call for artillery support. There was no finesse to it. The guns got the word and they opened fire on an indicated stretch of no man's land. That was all. No assessment of target, no correction of shot. With so few guns, and each one of them limited to a handful of rounds, it would have to do.

It was gratifying to hear the shells shrieking overhead, going in the right direction this time, and to see the white shellbursts flower in the air above no man's land, but the men in the Munster trenches could not see what execution they were doing, and the whole firework show was over all too soon. The machine-guns of the rifle battalion kept hammering away, and it was a lovely sound. So was the crackle of disciplined musketry. The Hun wasn't going to break through this line. The Hun was most likely already pinned down out there, the living huddling behind the dead and every man trying to crawl his way backwards to his own lines. Proper order.

And then the firing tailed off and the Munsters heard the Rifles cheer, and there was relief mixed with a sense of anticlimax. Men who had arrayed their ammunition clips on the parapet picked them up and wiped them off and squared them away in their pouches again.

'Is that it, do you think?' asked one of the youngsters.

'For a while, I reckon,' an old sweat replied.

'I didn't even get a chance to fire my rifle.'

'Saves you the bother of cleaning it then.'

And that was a blessing. Trying to boil water in a trench was a bloody bind, and if you managed it you should be allowed to make your tea with it, and not use it for boiling out your rifle barrel. And so thoughts turned easily to breakfast, with every third man stood down so as to allow him to have something to eat. On this fraught morning there was only biscuit with a little jam, but at least there was tea and it was hot. But they weren't given the time even to get that down them. Whelan was still only blowing on his mug when Moriarty shoved him down, causing him to spill the lot. The shelling had started up again.

This bombardment didn't last as long as the first one, but it was every bit as bad. The men had put up with the first one and it was almost unfair to expect them to do it again, especially on an empty stomach. The shells came down and the shuddering earth sent up gouts of black mud and the men of the Munster Fusiliers hung on under it all, cursing and blaspheming and waiting for the end.

They were spared any casualties this time, but felt no better because of it. In the ringing silence that followed the shelling Fitzmullen-Brophy strode up and down along the parapet, seeing what sort of a position was left to him, and offering congratulation and encouragement as he went. Then, as before, the firing started up front, and he clambered down without, he hoped, any undue haste. There was a definite difference now. Now there was the sound of only one British machine-gun.

It kept at it, merrily thumping away at targets still invisible to the Munsters. After a while it slackened slightly, and the bursts became shorter and more intermittent, but all along the line the firing never quite ceased, and that meant the German attack was still in progress. Then, clear as day, German soldiers could be seen rushing forward from some little bit of cover that hadn't been noticed before, and the Munsters saw them and knew that it was too late to stop them. Some men fired and one German fell, but then the Germans were in among the Rifles' positions. The lone machine-gun was silent – out of action, out of ammunition, overheated, who knew?

The Munsters waited tensely. A few Germans could be seen in the open and, regardless of orders, they were fired on. And then men could be seen climbing out of the front-line trench and making a run towards the Munsters' position. Not waiting for the command, men fired, while other men, and Fitzmullen-Brophy above all, told them to stop. Those weren't Germans. Those were British troops falling back.

And then all was confusion because there were Germans and British together, running and pursuing and fighting all the time. Some of the enemy were still helpfully distinguishable by their spiked helmets, but too many were wearing the flat forage cap, which was almost identical in silhouette to what the British cap looked like without its stiffener. Moriarty thought he might have hit a British rifleman and he felt sick, but drew a bead on another figure just the same. No point taking chances.

And then the Rifles were in among the Munsters, breathless and white-faced, and the Germans were falling back to consolidate the trench they'd just won at such high cost. From the rear, where there was no protective parapet, a trench wasn't as much of a defence as from the front, and the Munsters were happy to let fly at everything they saw moving.

'That's it, that's it, men. Keep their blasted heads down.' It was a Rifle officer who was speaking. He found Fitzmullen-Brophy and between them they organised an immediate counterattack. 'Organise' was perhaps too precise a word for it. The Rifles were taking back their trench and that was flat. If the Munsters chose to help, then all well and good.

In time of peace there was the usual rivalry between fusiliers and rifle regiments, with each thinking themselves smarter and just generally better than the others. Fusiliers wore scarlet and blue, topped off with great fur hats and all emblazoned with brass that shone like gold. Rifles boasted uniforms of green and black, with all their badges gleaming silver. Now the two regiments could look at each other and see only mirror images. The buttons of the fusiliers were dull and turning green, whereas the buttons on the riflemen were black and had never been supposed to be polished. The only other uniform distinctions were merely a matter of how far from the uniform any man might have deviated. All of them were just parcels of ragged khaki, darkened by damp and dirt.

Moriarty found himself sharing a cramped space with one of the riflemen. The man had come pelting in and had dived into the Munsters' trench without any regard for whomever might be underneath him. He was jostled so close that his equipment was snagging on Moriarty's. Fusilier and rifleman looked at each other.

'Are you right there, mate?' asked Moriarty.

The rifleman, eyes gaping, took a deep breath. 'All right, mate,' he gasped, and managed to shut his mouth and swallow a couple of times. And then the Rifles officer was working his way among them, a young man with a mission.

'Fix bayonets, men. We'll be going back directly. That's our ruddy trench and Fritz can ruddy well push off. Wait for the whistle.'

And Fitzmullen-Brophy was hard on his heels.

'Stand by to go in behind the Rifles. We'll give the Hun a taste of cold steel. He won't stand.'

Moriarty sighed and packed away his ready-use ammunition again, and pulled his bayonet free of its scabbard. It could have done with a good cleaning, but it was still good and sharp, and it slotted onto the end of his rifle with a reassuring click. His guts were at him, and there was a fluttering in his chest, but he wouldn't have said he felt scared. If things went amiss, the Rifles would be catching it first.

And then, in the anxious moment when the young Rifles officer climbed to the parapet with his revolver in his hand and his whistle between his teeth, another whistle was heard blowing, and men could see another counterattack going in from the right – a handful of determined men scrambling forward to retake the breach in the line.

The Rifles officer was taken aback, affronted even.

'That's Sanderson with B Company! Dammit, he can't just take my trench! Come on, men!'

And he put the whistle back in his mouth and blew for all he was worth while his men scrabbled back out of the Munsters' trench.

Fitzmullen-Brophy followed them only as far as the parapet and watched them go in.

'Wait for it, men! Stand by! Wait for it. Oh *jolly* good. Oh good show. Oh well done, the Rifles.'

Because it appeared they had done it. It was all hidden from most of the Munsters, but there in the trench ahead men were killing and dying at the closest quarters. There were just too few Germans and they were too isolated, and too racked by what they had endured. A few survivors could be seen making a run for it, and one or two of them were seen to fall, shot from behind by unchivalrous types. The attack was over.

'Cease fire! Cease fire, dash it!'

Fitzmullen-Brophy strode rapidly up and down the line, assessing the damage, and cheering the men's steadiness, but scolding them too for want of good fire discipline.

'Some of you are being over-eager, men. Mark your targets, and for Heaven's sake do wait for orders. Anybody hit?

'Roche, sir. He got a bit of a clip off a bullet in the head.'

'See what you can do for him. Anyone else? No? Good. Corporals – check ammunition. We mightn't have seen the last of it yet.'

But that was it for that morning, and for that day. They could hear firing from other parts of the line, and the German artillery kept up a sporadic and nasty fire on the British rear, but the footsoldiers in field grey had done all they could today. The British could see German wounded crawling painfully back the way they had come, and a few German stretcher parties moving furtively about in no man's land. Fitzmullen-Brophy was very stern indeed with those who thought to amuse themselves by firing on them. It was atrociously bad form. The Munsters were better than that, surely.

Belcher arrived in the afternoon. He was muffled up well against the weather but in bad temper, and splashed with mud from head to foot.

'Blasted German shell,' he explained, in tones that put the German artillery in the lowest orders alongside reckless cab drivers. He did not come armed to the front line, because getting into a scrap with the Germans was hardly any of his business.

'Buggers are playing hell with our lines of communication. Mail's been delayed. Damn well everything's been held up for that matter.'

But a seasoned campaigner like Belcher would never be completely at a loss, for he came with whiskey, and he shared it out among the officers as he put them in the picture. That was lunch – whiskey to wash down the bully beef sandwiches, eaten with everyone crammed around the doorway of the Piggery. Someone was having a look at the roof to see if it would last another night, and it had begun to drizzle outside, so the reasonably stout doorway was the place to be for the moment.

'Like this all up and down the line, I gather,' said Belcher. 'All the way from here up to Ypres, and the Frogs and the Belgians getting more of the same north of that. The Hun is putting on pressure everywhere at once. If he breaks through anywhere then he's broken through and that's our lot. As it is he's keeping all our reserves committed. But we have him there, gentlemen.' And he took a sip of whiskey and looked slyly over the rim of his mug at the small group surrounding him, his moustache twisting in a smile.

'How is that, sir?' asked Fleming, as he was expected.

Belcher grinned foxily. 'What? Why he's wasting his efforts in pinning down our reserves, you know, because we haven't any reserves left to pin down.' He gave a short bark of laughter at outwitting the Germans so cleverly.

'Well said, Tummy!' said Fitzmullen-Brophy. Fleming and Garvey chuckled politely.

After lunch Belcher had a look around the trenches.

'I say, FitzEm, they've left you in a dreary hole,' he said. 'Can't you do anything about all this damn wet? A chap could catch a nasty chill.'

'I hate to say it, Tummy old chap, but you have grown soft.'

'Have I? I suppose I must have. War is war after all. Can't postpone the match waiting for a dry wicket.'

He peered over the parapet but couldn't see much. 'Can't abide wet feet though,' he added absent-mindedly. 'Fancy a look-round up top? Avoid this blasted quagmire at any rate.'

'Capital idea. Just climb up onto that box and you should be able to get out that way.'

And the two majors strolled about in the open for a while, talking war and pointing with their sticks to things of interest, while occasional German shells arced overhead and exploded somewhere off behind the lines. There was still plenty of cover, even if one of Moyle's rowan trees had been knocked over in the morning.

60

My joy is the storm
That strews the ground with fruit –
Half-living, bleeding, and bruised –
From life's tree shaken.
I desire the flame of battle;
I desire gore-spouting wounds;
Flanks that are gashed, trunks that are headless
Heads that are trunkless in piles and in mounds;

—William Larminie, 'The Sword of Tethra', from *Moytura*

Private Roche died almost as soon as they lifted him onto the stretcher. The blood from his head wound had soaked through a yard and a half of dressing, and through the clothes of his mates who had tended to him, and left a crimson pool in the yellow water at the bottom of the trench and a black stain on the canvas of the stretcher where he died. He was twenty years old and had been at Étreux. When it got dark they buried him in a corner of a field right behind the line. There was nothing recognisable left of the other fatality, but the few anonymous bits and pieces gathered into a sandbag and put into the grave beside Roche, as if in afterthought, were at least included in the prayers.

'Eternal rest grant unto them, O Lord.
And may perpetual light shine upon them.
May they rest in peace,
Amen.'

There was no chaplain of any denomination, but because they had the time, a funeral service of sorts was held. Lieutenant Garvey led the prayers, as the only Catholic officer, and young and shy, he prayed in parade-ground cadences, and too loudly for the occasion, while the other officers and the few men attending stood by, bare-headed, in the attitude of mourning prescribed by army regulations. Whelan made sure he was there. He was no especial friend of either of the dead men, but he came to pay his respects so that he might be see how his mortal remains might be respected when it came to his turn.

> *'May their souls, and the souls of all the faithful departed,*
> *Through the mercy of God,*
> *Rest in Peace,*
> *Amen.'*

There was no volley fired over the shallow grave. Any firing might be construed as an alarm, and wake up the whole front. There would be firing enough tomorrow.

A short distance away the riflemen were burying their own dead. They took rather more time about it. The German dead from the front-line trench were buried too, but that was as much for the sake of neatness and hygiene as for anything else.

By rights the Munsters should have been out of the line that night, in dry billets farther back, but the German offensive had knocked all ideas of rest on the head. Everyone would be manning the line until further notice, and that meant little or no sleep, because where was there to sleep? There were precious few places to lie down, and even sitting was impractical with the water knee-deep in most trenches. So the men stood, and leaned against the parapet when they weren't on sentry duty, and they dozed where they might, with their knees locked and their feet freezing.

This would be their third night in the line, and three nights standing in cold water was no joke. Duffy kept a dixie of tea on the go constantly, and there was a relay through the night whereby men crept back toward the Piggery, and slept for an hour or two on ground that wasn't utterly waterlogged, and were given tea and a tot on waking. The Munsters in their support line were lucky to be able to do as much. The Rifles in the front-line trench enjoyed no such luxury.

The next morning came like the one before, with the distant booming of the German guns, soon followed by the nerve-racking howl of incoming shells. The Munsters were reminded how easy they'd had it the previous day when today the very first round to land on their position proved a direct hit.

It couldn't have been more direct. It landed on the very floor of a trench, and instantly turned the narrow excavation into a gaping great cavity. Three men were standing close enough that they were torn apart instantly. Another four men were picked up and thrown down as the blast was channelled in a vicious rush along the trench. Of those four, the man nearest the blast was practically filleted by a shell splinter, but it didn't matter to him, as he was already dead from a broken neck. His mate had enough ribs fractured to die from shock and asphyxiation in under a minute. The other two won for themselves various broken bones and lacerations, which ranged from disfiguring to fatal. They would last long enough for the stretcher party to waste dressings and frantic efforts on them.

A man sleeping in a hole dug around the traverse of the trench was unscathed, but the concussion kept him unconscious for hours, and when he came round it was found that his eardrums were ruptured. Everyone else was unhurt, but so shaken that some of them hardly noticed the continuing bombardment.

Wyndham had been sheltering in the Piggery when it happened. He'd heard the noise, naturally, but the first he knew of the carnage the shell had wrought was when the call went out for the stretcher party and for men to come quick with shovels. Dillon's section had been hit. Dillon's section was wiped out. It was in bits. Hurry.

Wyndham knew Lance Corporal Dillon as a sandy-haired young man who had no time for anything that didn't help justify the new stripe on his sleeve. Fussy and rather humourless, Dillon had nevertheless earned the grudging respect of the men – many much older than he – who'd had him set over them. In the first light of dawn Wyndham saw Dillon for the last time, but didn't know what he was looking at. The stretcher-bearers were blocking the trench, and Wyndham had a job getting around them and then, as he stepped past a casualty and caught his balance, he nearly choked on the stink, horribly familiar from that bad day above the Aisne. Robinson was there, directly in front of him, shovelling hard.

'Mind how you go, son,' he said, too late to stop Wyndham from catching his shin on some collapsed trench timbering. He looked up to see Robinson cease his digging and pull something free from the earth.

'Aw no. Too late for this poor sod. Here – find us a sandbag.'

It was still mostly dark, and it took a while for it to register in Wyndham's eyes that the slimy thing that Robinson had dragged from the mud was the better part of a human spine. While the cogwheels of recognition were still clicking into place, Wyndham turned away and leaned against the trench wall and took deep breaths, never mind that the air was so tainted.

Someone shook him by the shoulder. 'You hurt?'

Wyndham gulped and shook his head.

'Then get fucking digging. There might still be someone alive under that lot.'

But a little digging and a swift roll call revealed that no, there was not. After that the shovels were plied merely to rebuild the parapet. Wyndham was sweating at it for some minutes before he remembered he was in mortal danger, but the German bombardment seemed to be concentrated elsewhere for the moment. The dead bodies – those that were more or less intact, at least – had been lifted out and placed in the open behind the trench. The stretcher-bearers had been called away to where two more men had been hit.

There were yet more casualties to take into account before the German shelling eased off and Fitzmullen-Brophy was able to climb out of the trench once more and see what the day might bring. The mist was heavy this morning, but the sound of rifle and machine-gun fire from in front of him told him that another attack was beginning.

As before, the signal went up for the British guns to fire, and as before the British shrapnel whistled and burst all too briefly above the battlefield, to no visible effect. Maybe there were German soldiers out there in the mist, pierced and shredded, dying and dead, but the attack came on anyway. To Wyndham it all seemed to be devoid of drama and urgency. This was not an enemy host arrayed against them, but scattered distant figures that appeared and disappeared, while the defence was largely invisible, and indicated only by the sound of rifle and machine-gun fire. It was nothing like pictures of Gettysburg and Antietam that he knew from childhood. In fact, it put him in mind of a sport with which one is unfamiliar. For the participants and spectators it must be vital, but for the uninitiated there was no tension and no meaning to what was going on.

With nothing else to occupy him in the desperate moment, and loath to retire to his usual station in the Piggery, he stood nearby the major. Fitzmullen-Brophy had got back into the trench, but he now stood on a box, with his head and shoulders above the parapet, earnestly surveying the action.

He did not care for what he saw. Yesterday the Germans had

just come on until driven back. Today, better knowing their ground and the British positions, they were working forward with guile. When halted by British fire they didn't retire, so much as go to ground in any available hollow or hedge, and from there work their way into a more favourable position to push the attack forward. So yesterday where they had come forward with the bayonet, today they were answering bullet with bullet, firing from cover, inflicting losses, and keeping heads down while they edged forward as best they might.

The British line caved in somewhere over to the left, sometime around mid-morning. The Germans fought their way into the front-line trenches and held on there in the face of two determined counterattacks. Encouraged by their success, they poured in whatever reinforcements they had on hand and, during the afternoon, made a brave attempt at expanding their lodgement. A very muddy captain came up from Brigade to explain all this to Fitzmullen-Brophy, which was helpful only in so far as it explained why there were British troops retiring from left to right in a hurry and why the Munsters' left wing was now apparently the front line. The staff captain was not so helpful as to commit reinforcements or to promise greater artillery support. His word was the same word that had been coming from the rear all along: hold on.

The German artillery evidently still had ammunition to spare, because another bombardment came down before the day was out, and another German attack came in. This time the British were being put under pressure from front and flank, and this time the Munsters, from some of their trenches at least, had an unimpeded line of sight on their assailants.

Moyle's section was in its own little outpost still, but things being how they were, that outpost had been substantially reinforced, and now at last a trench had been dug to join up the Munsters' position. The major sent Wyndham there to see how things stood, and there was Moyle, his eyes bright, firing, and firing again. His movements were economical and automatic. He fired, worked the bolt, and acquired a new target as if hand, eye, and rifle were all part of the same mechanism. And as he fired he spoke quietly, to himself and to the Germans he shot at.

'I see you, you bastard.' *Bang*.

'I have you.' *Bang*.

'Bad luck to you.' *Bang*.

'I am a cunning artist.' *Bang*

'I am a salmon in the water.' *Bang*. And the last cartridge case would be ejected and a fresh five-round clip smoothly moved from pouch to breech and expertly thumbed home.

'And who's next?' *Bang*.

He might have been in a trance, except that the man at his shoulder jerked backwards and fell to the floor of the trench, and Moyle, never even turning his head for an instant, said, 'Hallinan's down. Have a look at him there, someone.'

Wyndham, not wanting to, came forward and knelt in the muddy water while Private Hallinan, a casual labourer in Limerick until his call-up came last August, thrashed and jerked for a second or two at the bottom of the trench. It was a bullet wound to the head, which had torn away a piece of scalp above the ear, and the blood pulsed out in gouts until it stopped, and just leaked out. Wyndham watched it happen, holding his hands above the dying man, unwilling to touch him, uncertain as to whether he could do the slightest bit of good.

'I think he's dead,' he said finally.

'I thought he would be,' said Moyle, not turning around. 'Is that Wyndham?'

'The major sent me,'

'Tell the major we're grand – I think. But you'd never run and get us some more ammunition, would you? Good man.' *Bang*.

Wyndham did as he was told, but when he came struggling

back under the weight of the ammunition box, the excitement was over for the day. It would be getting dark soon. The Germans wouldn't be attacking into the dark. Moyle was leaning against the side of the trench, with seemingly no more life in him than a scarecrow. He did raise his head when Wyndham came along.

'Good man. Do you have any water at all?'

Wyndham was a little flustered by the question, but he owned up to having what was in his water bottle – that was all.

'Give us a slug of it there, would you?'

He took the bottle and swilled the water around in his mouth before swallowing.

'You'd wonder how you'd get so dry in weather like this,' he said. 'Thanks.'

Robinson was there, and he asked Wyndham if there was only water in the bottle, and gave him a cheery wink.

'How are things everywhere else?' asked Moyle.

Wyndham told what he knew, and listed off the casualties as he was aware of them. He saw that Hallinan's body had been lifted out of the trench. An arm had flopped back in. Wyndham stared at it as he spoke, trying to work out what was wrong with the picture. If that was Hallinan's arm, and that was his head, then his body must be lying *that* way – so what was that thing that looked like a leg, and if it was a leg, what was it doing there?

It was a leg, but not Hallinan's.

'Gus O'Brien got hit by a shell earlier on,' explained Moyle.

'Bleeding shame,' added Robinson. 'Laugh a minute was Gussie.'

And that was when they heard sounds close by, from no man's land. They stood still, and confirmed that it was someone moving through the long grass, and calling out. Not calling, though – whimpering, more like. Robinson had a look, said, 'Stone me,' and heaved himself up for a better look. It was a wounded German, working his pitiful way forward on knees and elbows. Robinson pulled himself up further, until he was practically lying across the parapet, and he swung out one arm and caught the German by the collar. He dropped down again, pulling the German after him, and leaving him lying half in, half out of the trench.

The man was dressed in dingy grey, baggy and much muddied. Robinson lifted his head by hair that looked as if hadn't been cut since before the war, and they tried to make out what sort of a man their enemy was. They couldn't tell. He had been wounded in the face, and his face was a mask of earth and blood, clotted black.

'Jesus. Look at the state of him. No wonder he was going the wrong way.'

In the bad light and the mess of gore they couldn't tell what the nature of the wound was, but it had blinded the man, who was still making feeble animal noises in his throat. Robinson let go the man's hair and drew his bayonet. He punched it hard into the German's neck.

'That's for my mate Jim Dwyer,' he said, and he twisted the blade and pulled it free.

Wyndham was still in a daze when he met Moriarty.

Moriarty had looked after himself well and had staked out a dry enough place to sit down for himself and Whelan.

'Wyndham! Hey, Wyndham! What's up?'

Wyndham stopped, but couldn't think up any words of reply. He merely stood and blinked.

'You look all in, boy,' said Moriarty. 'Sit down and tell us about it. Shove up there, Whelan.'

Wyndham slumped down between them, even though there was barely room for two as it was, and after a few false starts he unburdened himself of what he had just seen. His comrades gravely took it in.

'Jesus,' said Moriarty.

'Jesus,' said Whelan. 'I wouldn't have thought Robinson was that sort of a man at all.'

'Neither did I,' admitted Wyndham.

'Just killed a Hun like that. That's bad. That's very bad.' Whelan shook his head.

'I wonder if there'll be trouble over it,' said Wyndham.

'Sure the Germans will never find out,' said Moriarty.

'No – I mean if he'll get into trouble for killing a wounded man. That's murder. Surely that's murder.'

'That's where you're wrong,' said Moriarty. 'How can it be murder if it's in the middle of a battle? If that was the way they could hang the lot of us twice over.'

'But what about the rules of war, and – and international law?'

'No,' said Moriarty. 'Robinson's still within his rights. It says in the Geneva Convention that the Germans have to sound the ceasefire or run up a white flag. If they don't do that then they're fair game. That's the rules.'

'Are you sure?' asked Wyndham.

'Fairly sure.' Moriarty broke a cigarette in two and with lordly generosity passed one half to Whelan. 'Another thing,' he said, 'Was the Hun wearing his cap, or his helmet or whatever?'

'No – why does that make a difference?'

'Because if he didn't have his hat on then he was out of uniform, wasn't he? Geneva Convention. If you don't make it plain what side you're on then you're fair game. Robinson was within his rights. I wouldn't tell the major about it, mind. He's kind of old-fashioned about things like that. He'd probably say it wasn't gentlemanly or something.'

Despite Moriarty's breezy air of authority, Wyndham was not reassured.

One of Duffy's assistants came round then. The good old cook sergeant was not going to leave his children go hungry, and even if hot food was too much to concoct under these circumstances, he had managed to find a quantity of bread, and if you had bread you could have bully-beef sandwiches. The man was doling them out from a sandbag.

'One each,' he said. 'There'll be tea along in a while.'

Moriarty and Whelan took theirs and started eating enthusiastically, pulling on their cigarettes between bites. Wyndham took his ration without any heart. He picked a piece of jute fibre from the wad and thought about what he'd seen shovelled into sandbags that day, and he looked at the jellied fat glistening in the dark red meat and his appetite went from him entirely.

'Here,' he said. 'Do you want to split this between you?'

'Are you sure? Good man yourself.'

'I should go and see if the major needs me.'

'Right you are. Mind yourself.'

It had been getting dark for an hour already but still wasn't night. This was as contrary as Ireland in June, where daylight seemed to last forever. Here in overcast Flanders it was either dark or getting dark. What was wrong with Europe? Why couldn't the sun just make up its damn mind and rise or set like it was supposed to?

So it was still light enough to see details on the bodies that were being collected for burial – the waxen skin and the black wounds. The lifting of the bodies was a job anyone could do, but attending to this rough and ready removal of the remains and recording it for the military authorities was a job for the company clerk. So Wyndham, in the last dim light of that savage day, was obliged to stand there with a clipboard and pencil, taking down the details of his late comrades. He was thankful that the men handling the bodies had gone beyond squeamishness, and showed no reluctance in going through pockets and opening clothing. It spared him having to do it.

Pay books and identity discs, sometimes sticky, were handed to Wyndham, and he peered closely at the details and thus didn't have to look at the bodies themselves. Most of the time, anyway.

'Here – this fella has no discs on him,' said one of the burial detail.

'He'd be one of the lads the major brought from Kerry. Them Special Reserve lads never got issued with the discs,' said his mate. 'Isn't that right, Wyndham?'

And it was right. Only a few days ago, when he'd been washing one morning, one of the regulars had joked about how his neck was bare of the identity tags that had been issued to all the men who'd come to the war through more regular channels.

'Don't get killed now, you hear, mate? Or if you do get killed, make sure to tell everyone who you are.'

He could hear the merry jibe so clearly that the burial man had to repeat himself.

'So who is he? He looks like your man O'Neill.'

Wyndham had a look and swallowed hard. Here was another victim of shellfire. Here was another example of what a shell splinter would do to a man's head. Half of the face was intact, and Wyndham thought he recognised the man from a scrupulously neat moustache. A pocket watch confirmed the identity.

'MacNeill,' said Wyndham, in quick businesslike tones, dropping the watch into the sack and scribbling on his clipboard. First name? Albert? Something beginning with A? MacNeill who was something of a dandy and had looked forward to the first time the recruits would be allowed out on the town in Tralee. Religion C of I, or something Protestant at least. He and Wyndham had attended the same church parades. Regimental number? Written in indelible ink on every article of kit. Next of kin could be found out easily by going through his letters. MacNeill had been a great writer and receiver of letters.

They buried all the dead where they had buried Roche last

night. Fitzmullen-Brophy read the burial service over MacNeill and another man who had died in the Anglican faith. His reading was solemn and genuinely moving. Wyndham held the close-shaded light so that Fitzmullen-Brophy could see the page, and he could clearly see the major's eyes filling as he came to the final Amen.

A Catholic chaplain making the rounds was on hand to conduct the service for the rest of the Munsters' dead. It was well that he was there, because Lieutenant Garvey, who'd performed the office last night, was among those shovelled under tonight.

61

And on the first day none of the kings or princes went into the battle, but only the common fighting men, and they fierce and proud enough.
And the battle went on like that from day to day with no great advantage to one or the other side.

—Lady Augusta Gregory, *Gods And Fighting Men*

With Garvey dead and in his grave there was considerably more sleeping space in the Munster corner of the Piggery. Fitzmullen-Brophy hated himself for thinking such a thing, but it was a fact nonetheless. The Piggery was home to the officers of the Munsters and to the battalion headquarters of the Rifles, and to officers' servants, and it was a place of work for the attendant signallers and a stopping place for runners and visiting staff officers and the occasional forward artillery observer. Storemen and cooks occupied the outbuildings or had set up camp in the yard and various odd corners roundabout – and all this in a space that had once provided accommodation for a small farming family and a small herd of pigs.

As commanding officer of the Munsters, Fitzmullen-Brophy could claim an enclosed space for his own, but that hardly afforded him any peace and quiet. Every muttered word and every scrape of a boot on the floor sounded right in his ear, and he had lived too long in middle-aged Irish domesticity to be at ease with these discomforts. The cold was abominable of course. The season was wet – the country was wet – so it was hardly surprising that the house should be damp. The roof leaked, and leaked all the worse since the shelling. Indeed, a sizeable portion of it had slid off and come crashing into the yard just that morning, and while that was over at the other side of the building, it hadn't done much for the integrity of the roof as a whole

And the cold came with the wet. It was November, so of course it was cold. But had it ever been so cold? Certainly not in a South African winter, but not even in the hills up towards the Afghan border either – or at least he couldn't remember it so bad. At least there one's feet weren't always wet. Susan would give him the very devil if she saw the way he was living. Going to bed in wet socks, indeed! He'd never hear the end of it. And how did he try to remedy the matter? Why, with Tummy Belcher's whiskey. A drop to set him up in the morning and another to warm him at night, with odd nips through the day. Wrapped in greatcoat and blankets and sipping whiskey in bed like a common sot. Disgraceful. No wonder this place was called the Piggery. Only fitting.

And then, on top of it all, there were the sniffles and the rheumy eyes, and the cough that just wouldn't clear up. Pitiful.

There was a fireplace in the main room, but it could not be lit by day because the Germans could see the smoke, and unless one slept right on top of it by night its benefits were not to be felt. Of course some men did sleep almost on top of it. Chaps who were coming and going, and didn't have a corner to call their own, tended to huddle down around the wretched little fire and smoke or snore for a brief hour, smelling like wet dogs.

Young Fleming was usually there. Turning out to be not a bad sort was Fleming. Conscientious. Always up and about in the line at all hours. Commendable. Of course that's why Fitzmullen-Brophy had brought him from Tralee. Spotted the boy's potential. Knew he'd have been wasted in the depot and possibly corrupted in the mess. Made friends easily. Lost them rather too readily too, and that was unfortunate, and hardly his fault.

He could hear Fleming now, being pleasant to Sweeney, even though Sweeney was far too shy to speak to an officer. If Sweeney was awake that was a good sign. It meant he was about the business of drying the major's socks. The lad would never have been first choice for an officer's servant in the normal run of things as he hadn't the first idea about looking after a gentleman's necessaries, but like Lieutenant Fleming he had a good heart and a kindly soul. He had burned the occasional hole in the major's socks, but that was a small fault when set beside his efforts to provide his master with an almost-dry pair every morning, and a dry change almost every time Fitzmullen-Brophy came in out of the wet.

And now Fitzmullen-Brophy could hear Fleming get up – it was surprising how, in this cramped life, one learned to recognise people by the noises they made in the dark – and come towards him. Fleming's sleeping space ('bed' was too fine a term for it) was next to the major's, with a blanket hung between the two. Fleming had a good heart but a clumsy great pair of feet and, when he was swathed in wet kit, an intrusive backside. The makeshift curtain bulged inwards and there was a noisy rummaging. Fitzmullen-Brophy grunted in irritation. That was unseemly. He regretted it instantly.

'That you, Bog?'

'Oh I'm fearfully sorry, sir. Didn't mean to disturb you, sir.'

'That's all right.'

'Just looking for a dry, a dry – never mind, sir. Awfully sorry.'

'Think nothing of it, my boy. Just about to get up anyway.'

And having said that, he had to get up now, hadn't he?

'What time is it, Fleming?'

That only flustered the young man further.

'Oh! – I'm afraid I can't see my watch, sir. Give me a moment and I'll strike a match, sir.'

'No need to trouble yourself. I'm just looking for a round about time.'

'Oh – in that case, sir, it's roundabout five.'

'That's what I thought,' said Fitzmullen-Brophy, even though he had come out of the uneasy doze that passed for sleep in the Piggery with no idea as to the hour. He unwrapped himself and budged past Fleming, and felt his way out into the kitchen. There was Sweeney, and there were his socks.

Sweeney was startled by the sudden appearance of authority. He was always apologising for doing his job.

'Major! I have dry socks here for you, sir. Give me just another few minutes, sir.'

Bless the man.

'No need just yet, Sweeney. Just make sure there's a pair ready when I come back from the line. Good man. And see if you can get me some hot water.'

It troubled him not at all to send Sweeney out after hot water under these primitive conditions. It was an officer's duty to keep up appearances, and thus it was his servant's duty to find the wherewithal for shaving every morning. Fitzmullen-Brophy slept in a balaclava helmet, and if he wore it through the day then no one would be able to see the state of his chin, but that was a shameful thought. An officer must be properly dressed at all times. Maybe if the worst came to the worst, and they were still in the line when it froze, maybe then he could go about in a balaclava. But as it was – why, if he wore it all the time he'd never get the benefit when he really needed it.

He lit his pipe while he waited for the shaving water, and when it made him cough he took advantage of his relative solitude to have a swift pull on his whiskey flask. Disgraceful.

When the hot water was provided, Fitzmullen-Brophy set to making himself presentable. Even by the light of a single candle he could see that the stubble on his face was pure white, even though his moustache was still a pepper-and-salt affair. He tried not to think about it. Thinking could only depress him. There was a mug of tea to be enjoyed. Think about that. Wherever water was heated in the army, there tea was made, and that was no small blessing on mornings like this one.

Feeling somewhat clean and awake, and warmed by tea and whiskey, he felt much better, and willing to face the day. He wrapped his scarf high around his neck to compensate for the absent balaclava, and went out to the yard to visit the outhouse and have another go at his pipe in the morning air. Quite a lot of fellows were up and about now. The German shelling might come early or late, but it was sure to come, and no one wanted to be caught napping when it did. Stand-to was in half-an-hour. That gave him plenty of time. He'd have a nose around while it was still dark. See if Fritz had done anything wily and Hunnish since he'd done the rounds just before midnight.

The action of the day before forced him to be more circumspect in his tour, and there were many familiar ways that had become dangerous or downright inaccessible. Nevertheless, it felt good to be out and about, and his chest didn't trouble him nearly so much when he was upright and moving in the fresh air. As usual at times like this, he thought how nice it would be to have a dog out here. Bringing a dog out on a pre-dawn ramble like this would probably not be a good thing, what with too many unpleasant things lying around in the undergrowth, but how fine it would be to come back to the Piggery and have a dog bounding up at one in welcome. Fitzmullen-Brophy never could understand people who didn't care for dogs.

The line north of Moyle's position was less a front today and more a line of outposts. There was no point in attempting to join them up, because there would not be enough men to man a continuous trench line, but efforts had been made to realign some of the existing positions so that they faced the new threat on their left. Trenches that had snaked around according to the landscape had now, with this new 'refused flank', become somewhat more L-shaped.

Fitzmullen-Brophy poked about, making himself known to sentries with whispers and passing on the encouraging word, until he could make out a faint greyish tinge to the east. Time to be under cover. Time for the dawn stand-to. Time for a spot of breakfast after that. Time to see what marvels Duffy had somehow worked this morning.

He had to hurry the last few steps. The German shelling was beginning. The first salvo was a good way distant. The next one was alarmingly close. Fitzmullen-Brophy flattened himself against the side of the trench and gave a reassuring smile to the white-faced soldier he found himself next to. Was that Hickey? Hard to tell in this light, what with the man so dirty and unshaven. He kept the smile frozen on his face as the ground shook and loose clods of earth came bouncing down the walls of the trench.

'A miss is as good as a mile,' he said to the soldier when it was finished, but the soldier (Hickey?) made no response. Matter of fact, Fitzmullen-Brophy couldn't hear himself either. Then he found as he straightened up that his knees didn't answer as well as they might. Ridiculous. He staggered round the corner of the trench, heading for home, and stopped dead. The Piggery had been hit. One corner of the building was smashed in, with half the roof caved in on top of it. A few men were crawling out of their various shelters to stare at the disaster. No one appeared to be hurt. That was something. The side of the building that was collapsed happened to be the Munsters' side. All his kit was somewhere under the rubble.

Fitzmullen-Brophy had a limited stock of strong language, so he tended to be at something of a loss when disaster struck or emotion overwhelmed.

'Bother!' he said. Then he shook himself free from shock and went to see what he could do.

Wyndham had been making unauthorised use of the outhouse that served as the officers' latrine when the explosion rocked him. His moment of private contemplation ended abruptly and he was out into the yard and tugging at his braces before the last piece of roof tile had landed.

'Anyone hurt? Anyone hurt?' it was the cry from almost every voice at once. By astonishing luck it appeared that no one was. Men who were thought to have been sleeping soundly inside came rushing up from somewhere else entirely, asking what was going on, and was anybody hit. Men whose business it was to be inside at this hour had, like Wyndham, just stepped outside before the shell struck.

But they couldn't find Sweeney.

They dug him out with some difficulty, but the beam that took an age to shift turned out to be the beam that had kept the worst of the wreckage off of Sweeney. Throughout all this frantic labour, a few shells were falling round about, but by now everyone was thoroughly, if unconsciously, attuned to what was really dangerous, and kept at it. Sweeney was white with dust when they found him, except for the dribbles of vivid red running from his nose and ears. By the same miracle that had preserved everyone else that morning, he was still sound enough in every limb, and even managed a few steps before he fell down and had to be lifted onto a stretcher.

Poor gentle Sweeney, apologising for the major's kit even as they laid him down. Duffy poured some rum down his throat as the medical orderly gave him the once-over.

'You're grand, son,' said Duffy. 'You're lucky to be out of it.'

And then the stretcher was lifted up and Sweeney was taken away, while the excavation of the Piggery continued. There were articles in there more important than officers' personal kit to be salvaged.

On their way out of the line the stretcher party came across the body of a sergeant, a storeman with the Rifles. He was stone dead, face down in the yard on the opposite side of the building to where the shell had landed. A roof tile had struck him in the back of the head and killed him instantly. It was the only tile to have been dislodged on that side of the roof. Duffy concluded that there had been so many miraculous escapes that morning that some poor bastard had to make up for it.

Major Fitzmullen-Brophy being busy with the impending German infantry attack, Duffy took charge of the rum issue, and was very open-handed about it too. Wyndham, bereft of his greatcoat and his blankets, and most tellingly of the two books he had carried in his haversack all the way from Tralee, accepted his tot this time. The rum didn't console him, and he had been warmed already by the digging, but it did renew and strengthen his belief that this was a just war. The Germans had shown their true colours once again. They had raped Belgium and burned down the library at Louvain and had now destroyed his copy of Lady Gregory. These were sins against civilisation and could not go unpunished.

He heard the one British machine-gun left in this sector open up, and the sound did not fill him with alarm as before.

62

I will fight for the men of Ireland with mutual smiting and destruction and wizardry.

—The Second Battle of Mag Tuired

The bite that the Germans had taken out of the British line was proving an inconvenience to everybody – not least the Germans, who still had to cross a deal of open ground to reinforce and resupply their men who were holding on in the captured British trenches. They still kept up their frontal attacks at various points along the line, but any German success brought the small benefit to the British of relief from the German artillery. With the two sides so close to each other, and even mingled in places, the Germans were reluctant to risk shelling their own, and so tended to concentrate on the British rear.

That wasn't enough to save the riflemen dug in in front of the Munsters. Late in the morning their lone machine-gun stopped firing and shortly after that a determined German rush pushed in their left flank and rolled up their front. The Rifles came streaming back in a hurry and piled into the Munsters' trenches.

Wyndham was an anxious onlooker to the hasty retreat. Two men, heavily burdened, were lagging behind their comrades, when one of them was hit. His mate went back, and with no small difficulty hefted the other's load, while the wounded man struggled to his feet and hopped and staggered along as best he could, with bullets clipping the earth and flying by him all the while.

As they came closer they were revealed to be the machine-gun crew, with one of them now somehow carrying on under the weight of both gun and tripod. He made it to the Munster trench, saw Wyndham, said, 'Give me a hand with these, Paddy,' and dumped his burden to go back for his mate. They both made it.

Wyndham was struggling to pull the tripod in off the parapet, and its surprising weight filled him with admiration for the machine-gunner's ability to carry it one-handed, even over a short distance. The thing was solid steel throughout.

The wounded man wasn't badly wounded. A bullet had torn a furrow through his calf muscle, which he admitted hurt like blazes, but did not injure him so badly that he was unable to tend to it himself or make it out of the line on his own two feet, even if he was reluctant to go.

'No – you clear off, mate,' said the No. 1 on the gun. 'Get that seen to. I'll be all right. This bloke here can give me a hand.' And he turned to Wyndham, who after all wasn't carrying a rifle or doing anything much to fight off the Germans. 'Ain't that right, Paddy?'

So with a 'cheerio' the No. 2 limped away down the now crowded trench, and 'Paddy' Wyndham prepared to be educated in the ways of machine-gunnery.

'What do I do?' he asked.

'Just pick up the tripod and we'll get the whole lot out of everyone's way.'

'You're not, um, siting it? Mounting it? You know – shooting the thing?'

'Nah, mate. The old bitch has packed it in. Going to have to strip her down somewhere quiet and take a look. There's fuck-all ammo left either. You and me might as well just pick up rifles from here on in.'

Wyndham helped the man to take the gun back to the Piggery, and left him there with it. Busy Rifles officers and NCOs were reorganising themselves and their mangled battalion and Wyndham didn't want to risk being roped into something extra-regimental. On a day like this he wanted to be with his own. He did pick up a rifle, though. There was a growing collection of them by the stretcher post. He had no specific intention of killing anyone yet, but he understood there could be no spectators in this war.

With the riflemen beside them instead of in front of them, the Munsters at last had an unobstructed field of fire almost all along their line and were taking full advantage of it. Moriarty and Whelan were standing side by side, in a good position, letting fly at anything that moved. They were content with their lot, and almost enjoying themselves. When the main German effort tailed off Duffy sent up tea, with every expectation of something to eat coming soon. There were still bullets flying, but the Germans were in a rotten position and few went to the trouble of showing their heads long enough to take aim.

'There! Left, left! Do you see him?'

'I see him, I see him!'

Then: 'Bollocks. Missed.'

'What harm? There'll be another one along in a minute.'

Moriarty was having a little smoke below the parapet when Whelan alerted him.

'There! Over by the hedge there!'

Moriarty had a look, but could see nothing.

'No – the far hedge. There beyond.'

That hedge had been serving since yesterday as the Germans' main line of communication, but they naturally tended to move along it at a low crawl. Unless someone kept his backside too high in the air, or the British artillery was being unusually effective, it was generally pretty safe. But now, when Whelan pointed to it, Moriarty could see definite movement.

'There's some fellas moving along there, They're standing up. Do you not see them?'

'I see them – the dirty bastards. Wait till they break cover. We'll have them,' said Moriarty.

Moriarty wasn't as good a shot as Whelan. Of course he never put it that way. He was as good a shot as anyone in the battalion. It was only that Whelan had younger eyes. The range was long and he thought he might as well finish his fag and let the boy see if he could hit any Huns.

'Can you get a bead on them yet?'

'They're hunkered down, but once they're past them trees I'll have them,' said Whelan. 'There's two of them.'

But then, instead of tightening his finger on the trigger, he took his eye from the sights and peered with both eyes on the target, bothered all of a sudden.

'What is it? What's wrong?' said Moriarty.

'I think they're carrying a stretcher.'

Moriarty had a look. The two Germans did indeed seem to be moving in tandem, just like a stretcher party. It would certainly explain why they were keeping upright. Moriarty made a tactical appraisal.

'Fuck it,' he said. 'Shoot them anyway.'

'Shoot stretcher-bearers? I will not!'

'They're only Huns.'

'I don't care. It's wrong. Sure they'll only start shooting our stretcher-bearers if that's the case.'

'Please yourself so.'

Moriarty had half a mind to take a shot himself, but he didn't want to upset Whelan. He did take up position, though, and have a good look at the two far-off Germans. They came into plain view for just a second, but that second was enough to make Moriarty fervently wish he'd kept his sights on them.

The German machine-gun was closely similar to the British

model, only the carriage was different. Where the British used a tripod, the Germans had something akin to a sledge, which could be collapsed into a handy, if very heavy, two-man carrying platform. That was what Moriarty was seeing now. He loosed off a wild shot, and missed by a mile, and swore. Other shots rang out at other points along the line, but the German team made it to cover. No doubt, crawling along just out of sight, the ammunition carriers were following, bringing box after box of little steel-pointed machine-gun bullets, ready to be loosed into the heart of the British line.

'Bollocks,' said Moriarty.

63

Then he grew half mad with fear, for the hours were passing, and he flung himself down on the ground in a lonesome spot, and wept and groaned in terror, for the time was coming fast when he must die.

—Lady Wilde, 'The Priest's Soul', *Fairy Tales and Folk Tales of the Irish Peasantry*

Things got bad from there on in. The German machine-gun had a range of more than a mile, but there it was dug in at what they reckoned at no more than seventy or eighty yards away. That was too close for comfort, but far enough to allow the gun crew to get a crack at any counterattack that materialised. The Rifles made that uncomfortable discovery for themselves when they vainly tried to retake their lost trenches.

Not only did they fail in that attempt, and leave more than twenty men on the ground they tried to cross, but they and the Munsters were obliged to evacuate a few of their own trenches because the German machine-gun had them effectively enfiladed. Bullet wounds to the head became worryingly common. Nerves were overwrought. It was all too much for some.

'Who is that man?' demanded Fleming.

'It's Hickey, sir,' said Moyle.

'But whatever does he think he's doing?'

Private Hickey was standing in no man's land, right out there in the open, with no rifle and with his equipment on anyhow.

He appeared to be talking to himself, but maybe he was just opening and closing his mouth compulsively. He was walking in rapid little steps but not going anywhere – just walking up and down and in little circles.

'He's touched, sir,' explained Robinson.

'Wandered,' said Moyle.

'Doolally,' clarified Robinson.

Fleming had never been posted out east, so had never been acquainted with the army's transit camp at Deolali near Bombay, where men who'd been too long in India waited to be shipped home and where young soldiers new off the troopship first learned about sunstroke. Hickey's symptoms were clear enough nevertheless.

'Do you mean he's off his head?'

'I think so, sir.'

'Oh,' said Fleming. He was at a loss. If the man had been wounded then he could have rescued him, but what was to be done with a man who'd run mad? The major would know, of course, but he couldn't go running off to find the major every time an unexpected problem arose. Genuinely perplexed, he turned to Robinson, as the oldest soldier present.

'What do you think we should do?'

'Well, sir – things being how they are, I'd leave him. It don't look like old Hickey is going to be much use to us one way or another.'

'But he's one of our men, Robinson!'

'With respect, sir – he's one of our men what ain't worth the trouble. Maybe he'll come in by himself in a bit.'

'No... No, I don't think that will do,' said Fleming. 'Hickey! I say Hickey! Come in, man – before you get hurt!'

But that brought no reaction at all from Hickey.

And then they heard catcalling in German. None of them spoke the language, so they were spared the finer points of their enemies' mockery, but it was galling all the same.

'You mind your own fucking business, Fritz!' called Robinson.

'That will do, Robinson!' said Fleming.

'Sorry, sir,' said Robinson. 'I'm only surprised they haven't gone and shot the poor silly bastard yet.'

'Perhaps the Hun has some decency after all.'

'Perhaps the Hun is just taking the piss – begging your pardon, sir.'

'It won't do. We can't allow the Germans to make fun of us – and we can't allow Hickey to be out there like that either. Stay here. I'm going to get him.'

And with that, Fleming was climbing out of the trench.

'Leave him be, sir! He ain't worth it!' shouted Robinson, and then, more quietly, 'I'll shoot the bleeder myself and save us all the trouble.'

But he didn't shoot, and neither did the Germans.

Moyle, watching, made to follow the lieutenant. 'Mind yourself, sir! Wait there and I'll give you a hand.'

But Fleming was having none of it, and told Moyle to stay where he was. He went forward upright and slowly, with his hands where the Germans could see them. He approached Hickey as he would a skittish horse

'I say – Hickey. Come on now. Come along with me.'

He knew that the man's Christian name was James, but he could hardly go and call a soldier by his Christian name. He put his hand on the man's sleeve, but Hickey shook it off in a quick nervous gesture, never looking at the officer. Fleming tried again, acutely conscious of all the eyes that watched him from the German trenches.

'Come along now. We'll go and get you a nice mug of tea.' And he took Hickey's arm more firmly. Again he was shaken off. He tried a stronger line.

'Now look here, Private Hickey: this nonsense has got to stop. Come with me this instant.'

But Hickey was paying no heed to officers this day, nor was he in any humour for a scolding. Fleming was running out of options. He knew he was looking foolish, but worse than that, he felt useless. He had been the butt of jokes many times in his life, and had felt the sting of a bullet only a month ago, and these were things he would face again if need be, but to be helpless when it came to commanding men in the field was just too much. If he couldn't shift Hickey then he was letting down the major and the regiment, his king and his country, his school and himself.

Bog Fleming hadn't been a star of the rugger team by any means, but his schoolmates would happily have conceded that he'd had spirit. Now he bunched his shoulder and tackled Hickey so as to knock the man off balance. He knew it was a terrible sin for an officer to lay violent hands on a soldier, but affairs had become desperate. Hickey stumbled, and Fleming grabbed hold of his arm again and pulled hard, and this time Hickey followed along. He heard a derisive cheer raised in the German line, and he didn't care. It took a deal more pulling before he got Hickey back, but get him back he did, and that was an immense relief. There was quite an audience waiting for him.

'Good man yourself, sir.'

'Bloody well done, sir.'

And, in the background: 'Told you he'd do it. Two francs you owe me,'

They were less welcoming to Hickey. Moyle gave him a shove.

'What's wrong with you, you fool?'

Hickey didn't react, but bounced into Robinson, who slapped him round the back of the head.

'Idle bugger! Getting Mr Fleming nearly killed.'

There was much of the same from others, but Hickey never said a word. The medical orderly brought him away in the end, and some said they saw tears in Hickey's eyes as he was led out of the line. Proper order. The man should have been bloody well ashamed of himself.

64

And there was great slaughter, and laying low in graves, and many comely men fell there in the stall of death. Pride and shame were there side by side, and hardness and red anger, and there was red blood on the white skin of young fighting men.

—Lady Augusta Gregory, *Gods And Fighting Men*

Like a heavy-handed assistant to autumn, the shelling had stripped away the last of the leaves, and taken twigs and branches as well, and a few whole trees here and there. The wet places were all pools and bare earth was mud, spreading and getting deeper with every footfall. To the autumnal litter was added the rubbish of armies, so that fallen leaves and rotting vegetation were scattered about with empty food tins, spent cartridge casings, old bandages, and less-identifiable scraps and rags. What would have been just depressing had been made ugly. And it was raining again.

Some blamed the next German successes on the rain. Although it rained upon the just and the unjust alike, it could be especially dispiriting to keep watch on a rain-swept field, risking a bullet to the head, and all when you haven't really slept in days and haven't had anything to eat besides bully and biscuit, and can't quite feel your feet, except as a dull cold pain somewhere below your knees. So men who should have been vigilant tended to keep their heads down out of the weather, and let their mates keep an eye out.

The Germans loosed off a belt of machine-gun fire, and with no more warning than that they rushed the British line. Their feet must have been bad too, and heavy with mud, but desperation pushed them on, and with the incremental advances of the previous days they didn't have very far to run. The British saw them coming, and fired more than a few telling shots, but with no machine-gun in this sector, and no artillery support worth a damn, they could not halt the attack.

It was fortunate for those who were not killed then and there that the Munsters' position had grown into a more complex affair than it had originally been. To answer the German threat from the flank, new trenches had been dug in new directions, so that for the men driven back there was some sort of refuge not far distant. From one of these soggy excavations Moriarty and Whelan watched in horror at the collapse of their forward line, and loaded and fired like men possessed.

The British service rifle had more than a few little drawbacks, but in order that the same weapon could be shouldered by an infantryman and carried in a saddle bucket by a cavalryman, it had been made considerably shorter than the standard design. That compactness was proving handy in a battle fought from holes in the ground, and there were one or two men now who owed their lives to the relative unwieldiness of a long German rifle, with long bayonet fixed, in a narrow trench. On the other hand, the short length of the British Lee-Enfield contributed to its vicious kick, and the general filthiness of conditions in the line meant that the mechanism, which should have moved smoothly, was proving stubborn. Keeping the fiddlier bits of the rifle in working order was an uphill task. Every rifle came with its own cleaning kit, but the single four-by-two-inch patch of flannelette did not last long here, and a patch torn from a shirt tail was a common substitute.

Likewise, when Moriarty fired, a sharp nose could have made out, mingled with the smell of cordite, an undertone of bacon. Rifle oil was in short supply, and Sergeant Duffy had supplied fat on request. There were misfires and stoppages and jams, with plenty of cursing. At least the ammunition held out, and it was not wasted. As had been the way at Mons, and every battle since, the Germans were finding out what a British soldier in possession of his wits could do with nothing more than a five-round clip.

Wyndham had been summoned to the fight, and Duffy had festooned him with pale cotton bandoliers and told him to play delivery boy. Now he edged in beside Moriarty and Whelan and asked if they needed any ammunition. The action had become less frantic now that the Germans had taken their initial objective and were consolidating their gains. Moriarty had time to look up from his work.

'I will, thanks. Just hang it around my neck there. Good man. You don't have any cigarettes, do you? No? Shite.'

But he had one himself, kept dry enough inside his cap, and battle or no, he took the opportunity to fish it out and light up. He saw that Wyndham had a rifle slung.

'Well look at yourself,' he said. 'Welcome to the war. Here – you can take over awhile while I have a fag.'

Wyndham wasn't going to argue. If he was going to pick up a rifle it followed that he was going to use it.

'Straight ahead of you,' Moriarty told him. 'About thirty yards. And keep an eye on those bushes a bit over to your right. If they're coming in again they're coming from there.'

And Wyndham, not quite knowing what he was doing, took a hold of his rifle with new purpose, and raised his head above the parapet. Whelan was poised beside him, eyes glued to the sights. He confirmed the directions that Moriarty had given. Wyndham pushed his rifle forward, and got mud on it straight away. He moved to wipe it off.

'Leave it,' said Whelan. 'Doesn't matter. Here – do you have one up the spout?'

'I beg your pardon?'

'Do you have a round in the breech like? Do you know if the thing's loaded at all?'

Wyndham pulled on the bolt and nothing happened. He flicked the bolt upwards and was relieved to see that that worked. But then when he pulled it back, it stuck. He pushed on it and pulled again and this time the breech opened and a perfectly good cartridge, all shiny brass, sprung out into his face and tumbled into the mud at the bottom of the trench.

'Oh dear,' he said.

'Sure 'tis loaded anyway,' said Whelan.

Wyndham tried to close the bolt again but it wouldn't move at all this time. Exasperated, Moriarty took the rifle away from him, and worked the bolt with impatient competence and made everything right again. He thrust it back at Wyndham.

'There you go. It's safe now. Don't do anything with it.' And leaving Wyndham feeling rather small, he took up post again, and levelled his own weapon at the German line. His aiming eye squinted more than usual from the sting of smoke that rose from the dog-end still between his lips.

'Put out that cigarette, that man!'

That was Major Fitzmullen-Brophy, keeping an eye on everything at once. He knew these were trying times, but standards had to be upheld. Allow a man to smoke a cigarette in the middle of a battle and who knows where you'll be next. Shocking – and bad for a fellow's wind too.

65

It is my Royal and Imperial command that you concentrate your energies, for the immediate present, upon one single purpose, and that is that you address all your skill and all the valour of my soldiers to exterminate first the treacherous English and walk over General French's contemptible little army.

—Emperor Wilhelm II

And the fighting went on from day to day, and at last Finn said to Fergus of the Sweet Lips: 'Go out, Fergus, and see how many of the Fianna are left for the fight to-day.' And Fergus counted them, and he said: 'There is one battalion only of the Fianna left in good order; but there are some of the men of it,' he said, 'are able to fight against three, and some that are able to fight against nine or thirty or a hundred.'
'If that is so,' said Finn, 'rise up and go to where the King of the World is, and bid him to come out to the great battle.'

—Lady Augusta Gregory, *Gods And Fighting Men*

Fitzmullen-Brophy's command was reckoned a company for convenience's sake, but a company at full strength should have amounted to more than two hundred men and Fitzmullen-Brophy had never boasted much more than a hundred and twenty at the best of times. He had eighty-odd under his command when the German offensive opened, and that was down to fewer than fifty by the time they were driven back on the Piggery. That was where Robinson killed a man with a shovel.

British troops were falling back in haste, with a few Germans in hot but unwise pursuit. The riflemen and fusiliers were running, but they weren't panicking. As soon as they reached a position that looked halfway defensible they turned and fought. A German soldier crashed through the bushes and lost his footing on the sudden dip into the yard, and Robinson took him with the bayonet in textbook style. The blade went in deep between the victim's ribs and stuck there fast. Given time, Robinson could have worked it free, but time was pressing. He left his rifle where it was, picked up a handy shovel, and walloped the next man along with such force that the single blow might have killed him there and then. Robinson wasn't taking any chances though. Seeing as no one else was immediately threatening his life, he swung the shovel again and again in brutal chopping strokes until he was satisfied that his man wouldn't be getting up. He went to retrieve his rifle from the body of the first man he'd killed and could only manage it by firing into the corpse and yanking the blade loose as the bullet punched its way in.

'Shooting a dead man, eh?' he said to no one in particular. 'Fancy that.'

And then Duffy was there with a gentle hand on his shoulder and a discreet swig from his special water bottle.

A few more Germans had attempted to storm the Piggery, but they'd been similarly dealt with. The defenders had their wits about them – up to a point. One of the Munsters, coming in too late, was shot by a nervous comrade, and there were probably a few near misses too that no one felt the need to own up to.

There were wounded out in the open, but the mood was too

tense for even a hint of a truce to allow them to be brought in. One poor soul, lost among the tall weeds, stuck his head up too high, and a fusilier, either jumpy or just plain vindictive, put a bullet in it. This provoked a few scattered shots from the other side and – oddly enough, seeing as no one knew the nationality of the dead man – shouts of protest. The Munsters answered in kind, and for an angry half-minute the Irish and the Saxons cursed each other for English swine and Prussian bastards.

Fitzmullen-Brophy took stock. With the men and the ammunition on hand, the Piggery was a position well suited to all-round defence, and if this were, say, Chitral, then he would have had grounds for hoping that he and his remaining men would go down in history as the heroes of Chitral. But the men of German XIX Corps were not discontented Afridis or angry Afghans. They had the manpower to swamp the Munsters and, failing that, the firepower to pound them into the mud. The prudent thing to do would be to withdraw completely, but that was contrary to orders, and just as bad, would leave the neighbouring battalions in the lurch. If anyone failed, it would not be the Munsters.

But the correct spirit might not be enough to save them. They had been making a grand display of dogged resistance for days, in the proudest traditions of British infantry in adversity, but all it had won them was what they had now. They may have punished the Germans for their advance, but the Germans had advanced nonetheless. The Hun had been made pay a high price for the ground he had won, but he'd paid it and won it, and now the Munsters were backed into a corner. Ticklish.

Fitzmullen-Brophy calculated that he had an hour or two before the Boche gathered himself sufficiently, and then maybe there would be another attack, or maybe the attack wouldn't come until tomorrow. That meant another wakeful, soul-sapping night in the cold, waiting for the worst, with perhaps another bombardment as in previous days. With the unit all crowded in together like this, an artillery strike could do terrible damage.

Wait for the Hun to come on again? No. Better to take the fight to him. Knock him off balance. Punish him. Show him Irish steel.

The decision made, there wasn't a moment to lose. He summoned Fleming, and his two sergeants Duffy and Hegarty. He hadn't much, but he was pleased with what he had. Hegarty, originally dismissed as an old man, was unshaken by an ordeal that had seen the end of much younger men. His nose dripped and he coughed all the time, but he never complained and he kept his men in line. That was how the army had bred soldiers in the old days. Duffy had proved himself time and again to be steady as a rock, strong as a bull, and resourceful as bedamned. It was a lucky day indeed that had charmed Duffy from his cookhouse in Ballymullen.

And then there was Fleming: Fleming who was proving himself every day to be the right sort. Still learning, and not particularly bright, but trustworthy and faithful, young Fleming would restore a chap's faith in the younger generation at a glance.

'We're going back at 'em, men,' he said. 'They won't stand. They're tired, they're muddled, and in the last reckoning, gentlemen, they are no match for British soldiers. We will go in two waves. I will lead, and Lieutenant Fleming will follow. Duffy, you are with me. Hegarty, you are with Lieutenant Fleming. We will break out to the left. Aim for the stand of trees that used to mark Moyle's outpost. Our objective is to recapture those trenches and re-establish our line, or at the very least, give the Hun second thoughts about just waltzing into our trenches. Everybody clear?'

They voiced their assent with varying degrees of animation. There was no need for any more elaborate preparation. The whole company was within earshot. The order was given to fix bayonets and stand ready. Although there was no reason why they shouldn't just push off directly, ingrained military habit had caused Fitzmullen-Brophy to set an exact time for the assault to be launched. As the few minutes ticked away to the fateful hour of three-fifteen, and the major stood, his pistol loose in its holster, his whistle in his hand, and his eyes fixed on the creeping minute-hand, Duffy approached.

'Begging your pardon, sir, but do you think that maybe the lads should have a tot before they go over?'

A Munster Fusilier did not need Dutch courage to face his enemy, but there was no denying that rum would be just the thing to put heart into tired men – to put them in better fighting trim. Also, there was the unspoken certainty that a drink of rum now would be the last drink that some of the men assembled would ever drink.

'A sound idea, Duffy. Just a tot, mind – to keep out the chill.'

It was a generous tot, and Fitzmullen-Brophy drank his alongside the men. It seemed that he should mark the occasion with a toast, but Fitzmullen-Brophy couldn't think of anything fitting to say, and was doubtful if it was even proper for an officer to bend his elbow with the men and utter hearty words at a time like this. No. He felt cold, and any appetite he might have had for melodrama was stilled by a heaviness of spirit that in another man might have been taken for nerves.

He swallowed his rum in silence and didn't even wish them luck. He did though, as the second hand ticked through its last arc, order the smashing of the rum jar, and he made sure he stayed to watch it being done.

At the last second Fitzmullen-Brophy decided against blowing his whistle to signal the attack. Instead he silently waved his arm and the men followed him up and over. As always, there was the moment of disorientation to find oneself above ground, as if you had just climbed out onto a roof, but this was no time for hesitation or fanciful thoughts. The enemy-held trenches were largely invisible, but the objective, marked by the clump of trees, was clear ahead.

The great danger was the German machine-gun, but the major knew his ground well. That gun was over *there*, angled *that* way, and there was a hedge between to obstruct the view, and the slightest rise in the ground to spoil the aim. If they moved quick enough the gunner might not even be able to get a shot at them. It occurred to him – suddenly and most unpleasantly – that the Germans might have brought up a second gun, but it was too late to be worrying about that now. Behind him the men lumbered forward, sore-footed on uneven ground, and in no semblance of order. Fleming's men were hard on their heels. Fleming should have left a longer interval before following Fitzmullen-Brophy, but he was afraid to be left too far behind. Men stumbled, but recovered quickly. They were eager to be at the Germans. It would mean that this terrifying venture would be over.

They made it surprisingly far before anyone was hit. The German sentries had seen them coming the moment the Munsters broke cover, but the sentries had to sound the alarm, and their mates had to stand up, and level their rifles, and take aim, and all of that took seconds and in those seconds the distance was closing. German soldiers were, for the most part, civilians in uniform, and either did not set such great store in marksmanship or enjoy so many hours of training on the range. The German rifle was every bit as good as the British one, but the shooting was poor. Even being fired on from two directions at once, the Munsters were aware of the bullets flying by and overhead before any of them fell.

An old sweat called Sloan took a bullet square in the chest and was stone dead before he hit the ground. Moriarty, right behind, instinctively dived for cover behind the body, but got up again quickly as his mates ran past him. Safety in numbers. Two other men were wounded but one of them kept moving regardless.

The unit's other Private O'Brien made it all the way to the lip of the German trench unscathed, but found himself poised to jump down on top of a German soldier who had the presence of mind to shoot first. O'Brien was hit in the throat, with the bullet travelling upwards into his head. At such close range, it still had plenty of punch left to lift O'Brien's cap off his head, along with several shards of his skull. He did his duty to the regiment even in death, though, for his body pitched forward, landing on his killer, and obliging his killer's mate to get out of his way in a hurry. Then Sergeant Duffy was in among them, swinging haymakers with his rifle butt.

Fitzmullen-Brophy jumped into the trench a moment later and landed badly. Thank heavens for the softness of mud. His revolver came with a length of lanyard that looped round his neck, so he didn't lose it, but it was all covered in mud now. Duffy helped him up, or at least grabbed him by the collar and yanked him unceremoniously to his feet. He let go then but stuck very close, and acted as the major's shield against any possible assailants to the extent that the major couldn't see what was going on.

Fleming's revolver was still in working order, and a reassuring weight in his fist. When he reached the parapet the trench below seemed so busy with Germans that he hesitated to jump. He pointed his pistol and started shooting. After three rounds the hammer snapped down on a spent cap. He'd forgotten to check to reload.

'Oh you fathead,' he said to himself, and jumped, ready to grapple the enemy bare-handed if it came to that. Moyle and Robinson were right behind him, and as soon as they slid down into the trench the Germans ran for it. Fleming straightened up and saw that they hadn't left any dead or wounded behind. Three shots at a range of no more than a few feet and he hadn't hit a blessed thing. He hustled after the fleeing enemy, the others close beside him, and he still hadn't reloaded his revolver.

There was some ugly work with butt and bayonet in places, and with fist and boot too, but Fitzmullen-Brophy had been right in his instinct. The Germans who had taken this trench had been caught off balance, with neither the numbers nor the appetite for further combat that day. They'd had a hard time of it fighting this far forward, and when you're facing angry hooligans with sharp blades in a narrow space, a wet trench just isn't a prize that seems quite so valuable any more. One German sergeant was trying to organise a defence when he was bayoneted. Another was ordering a retreat, and he was getting more takers.

Some vengeful Munsters fired after the withdrawing Germans, but a rifle with its bayonet fixed was a badly balanced thing for fine shooting and little execution was done. Many of the Munsters never even saw the Germans go. Moriarty and Whelan had tumbled into a trench that was in uproar. Like Portsmouth on a Saturday night, Moriarty said later, only muddier, and with not so much broken glass. They snarled and jabbed, but only to make space for themselves and, in the moment it took to get their bearings, the place was nearly empty again. A couple of the German wounded were being finished off, but everyone else in grey had vanished. The two fusiliers stood back to back, trembling with nervous release, and the sweat going cold on them.

'They've scarpered,' said Whelan.

'Jesus,' said Moriarty. 'They have and all.'

Fitzmullen-Brophy watched the Germans fall back, and had everyone make sure that there were no spiteful stay-behinds waiting around the next traverse. All was well. His own casualties had been low. He had made a decision, launched a surprise counterattack, and got away with it. He told himself that all was well. He'd forgotten how thoroughly frightening this sort of thing could be.

66

'Who are you?' cried the king.
'My name in Erin is Dyeermud.'
'What brought you hither?' asked the king.
'I came,' replied Dyeermud, 'to succour my chief, Fin MacCool.'
The king let a laugh out of him and asked, 'How many more men come besides you?'
'When you finish with me, you may be looking for others,' said Dyeermud.

—Jeremiah Curtin, *Hero-Tales of Ireland*

Not everyone had joined in the attack. Wyndham had been left behind as a token headquarters detail. The stretcher party was there too, as were a few odds and sods from the rifle battalion, but the Piggery was suddenly an empty place. Wyndham watched his bold commander lead the remnant of the company across the muddy fields, and he held his breath when the shooting started.

Then the Munsters were out of view in the German trench and he became aware of other spectators to the action, and it wasn't just some stretcher-bearers or signals-wallahs either. A small party of officers had arrived, and were taking in the scene with interest. Wyndham wasn't versed in the markings that distinguished senior officers or staff officers, but these gentlemen, and the leading pair in particular, were obviously very important. For all that they were spattered in mud, their uniforms were positively spruce. Their khaki was merely muddy, and not greasy. It still was of a colour that conformed to dress regulations, whereas everyone else was wearing a tone darkened with ingrained sweat and grime and damp. And the officers had obviously shaved that morning, and most likely breakfasted well too, for their faces were smooth and pink.

Wyndham straightened up and saluted. The junior of the important pair returned the salute in a manner casual and lordly. He looked at Wyndham's badges.

'Afternoon, Private. Munster Fusiliers, yes?'

'Good afternoon, sir. Yes, sir.'

'That Major Fitzmullen-Brophy went off just now?'

'Yes, sir.'

'Thought so. Where's the rest of his company?'

'I'm afraid I'm it, sir.'

'Hmm.'

And with that the officer turned to his superior and didn't pay Wyndham another glance. Wyndham didn't think he had been dismissed, and he hadn't been going anywhere anyway, so he stayed where he was, not sure whether he was conspicuous or invisible. After a little while he relaxed from his position of attention, and just eavesdropped.

'I think they've done it, sir,' said the officer who'd spoken to Wyndham. 'They're not coming back just yet at any rate.' He was identical to fully half the more senior officers that Wyndham had ever encountered, being maybe forty, and maybe a major, or maybe forty-five, and maybe a lieutenant colonel. Precise manners, well-kept moustache, expensive boots.

'Stout fella, that Fitzmullen-Brophy,' said the other man, slightly older, slightly heavier. 'That's the stuff to give 'em. Absolutely first-class effort.'

'First class, sir. Absolutely.'

'Bit awkward, mind. Damn all support available.'

'Quite.'

'I'd send reinforcements, of course, except that technically the Munsters *are* reinforcements. Still: see what we can do.' He lowered his field glasses and looked at Wyndham for the first time. 'You there – Private.'

Wyndham braced his knees and squared his shoulders.

'Cut along to Major Fitzmullen-Brophy. Take him this message.' And he turned to one of his underlings. 'Charles? Charles? A notebook, if you please.'

He scribbled out a note and handed it to his second-in-command, who passed it to Wyndham. Wyndham took it and saluted.

'Right then. Off you go,' said the officer.

Wyndham knew better than to voice the thoughts that were clamouring in his brain.

Who me? Over there? Now?

He let obedience guide him. That was enough to get him on his way. An officer was sending him on a mission. Then, when he was out in the open, in the cold air, obedience wasn't quite enough. He kept low. He probably couldn't have stood up straight if you paid him. There was a very inviting hollow, over there by that broken fence, but that was out of his way and it led nowhere. He told himself to keep moving straight ahead. Major Fitzmullen-Brophy needed him. The message must get through. Daniel Wyndham had been called. This was his hour.

Listen, my children, and you shall hear
Of the midnight ride of Paul Revere,
On the eighteenth of April, in Seventy-Five:
Hardly a man is now alive...

That last line was unfortunate.

A bullet cracked in the air close by, and there was a sharp thump on the ground behind him that could well have been another one.

After that he just trusted to luck and sprinted. When he made it to the trench no one seemed to think much of his heroism.

'What made you come the long way? Did you not see the trench running there alongside?'

That was Whelan. Breathless, all Wyndham could say was, 'What?'

'The trench that's at an angle to this one – you could have jumped down in there. You didn't need to come all this way in the open at all.'

And then Duffy: 'What are you doing here, man? Weren't you told to stay back?'

But Fitzmullen-Brophy was welcoming at least. 'Good show, Wyndham. But you really shouldn't dawdle about in the open, you know. It's really quite dangerous. Now what's this message, eh?'

The message was from Brigade, which meant that the exalted personage back at the Piggery was none other than the Brigadier General himself, with all his tremendous staff about him. The message was congratulatory, but not wonderfully encouraging. There were no supports, no reinforcements, and no artillery. The Munsters should hold on as best they could for as long as they could, and get well out of it when they couldn't. None of this was a particular surprise to Fitzmullen-Brophy, but it was galling to be told that his gains would have to be abandoned. And abandoned they most certainly would be. There were forty-three men – forty-four now that Wyndham was here – and around eighty yards of trench. They had the ammunition each man had carried with him, and anything else would have to come by the same path Wyndham had just risked. The Germans, having been in much the same state, hadn't left anything behind, not even food and water.

At least it would be dark soon enough, so there was little cause to fear any further enemy action. If this had been a proper sort of fortification they could wreck it and thus deny it to the enemy, but apart from actually filling the thing in, there wasn't a great deal they could do to demolish a trench.

Moyle and Robinson volunteered to try stalking the troublesome machine-gun, but Fitzmullen-Brophy, after giving it some serious thought, reckoned it wasn't on. They'd have had to move across ground that was under direct observation, and even in the dark the opposing sides were too close to chance that. More than that even, they'd actually have to cross a German-held trench, and these were two men that Fitzmullen-Brophy could ill afford to lose.

He had the men keep up a scattered fire as the night came on, intensifying it as the small force withdrew by sections. The last few men to leave were rattling out full-on salvoes. They regained the Piggery without loss. They had done remarkably well for themselves, but it had all been for nothing.

67

Now hope all ending, and death befriending
  His last aid lending, my cares are done.
No more a rover, or hapless lover,
  My griefs are over—my glass runs low;
Then for that reason, and for a season,
  Let us be merry before we go.

—John Philpot Curran, 'The Deserter's Meditation'

There was no rum, and tobacco was running low. All there was to eat was whatever was left over from yesterday. Duffy had been otherwise engaged and the normal supply routine had been disrupted. So there was tea, as always, and bully and biscuit, as always, and the more companionable souls shared out their few cigarettes. Have a drag, have another one, and pass it on.

The ruined Piggery, although a dismal place on this unhappy night, had the advantage over the trenches of being hardly flooded at all. Men could sit down, and even lie down in some places. At Fitzmullen-Brophy's insistence they took off their boots. The puttees that wrapped their lower legs were there to keep the trouser bottoms from flapping and to present a clean and soldierly appearance. They were cheaper than leather gaiters and were fiddly and troublesome in a manner beloved of the army, and only a proper and diligent soldier knew how to wind them in a precise and seemly fashion. Out east, where the fashion had originated, they had the great benefit of protecting against snakebite. Here in Flanders, with venomous snakes being less of an immediate hazard, puttees collected mud, but then so did everything else. There was also the less happy feature by which, tightly wound and soaking wet, they constricted the circulation to the feet. So on the major's orders the men in relays took off their boots for the first time in days, and wrung out their socks, and vigorously rubbed their feet. It was a disgusting sight, and a painful exercise for many of the men, but most of them, having privately damned Fitzmullen-Brophy for an old woman, felt the benefit afterwards.

The Piggery belonged solely to the Munsters now. The neighbouring battalions, ground down and strung out, were dug in wherever they might, and each battalion's troubles were its own. The farmhouse itself was now cookhouse, magazine, and aid post, with a kitchen table in one corner serving as headquarters. The chimney had been destroyed by the shelling so the only heat came from a wretched brazier fashioned from a bucket, the only light from a candle stuck in a whiskey bottle. There was another whiskey bottle, but Fitzmullen-Brophy kept it hidden. It was for medicinal purposes only. He didn't want to corrupt young Fleming with a love for strong drink. Tea made with lots of condensed milk would be just as good for fortifying the young man. Cocoa would be better still, but there was no cocoa. The two officers sat across from each other, and Fitzmullen-Brophy told tales of South Africa, and of soldiering as it had been when he was young. Fleming felt immensely privileged, but had great trouble keeping awake.

Outside in the dark, Wyndham told on request the story of Oisin and Niamh. Wyndham was obliged to reveal that yes, Niamh had big tits, but that bit of ribaldry was included merely from habit. The men who listened to the story, even though they'd heard it from Wyndham before, were more reflective than was usual.

'Can you imagine?' said Whelan. 'You go away for a year and when you come back you find out you've really been gone a hundred years.'

Moriarty said that wouldn't bother him in the slightest, and that if some blondie young one came along on a big horse and offered to take him away from all this shite, then he'd be up on that horse like a shot and he couldn't be arsed how many years would go by.

But while there were heartfelt noises of agreement at this, there was a silence thereafter. Perhaps they wondered. Perhaps they might come home from this to find all who knew them long dead, and Ireland populated by lesser men, for whom the heroes were no more than faded legends.

68

A grievous descent was made on his native place,
The price of mead in the hall, and the feast of wine;
His blades were scattered about between two armies…

—The Gododdin

In the morning, which was a very long time in coming, the Germans retook the trenches from which they'd been driven the day before. After that they came and took the Piggery.

There was no preliminary bombardment, so although the Munsters were expecting them, they weren't expecting them just yet. The Germans had re-sited their machine-gun during the night, and now it spat out bullets that chewed up the sandbags and cracked against the walls and kept everyone close to the ground. And then, when the firing shifted to allow the attacking infantry to move in, and the defenders raised their heads and prepared to give them some of that tried and tested rapid independent, they saw that the Germans were close, very close.

Whelan brought up his rifle and saw a German not twenty yards off and closing fast. By reflex, or training, or by pure fluke, he shot straight and the German fell, but he fumbled the bolt then, and didn't have time for a second shot before they were on him. He stumbled backwards, waving his rifle around like a club.

Moriarty didn't even manage to loose off a first shot, but he did hear old Sergeant Hegarty shriek at them to fix bayonets, and he did as he was told, but he was falling back as he did so.

Fitzmullen-Brophy stood his ground and fired off all six

chambers of his revolver into the advancing mass. Only it wasn't an advancing mass: it was a Hun here and a Hun there, and all moving fast and dodging about, and his own men suddenly getting in the way. But there were enough of the blighters to convince him that a few pistol shots weren't going to make a blind bit of difference. Moreover, an officer's job was not to fight but to command, and right now, with his front being driven in, that probably meant organising a new line of defence, followed by a counterattack or – God forbid – a withdrawal.

Over the next minute, even while Fitzmullen-Brophy made a very decent fist of keeping some sort of control over his command, the Munsters were overwhelmed. The record, if it ever got round to being written, would describe the defence as gallant, which was more polite than calling it savage. The little yard at the back of the Piggery was a brawling mass in no time, but it was clear that the Germans were getting the better of it. The main building itself had been readied for defence, with loopholes knocked in the walls, but the men at the loopholes could see nothing beyond a confused struggle of khaki and field-grey at extremely close quarters that presented no clear target. They were still there, uselessly, when a few men tried to retreat through the half-ruined farmhouse, the Germans so hard on their heels that the men garrisoning the house were unable to take advantage of their position. They couldn't shoot with their mates in the way, or spring any sort of ambush. There was a short and ugly fight in the kitchen, but the Germans had momentum on their side and soon got the better of the situation. Some of the Munsters made it out and some were trapped like cornered rats. Outside, the rest fought their way back, or just ran for it, around the side of the building, where the men in the front yard were already looking to their own way out.

It was Robinson who probably saved the day, or at least gave everyone a chance to get away. Robinson was drunk. Not cosy and contented drunk, as he had been for weeks, but properly drunk – wild and stumbling drunk.

He had most likely taken possession of Duffy's secret store of rum the night before, or stolen the major's whiskey, but when morning and the German attack came he was, as the Royal Munster Fusiliers would have put it, bladdered, half cut, stocious.

Rotten mouldy drunk.

But not paralytic. Not useless in a fight.

When the Germans rushed the Piggery he turned from being sleepy and placid to roaring. His mind was fogged but his hands remembered how to fix a bayonet, and then there was no stopping him. When a brave young German lunged at him he was too clumsy to parry, or maybe never even thought to do such a thing, but lunged right in himself. The two men stabbed each other without either doing serious injury, but the German had sense enough to get out of the fight fast. He backed into one of his mates, and that was how, in the narrow space by the side of the main building, the whole German attack was briefly stalled. As another man shouldered passed them, Robinson was ready for him, and he lunged and stamped and shouted as to warm a drill sergeant's heart. The German stepped back, the point of the blade stabbing at his face, and he stumbled, and the bayonet was scraping on his collarbone and he fell. The man behind him was battered on the side of the head with Robinson's rifle butt. After that a German officer stepped in and shot Robinson with his pistol. A more sober man might have noticed it, and sat down, and had no more to do with the fight, but Robinson was having none of it.

He staggered under the shot, but he was staggering anyway, and might not even have noticed the bullet. Then he was trampling over his stricken foes and was out again in the more open space of the yard, where he got a good swing in and obliged his assailants to scrabble backwards to give themselves some fighting room, or at least to get out of reach of this madman. The German officer did not deign to fall back, and that was his mistake. He stood his ground and squeezed off two more shots, and one of them hit, and the other missed, because by then he had Robinson's bayonet in his guts. A German corporal had to wait until his officer had fallen down and given him a clear line of sight. Then he shot Robinson in the chest, and that was the end of that.

69

And here upon the turret-top the bale-fire glowers red,
The wake-lights burn and drip about our hacked, disfigured dead,
And many a broken heart is here and many a broken head;
But to-morrow,
By the living God, we'll try the game again!

—John Masefield, 'To-morrow'

The retreat from the Piggery was more like a stampede at first, but the banked-up laneway at least kept everyone together. Everyone, once they went to ground in some handy shell holes by a bend in the lane, was discovered to amount to little more than thirty souls, and several of them wounded. Duffy was carrying two of these in a double fireman's lift – one slung over each shoulder. Champion of the ring in his day, and hero of the tug-of-war he might have been, it yet was a wonder how he'd ever managed to hoist them both up like that. The sweat was streaming off his red face, his chest was working hard and his mighty belly was heaving. His tunic was dark with other men's blood.

Lieutenant Fleming made it in on his own, but they could tell as soon as looking at him that he was hurt too. He assured them he was quite all right, really, as he keeled over, and when he thumped down hard against the earth bank a spray of blood was forced from his mouth. Fitzmullen-Brophy was at his side in an instant, pulling at Fleming's gear to try and find the wound. It was easily found. He'd been shot in the chest, or possibly in the back. It was hard to say as things were now, with the blood coming thick and fresh from the two ends of the hole that had been bored through him, front and back.

Fitzmullen-Brophy roared at the medical orderly to come at once, and Sergeant Hegarty, uncomplaining, was left to bandage his own hand, scored across in a bayonet fight.

'Clean through the lung, sir,' the orderly verified. 'Most likely chipped a rib on its way. We'll get him back directly.' Besides the orderly, the medical team were down to two men, and that meant only one stretcher now. Fleming said that someone else should take it, and that given a minute, he'd be perfectly able to walk back to the dressing station. Fitzmullen-Brophy overruled him while the medico bound him up. All in all, it wasn't such a terrible wound, and a healthy young man stood a very good chance of surviving it, provided he didn't bleed to death any time soon, or succumb to shock, or drown in his own blood, which was a real risk in cases like this. If he escaped all of that, there was also a chance of an infection introduced by scraps of filthy clothing carried deep inside the body, but infection wasn't the orderly's business. Let the buggers back at base hospital deal with that problem. Insisting on hygiene out here at the front was rubbish.

'Awfully sorry to be putting you to this trouble, sir,' said Fleming, and he clearly meant it.

'Nonsense, my boy,' said the major, patting his hand. 'You've done very well indeed. You deserve a rest. Don't worry about us at all.'

Fleming said something else, but his voice was too faint to make out.

'Not another word, lad,' said Fitzmullen-Brophy, and left the stretcher party to their work. The last anyone saw of Fleming he was pale but still breathing. They could see he was breathing by the red bubbles around his mouth. The same bubbles would be frothing around the hole in his chest, but there was a bandage tied over it by then.

Fitzmullen-Brophy was sick to leave the boy like that, but he had other business to see to. This fight wasn't over yet. It wasn't lost yet either – not if the Munster Fusiliers had anything to do with it. He saw that Moyle was still with them, and better yet, he was keeping his head and keeping the Germans at bay. Young Whelan was there beside him, kneeling near the top of the bank, and firing steadily. The two men were dangerously exposed, but were otherwise in a perfect position to shoot any Hun who thought to pursue them. The bodies of several who had been discouraged in their pursuit already lay in the laneway by the broken gate of the Piggery.

Still and all though, it wouldn't do. Another concerted rush and they could be pushed out of this rather sorry excuse for a defensive position, and that would give the Boche a clear run all the way into the British rear as far as the canal. No. Something must be done.

Wyndham was sitting shivering when the major called him, and he was called twice before someone punched him on the shoulder and told him to get a move on. He hadn't so much as fired a shot, or thrust with a bayonet, or even thrown a punch during the fight in the yard. He'd lost his rifle somewhere. The moment the Germans arrived he was moving backwards – not out of cowardice, of course, but from a polite desire to get out of everyone's way. Close-quarter combat wasn't for novices like him. Better to step aside and let the experts at it. But he hadn't stepped aside quite fast enough, and here he was now, compulsively fingering the rent in his sleeve. A man he'd never met before, a man red-eyed and bearded, had tried to run him through, tried to drive a long blade into his body. He'd missed. He'd missed because Sergeant Duffy was suddenly there, grappling the German from behind. 'Grapple' was the wrong word. Duffy had wrapped one arm around the man's head, swung him off his feet, and thrown him to one side. The man managed to land on his feet, and even managed to keep one hand on his rifle, but his balance was gone, and he hadn't even straightened up before Lieutenant Fleming shot him with his revolver. And then Duffy had pointed to the lane leading out of the Piggery and bawled at Wyndham to bloody run.

And now Wyndham's sleeve was torn, and he could steel feel the point of the German bayonet catching there, and the terror of what had been certain to happen next.

'Wyndham! Go on – the major wants you.'

It was another message to be got through.

Enemy in possession SUTHERLAND FARM. Holding position in sunken lane 50 yds W of farm with 30 men. Request reinforcements. Urgent. Request artillery fire on farm. Urgent. Fitzmullen-Brophy Maj. 2/RMF

'And hurry, Wyndham. You must hurry, do you hear.'

It was barely daylight, and rain was blowing in again from the west.

70

Forget not our wounded companions, who stood
  In the day of distress by our side;
While the moss of the valley grew red with their blood,
  They stirr'd not, but conquer'd and died.

—Thomas Moore, 'Remember the Glories of Brien the Brave'

The Germans who took the Piggery stayed in the Piggery. Maybe they were in as bad a shape as the Munsters. Maybe they thought it a miracle they had made it that far. Maybe their reinforcements were being called away to the other fights that were sparking up every day all along the line. Whatever it was, they stayed where they were, and they rebuilt the defences to be on the west side of the farmyard instead of the east, and they kept their heads down while they worked, because Moyle made sure of it.

A mile to the rear Wyndham handed over his message, and the powers at Brigade set about scraping again the bottom of the barrel for something that might do poor old Fitzmullen-Brophy some good. As it happened, Tummy Belcher was already seeing about the matter.

The news from the front had been grave these last few days, with the British being pressed hard and sometimes pushed back. The Germans hadn't broken through anywhere yet, but it had been a close-run thing on more than one occasion. Reserves – there were none, but an army could always find a few extra bodies somewhere. It was one of the unexpected benefits of the musketry proficiency scheme that men who would, in the normal run of things, have no reason to pick up a rifle, had gone to the effort of earning their sixpence proficiency pay. Cooks and clerks, bandsmen and drivers, had gone out to the range and fired off their ammunition allowance and won their marksman's badges and the extra pay that came with it so now, when it seemed that every man had been thrown into the fight, there appeared more men, and from all sorts of odd corners.

Giving a cook a rifle and a fifty-round bandolier was all well and good when you had the cooks in the first place. The Munster Fusiliers, not yet being a properly constituted battalion, had little by way of support personnel, and in the case of Fitzmullen-Brophy's little commando, the rear echelon comprised Major Belcher and Corporal Thompson, and whoever in the company was detailed to carry rations on any given night, and that just wouldn't do. Nevertheless, as Belcher knew full well, that was no reason to leave a comrade in the lurch. One didn't let the regiment down simply because the situation was hopeless. Even before Fitzmullen-Brophy raised the alarm, Belcher was doing what he could.

At the very hour that the Fitzmullen-Brophy was launching his desperate counterattack to retake the lost trenches, his old chum was visiting the hospital, smelling out any men of the battalion who might not be as unwell as the doctors made out.

'The doctors don't know everything, Noonan,' Belcher told one bed-bound fusilier in tones that brooked no argument. 'I mean to say, man, what's supposed to be wrong with you? Influenza? Nonsense! You have a chill, that's all – and when did a Dirty Shirt cry off with a chill, and his regiment in need of him, eh? Come now,' he said, and winked, soldier to soldier, 'You've done a fine job bamboozling the medicos and you've had your rest, but it's time get back to work, what?'

Private Noonan had been able to walk unaided to the latrine since the day before yesterday, and that meant he was able to dress himself, and stand up, and discharge himself from hospital. It wasn't what he had wished, but it made the major stop shouting at him.

By the time Belcher had finished his rounds of cajoling and bullying, Noonan had been joined by a jaundice patient, two cases classified as pyrexia of unknown origin, two victims of trench foot, and one gunshot wound. All had had their better nature well and truly appealed to.

Lance Corporal Byrne, who had a hole in his right arm packed with sterile gauze, couldn't hold a rifle, and the trench-foot cases discovered, unsurprisingly, that they couldn't walk very far. But Byrne could take charge of the others, and carry ammunition with his good hand, and the men with the bad feet could leave their boots unlaced for the time being. Belcher had not come unprepared, and had a wagon laid on for the comfort of his invalids. A little ride in the fresh air would do them a world of good, and then they could rest up in the storehouse at Three Poplar Farm until tomorrow. Then, if fresh air hadn't done the trick, there was always rum. What mattered was that there would be a few more men upright in the line tomorrow. If all went well, then their addition might be enough to deter the Germans, and if things didn't go quite so well, he was confident that these men would rediscover their fighting spirit when put to the test.

The balance of war, however, could not be expected to be tipped by a mere handful of men, but Belcher had a plan too for improving their chances. After getting the convalescents settled in, and arranging for them to be fed, and well swaddled from his great store of blankets and woollens, he slipped a bottle of whiskey into each of his greatcoat pockets and set out across the fields. His first stop was Brigade, where a staff captain only just back from the line filled him in on the latest exploits and present plight of the Munsters. Belcher was concerned enough to jeopardise his diplomatic standing with the staff by requesting special treatment, but the strings he had to pull were few and Brigade was too weighty to be shifted by mere string. He didn't bother to offer bribes of whiskey. The staff would certainly have enough whiskey as it was, and he had more useful recipients in mind.

The artillery lines were silent, but he knew well enough where to find them. There were positively herds of horses, and absolutely masses of men, and hardly a man jack of them doing anything worthwhile, and all this great panoply of military might was there to serve a battery of a mere six guns. Belcher accosted one idler with a stripe on his sleeve.

'You there! Corporal! Where do I find the commanding officer?'

'Major Ferguson, sir? Over there, sir. You see that tent with the light burning?'

'Much obliged. Wait – did you say Ferguson? Is he an Irishman, by any chance? Tall gentleman? Sandy hair?'

'That's him, sir.'

Well fancy that. I wonder.

'Darky Ferguson! You old dog, you!'

'Tummy Belcher! Well damn me!'

Major Samuel Beresford Ferguson, Royal Field Artillery and Master of Fox Hounds, rose from his canvas chair and seized Belcher by the hand. 'Why this is capital! Haven't seen you in an age or more. Pull up a pew and have a drink, Tummy.'

'Matter of fact, Darky, I thought I might offer you one.'

And after that all was merry as could be, with talk of the war, and talk of hunts from Ballyhack to Two-Mile Borris, and trout and salmon of bygone days.

After a decent while Belcher said, 'Before I forget, Darky old man, I've come to beg a favour.'

'Beg away, my son.'

'Not from you personally, mind. Didn't even know you were here until I stuck my nose in your tent. A favour from the artillery. A professional matter.'

'Speak on, Tummy.'

'Now I realise that you must have all sorts of calls on your time and so forth, but poor old FitzEm's in something of a hole, and I'd be ever so grateful if you could see your way to giving the Hun a proper seeing to in his sector.'

'Tummy, everything I have is yours – yours and FitzEm's – but everything I have amounts to five piddling rounds per gun per day, and I've already spent Friday's allowance and it's only Tuesday. The ammunition bailiffs will be pounding on my door any minute now, I expect.'

'Damn,' said Belcher.

'And another thing,' said Ferguson. 'Even if I were able to find a few shells more – and that's quite something of an *if*, you know – it wouldn't do much more than annoy the jolly old Germans. This indirect firing is rather a bind you see. Hard to hit the target when you can't see the bloody thing. A handful of rounds and you probably wouldn't hit a soul.'

Belcher scowled.

But Ferguson was a sportsman to his fingertips yet.

'I'll tell you what I *might* be able to do, though,' he said.

There was a bite to the wind that night, and the promise of rain, but Belcher did not feel the cold as he walked back to his billet. It would not be fair to say that he had high hopes for the morrow, but he had a definite purpose, and that was good enough. The mean farmhouse was warm with the fug of sleeping men in newly deloused clothes, well supplied with tobacco. He let them sleep, but he roused Corporal Thompson out from his hidey-hole among the heaped stores.

'We're going into the line first thing tomorrow, Thompson.

Full fighting kit and all the ammunition you can carry, and I don't want to hear a word about your feet. Make sure there are dry socks for me and I want my boots well greased. Breakfast at six sharp, you hear?'

Thompson rubbed his face and blinked in the candlelight.

'Six sharp. Right you are, sir.' Then, as the instructions seeped into his brain, he thought to ask:

'What about the stores, sir?'

'I don't think we need worry about the stores any longer, Thompson,' said Belcher, looking round dismissively. 'And bring whatever personal effects you might have. I don't expect we'll be coming back.'

71

He drank a drink, and he washed himself, and he returned back again to his death, and he called to his enemies to come and meet him.

—Lady Augusta Gregory, *Cuchulain of Muirthemne*

'Morning, FitzEm.'

'Tummy! Bless me! How very good to see you.'

'Heard you'd been turfed out of your digs, old boy. Thought I'd come along and help you win back that beastly spot you've been calling home these past weeks.'

Fitzmullen-Brophy managed a smile. 'Might be some difficulties there, Tummy. I'm afraid we're in rather a fix at the moment.' And he gestured to the men of his wasted command, wet and dispirited, hanging onto these last hollows in the earth.

Belcher looked around with disapproval, but there was yet a lightness about him that his friend hadn't seen in many a year. 'Yes,' he said. 'Saw your signal to Brigade. Sounded like you were at the end of your tether. Don't blame you. You have had a rough time, haven't you?'

Fitzmullen-Brophy could only gesture again.

'Well that can't be helped, I'm afraid,' went on Belcher. 'You mayn't have heard yet but the rest of the brigade is in much the same boat, as is the division, as is the whole blasted front, I gather. Spoke to a staff-wallah earlier. I expect he'll be around in a bit to tell you in person.'

'Tell me...?'

'Counterattack. Push the Boche clear out of the parish. Bedfords are going forward on the right, and the Rifles, who are, apparently behind our left as of last night, will pivot on us, or rather on the Piggery, which we are to have in our possession by the appointed time, which is ten, or maybe half-past – I forget.'

Fitzmullen-Brophy was aghast, but didn't want to imply funk.

'It's a rather tall order, Tummy. Do they have any idea what they're asking? Do they know how few men I have left?'

'The line can't go any farther back, and seeing as where it happens to be is considered unsatisfactory by our lords and masters, it must go forward again, and ours not to reason why. They tell me that there's a battalion of territorials somewhere in the mix too. They said it as if it were good news. Territorials – I ask you.'

Fitzmullen-Brophy was quiet. He was sitting against the steep bank, and now he slumped, his backside sliding down until his knees were almost up to the level his shoulders. His uniform was somewhat shapeless with the layers of woollens worn underneath and he was wearing his balaclava helmet instead of his cap.

'Oh cheer up for heaven's sake, man,' said Belcher. 'It's not as bad as all that. Have a drink.'

He had brought his spirit flask, because he never went anywhere without it, and he had brought another, just in case. When girding himself for battle that morning he had loaded his revolver and considered putting a packet of cartridges into his tunic pocket, but plumped for a spare whiskey flask instead. It bulged in his pocket alongside a packet of sandwiches and a bar of chocolate, all of which would doubtless prove their worth far more readily than a few silly bullets. There would be quite enough bullets flying about for an officer of his rank and station to be adding to them. Besides, a chap needed to be fortified against the chill if he was obliged to go out without his greatcoat. Greatcoats should not be worn in the front line. Bad form. A fellow might as well carry an umbrella. He was glad in a way. A greatcoat would have hidden his badges and his medal ribbons, and the Germans should see what a real soldier should look like – a real fusilier and an old South Africa man. For the same reason he had Thompson brush down his uniform before they left. It would make little difference with all this mud, but still. He did not carry his sword. No one did these days. Swords had gone suddenly out of fashion, it seemed.

'Better not,' said Fitzmullen-Brophy.

'No? Might do you some good. You look perfectly ghastly.'

'What a thing to say! I feel all right, thank you.'

'Well never mind that. What I meant to tell you is that I've brought you some reinforcements. Not many, but stout-hearted chaps who left the hospital as soon as I told them you needed them. They should be along directly. Tried to drag an ASC driver along too, but he was having none of it. Poor sort. Better off without him.'

'How many men, Tummy?'

'Seven, including Thompson. All a little under the weather still, I must warn you, but frightfully keen, I'm proud to say.'

'Seven,' said Fitzmullen-Brophy in a tired voice.

'Oh yes – and one more thing. Never guess who I ran into last night.'

'Who?' Fitzmullen-Brophy's question was listless.

'Darky Ferguson. You remember Darky. Commands a battery of 18-pounders these days.'

Fitzmullen-Brophy looked up warily. The mention of artillery might mean something.

'So we had a little chat, and I asked if there was anything he could do for us, and do you know but he came up trumps.'

'How's that, Tummy?'

'He's giving us a gun. Two of 'em actually – if he can spare them. Not really giving, mind, but bringing them right into the line. He can't whistle up any extra shells, but he says he can make damn sure the few he has get delivered to the right address. Should be along soon, and you'll never hear me say a bad word about a gunner again.'

Belcher's invalids came up presently. Sick and lame they may have been, but they looked considerably better to the men who'd been holding the line. They were anything but pleased to be back, but they were welcome. They had, after all, brought all the cigarettes that had been in Belcher's store, as well as a few tins of food that wasn't bully beef, and a half a gallon of rum. Fitzmullen-Brophy wasn't wholly pleased about the rum, but he reckoned that, fairly distributed, there wasn't enough to make a man wild like poor old Robinson.

They were all sitting around eating biscuit with jam when the artillery was heard rolling up. Men stuck their heads up to take in the spectacle of horse teams and gun crews going about their business with such swift efficiency. And the work was swift, because this was dangerously close to the German line and a couple of teams of gun horses made no small target. In half a minute the guns were emplaced in the field not two hundred yards back, and the horses were being driven away at speed. The Germans appeared to take no notice.

Ferguson, who had ridden up on a magnificent chestnut hunter, came forward on foot to have a proper look at the ground ahead, and the Munster officers met him half way. There were hearty handshakes all round.

'That it?' asked Ferguson, pointing to the Piggery. A German bullet whined close overhead by way of an answer. Ferguson didn't deign to duck.

'Only got six rounds,' he said, as if nothing had happened. 'And I was saving those for Christmas. Only shrapnel, mind. Mightn't have the desired effect if they're all indoors out of the rain. Have to shorten the fuses as low as they'll go. Could be a bit dicey. Still, though – firing over open sights, what? Like in Wellington's day. Ripping stuff.'

And he shared a stirrup cup with Belcher before going to see to the finer points of his proposed bombardment, and after that there was nothing to do but wait.

72

God of Heaven! Would that I had not gone to the fierce battle!

—The Frenzy of Suibhne

'Oh, lads. I'm not able for this at all,' said Moriarty.

The rain came and went through the morning, and anyone who had got out of the Piggery got out in the clothes he stood up in, with no blanket or groundsheet to keep him from the November elements. At first there was the exhilaration of the fight and the escape to keep their minds from lesser troubles, but after the passing hours had soothed jangling nerves, and breakfast was shared out, there was occasion to dwell on their unhappy lot. The proposed counterattack was just too much.

Moriarty in his woollen comforter, without so much the peak of a cap to shield his face, was trying to light a cigarette. The matches were damp, and he went through half a box of them until the sludgy heads were all scraped off, and by the time he'd prevailed on a comrade to give him a light off a butt, a fat raindrop had landed on his cigarette.

'*That is the drop that brings a man to the ground,*' said Wyndham cryptically.

Moriarty fixed him with an accusing stare. It wasn't like Wyndham to be mocking fellas like that. Wyndham saw the look, and shook himself like a man waking from a reverie, and apologised, saying that it was just something from a story that he remembered. Moriarty reflected that the Yank had gone a bit funny, but then he must have been half mad to go joining the army in the first place, and all mad to have followed Major

Bloody FitzEm to the war. Moriarty went to stow the cigarette in his hat to dry it, but his hat was sodden too, so he threw the fag away in disgust and took more care with the next one.

For his own part, Wyndham was trying to withdraw into himself, but his bodily discomforts made it difficult. There was grit under his fingernails. His nose was running and he had no handkerchief. The cold was painful, and he had long since lost any sensation in his feet. Worse than that was the confirmation that he was lousy. He'd suspected it and feared it, but told himself it was just an irritation of the skin, but now, with his hands in his armpits to warm them, he had definitely felt something move that was not of his body. It was disgusting. It was distressing. And there was nothing to be done about it. He'd only be laughed about it if he complained. His comrades would scoff at the soft American in his lah-di-dah uniform and his cushy indoors job, grousing about what had already been afflicting everyone else for ages. And now soon he would have to stand up in this wet and cold, and follow the major to confusion and death. And he would die lousy. What would Mother say? He hugged himself close, while Moriarty went on, holding forth whether anyone was listening or not.

'It's bollocksed, lads. It's all fucked.

'Did you see the state of the poor eejits that old Belcher dragged in? Thirty-odd of us, and we're half dead as it is, and that's supposed to be our reinforcements? Come on. I should be in the bloody hospital myself.'

He puffed fast and hard on his cigarette, taking what he could from it before the rain got it, and then, when it was down to a harsh hot stub in damp, yellow-brown paper, he passed it on to Whelan.

Whelan took it without comment. His thoughts, like Wyndham's were elsewhere. He had seen that a German shell had landed in their temporary cemetery and disinterred things that should be properly hidden. Whelan had enough reminders of mortality to be getting on with, and he didn't need a rifleman, three days dead, to be lying there like an old rag doll, saying, '*As you are now, so once was I; As I am now, so you will be,*' or whatever was written on gravestones. No – he was a soldier and death was one of the risks of the job. He'd been facing his own mortality since Étreux. Maybe this hour was the hour of his death. It might be a good death or a bad death, but either way it would be the end.

But that man, that poor old rifleman – it hadn't been the end for him. He had done his duty and fought and died and now those bastards had dug him up again and that was all wrong. He was out of it. He'd earned his discharge. He should have been spared this last punishment. Whelan had spoken to the padre and confessed his sins, and the padre had told him not to worry, and that soldiers were granted all sorts of dispensations, and Whelan chose to interpret that as tacit permission to hold onto those pictures of the girls for the time being. He'd confess to God in person if it came down to it. But he wanted to believe that while he was dead, and getting his sins squared away, his body wouldn't be lying out in a field like old rubbish, where anyone could look at it. A body underground was a thing for reverence, but a body in a field was just disgusting.

Moriarty was still going on. Maybe he'd been looking at the old corpse too.

'Do you know why they want us to take our old trenches lads? It's because we left all our kit behind us. They're making us get our blankets back so they can bury us properly. Regulations say you have to bury a man in his blanket, and the cost of it is deducted from your final pay.'

Somebody must have been listening to him because someone told him to shut up.

'I'm only talking,' said Moriarty.

'You're only bloody blathering, and I'm bloody sick of it. I'm in no humour to listen to that class of talk at a time like this.'

'Do you want we should maybe say a decade of the rosary instead? Maybe Wyndham can tell us one of his stories.'

'And maybe you could just shut up.'

Moriarty did. He had nothing to say anyway. It was only his nerves at him. The major said they'd be moving at ten or half-past. What time was it now?

No one did turn up from Brigade, as it happened, but at ten sharp there was the sound of gunfire from north and south, and after a hurried consultation among the officers, that was agreed as the 'go' for the attack. Perhaps that small loss of synchronisation made all the difference. The Germans, who had been expecting something of the sort, stood to their arms around the Piggery. Those among them who had been keeping out of the rain in the farm buildings grabbed their rifles and joined their comrades at the defences, whereas they'd have stayed put if they'd been under shellfire from the outset. Even the damaged walls and roofs could provide an adequate defence against the British shrapnel shells. But now, nearly a minute after the scanty bombardment had come down on the neighbouring positions, and while the shivering German soldiers were waiting for the Munsters to come at them, Major Ferguson's guns opened up, and Major Ferguson's shells screamed in so low and fast that it was too late to do anything about it. There were only five rounds all told, and two of them missed or detonated too late to have any effect, while another smashed into the roof of an outhouse before it could burst, but the other two exploded in most satisfactory manner directly above their target. One blew in textbook fashion a few yards above and in front of the barricade that had been built across the farm's gate, and hundreds of tiny bullets exploded directly into the faces of the defenders. Shrapnel sliced and drilled down on men's heads and backs as they cowered around the yard. Even the small blasting charge, at such range, could batter and stun. The Germans had no notion of the number of shells to which the British guns were rationed, and they were in no position to keep count, so the survivors were still keeping their heads down for vital seconds after the last shell had struck. By the time the alarm was shouted, the attacking Munsters were already half way on them.

The Irishmen came in at the rush, with no semblance of order or formation. Each man wanted to get this done with fast. There was no hanging back. There was no safety in numbers because there were not the numbers. Urgent and grim they closed the distance, running low and hurdling obstacles, their middle-aged officers unable to keep up. They were on and over the barricade in moments, and after that the Germans did not seek to contest the position. Any man who was too badly hurt to run was left behind to the mercy or otherwise of the victors. Some were bayoneted because they were too slow to surrender. Some died because they were too wounded or dazed to even raise their hands. Whelan stabbed a man who was already dead, but whose body had remained half-upright in a tangle of smashed timbers at the barricade. Three Germans were taken alive and on their feet.

Fitzmullen-Brophy came jogging in to the scene of his triumph, puffing hard. He was delighted by the success of the action, but disappointed to have missed it, and rather disgusted with himself for not having sufficient wind to be in the lead. Belcher was there shortly afterwards. He knew his limitations and had not even tried to hurry. For an officer of his age and physique it was better to risk a bullet by setting an example of calm than to look foolish by trying to run.

'Oh well done!' he said. 'Well done, indeed! You all right FitzEm? Not a scratch, eh? Good show!'

Everyone was rather dumbfounded by their success. The more tactically minded saw to consolidating the position. Others went to see if they could retrieve any of the kit they'd left behind when they'd been forced out earlier. A few fell to shameless looting, even though the Germans had little enough to take. Wyndham, who had taken part in the attack empty-handed, keeping well back beside Fitzmullen-Brophy, thought to pick up a rifle, but whether or not it was in working order he couldn't tell. Duffy confirmed that there had been no casualties and reported as to the situation as he saw it.

'Two of the Huns are hurt very bad, sir. One of them might make it. I suppose we could get the others to carry him back – if you think he's worth the bother, sir.'

'I suppose it's the thing to do.'

'They hadn't got around to burying our own lads yet, but they've all been shoved out of the way in the lee of that wall. If there's time, sir, I could get the lads digging.'

'If there's time. I'd leave it a while, Duffy.'

'You're right, sir. The cold will keep them from stinking up the place for a fair bit longer. Mind you, one of the shells is after knocking down the kharzi, so there'll be a rare hum of shite about the yard, if you'll pardon me, sir.'

'Quite. Carry on, Sarn't Duffy.'

The tension and terror of the attack was giving way to a mood of quiet congratulation when the staff officer from Brigade found them. He found the attack he had come to order complete and successful, which put him out a bit. He bore tidings of partial success at various points, but also came with the unwelcome confirmation that more was expected of Fitzmullen-Brophy's tiny force, seeing as they hadn't been annihilated yet. In essence, the action of yesterday was to be repeated. The Piggery as an isolated strong point was not reckoned viable, and much of the former front line had to be recovered. The only consolation was that this time the Munsters would not be alone. Their attack was to be made in conjunction with what was left of the rifle battalion, at such a time as the Rifles might have won their way far enough forward to make such an undertaking possible. To counter this comfort, there was the unhappy fact that there was no more artillery support.

'I've done all I can,' said Ferguson. 'Come take a look at the ammunition limbers if you don't believe me. The cupboard's bare, and the beasts at divisional artillery won't even answer my letters anymore.'

As it happened, looking in the limbers wasn't really an option, as Ferguson had ordered his guns out as soon as they had done their work. They had obeyed with such speed that Ferguson tarried a while not just to pay his compliments to his friends in the infantry, but to show that not all gunners were shy of being this close to the enemy. His parting words to Belcher were:

'And another thing, old man – this is absolutely and utterly unauthorised, d'you hear? Breathe a word to HQ and they'll be sending me to bed without any supper. Wouldn't have missed it for worlds, though.'

And then he was on his merry way.

And so, as the grey morning wore on, the men waited for the time when they would have to do again what many of them had thought would have been their last act on this earth.

73

Finn and the Fenians will not see me alive after this. I will rush into the midst of the foreigners; and they will fall by me, till I fall by them.

—Jeremiah Curtin, *Hero-Tales of Ireland*

In the last nervous hour before the attack the Piggery had one more visitor. A boy with spurs on his boots and mud plastering him from head to foot tumbled in with the breathless news that two troops of dismounted yeomanry were moving up in support and that their arrival would signal the opening of the show. The bright young thing pushed on to spread the word to neighbouring units, leaving the Munsters with the impression that they might expect old Etonians and the flower of the English counties to sweep in at any moment. Such a reinforcement was hardly a guarantee of victory, but it was enough to convince Fitzmullen-Brophy that he could perhaps afford now to leave Wyndham out of the attack.

He'd had no qualms about leading the young man off to war, but almost-certain death was another matter entirely, especially as the American's enlistment and service rested on such unsafe legal and moral grounds. And another thing – looking at the fellow now, he was looking rather played out. No surprise really. He had neither been inured to hardships from an early age, like the rankers, nor had he been toughened up in a proper school like the officers. He had done very well, but he deserved a rest.

For the sake of face, Fitzmullen-Brophy detailed Wyndham

to take charge of the few prisoners. As predicted, one of the severely wounded had died, but the other had been taken care of by the British stretcher party – the other Germans all being hurt to one degree or another that no two of them were capable of carrying a stretcher very far over broken ground. So Wyndham was now advised to find a bayonet for his rifle and escort them to the rear. Wyndham accepted the task without any expression of relief or disappointment. It was an unfailing soldierly quality in the young man that the major had noticed before and always admired. Clearly he had been right in recruiting the lad. A pity the war had come along when it did, or rather a pity that it was this sort of a war. Wyndham's experiences thus far would probably be the making of him, but a sharp little campaign in the cool season in India would really have been much better.

The major thought about that diffident and apologetic tourist whom he'd rescued in Tralee (and he really did see it as a rescue – from the stifling confines of a little life), and compared him to the man standing before him now. Wyndham muddy, Wyndham unwashed and unshaven, but Wyndham with a rifle in his hand, accepting without a qualm responsibility for three enemy prisoners. Fitzmullen-Brophy had much to be proud of.

'Now you know what's expected of you?'

'Yes, sir.'

'Don't take any nonsense from them. All the mischief has probably been knocked out of them, but you don't want them getting any ideas when they find there are three of them and nobody but you. Prod them with the bayonet from time to time if you feel the need to – that one there, the biggest one. He'll do.'

'Yes, sir.'

'Jolly good. Once Brigade has taken them off your hands you can come back, but I don't expect we'll be here by then.'

Wyndham nodded. Fitzmullen-Brophy took the plunge.

'What I mean to say – and it's probably fearfully bad luck to say such a thing, but well, you know. What I mean is that this next attack is going to be a very serious business and well – well it's possible we might not meet again, Wyndham. Do you see what I mean?'

He didn't wait for a response, but pushed on.

'Look here – what I mean to say is that if the worst comes to the worst and I don't come through, I would like you to tell Susan – Mrs Fitzmullen-Brophy, that is – when you are stopping in Tralee to retrieve your things, I mean – I would like you to tell her that well… tell her I was thinking of her, and all that sort of thing. Do you think you could do that, Wyndham?'

Wyndham, his eyes wide with sorrow, nodded again. 'Of course, Major,' he got out finally.

'And well – while I'm spouting on like this – I should just like to say what a dashed fine fellow you've made of yourself – what a dashed fine fellow you *are*, Wyndham, and how tremendously pleased I am to have met you.' And with that the major impulsively held out his hand to the private and, after the briefest hesitation, Wyndham took it and squeezed it hard.

'God go with you, my boy.'

'And with you, Major.'

Wyndham thought he might start crying, but couldn't quite think why. He was cold and weary and nerve-racked, but that was physical rather than emotional. Surely there was no call for tears. Nothing could kill Major Fitzmullen-Brophy. He at least wanted to come to attention and salute, but the gallant old soldier had already turned on his heel and, quickly wiping his moustache, was about other business.

Standing to one side through this exchange was Whelan. He shyly came forward now.

'Are you going so, Wyndham?'

'I'll be right back, Whelan.'

'Ah sure, don't hurry yourself. Listen – I was just wondering, like. Would you ever take these?' And he handed over a grubby envelope that Wyndham thought he knew.

'But those are your – your photographs, Whelan!'

'I know, I know. And thanks for them and everything. It's just that I don't really want them anymore.'

Wyndham understood. What if Whelan's personal effects were sent home to his next of kin? Then it selfishly occurred to Wyndham that he might get killed himself, and weeks later an envelope full of naked ladies would land on the mat in Lowell with devastating results. He took the packet from Whelan, but resolved not to keep them for long.

'I'll give them back to you afterwards,' he said.

'You're grand.'

In that case then he'd give them to one of the German prisoners. For some reason he believed that it would be the worst of bad luck just to throw them away somewhere.

'Take care of yourself, Whelan,' he said.

Whelan stood there a moment longer, working something over in his mind. Then he just said, 'Good luck,' and turned to leave. Then suddenly he was back, gripping Wyndham's sleeve and talking close into his face.

'Listen,' he said earnestly. 'Would you do something for me? Would you light a candle for me?'

'I will,' Wyndham assured him. 'I certainly will. You needn't worry on that score, Whelan.'

Whelan let him go, looking embarrassed. 'Thanks,' he said, and he was gone.

The last to say his goodbyes to Wyndham was Sergeant Hegarty. They had hardly spoken before, but here the old man was now, with his bandaged hand and running nose and wheezing breath.

'Are you off?' he said.

'I am,' said Wyndham.

'Will I tell you something?'

'Please, Sergeant.'

Hegarty gave a conspiratorial look left and right and leaned in close. 'Make them walk in single file,' he said in a rasping undertone.

'The prisoners?'

'Yeah – the prisoners. Walk behind them, all four of ye in a row, and then when you shoot the last one in the back the bullet will kill the fella in front of him too. It might get all three of the bastards – you never know.'

'Sergeant?'

'The one in front won't know what's going on, and you can have your bayonet in him in a second.'

And he winked then. 'Right – on you go.'

Some of the men who watched Wyndham go envied him, and some were forthcoming enough to curse him for a lucky bastard, or even a skiving, malingering Yank bastard, sloping off when the sloping was good. Lance Corporal Moyle let them mouth off. Some fellas were always moaning, and there was usually no harm in it. But then he heard a man in his section called Dennehy not just grousing, but on the verge of causing trouble. This had nothing to do about Wyndham. This was about Dennehy trying to huckster with the army, trying to bargain with fate: trying to cheat the war itself.

'Them yeomanry lads,' Dennehy was saying. 'We've never seen them fuckers before, have we?'

'We've seen no one but a few Rifles, and they're down to two men and a dog,' admitted a mate.

'Them yeomanry lads will be fresh as fucking daisies, won't they? You saw that kid of an officer? Raring to go, he was. All the rest of them will be like that. Two troops of them.'

'How many is a troop?'

'I don't know. A couple of platoons or a couple of companies or something. I haven't a clue about the horsey fellas – shower of stuck-up bastards.' That was Moriarty. He had wandered over in search of tobacco and conversation. Now, having confessed to ignorance on one point, he was obliged to make up for it by advertising his wide knowledge.

'Yeomanry,' he said. 'They're not even real soldiers, you know. Militia on horses – that's all. Landlords and big farmers. You know it was the yeomanry that put down the rising in 1798? That's the class of characters they are.'

A few men rumbled in patriotic solidarity at the mention of '98, but Dennehy was quick to get his argument back on the rails.

'Couple of companies,' said Dennehy, 'and fresh as fucking daisies.'

'What are you saying, so?'

'I'm saying let them do the fighting if they're so keen on it. Haven't we done our bit?'

'You mean we should hang back or something?'

'We should hang back. Let the bloody yeomanry do a bit of hard work for a change.'

'The major wouldn't be having any of that.'

'So we don't let on to the major, so. We could just be a little slow off the mark when he blows his whistle. With all the yeomanry fellas, sure no one would miss us.' He looked up at Moyle for approval. 'Isn't that right, Moyle? Isn't that right, Corporal?'

Moyle was having none of it.

'You'll be going over the top when the major blows his whistle, even if you're going with my boot up your hole. Do you hear me, Dennehy? You'll do as you're bloody told – all of ye! Do you hear?'

He looked at them with scorn.

'You're all awful fools if you think you can shirk anything now. You've taken your shilling and this is good enough for you. You'll go in behind the major in half an hour and tonight they'll wrap you in your blanket and if you're lucky they'll fire a volley for you. Stop your bloody whingeing.'

And he turned away from them dismissively, and set his red-eyed gaze on the world beyond the parapet, his jaw quivering slightly.

'And haven't I seen the banshee below at the canal washing all yere dirty shirts for ye?' he said, but more to himself than to anyone else.

The counterattack was launched on a front of no more than three hundred yards, with yeomanry on foot, keen and fresh on the wings and, in the centre, fusiliers and riflemen looking like tinkers. Someone had whistled up some meagre artillery support, but perhaps it was intended purely to keep the Germans from bringing up more troops, because the shells could only be seen exploding in the distance. The German artillery's response was not slow in coming, and it was more vigorous. The single German machine-gun was even quicker to be heard, and the British were hardly off their own start line before they heard its bullets chopping into the vegetation all around.

The yeomanry suffered the worst. They presented a good large target, and they were coming on with more dash than the tired infantry, who were experienced and prudent enough to use all the cover there was. The men of the yeomanry, stalwart countrymen as Moriarty had said, and so bright and ruddy compared to the other units, were new to the war, and their training in dismounted action might have left something to be desired. On the other hand, the German machine-gunners were getting good at their job. They had learned to set their sights low, and now they were rewarded with a picture of British soldiers tumbling. Bullets sliced leg muscles and smashed kneecaps. Bullets broke legs and wrecked pelvises, sending bone fragments spiralling into guts. Bullets struck stones and tree stumps and bounced up to catch in shoulder or throat.

The attention paid to the yeomanry did the Munsters no harm at all. They covered the first thirty yards in a rush and went to ground in a hollow. The idea was to get their bearings and coordinate for the next rush, but Fitzmullen-Brophy didn't like it. Hollow ground or not, there was no real safety here. That was proved when a bullet took one man in the head. But worse than that was the prospect of the attack stalling. They must get up now, and cover the last length at the charge while their blood was still up, and before the machine-gun traversed their way. A shell landed close, and before the debris had stopped falling Fitzmullen-Brophy was back on his feet, feeling light-headed, but standing tall on the battlefield. His whistle was dangling loose somewhere at his waist. He didn't need it. Everyone could hear him.

'Stand up, Dirty Shirts!' he shouted, and waved them forward. He didn't wait to see if anyone was following. He just went forward as fast as he could. Despite the din of small-arms fire, his breathing was loud in his ears. Wheezing like an old carthorse. Still hadn't quite shaken that chill. Soon be too old for this game.

A bullet cracked by his head, and he saw the man who fired it, not very far ahead at all. A nasty little fellow in a scruffy cap. Fitzmullen-Brophy raised his revolver and snap-shot twice. In doing so he missed his footing and caught his shin on a fence timber lying in the grass, and he pitched forward and saved himself from coming a cropper only by the wildest luck. By an even more remarkable fluke he appeared to have hit his man, or at least something had. There was another one taking aim at him now. Couldn't be the same fellow. This one had one of those ridiculous spiked helmets. He saw the muzzle flash but didn't hear the shot.

There was a loud thump from just behind him, and he saw from the corner of his eye one man falling and rolling.

Fitzmullen-Brophy fired again, to no effect, and then his men were rushing past him. Some jumped straight into the German trench, and others stopped on the parapet and fired their rifles down. It was magnificent. That's the stuff to give 'em. He was going to jump down himself, but the trench just here was deep and jumbled, and he suddenly felt that his knees weren't quite up to it. He hurried along the line of the trench and loosed a few potshots where it seemed opportune. It wasn't so dangerous to be above ground just here. They were out of the machine-gun's arc of fire. By the sound of things the yeomanry were not. The gun was still firing, but in shorter and more intermittent bursts now. Of the yeomanry troop he could see nothing.

He watched Sergeant Hegarty getting the worst of a bayonet fight. The man was vicious and wiry but he was too slow and, with a bandaged hand, too clumsy. Fitzmullen-Brophy hurried along the top of the trench to help, but he was too late. The veteran sergeant was impaled on a long German blade, once and once again to be sure. The killer was quick on his toes because he was poised and recovered and fighting his way skilfully backwards as more Munster soldiers crowded in on him. One of his comrades, covering from behind, saw the tall Irish officer above and loosed a shot, but it went wide. It was enough, though, to convince Fitzmullen-Brophy to climb heavily down into the trench. It was partly fallen in here, which made things easier.

He saw Belcher coming in at what passed for a jog. The man hadn't even unbuttoned his holster, and was going into battle with no more than his stick. By heaven, there was a cool one. Nothing rattled old Tummy much. He caught a glimpse of some Germans escaping across open ground. It did not look anything like a panicked retreat. As Fitzmullen-Brophy knew well, this ground was a maze of snaking little trenches. No one needed to go very far to find another defensible position. That meant that the momentum of the attack had to be kept up. He found an observation point and climbed up on a step to see isolated figures moving over on the right. Those were the other yeomanry troop, or possibly the Bedfords. The clamour of combat was clearly heard on his immediate left. Those were his own men or the Rifles. German shells were still exploding at intervals, but as soon as news reached the German batteries that the British had taken this line and were massing there, they could expect a real bombardment. And there was still that infernal machine-gun.

He climbed down and jostled his way along the trench. Duffy was nursing a wound, but was upright and making no complaint. There were a few men down, white-faced and struggling to breathe, and a few faces missing altogether. But at least he had Duffy, and Moyle was there too, and with NCOs of that stamp, and twenty-five or thirty good men besides, he could jolly well keep pushing on.

He muttered a few congratulations as he moved among them, but refrained from making any speech. When he had them all under his eye, all he said was, 'Right, men – one more effort. That machine-gun has to go. Form up.'

And they did, and he led them over the top one more time.

It was worse this time. There was a little more cover among the trees and thickets, but the leaves were all fallen and the Germans could without difficulty see them coming. Also, the machine-gun crew and the other pockets of German infantry had fewer distractions this time. Fitzmullen-Brophy thought he saw a few men rise up from the ground where the yeomanry had been cut down, and if that was the case then bravo, and the more the merrier, but he had other things to occupy his attention. A hedge ran athwart the Munsters' line of advance. One party moved to swerve around it and, bunched together, they suffered for it.

Moyle tried to lead what was left of his section through a gap he forced in the hedge. He was thrusting the slapping branches aside when someone shot him. He thrashed for a bit before falling forward, his body limp in the hedge and his tunic darkening.

A German shell landed close by, and men who still had their hearing heard screaming. They also heard the howl of another incoming shell, and they took cover. In the lee of the blood-spotted hedge, with clods of dark earth falling down on them, the Munsters' attack was stalled.

74

...A shroud and a coffin –
For a big-hearted hero
Who fished in the hill-streams
And drank in bright halls
With white-breasted women.

...On me is the grief
There's no cure for in Munster.

—Eileen O'Connell, 'The Lament for Art O'Leary'

It looked like more rain. Not surprising really. Damnable weather in this part of the world. Then again, it was probably much like this at home this time of year. Thing was though, that one tended not to lie out under it at home.

Tummy Belcher was lying flat on his back, or at least he thought it was flat on his back. To be quite honest he wasn't sure about his lower body, which he suspected might be twisted into an uncomfortable posture. Knocked about quite a bit, even. He'd seen the like in South Africa. Boer shell. Old Whatsisname, with one leg off and his insides out, scarcely aware there was anything wrong with him and chatting away quite calmly. Got a bit light-headed soon enough, mind, and then he was dead, which was a mercy really. Belcher suspected there might be something similar the matter with him. Suspected, but not feared. Not that he was feeling especially brave, that is. Just that it didn't quite concern him. Either the medicos would find him in due course and he'd be patched up, or they wouldn't and he'd die here in this wet Belgian field, and at the moment that was all the one to Tummy Belcher.

All in all, counting one's blessings and all that, it was good to get a rest from all the bother of the past months. His mind did not dwell on the notion of being mortally wounded. Maybe he was. Maybe he wasn't. The immediate present was enough for the time being, and at the present there was something to be said for having a bit of a lie down.

Pity about the cold.

Damnable cold.

He thought about how a drop whisky might be the thing, but he knew that rummaging for it was out of the question. Was there even any left? Couldn't quite recall. So grin and bear it, old boy. Wait and see.

The noise must have been shockingly loud, but for some reason it wasn't hammering in his ears as it had been earlier. Blast might have deafened him, of course, but really, the battle just wasn't his concern any more. That was that blasted German machine-gun off in the distance. Probably just the next field, but as far away and immaterial as dreamland. That was somebody shouting, quite nearby. Was that FitzEm? Hoped that FitzEm was all right, the silly ass. Susan would have his hide if he let anything happen to FitzEm. There was explaining enough to do as it was, what with this ridiculous jaunt they'd conspired in. Probably not have to face the music on that one. Not the way things were right this moment at any rate. Explain yourself to Susan Fitzmullen-Brophy or to your Lord and Judge. Which would you rather?

A fat raindrop hit him square in the eye, and he found it oddly refreshing, despite the cold. In for a spot of rain again. There was another voice, and for a second he could have sworn it was Hornsby, who'd captained the First Eleven in rugger. Years ago now, but similar circumstances in a way. '*Get up, Belcher! Come on, old man!*' He'd got up that time. Tackled by some brute twice his size and got up anyway, shaking off the concussion and putting his solid frame into the scrum like he was told. They'd lost the game, mind you, and Belcher hadn't been able to move his neck for a week afterwards, but there you were. No good Hornsby shouting at him now. Ask one of the younger men.

He felt two more raindrops. One of them ran up his forehead and across his scalp. Chilly. Hat must have come adrift. Obvious really. If something is powerful enough to lift a stout old gentleman off his feet, then naturally it will blow his cap off.

He thought about the rain in Burma when he'd been a youngster. Now there was rain. Came down in absolute torrents, warm as milk. Lie out in that and you'd drown, no question. But so refreshing after the interminable hot spell. Wouldn't mind a bit of that heat now, though. Make a nice change.

Poor old FitzEm. Hated to leave him in the lurch like this. Encourage him in that madcap scheme of his and then get bowled out like this, leaving him to carry the can? Not on at all. A decent fellow. Thoroughly decent fellow, but not the most capable of chaps. Too flustered. Too innocent. Never have got on in life without people like himself and Susan and old Colonel Barnard. And Barnard was long gone now, and Susan was far away in Kerry, and here was useless old Tummy Belcher lying in the mud while poor old FitzEm was no doubt getting into a hopeless muddle as usual. *Get up, Belcher. Come on, old man.*

But it was no use. Even the thought was too much of an effort.

And then he heard another voice from out of the past. Not so much a voice. A laugh. Louisa Cartwright-Jones. Well bless me, but it had been a long time. But it was her all the same, no doubt about it, giggling right into his ear and ruffling his hair. He'd had a full head of hair then.

'Dear old Tommy,' she was saying. Nobody ever called him Tommy. 'Dear old Tom-tom.' He could hear her plain as day. He felt the slightest twinge of embarrassment then. He feared he hadn't quite played fair with old FitzEm on that one. But he let the guilt slide away, because there was Louisa right beside him. Thirty years ago now, or near as dammit, and her voice clear as a bell in his memory. He'd never told FitzEm, of course. Never told anybody for that matter. Couldn't do that. But before he'd shipped out for the East that first time long ago he'd been to see the girls. How unexpectedly that had turned out. Unexpected. Delightful. Delicious. Louisa Cartwright-Jones curled beside him, laughing and ruffling his hair, and Alice Cartwright on the other side, laughing too, and playing her fingers across his broad belly. Alice and Louisa and Tom-tom, all together.

Tummy Belcher blinked away the water from his eyes, and then he closed them, because that was easier.

75

Hugh marched forth to the fight—I grieved to see him so depart;
And lo! to-night he wanders frozen, rain drenched, sad, betrayed –
But the memory of the limewhite mansions his right hand hath laid
In ashes, warms the hero's heart!

—James Clarence Mangan, 'Ode to the Maguire'

Wyndham met Moriarty on the road back. It was not a road that was shown on maps or had existed a month before, but the real road was known to the Germans and did not lead anywhere that a soldier up the line needed to go, and the smaller byways, never important enough to be surfaced, were now no more than deep muddy ruts. This road was a track through the fields, made of planks, and winding as the waterlogged landscape and enemy observation dictated. Even that was breaking down now, and Wyndham had just leaped across a section recently torn out by a shell. If he hadn't been along here only an hour before with the prisoners he might have doubted his way. Trees that had guided him were fallen, or knocked into reduced and unfamiliar shapes. There was more military rubbish, and some, already rusty and decaying, looked to be of an archaeological age. The bodies of men had been taken away, but discarded personal equipment and a few rags of bandages showed where the fatal dramas had been enacted. The bodies of horses and mules lay yet where they were.

And there, catching his balance on the far side of the shell crater, and holding his breath against the smell of a wagon team, tangled in their harness and broken traces, Wyndham met Moriarty. The skyline was altered, but he was sure that the broken roof just ahead was the Piggery, and then he saw that the figure approaching, as brown and battered as the landscape, was his comrade.

He looked dirtier and more haggard than before, and so much older too than he had this morning. He didn't raise his head to acknowledge Wyndham, and for a moment Wyndham wondered if it really was Moriarty, or maybe the ghost of a Moriarty who was already dead and whose body lay somewhere in the fields beyond. He grabbed at the apparition's sleeve more forcefully than he'd have meant to, and Moriarty's head jerked up, and his eyes opened in recognition, and his dirty face broke into a grin.

'Is it Mr Wyndham? How are you, boy?'

'What happened, Moriarty? Where are you going?'

'I'm the luckiest gobshite alive – that's what. We're the two luckiest fuckers that ever walked.'

'What happened, Moriarty? Where are the others?' Wyndham wouldn't let go the man's sleeve, and now he was shaking him. Moriarty looked confused and vaguely affronted, and for a moment they were like two drunks, colliding in the street, neither knowing what the other one was about.

Moriarty swayed a little, and blinked a few times, and looked around him.

'The others? They're, eh –' He looked back over his shoulder. 'They're back a bit that way. Jesus – I've come too far. Come on, I'll walk back with you.'

'Tell me what happened, Moriarty.'

'Come on. We'll go back. I'll tell you.' And Moriarty turned, and stumbled, and righted himself. Wyndham trotted after him on sore feet.

'Jesus, it was bad,' said Moriarty. 'Jesus, but I'm lucky. I'll tell you that for nothing. Where are you off to anyway, Whelan?'

'It's not Whelan – it's Wyndham.'

Moriarty stopped dead and Wyndham bumped into him. 'You're right, you're right,' said Moriarty, his voice perfectly clear and bright. 'Sorry about that. Sure of course Whelan's dead.'

'Whelan's dead?'

Moriarty suddenly shook himself like a dog. 'That was a bad one.'

Then: 'I'll tell you.'

Whelan was dazed by the blast but he was still up and moving. He pushed in behind Moyle, wanting to get through the gap in the hedge, and then he saw Moyle was dead. He knelt down, using the body for cover and as a rest for his rifle. Someone was crouching behind him, using *him* for cover, the windy bastard, and a couple of men were alongside him, hugging the ground close. Moriarty was one of them. He could feel his buttons digging into his chest and the wet earth cold against his face, but there was too much angry air about him still.

Someone was screaming blue murder close behind. Moriarty supposed that a few fellas must have got caught by that shell. He wasn't going to raise his head to look. There was a terrible hammering on the earth in front of his head and Whelan fell down beside him, cursing. In the briefest lull in the firing Fitzmullen-Brophy's voice, plaintive, almost querulous, was heard urging the Munsters forward. Boots thumped by Moriarty's head and someone forced his way through the hedge in a crashing of twigs, and then Whelan was staggering to his feet, and to his undying amazement, so was Moriarty. He was a little slow off the mark as always, and in time to see Duffy, huge and unstoppable, charging the German position like a maddened bull, with Whelan and one or two others hard on his heels.

Duffy'd had a fair few drinks in him that morning, he didn't mind saying. It was cold and wet and he'd had no sleep for days, and he had to go and get into another fight, hadn't he? A drop of rum was what would set a man up. Just a drop, mind. That was what poor old Robinson had forgotten that one time, God be good to him.

Now, after a swallow of rum here, and another swallow there, all through yesterday and into today, he wasn't drunk at all, but he had that unsettled sick feeling all the same of a man sobering up. His head was bad and his temper was bad and his nerves were bad. He had hurt his hand and the rum hadn't done the slightest thing to cushion the pain. And now the attack was all going to shite and the men were getting killed left, right and centre. That was all wrong. He had seen poor Major Tummy get knocked over and the same thing was going to happen to Major FitzEm in a minute if he didn't do anything about it.

So forward he went, and something slapped him in the face, but forward he went anyway, with Whelan and a few of the lads after him.

'That's the way, men!' shouted Fitzmullen-Brophy. 'That's the way! Come on the Munsters!'

But they hardly needed the encouragement now. The job was done. Duffy, his face streaming blood, had led the way into the German trench, had positively trampled the Hun underfoot, and then the others were in with the bayonet. Not many others, but not many Huns either, thank God. Besides those devils on the machine-gun there had only been four or five others, and four or five Boches were no match for an Irishman when he's roused. They'd done for poor young Whelan before it was over, though. Dreadful shame. A decent lad, with the makings of a fine soldier, and cut down here at the moment of victory.

Because this was victory. A few Germans could be seen, but they were retreating, and the few figures coming up were British. The field was theirs. This vast emptiness, with its dripping hedges and torn trees rising from a sombre waterscape, had been won. And it would be held.

Raindrops hissed on the machine-gun.

'Well done, men. Jolly well done,' he repeated, but more to himself. But what to do now? Consolidate, one supposed. But with what? Who was left?

He turned from the battlefield to his men. Was Tummy there? Where was Tummy? He turned around, a little unsteady on his legs for some reason, and anxiously scanned the lumps and bundles that strewed the ground across these fields. Where was Tummy?

Oh Lord please not poor old Tummy.

But no. That must wait. What mattered now were the men still with him, whoever, however many there were left.

'Duffy? Who's left?' he asked, and something struck him hard in the side, and he fell down.

'Major Belcher's dead too, I think,' Moriarty told Wyndham. 'Major FitzEm was still alive when they got him on a stretcher. Some other mob picked him up. It was the Rifles, I think. I forget. It wasn't our lads anyway.'

'Where would they have taken him?' asked Wyndham. 'The major, I mean?'

'To the Piggery, I suppose. No – I'm wrong. We're back at the Piggery. They went and took the major somewhere else. Do you want a fag? They're German. They're a bit queer. Turkish, I think. There was one fella with a pocket full of cigars. Cigars! There's style for you.'

But Wyndham didn't say yes or no, and Moriarty didn't take one himself either. They came to the Piggery, and there were troops there that Wyndham didn't know. They found a few Munsters over in one corner. All were more or less wounded. Duffy looked like having lost a finger and probably more from one hand, but his face was the main attraction. There was a gash in his cheek so big he could breathe through it, and as Wyndham watched, a stretcher-bearer extracted a broken tooth through the side of Duffy's face before pressing on a big pad of gauze. Duffy didn't seem too perturbed, but he wasn't his usual hearty self either. Dennehy, the shirker from Moyle's squad, appeared to have got off the lightest. He had a single straight-through bullet wound to his left hand.

Wyndham asked after the major, but no one answered. He asked again, asking each man in turn until someone told him that Fitzmullen-Brophy had been hit and taken to the rear, but there was no answer to be had better than that.

Tea was being served out, and first-aid parties were doing the rounds. The rain intensified and then eased off. German shells were still bursting here and there in the distance. One landed no closer than two-hundred yards off and a few of the men in the yard ducked, but they were only newcomers. These were the territorials, a whole company of them, and a whole battalion, to hold the ground that a few handfuls of exhausted regulars had held all by themselves for days – ground that had been lost and won back.

Moriarty said something bitter about the territorials. Effing nancy boys, he called them. Bloody weekend warriors. He was sitting with his mates, staring at the ground, letting the bitterness run out of him in a heartfelt undertone, his nose running and an unlit cigarette slipping off his drooping lower lip. Wyndham left him to it, and climbed up out of the Piggery, past the neatly laid-out bodies of Robinson and the others. Evening was coming on, far too early. Another shell struck far off, but the dark explosion was barely visible. Here and there bullets still sped low over the desolate ground.

He took his bearings on what he thought were Moyle's rowan trees, and he set out to look for the major.

76

'I ask no more delays, for I have drawn the sword, and told the truth, and lived my dream, and am content.'

—W.B. Yeats, *The Secret Rose*

Fitzmullen-Brophy was still alive. He had been shot in the hip, and by the time Wyndham had found out as much, the major had been carted off to a field hospital. Wyndham did find the hospital, but the major had already been moved on, and would be half way to Rouen by now. He came across Lieutenant Fleming though, pale as death in the officers' ward and weak as a day-old kitten, but doing well, and reckoned to be sufficiently out of danger to be marked for home.

Fleming was touchingly pleased to see Wyndham, and said how he was so very sorry to have been bowled out when the regiment needed him so. Wyndham chatted awkwardly for a while, as one does to an invalid, and then squeezed his hand and departed.

The hospital was by a village, and seeing as he had come this far, Wyndham visited the church, and found the curé, and asked if the priest would be so good as to light a candle and say a prayer for the soul of Timothy Whelan, because Wyndham felt it might be blasphemous if he were to do so himself. The priest solemnly agreed to the undertaking and Wyndham found he had not a sou to give the man. It was the first time he had been financially embarrassed since that hellish night in Tralee in June. The curé did not appear to want payment, but Wyndham apologised all the same, and presented the good father with some German cigars he'd been keeping dry in his cap, and that seemed to satisfy all parties.

It occurred to Wyndham, after he left the church, that there were other Munsters whose souls might have felt the benefit of a prayer, but none of them had specifically requested one. It was too late now. They were all dead, and the church was back there.

He went around a corner, out of sight of any passers-by, because he had to sit down. He experimentally lit the one cigar he had kept, but it was no use. He was crying and shaking too hard to smoke it.

Moriarty was much better after a long sleep, but was genuinely aggrieved that there were eight fusiliers still hale and unwounded to be counted. He was not a sole survivor. He was not distinguished. He wasn't even in charge. Belcher's assistant Corporal Thompson, even though he never stopped complaining about his bad feet, never reported sick either, and assumed command of the survivors when they moved into rest, and from there to the battalion.

For the battalion was finally being reconstituted. The new colonel had badgered and nagged and pulled strings, and carefully husbanded what few resources came his way until the high command finally acknowledged that the 2nd Royal Munster Fusiliers existed once more. The reformed battalion was as yet no more than half the size of the old one, but after the carnage at Ypres, that put them far ahead of most units still on the order of battle.

That was another thing that irked Moriarty. What had befallen Fitzmullen-Brophy's command was a story known to many. Everyone had suffered. Everyone had old soldiers' tales to tell. No one was interested. He arrived at a rest camp, and was assigned to a platoon and a billet, and while he was accepted without hostility, he was also accepted without comment.

They made room for him, but nobody treated him like he was special. The new battalion was a disappointment. Moreover, there was something wrong, after these past months, to see the tiger on the cap badge but not to know the face beneath.

The one advantage for Wyndham was that it was new. The disparate elements that had been serving in penny packets all along the front these past weeks had never functioned together as a battalion, so now the colonel had instituted a comprehensive training scheme, and that meant that Wyndham was back on the parade square, learning the fundamentals, continuing his military education where it had broken off. He even had the same teacher. Lance Corporal – now Corporal – Sheehan was one of the familiar faces from Ballymullen. He was nonplussed to recognise Wyndham, but didn't single him out in any way. It's hard to victimise and belittle a handless recruit when he has served more time in the seat of war than you have yourself.

All the same, Wyndham thought better than to approach Sheehan with the matter of his enlistment. His six months with the colours would be up next month. Had Major Fitzmullen-Brophy still been in charge it doubtless would have been a simple matter to arrange a discharge, but it was hard to imagine, looking at the brusque and harried officers, that the new colonel would happily part with Wyndham with a handshake and good wishes for the future. Maybe when Wyndham knew his way round a little better he might broach the subject – explain that he was not, in fact, a British subject. He had lost the shilling he'd been given in Tralee, but he hardly thought they'd be asking for it back.

There was much talk as to whether the war could last much longer. The Germans were beaten – that much was clear, but the British and French would need time to gather their strength for one more big effort to turf them back across the Rhine. That wouldn't be till spring, and that meant a winter in the trenches. The battalion was marched into the line in the last week of November and took up positions at a place called St. Yvon, on the southern end of the Ypres salient. It was much the same as the line in front of Armentières had been. Too much mud and too much water. What passed in this place for high ground was in the hands of the Germans, and the Munsters watched with disapproval as, day by day, German soldiers in canvas working suits carried timbers into the line to floor and wall their trenches. They may have been beaten, but they would be spending this winter in some sort of comfort all the same. When it was quiet the working of pumps could be heard, and runnels of dirty water ran downhill from the German line. At the same time the British trenches were filling up, and the Munsters, new-formed in this world, were deficient in waterproofs. As for good timber, it could not be had for love nor money.

A tacit policy of live and let live prevailed. Artillery ammunition was too scarce yet to be wasted in vindictive little quarrels that wouldn't win anything for either side, but some men stood in thigh-deep water and heard the German pumps, and thought it was all a bit much.

'I'm going to have that big bastard yonder,' said Moriarty one day. He and Wyndham were manning an outpost in a forward sap, and the Germans' activities could be seen clear as day, not two hundred yards distant in their support line. The two of them had been assigned to the same section, and they stuck together now. Wyndham's carefree wanderings were over. He did fatigues and stood sentry and no one asked him for stories any more. He carried a rifle, and he had a better idea of how to use it now. There were a few old reservists who hadn't shouldered a rifle since rifles were a simpler breed of beast, and who needed instruction in the workings of the Lee-Enfield. There were also the idle soldiers who might have dodged out of musketry courses on their way back into the army, and the colonel, a thorough man, was doing his best to ensure that his battalion would be a battalion that could shoot. So Wyndham had learned with them that last essential of soldiering, and with the resources available had fired a few rounds at a target without disgracing himself or the regiment.

And now here he was with Moriarty, close enough to the German line that they could see the breath of their enemies steaming in the November air. Mostly the Germans were furtive and circumspect in their movements. Live and let live might have been the custom, but no one was going to let the other side take liberties. They mustn't have known about this forward post though, unobtrusive behind a thicket at the end of a long, zig-zag approach trench, because they were not acting like men who could be clearly seen by their foes. The working men, plying shovels and humping sandbags, were just working men, and Moriarty might almost have sympathised with them, but there was one tall fellow standing by – sentry or overseer – and Moriarty hated him on sight.

'Look at the fucker. Big warm coat on him and big stupid spiky hat. He's got sergeant written all over him. Him and his bloody hat. I'll have that bastard.'

Wyndham didn't think much of what Moriarty was saying. The man was always talking about something and though often good-natured still, he had an unlimited stock of grudges and grievances. But suddenly Wyndham saw Moriarty bringing his rifle to bear.

'Don't do that,' he said.

Moriarty stared down the sights, but then raised his head.

'Sure I probably couldn't hit him from here anyway. Be good to scare him, mind. Make him jump in a hole. Get him all cold and wet – him and his good coat.'

And that didn't seem like such a dreadful idea to Wyndham. 'All right then,' he said. 'Give him a fright.'

And Moriarty squinted along his rifle again, and rubbed his

eye, and fiddled with the backsight, but that was all he did. Wyndham wasn't mischievous so much as bored. He wanted Moriarty to fire or shut up. Then Moriarty, reading his thoughts perhaps, looked him in the eye.

'You do it,' he said.

'Me?'

'Go on.'

'I've never shot at anybody.'

'Time to start then, wouldn't you think?' And Moriarty grinned like old times. 'Go on – what did you become a soldier for anyway?'

'I'm not sure.'

'Go on.'

And Wyndham hunkered down against the lip of the trench – there wasn't even a proper parapet – and pushed his rifle forward through the dead grass, and settled himself behind it.

'I don't know,' he said, but he set his sights to two hundred like he'd been taught.

'Go on. You're doing grand.'

The picture framed by the foresight guard showed, after a brief search, the large German NCO. Looking at him like this, Wyndham could understand something of Moriarty's attitude. The man did look haughty – arrogant even – standing there while others worked. And he was clean and dry – maybe the only man in the entire front who could boast such comfort. Wyndham's own feet were coated in whale oil and he was wearing two pairs of socks, and it did no good. He was cold and wretched.

'I'm not shooting him, though,' he told Moriarty.

'So don't shoot him. Just scare him. Knock him off his high horse.'

'I don't know.'

'He's taking the piss, boy. Look at him. He's taking advantage of our good will. He knows we're not shooting and he's standing there with a rifle, cool as you please.'

It was true. The man had a rifle slung.

'The Geneva Convention would take a very dim view of that,' Moriarty assured him.

Wyndham kept his eye where it was. His target did look like the sort who'd have committed atrocities in Belgium. Just the type to break furniture and outrage women and bayonet nuns, and all because they wouldn't salute the German flag or step out of his way. Wyndham wasn't prepared to kill him for it – not on this bleak day with his blood cold – but right then it seemed a fine idea to shoot the spike right off this Prussian bully's helmet. Him and his bloody hat, indeed.

Not that he could hit it at this range, of course. Probably couldn't even hit the man for that matter. Someone like Whelan could have done it easily, and someone like Moyle could have done it with his eyes closed, but Wyndham knew his limitations.

'Are you going to have a go or not?' asked Moriarty.

Wyndham didn't answer, but the rifle still hugged tight to the shoulder and the finger on the trigger guard were answer enough.

'Aim high,' said Moriarty. 'Aim right over his head so he knows it's for him.'

Wyndham nodded so very slightly, keeping his aim steady. He raised the muzzle a fraction so that the German was below his minuscule field of vision.

The rifle was a good weight, a comfortable fit. He pulled the trigger. He remembered too late that he should have squeezed and not pulled, but the report was loud in his ears and the stock was kicking back in his grip.

'Shot, boy!' exclaimed Moriarty, and slapped him on the shoulder.

With both eyes open now, Wyndham tried to see what he had wrought.

'What happened?'

'You got him! Jesus! Good man yourself!'

'What?'

He gazed but could see nothing. There was nothing to be seen. Everyone had taken cover in an instant. He stared across the grey and brown landscape, his ears ringing and a wisp of cordite smoke dissipating in the air. Far off where the man had been standing there was a shape on the ground, but it might have been anything.

'What happened?' asked Wyndham.

'Thou hast taught Man to kill, and he is no slow learner.'
—Tha, the Lord of the Jungle, to the First of the Tigers

—Rudyard Kipling, *The Second Jungle Book*

Dirty Shirt

by John Ware

When unassuming American tourist Daniel Wyndham arrived in Tralee, he was searching for whatever strain of Irish mysticism inspired W.B. Yeats and Lady Gregory.

But instead of a Celtic Twilight he found the hard-drinking redcoats of the Royal Munster Fusiliers – the Dirty Shirts.

Ireland was on the brink of civil war, Europe was on the brink of world war, and Wyndham was about to find out what the heroes and fighting men of Irish legend looked like in the twentieth century.

* * * * *

"…a fascinating tale – **fun, fast and furious** – and it shows an aspect of the Great War in a way never attempted before."
— Sue Leonard, *Irish Examiner*

"… **a distinguished first novel** … written so well that the military historical instruction it affords is a pleasure to absorb."
— Kenneth Ferguson, *The Irish Sword*

"**Ware has an unerring eye for detail**, telling his story not from the point of view of strategy and troop movements, but compassionately and humanely from that of the soldier right there in the trench ..."
— Katherine Mezzacappa, *Historical Novel Review*

A Green Bough

by John Ware

Daniel Wyndham, misguided American tourist, has seen the Royal Munster Fusiliers – the Dirty Shirts – go down into the mud of the Western Front.

Now, in the fields of County Cork, he watches a new army being improvised: an Irish army.

Wyndham's romantic dreams still have breath left in them, and to him it seems that the heroes of legend will march once more. But fighting for Ireland is taking on a new meaning, and 1916 will prove a bad year to be an Irishman in the King's uniform.

* * * * *

"…**meticulous, moving and often very humorous**.... An abundance of delightful, unforgettable ideas and endearing characters."
— Julia Stoneham, *Historical Novel Review*

"**Ware's words draw the reader like a magnet**, and he is truly a gifted storyteller. ..."

— *Amazon customer review*

"Ingenious, well-written, characterised by apt quotation and a sure touch for military detail, **this is literature in the making**, fun to read as it emerges hot from the press.

— Kenneth Ferguson, *The Irish Sword*

The World in a Sandbag

by John Ware

Daniel Wyndham, starry-eyed American tourist, is lost. The Battle of the Somme has led him to think that joining an Irish regiment of the British army was perhaps a mistake.

Now he's looking for a way out and a way home. But as all the ties that bound him to the Munster Fusiliers are falling away, he's finding a reason to stay in the war.

Miss Nora Maxfield, of the Voluntary Aid Detachment of the Red Cross, wouldn't be everyone's idea of a war aim, but she's what Wyndham is fighting for now.

* * * * *

"**A splendid sequel** ... Despite its underlying themes, this novel is full of humour – real laugh-out-loud moments."
— Julia Stoneham, *Historical Novel Review*

"...**does not disappoint** as another stunning example of Irish historical fiction ..."
— *Amazon customer review*

"The Royal Munster Fusiliers ... are benefiting from **a remarkable imaginative renaissance**."
— Kenneth Ferguson, *The Irish Sword*

www.ingramcontent.com/pod-product-compliance
Lightning Source LLC
Chambersburg PA
CBHW071552080526
44588CB00010B/880